The Destruction of Glubokie (Hlybokaye, Belarus)

Translation of
Khurbn Glubok

Original Book edited by:
M. and Z. Rajak, Former residents' association in Argentina

Published in Buenos Aires, 1956

Published by JewishGen

An Affiliate of the Museum of Jewish Heritage—A Living Memorial to the Holocaust
New York

The Destruction of Glubokie
(Hlybokaye, Belarus)
Translation of *Khurbn Glubok*

Copyright © 2021 by JewishGen, Inc.
All rights reserved.
First Printing: May 2021, Iyyar 5781

Editors of Original Yizkor Book:
M. and Z. Rajak, Former residents' association in Argentina
Project Coordinators: Anita Frishman Gabbay
Layout and Name Indexing: Jonathan Wind
Cover Design: Rachel Kolokoff-Hopper

This book may not be reproduced, in whole or in part, including illustrations in any form (beyond that copying permitted by Sections 107 and 108 of the U.S. Copyright Law and except by reviewers for public press), without written permission from the publisher.

Published by JewishGen, Inc.
An Affiliate of the Museum of Jewish Heritage
A Living Memorial to the Holocaust
36 Battery Place, New York, NY 10280

JewishGen, Inc. is not responsible for inaccuracies or omissions in the original work and makes no representations regarding the accuracy of this translation. Digital images of the original book's contents can be seen online at the New York Public Library website.

The mission of the JewishGen organization is to produce a translation of the original work, and we cannot verify the accuracy of statements or alter facts cited.

Printed in the United States of America by Lightning Source, Inc.

Library of Congress Control Number (LCCN): 2021936851

ISBN: 978-1-954176-12-6 (hard cover: 462 pages, alk. paper)

Cover Credits

Front and Back Cover Background Texture and Color: Rachel Kolokoff Hopper

Front and Back Cover Background Photograph: Rachel Kolokoff Hopper

Front Cover Photograph:

Wedding of Moshe Leib Rodstein (well-known communal worker of the Chasidim of Chabad) from the book, page 25 [page 27 of original book].

Back Cover Photograph:

A Street in Glubokie, from the book, page 262 [page 272 of original book].

Back Cover Poem:

Remember! Dr. Mark Dworszecki. From the book *"Jerusalem of Lithuania in Struggle and in Destruction."* From the book, page 4. Translated by Jerrold Landau

JewishGen and the Yizkor Books in Print Project

This book has been published by the **Yizkor Books in Print Project**, as part of the **Yizkor Book Project** of JewishGen, Inc.

JewishGen, Inc. is a non-profit organization founded in 1987 as a resource for Jewish genealogy. Its website [www.jewishgen.org] serves as an international clearinghouse and resource center to assist individuals who are researching the history of their Jewish families and the places where they lived. JewishGen provides databases, facilitates discussion groups, and coordinates projects relating to Jewish genealogy and the history of the Jewish people. In 2003, JewishGen became an affiliate of the **Museum of Jewish Heritage—A Living Memorial to the Holocaust** in New York.

The **JewishGen Yizkor Book Project** was organized to make more widely known the existence of Yizkor (Memorial) Books written by survivors and former residents of various Jewish communities throughout the world. Later, volunteers connected to the different destroyed communities began cooperating to have these books translated from the original language—usually Hebrew or Yiddish—into English, thus enabling a wider audience to have access to the valuable information contained within them. As each chapter of these books was translated, it was posted on the JewishGen website and made available to the general public.

The **Yizkor Books in Print Project** began in 2011 as an initiative to print and publish Yizkor Books that had been fully translated, so that hard copies would be available for purchase by the descendants of these communities and also by scholars, universities, synagogues, libraries, and museums.

These Yizkor books have been produced almost entirely through the volunteer effort of researchers from around the world, assisted by donations from private individuals. The books are printed and sold at near cost, so as to make them as affordable as possible. Our goal is to make this important genre of Jewish literature and history available in English in book form, so that people can have the personal histories of their ancestral towns on their bookshelves for themselves and for their children and grandchildren.

A list of all published translated Yizkor Books in the project with prices and ordering information can be found at:
http://www.jewishgen.org/Yizkor/ybip.html

Lance Ackerfeld, Yizkor Book Project Manager
Joel Alpert, Yizkor-Book-in-Print Project Coordinator
Susan Rosin, Yizkor-Book-in-Print Associate Project Coordinator

This book is presented by the
Yizkor-Books-In-Print Project
Project Coordinator: Joel Alpert
Associate Project Coordinator: Susan Rosin

Part of the Yizkor Books Project of JewishGen. Inc.
Project Manager: Lance Ackerfeld

These books have been produced solely through efforts of volunteers
from around the world. The books are printed using the Print-on-Demand technology and sold at near cost, to make them as affordable as possible.

Our goal is to make this intimate history of the destroyed Jewish shtetls
of Eastern Europe available in book form in English, so that people can
experience the near-personal histories of their ancestral town on their
bookshelves and those of their children and grandchildren.

All donations to the Yizkor Books Project, which translated the books,
are sincerely appreciated.

Please send donations to:

Yizkor Book Project
JewishGen, Inc.
36 Battery Place
New York, NY, 10280

JewishGen, Inc. is an affiliate of the
Museum of Jewish Heritage
A Living Memorial to the Holocaust

Acknowledgment

As I am writing this introduction to the "Destruction of Glubokie" during the month of April, 2021, 76 years after the Liberation of the Holocaust, an "uniquely evil event in the history of mankind", reading each story of these horrific genocides, first-hand accounts, to kill off a people belonging to a particular group, I am truly humbled and honored to participate in the translation of these Yizkor books. The cruelty involved in all these situations is almost beyond comprehension. The more the years pass, the more I am struck by the fact that the Holocaust was a uniquely evil event, none of which is to diminish other horrific genocides.

Where the Holocaust entered into new territory was the fact that Jews were not in conflict with those that murdered them, that the murder of Jews took place across many borders, that Jews that lived on both sides of the war that was taking place were murdered equally, that bystanders in many countries stood by idly when Jews were being taken away, and that *children* were a particular target of the murderers.When all the elements come together, they explain why, as the years pass, the emotions about it all remain as strong as ever. How could humanity have sunk to such a level, even recognizing that antisemitism was deeply embedded in Western culture? Why were there not more people ready to stand up and say no to the mass murder that was taking place right before their eyes?Think of all the poems that were never written, the medical cures that were never developed, the leaders that never appeared because of the devastation that took place.

Our best revenge was to build a healthy democratic society in our *state of Israel*. The destruction of one third of the world's Jews in the SHOAH can never be forgotten and the potential loss of human accomplishment can never be replaced. For us, the living, despite it all, there is a message of hope and responsibility: to create a better world and live up to our highest moral standards. Pass on the memory of our "lost world" to future generations. *Never forget…Who will remember them….*

Anita Frishman Gabbay, project coordinator of the Kobylnik and Sventzian Yiskor Books, whose roots are from Kobylnik and Sventzian, assisted in the completion of the last translations:

IN MEMORY OF THE YAVNOVITCH AND GILINSKI FAMILIES OF KOBYLNIK whose link to GLUBOKIE came from the autobiography of the late *Meir Yavnovitch*(Meir Yavnai z"l, of Tel Aviv), who went to GLUBOKIE to continue his education and lived with his mother's (Raiza Gilinski) cousins, SHALOM AND GITA(?) of Glubokie (whose business was seeds, oil, grease for the Carriage wheels, etc). This was about 1921-1925 where he studied with a private tutor. He was not embarrassed to write about his romances with the beautiful girls of Glubokie, Gite Gordon was one of them (mentioned in this book, pag3 97-the lover of a German officer-Shultz, Gite was later murdered) which adorns his photo album. Translating these Yizkor books opens up a window for many children of Holocaust survivors who never met their murdered relatives, a never-ending story in which many, many intriques are discovered and adds dimension to one's family history….

After completing the Glubokie book, and reading through several of the chapters and dedications, I will attach the tombstone that I came across on a recent trip to Postavy in 2018. It is significant because the Reichel family, whether in Argentina, Israel or elsewhere can add this to their family memorial. It is the tombstone of Dov Yacov, son of Ber Reichel. This is one of many that lie beneath the covered garden of this Gentile, Victor[?].

It is painful to read about our history, our final days, memories erased, but thanks to this book and others, we can memorialize "a shtetl and it's people".

Anita Frishman Gabbay
Montreal, Canada April, 2021

Notes to the Reader:

We apologize ahead of time for the poor quality of images in the book. Often these images had been scanned from the original Yizkor books which were of poor quality to begin with, being copies of old photographs. Each transfer results in loss of quality. We have done the best we could, given the original material and the resources and technology at hand. Even though images often appear of higher quality on computer screens, that does not transfer to high quality images in print. A reader can view the original scans on the web sites listed below.

Within the text the reader will note "{34}" standing ahead of a paragraph. This indicates that the material translated below was on page 34 of the original book. However, when a paragraph was split between two pages in the original book, the marker is placed in this book after the end of the paragraph for ease of reading.

Also please note that all references within the text of the book to page numbers, refer to the page numbers of the original Yizkor Book.

The original book can be seen online at the New York Public Library site:

https://digitalcollections.nypl.org/search/index?utf8=%E2%9C%93&keywords=gluboke

or at the Yiddish Book Center web site:

https://www.yiddishbookcenter.org/collections/yizkor-books/yzk-nybc313765/hurbn-glubok-sharkoystsene-dunilovitsh-postov-droye

In order to obtain a list of all Shoah victims from Glubokie, the reader should access the Yad Vashem web site listed below; one can also search for specific family names using family name option. These lists are continually updated by Yad Vashem, so it is worthwhile to periodically search these lists.

There is much valuable information available on this web site, including the Pages of Testimony, etc.
http://yvng.yadvashem.org

A list of this book and all books available in the Yizkor-Book-In-Print Project along with prices is available at:
http://www.jewishgen.org/Yizkor/ybip.html

Geopolitical Information:

Globokie (Hlybokaye), Belarus is located at 55°08' N 27°41' E and 85 miles N of Minsk

	Town	District	Province	Country
Before WWI (c. 1900):	Glubokoye	Disna	Vilna	Russian Empire
Between the wars (c. 1930):	Głębokie	Dzisna	Wilno	Poland
After WWII (c. 1950):	Hlybokaye			Soviet Union
Today (c. 2000):	Hlybokaye			Belarus

Alternate names for the town:
Hlybokaye [Bel], Głębokie [Pol], Glubokoye [Rus], Glubok [Yid], Glubokojė [Lith], Glybokoje, Hłybokaje, Hlybokae, Hluboka, Glebokoye, Globokie, Glubokie, Gleboke, Glembokie

Nearby Jewish Communities:

Yasevichi 8 miles ESE
Halubichy 11 miles E
Plissa 12 miles ENE
Dokshytsy 16 miles S
Luzhki 17 miles NNE
Parafyanovo 18 miles S
Sharkowshchyna 18 miles NNW
Dunilavičy 18 miles WSW
Germanovichi 19 miles NNE
Prozoroki 24 miles ENE
Kublichi 26 miles E
Budslav 26 miles SSW
Novy Pahost 27 miles NNW
Iody 28 miles NW

Jewish Population: 3,917 (in 1897), 4,000 (in 1925)

Map of Belarus with Glubokie

Title Page of Original Yizkor Book

מיכאל און צבי ראיאק

חורבן גלובאק • שארקויסצענע
דונילאוויטש • פאסטאוו
דרויע • קאזאן

דאָס לעבן און אומקום פון ייִדישע שטעטלעך
אין ווײַסרוסלאַנד — ליטע (ווילנער געגנט)

רעדאַקטאָר: שלמה סוסקאָוויטש

אַרויסגעגעבן דורך
לאַנדסלײַט פאַריין פון שאַרקויסצענע, דונילאָוויטש, פאַסטאָוו,
גלובאָק און אומגעגנט אין אַרגענטינע

בוענאָס איירעס, 1956, תשט"ז

Translation of Previous Page

Michael and Zvi Rajak

The Destruction of Glubokie · Szarkowszczyzna Dunilowicze · Postavy Druya · Kaziany

Memorial For The Jewish Communities of Glubokie, Szarkowszczyzna, Dunilowicze, Postavy, Druya and Kaziany,
(in Belarus and Lithuania-Vilna region) perished by the barbaric hands of Nazi Germany

Editor: Shlomo Suskovich

Published by:

Landsleit Fahrein (Association) of Sharkoystzene, Dunilovitch, Postav, Gluboke and the Surrounding Area, in Argentina

Buenos Aires, 1956

TABLE OF CONTENTS

Yahrzeitn (Remember)		3
Remember	Dr. Mark Dwerdeshetzki	4
Forward	Society in Argentina	5
Dedicated to the holy memory	Michael and Zvi Rajak	7

Glubokie

The Destruction of Glubokie	Michael and Zvi Rajak	8
To the Reader		8
To the Story of Glubokie	Michael and Zvi Rajak	10
The Outbreak of World War II	The Rajak brothers	30
The Jews Under the First German Influx		47
The First German Provocation		48
Russian War Prisoners		50
The Agreement Between the Magistrate and the Mayor		54
Bread Rationing		55
Death Sentence for having Extra portion of Flour		56
Forced Labor		57
The Isolation of the Jews		58
The Police		59
The Judenrat		60
The Gestapo in Glubokie		62
The German Civil Administration		64
The Jewish Police		67
Confiscation of all the Jewish Property		70
Confiscation-Money Action		71
Village population under Terror		72
The Gypsies' Chase		73
The Ghetto		74
Bemma, Commandant of the Glubokie Slaughter House		83
The Abuse of The Jews from Krulevshchizna		85
The Murder of Forty Souls		86
The Great Exodus from the Vilna Ghetto		88
Mass Murders in the Surrounding Shtetls		90
The Murder of One Hundred and Ten Jews		91
The Ghetto Space allowance Decreases		94
The "Black Students"		97
The Extermination of the Jews of Surrounding Shtetls		100

The Second Ghetto	106
The Second Ghetto is about to be Liquidated	108
The Liquidation of the Second Ghetto	115
After the Slaughter	123
The Reduction of the Ghetto size	128
The German Spy Vitvitzki	132
"Warehouse"	137
Workshops and the Office of the GEBIT Komisar	139
Glubokie Ghetto; A Concentration camp for the Remaining Jews of the surrounding liquidated Shtetls	144
The First Glubokie Partisans	150
The Arrest of Moshe Abramovitz	155
The Germans Arrest the Judenrat Elder	156
The Germans Swallow Jewish Victims	158
The Radianovtzes Join The Partisans and Fight The Glubokie Germans Gendarmes	166
The Criminals liquidate the Glubokie Ghetto	168
The Last Night	170
Friday, August 20, 1943; A Day of Pandemonium and carnage	172
The Ghetto is Burning	174
Before the Final Hour	179
We Wander Aimlessly and Come to the Partisans	185
The Principal Murderers of the Glubokie Jews	188
At Combat against The Enemy	193
After We Separated	197
After the Liberation	230
Glubokie Necrology	232
Pictures	260

Szarkowszczyzna

The Destruction of Szarkowszczyzna	274
The First World War (1914 - 1918)	279
R' Yehoshua Estrin	283
When the Red Army Entered Szarkowszczyzna	284
Szarkowszczyzna Survivors Relate…	300
Sonia Szmuskowicz-Pajkin	309

Dunilowicze

The Annihilation of Dunilovichi	311
June 1941, The Germans' entrance to Dunilovichi	339
The 11th Yahrzeit of Hirshke Trotzky	346
Dunilowicze Jewish residents in 1939	348

Jewish survivors who were in Dunilowicze during the war	356

Postavy

The Topographical Situation	358
Postavy History Until 1914	359
A Blood Libel	360
Preventing a Pogrom	361
The First World War - 1914-1918	361
The Return to Postavy	363
The Soviets Entry in 1939	365
The Arrival of the Germans	366
The First Victims	366
Incarcerating the Potsavy Jews	368
The Liquidation of the Postavy Ghetto	369
The Survivors of the Postavy Ghetto	372
Partisans of the Postavy Ghetto	373

Druya

Druya	377
Druya Noted Personalities	386
Snapshots of Druya School Life during the 20th Anniversary of the Druya Folkshule	390
The Liquidation of the Druya Ghetto	394

Kaziany (Kozyany)

The Destruction of Kazan	395
Baile Reichel	398
Former Kazan Partisans in Israel	401

Pictures

	402
Landsleit Organization of Skarkowszcyzna, Dunilovitch, Postov, Glubok and Environs	420
[Introductory Spanish pages]	425

Name Index   427

The Destruction of Glubokie (Hlybokaye, Belarus)

Translation of *Khurbn Glubok*

Edited by M. and Z. Rajak, former Residents' Association in Argentina

Published in Buenos Aires, 1956

Acknowledgments

Project Coordinator

Anita Frishman Gabbay

Emerita Coordiantor: Eilat Gordin Levitan

Note: Jerrold Landau made a light editing pass over the entire book to correct obvious translation error,
fill in missing photo captions, and ensure proper pagination. Some inconsistencies and errors may still remain.

This is a translation from: *Khurbn Glubok*
(The Destruction of Glubokie),
Editors. M and Z. Rajak. Buenos Aires, 1956:

Former Residents' Association in Argentina (H)

TOC translated by Eilat Gordin Levitan

Michael and Zvi Rajak

Memorial For The Jewish Communities of Glubokie, Szarkowszczyzna, Dunilowicze, Postavy, Druya and Kaziany,
(in Belarus and Lithuania-Vilna region) perished by the barbaric hands of Nazi Germany

Publisher: Salomon Suskovich

Edited by the Society of the Residents of
Szarkowszczyzna, Dunilowicze, Postavy and Glubokie in Argentina

Special Thanks for Sonia and Noach Katzovitz of Postavy
For their generous financial donation for the book

Buenos Aires
1956

Remember

Translated by Jerrold Landau

The Yahrzeits of our beloved and dear ones who were killed in the mass murders are as follows:

Destruction of Glubokie, 6,000 souls	August 20, 1943; 19 Av 5703
Destruction of Szarkowszczyzna 1,800 souls	July 18, 1942, 3 Tammuz 5702
Destruction of Dunilowicze 900 souls	November 22, 1942; 13 Kislev 5703
Destruction of Postavy 2,500 souls	December 25, 1942; 15 Tevet 5703
Destruction of Druya 2,500 souls	July 17, 1942; 2 Tammuz 5702
Destruction of Kaziany 300 souls	August 20, 1943; 19 Av 5703

* * *

We request from all our townsfolk that the elder of the family read chapters of the book to the family on the day of the Yahrzeit. We permit ourselves to unite with our dear beloved ones who were killed in sanctification of the Divine name.

On the day of the Yahrzeit, none of our townsfolk should celebrate a private joyous occasion or a communal celebration.

Remember!

Dr. Mark Dworszecki

From the book "Jerusalem of Lithuania in Struggle and in Destruction"

Translated by Jerrold Landau

Remember the destruction of Israel – remember the battle and the killing – and learn a lesson from it.

Let the memory of the destruction be the salt in your bread, and let it flow through your blood, in your flesh and bones.

Grit your teeth and remember! And when you eat – remember! And when you drink – remember!

And when you hear a song – remember! And when the sun shines – remember! And when night falls – remember!

And when you build a house – break a wall inside of it – so that you will always see the destruction of the House of Israel before your eyes!

And when you see a plowed field – place a mound of stones in it – as a testimony and a memorial for brethren who did not merit a Jewish burial.

And when you lead a child to the marriage canopy – you must remember the Jewish children who will never be led to the marriage canopy! – And for whom nobody will ever recite kaddish.

Let us be as one! The dead and the living; the ones torn away – and the ones that remain; those who are away – and the remnant of Israel.

Listen and listen, as it calls to everyone one of us – the lesson of our people's misfortune – Be uncomfortable! Be uncomfortable!

Forward

Landsleit Fahrein (Association) of Sharkoystzene, Dunilovitch, Postav, Gluboke and the Surrounding Area, in Argentina

Translation suppied by the Kotz family

Edited by Eilat Gordin Levitan

With a sacred trembling, we commemorate our beloved and dearest, who perished at the hand of the German murderers and the local Christian population. They were banded in life, and likewise in their deaths. We allude to the communities of the towns of Gluboke, Sharkoystzene, Dunilovitch, Postav, Druya and Kazan. They are all part of Belarus (Reisn). They are considered to be in the Province of Vilna. The Jews of all of these towns are called "Litvaks", even though they didn't know a word of the Lithuanian language. The language that was commonly spoken in our area was Russian.

The major portion of this book is devoted to recounting the destruction of Gluboke, which the two siblings, Michael and Tzvi Reiyak, who were Gluboke teachers, wrote. Glubokeites had the privilege of having, among their survivors, those who had talent, and the will to pass on to future generations, that which they saw in the "Valley of Death". They recorded these pages after the destruction of Gluboke, while they wandered, famished and destitute, through forests, fields and swamps, and while death lurked about them, on all corners. Their recounting has the distinction of maintaining but limited rhetoric. They've compiled only actual events, which are authenticated with hundreds of names and endless data. They have relied, not only on what their own memory and experience dictate, but also on the testimony of others. Thus, a detailed description of the life, struggle and destruction of the Jews of Gluboke. We see them from within. For us, they Live! The Gluboke Ghetto was destined to be a temporary shelter for the surviving remnant of the encompassing, slaughtered towns. The Jews, who saved themselves from the slaughter in their own towns, could find no place of refuge. At the time, there were revolts yet no organized partisans, so there was nowhere to flee. They lay scattered, starved and exposed in the forests, fields and swamps. When the deceitful call came from the Judenrat, that the remnant of survivors come to the Gluboke Ghetto, most of the Jews consented. They had no alternative, for death lurked on all sides. Tens of victims fell daily, so they latched on to this call. The brothers Reiyak also tell about these Jews. They left no corner unturned. Afterwards, they describe their own wanderings and recovery. But that is a chapter by itself!

The narrations about the other towns, that are included in this book, have an entirely different character. These are the jottings that the Jews from the "stetetlach" (small towns) related. That's how it is with the information that was relayed about the towns, before their destruction, and, at the time of their destruction. Most of the narration was done collectively. We assembled fellow townsmen (landsleit), and from them, elicited the important information. We also made use of letters. Our chairman, who is the editor of this book, is the one who wrote up all of the information about the towns. The annihilation of these towns, that we recall here, began somewhat sooner than elsewhere, at the beginning of 1942. Also, the uprising, or resistance against the murderers, began a lot sooner then in other places. On the 18th of July 1942, a fullblown uprising took place in the Sharkoystzener Ghetto. Thirty minutes before the heavily armed German police pounced on the Ghetto, the Judenrat succeeded in breaking down the Ghetto fence and setting fire to the town. The Judenrat was arming those few who did not let themselves be fooled by the murderers. That's how about 80% of the Jews of the town were able to save themselves. However most perished later from hunger, hardship, and the murderers' bullets. The remnant perished when the Gluboker Ghetto was annihilated.

The monstrous enemy could not condone such a rebellion. Ironicly, at the time, many Jews considered this uprising as a tragedy for the Jews of the entire area. They maintained that it had inflamed the enemy!

We hope that chapters of the Memorial Book will be read by our landsleit (fellow townsfolk), at the very least, on the annual memorial day of the annihilation of each of our beloved "shtetlach". Let everyone read it to his family!

Let this Memorial Book serve as an eternal reminder to bind us to our beloved and dearest ones, who were robbed of their human rights and dignity, and whose blood was wantonly spilled, and whose lives were so cruelly cut short! Almost all of the landsleit contributed to the publication of this book. We must give credit to our prominent "landsman" (townsman), Noah Katzovitch, who covered half of the costs.

Dedicated to the Holy Memory

Michael and Tzvi Rajak

Translated by Jerrold Landau

Of our dear mother Sara-Rachel of blessed memory.

Of our wife and sister-in-law Dr. Helena Wilkomirska-Rajak and son Aharon-Yitzchak.

Of the devoted, dedicated teachers in our institutions of learning.

Of our hundreds of students and their parents.

Of the entire Jewish community of Glubokie.

The memory of them all, who were so cruelly murdered by the German murderers and their assistants.

To our students, may they live long, in Israel and in the wide world – a cup of comfort.

[Page 11]

Glubokie

The Destruction of Glubokie

By Michael and Zvi Rajak

Translation supplied by the Kotz family and Eilat Gordin Levitan

Zvi Rajak

To the Reader

As we commence to depict the events that befell upon us, the horror of the plight of the Jews and their eradication.... Their slaughter by the German murderers. We will pause briefly to describe the circumstances under which the writing of this testament was carried out.

This dairy was written after fleeing from Glubokie at the time of the abominable slaughter on the 19th of the month of Av in 1943. It was written during the time of our wandering - wandering in numerous forests, fields, swamps, etc., where we had to hide from the Germans and their local assistants. And there we wrote on one side of the page something of our encountering, but we were not able to write the other side of the page, aware that we were constantly forced to change our "dwelling place", migrating from one mire to another, from one forest into another.

Frequently, we changed location several times in a 24-hour period, where we were during the day, we were not during the night and vice versa. Very often, while gathering our thoughts to proceed with the task of recording we were ed: "Germans are about"... and we had to run... not knowing how or where to....

[Page 12]

Secondly, we constantly found ourselves in a condition of starvation, and many a time, the hunger made itself so strongly felt that our heads swarmed from dizziness, and we had to abandon our writing to scavenge for something to eat. Seeking this type of "hospitality" was fraught with great danger on the one hand, and with difficult moral choices on the other. Besides which, we were not always too successful in finding something. And if there were those who were "humanitarians" and did toss us something to eat, no sympathetic expression was ever displayed.

The main impediment to our task was our dreadful mental state. It was written after the liquidation of the ghetto of Glubokie on August 20, 1943. During a time that those earlier deep wounds had not yet even begun to amend. We refer to the wounds inflicted on us 13 months prior to the final Destruction, the day the Germans murdered our beloved mother.

Added to those deep wounds; I, (M. Rajak), involuntary parted with my dearly beloved wife, Helena, and dearest beloved child, 8 years old Aaron Yitzhakel..., may their memory be blessed.... As the Glubokie ghetto, with its Jewish inhabitants was burning, we were able to flee together at dawn on August 22nd. As we arrived about 3 kilometers from the city, German vehicles with the Glubokie hangman, Vitvitzki, at the head, overtook us, and for 2 hours shot at us with machine guns and rifles. Being confused, we ran from the firing without presence of mind to varied directions, not knowing for many months who ended up where. As it turned out, we were separated forever! That was the most grievous and catastrophic moment of my life. We were "saved"! Saved in body! My soul remains throughout eternity with my wife and child. My wife was a dear, compassionate woman, but also a renowned, beloved physician, who had saved many children. (She was a pediatrician.)

Feeling the sacred obligation to eternalize the gruesome events that befell the Jewish community of Glubokie, which came to such a violent end. In order to set up a memorial, such as it is, for the holy Glubokie community. For the thousands of Jews who perished with their wives and children, for our dearest and most beloved, who fell for the "Sanctification of the Name", we have, in spite of our personal devastation and ceaseless despair, sanctified this immense, significant and sacred task.

[Page 13]

To the Story of Glubokie

By Zvi and Michael Rajak

Translation provided by the Kotz family and Eilat Gordin Levitan

Glubokie is an old city, her roots go back to the early 1800's. She lies on a low plain, enveloped by hills. From her topographical image originated the name; "Glubokie", suggesting certain "depth". She is located about 200 kilometers northeast of Vilna and 90 kilometers from Polotzk, covering a distance of about 8 square kilometers. Among her monuments most significant is the old castle on the Polish "cemetery" that was named "Napoleon's Tower". Likewise, the thick checkered boundary of about half a meter that encompass the city public garden (park). It was to some extent ruined. Also, in Glubokie of that bygone time, there was old synagogue with a high, far-reaching cupola which made for a splendid vista. Inside, on the wall of the synagogue, there was a very beautiful, skillfully carved Holy Ark, above which, there hung a large Czar's eagle. The eagle was fastened to the very top of the ceiling right into the cupola. In 1920, when Glubokie was taken over by the Poles, the Russian eagle was removed.

Michael Rajak

Two kilometers from the city stood an old Berezvetsher monastery. Here, nature was abundant and kaleidoscopic - blessed with a exquisite forest, orchards and gardens.

[Page 14]

The lake, which was called "Lake Berezvetsher", gave the city a distinctive aura. On the other side of the lake was the Jewish cemetery, in which, until the devastation, one could come upon tombstones erected more than 150 years ago (c 1790). Until the war, Berezvetsh had a laboratory that analyzed flax, hemp, and alike. Students, who were specializing in this field, would come there from all over Poland.

A small stream divided the city into two parts - eastern and western regions. A bridge linked them. The stream banded Lake Berezvetsh with the lake to the south of the city. There was a very picturesque nook by the lake, so called, "Kopanitze": An avenue lined with trees on both sides. At some places the walk took you deep into the lake and the lake penetrated into the dry land, so there came about a system of inflow and outflow, creating an intricate panorama of peninsulas and islands…

On Shabat afternoons, during the summer, the Jews of Glubokie would serenely stroll on the esplanade. Here you would meet the town's teacher, who after an exhausting week of teaching the children in a dampen, confined room, would come to catch his breath and fill his lungs with a little fresh air. Here, adorned in their Shabat finery, would promenade the shoemaker, the tailor and denizens with their wives and children. Here, a young couple would set their rendezvous and go on "dates". Very often the Shabat tranquillity would be "agitated" by the joyous playing of Jewish children, who were released on the Sabbath day from school and studies. The air would resonate with their juvenile, high-pitched voices. Their joyful chatter clustered with their adolescent laughter would be heard from afar.

The "Kopanitze" was a part of the town garden (park). There on a Shabat day, the Jewish youth, children from the orphanage, Cheder students and school children milled about. Very close to the city, was the railroad line - Vilna - Kruleveshtzine - Polotzk. It was a very busy line. The tie with the center, with Vilna, was very firm. Three or four passenger trains a day would pass through, going to and from. On each trip the trains would be overflowing with Jews. Besides which, various freight trains, with imported merchandise, and commodities for export, would pass through. From Glubokie they would send flax, grain, eggs, pelts, rags, hogs-hair, and alike. Merchandise from the provinces, manufactured goods, grocery wares, fancy goods, and the like were imported. The entire business was in Jewish hands.

[Page 15]

The city, in general, was a large trade center and densely populated. In recent times Glubokie was called "Little Danzig". Up to the war, the population numbered 11,000. Jews made up about half of the population, Poles about 48% and the remainder, White Russians and other nationalities.

A class in the Hebrew Gimnasia (high school)
The authors; Michael and Zvi Rajak were the heads of the school

The Jewish dwellings were concentrated mainly in the central streets and around the market place. The humble Jews lived in the old and new Kishelaike and pubrove and Polne Streets and at the end of Vilna Street, and alike. The so-called "Mashiach's Colony" was very prevalent, due to the fact that in that area there lived a prolific family, named "Tzemach", a synonym for "Mashiach", which means Messiah. The residents of the area were made up of strong Jewish porters, draymen, and ordinary working Jews, with whom Jewish Glubokie had to reckon. The family rapidly multiplied, and if not for the catastrophe, they would have contributed greatly to the increase of the Jewish population in Glubokie.

[Page 16]

Most of the Jewish businesses, stores, workshops, and similar, were in the center of the town. On the edge of the town were the mills, leather factories, a sawmill, and alike. In Glubokie there were 2 cinemas that also belonged to Jews. The electric station belonged to the municipality. On the outskirts of the city lived the so-called "town peasants", they were involved with cultivating the land. There were small-scale fairs but, once a week, on Thursday, there were large fairs. Christians and Jews would arrive from far-away places. Even Jews from Vilna would come to the fairs. With the development and expansion of the commerce, the prosperity of the population increased. The majority of the Jews were well to do. The cinemas showed movies on a daily basis. Very often, a Jewish or a Polish troupe would come to present a play, and the performances would be well attended. During the summer Jews would go to repose in their summer homes. In town there were about 1,100 dwellings, many two-storied and a few even three-storied.

The Jewish Executive Committee of the Community of Glubokie was a wealthy one. It owned a large amount of land dubbed the" Jewish Pasture". The Glubokie Jews also had their personal meadows for feeding their cattle, and from it, the community derived a nice income. The community also had, in the center of town, its own shops, which were rented out to Jewish shopkeepers_ The Jewish population paid, into the community chest, a special tax. Besides that, the community had income from birth certificates, weddings, circumcisions, burials, and similar activities. For its part the community supported the Rabbis, ritual slaughterers, various communal institutions, insolvent individuals, bankrupt Jews, and other needs. The head of the Glubokie community, before the war, was Rabbi Mordechai Lev, of blessed memory, an enlightened Jew, a master of the Talmud, and a fervent Lubavitch Hassid. He was also a writer, with an elegant, enticing mode of speech. He conducted a daily study group in Talmud, in the Starosyelier Synagogue, which was always very well attended. Outwardly, he did not make a very powerful impression. The reason was that he supplemented his income by being a flour merchant, and except for Shabat and holidays, was always dusted with flour. His integrity and eloquence could only be truly appreciated when one conversed with him and became better acquainted him.

The chidren organization in the Yiddish school

The organization, "Toz", helped sick Jews. "Toz" had its own infirmary for out-patients. Over the years all kinds of doctors had worked there. During the last few years, Dr. Yitzhok Britanishsky of Vilna, was employed there. He was also the deputy mayor of the town. There was also a children's' consultation clinic, administered by a woman physician, Dr. Vilkomirska-Rajak, (the wife of M. Rajak). She, and their 8-year-old son, were murdered by the Germans on the 21st day of Av, in the year 5703 (1943).

[Page 17]

The women's' association in Glubokie was composed of local, dynamic women, who would aid poor brides, support orphans, help out during childbirth, and other comparable activities. A unique institution in Glubokie was the Child Protection Society. Jewish youth, regardless of their social standing or economic circumstance, cared for the destitute Jewish children. They would go to the cheders (one-room schools), schools, children's' homes, and also private insolvent homes, and concern themselves with the children, their circumstances and necessities, and they would do their utmost for them, especially those in greatest need. They would provide them with food and clothing. The Jewish youth organization would especially display their efficiency during the cold autumn and winter months.

[Page 18]

The Jewish bank, which was held in esteem, did an enormous volume of business. For both the large and small merchants, the bank would grant assistance in the expansion of their enterprises. In volume, the Jewish bank outdid the local Polish Government Bank. A very important institution was the "Free Loan Society". They would lend out money, for a long-term duration, without charging any interest, and the repayment would be made in installments. Hundreds of craftsmen and small shopkeepers were put back on their feet by the Jewish "Free Loan Society".

A Merchants' Union and a Hand-craftsmen's' Union was established. Both vibrated with activities for the mutual benefit of the members. The task of the "Bread for the Poor" Society, was to provide impoverished Jews with "challahs", meat and other necessities for Shabat. They also saw to it that Jewish prisoners would attain kosher food on weekdays, Sabbaths and holidays. On the High Holy Days, the Society would arrange for a "minyan" (quorum of 10 adult males) for the incarcerated Jews. It is worth mentioning some of the names of the participants in these good enterprises: David, the carpenter, of blessed memory, who died before the war. He was an elderly Jew, who, during his entire life, enjoyed working with his hands, and sought to help the needy in whatever way necessary. He stuttered, but everyone could comprehend what he said. The entire Jewish community of Glubokie properly honored His valuable activities. Often, he would leave his workbench, cut short his work, which was his livelihood, and go out to collect money for the "Bread for the Poor" Society. Not a single Jewish home would deny him a donation. Everyone contributed joyously. The Jews of Glubokie respected his dedication, which was completely selfless. On a holiday, he and another person would go out with a large basket from house to house, gathering "challah", fish, meat, and alike., for the Jews who had been arrested. "They also have to eat!" he would contend. "It's a holiday!" He would organize other fairs to help carry out these righteous projects. And thus, it became a tradition for the Jews of Glubokie, to bake and cook for the Jewish prisoners in the local jail, before a holiday.

R' Shlomo Bogin, now in America, the former editor of the local Jewish newspaper, also helped this Society. A very active participant in the leadership of local Jewish and social institutions, was David Munvoz, who came to a tragic end. He would work everywhere, whenever he was needed, the House of Study (Beis Hamedrash), the library, Mizrachi or Poale Zion, religious or secular enterprises. He never refused a call for help. Everywhere he was "exploited". Very often, he would put out money for one or two institutions and be paid back in installments. He was a devoted director and put the needs of the public first. He was the Gabbai (man who distributes honors and keeps order) in the big Synagogue. He worked tirelessly until the day he was murdered by the Germans - may their names be blotted out.

[Page 19]

The Glubokie Library on a Flower Day

The town had a library with a massive number of books in Hebrew, Yiddish, Polish, Russian, and other languages. There were numerous readers who were adequate in all of these languages. The number of books would constantly increase and would be loaned out to local readers as well as readers from the surrounding provincial towns and villages, for their Jewish youth.

Glubokie was known for her varied Zionist organizations, beginning with the god-fearing Mizrachi and all the way to the Socialist Poale Zion and Hashomer Hatzair on the far left. All of them conducted a broad range of activities. Their accomplishments for the Jewish National Fund and the Keren Hayesod (Foundation Fund) were done in a united way. All worked for these funds with devotion, without any distinctions. One of the strongest and most effective organizations was the Hechalutz. (Pioneers) The Glubokie branch was well known throughout the Vilna district. The youth of Hechalutz was active in all aspects of community life in Glubokie. Most effective was their Hachshara. (Pioneer preparatory training camp for those preparing to go to Palestine.)

[Page 20]

There were also Bundists and Socialist Democrats (non-Zionist left). They were small and weakly organized groups. Strongly established were the so-called "Yiddishists". They were against speaking Hebrew and preserving the Yiddish essential quality. Their influence was strongly felt. In Glubokie there was also an underground Communist cell. Active in it were also Jewish young people, some of them, due to their activities, spent many years in the Lukishker Prison in Vilna. They were Chaim Svidler, David Veitzkin, Chaste Tzeitel, Sarah-Riva Baoudin, Rachel Glaz, and others.

The Hebrew School in Glubokie, under the supervision of the writers of these lines, not only occupied the most prominent position of all local institutions but was also popular and well known far beyond the boundaries of Glubokie. In celebration of its 20th anniversary, in 1927, the school became a middle school, and graduated hundreds of male and female students - proud of their national heritage and well educated in all spheres. Many of them later became famous. Who, in Vilna, was not acquainted with the prodigy, Aaron-Yaakov Lazavik, of blessed memory, who most certainly would have become of the true great in the land of Israel? From that school, a large proportion of the youth later went on to study in schools of higher education, and later distinguished themselves. Moshe Chaves and Aaron Godin as doctors; Liptshe Gurevitsh, Freidl Tzentziper, David Pliskin, Raphael Valstein of Nei-Fahast, and others as teachers, Aaron-Zelick Pliskin as an actor. And many, many others....

Among the brave fighters of the Haganah, there is to be found an admirable list of former students of the above-mentioned institution, who distinguished themselves by their bravery in the liberation of Israel. They were Shloimke Chevlin, Shimon Shapiro, Tzvi Slabodkin, and others. Youth, not only from Glubokie, but from the entire surrounding area, attended that school, in order to learn Torah and acquire an all-round education Besides the Polish government mandated curriculum, and besides the general secular studies, a student, in ending the course of study in the school, had to be well versed in Bible, Jewish History, Hebrew and Yiddish literature, the Aggadah, and alike. It is worthwhile dedicating a few words to the role played by the Yiddish-Hebrew School in Glubokie; of her educational value, not only for the youth and children, but also for parents, for Jews of all sorts, and in general.

[Page 21]

The city, for example, would often have undertakings of various functions. The traditional, open to the public, school activities during the year, consisted of: Chanukah evenings, Purim evenings, Lag Lag B'Omer activities, Passover and Succot celebrations and Tu - B'Shvat projects. The evening celebrations would revitalize not only the school youth and children, but also the older people of the entire city and surrounding area.

The graduation of the "ladies seamstresses" from the ORT Society

For the Chanukah and Purim evenings of the school, the Jews would wait even more anxiously than for the other holidays of a more religious character. The tasteful Yiddish and Hebrew songs of the school choir became the hit songs for everyone, a heritage of Jewish Glubokie. They would immediately be sung at weddings and circumcisions, and in the branch meetings of the various organizations, in informal and social clubs, and the like. Even on Simchat Torah, during the Hakafot (circling the synagogue, holding the scrolls of the Torah), they were sung in the House of Study. The presentations of the musical operettas: "Bar Kochba", "Hannah and Her Seven Sons", "Chanukah-Gelt", "Ahashverosh", "The Errant Maiden", "Yisroelik", and many, many more, still remain in the memory, to this day, of those who survived. It is enough to mention that a Chanukah or Purim evening, performed by the school children, would, at the public's request, have to be performed 2 or 3 times. Even considering

[Page 22]

the large size of the auditorium, "The Liyudovi", there wasn't enough room for all those who wanted to see the performance.

On Lag B'Omer, the school holiday wasn't restricted to the four walls of the school building. On that day there would occur a real Jewish National street celebration. Hundreds of children and young people, with flags, with posters and banners of all sorts, would march out to the woods. The little ones would be transported in tens of wagons, and in later years, in automobiles and the like. The queue of youth would sing their Lag B'Omer repertoire of songs as they marched through the entire city, and into the forest. The children' singing rang out in the spring air, so sweet and delicious. On both sides of the street, there would stand Jewish and Christian onlookers. The Jews, naturally, would enjoy and "kvell" with happiness. Many Jews would leave their enterprises for the day and make it a holiday instead of a workday, join the children and let themselves be dragged alone to the forest by the stream of adolescence. This weekday holiday became, through the Jewish school, a true Jewish Holiday. This sort of demonstration would also leave a strong impression on the local non-Jewish population.

The arrival to the forest would herald the commencement of the real celebration of the holiday. There would be a Lag B'Omer picnic feast, sports, presentations, singing, orations, and alike. No one would even pay attention when this jovial day came to an end, people would linger on.... At night they would return to the city, singing, and causing a stir, so that they were greeted with joy and enthusiasm by the city populace. For this Lag B'Omer celebration, Glubokie Jews would wait.... In mentioning school holidays, we cannot skip over Tu B'Shvat (the 15th day of the month of S'hvat, New Year of, the Trees). This holiday likewise had its special merit and value, and not only within the four walls of the school. If not for the school, the Jews of Glubokie wouldn't know and wouldn't appreciate this particular holiday. Religious people would have observed it by not reciting the mournful daily prayers., and making the special blessing ("She'eche'yanu") over a new fruit, and those who observed only Rosh Hashanah and Yom Kippur, and didn't' recite blessings at all, would know absolutely nothing about the New Year of the Trees. The school would celebrate this holiday in a most original way. Already, a few weeks before the holiday, the Jewish National Fund of Warsaw would send packages of pictures and information about life in the land of Israel. The small, illustrated bags, which were included, would be filled with the fruit of the land: Carob, figs, raisins, and also chocolate, candies and other goodies. For the evening, the auditorium was decorated, and on the walls were inscribed slogans of the day. In the center hung a silvered Star of David, with a fruit laden tree in its midst. The children would come adorned in their holiday finery, and would bring their parents, brothers, sisters and just any guests.

[Page 23]

The Hebrew Gimnasia and brothers Rajak

For such a celebration, there would occasionally appear a "grandmother"; but what a grandmother! A lively, jolly, Jewish old lady, who couldn't get enough of the "nachas" of the "Land of Israel" within the four walls of the Glubokie Jewish school in the heart of winter.... Older children would present different Land of Israel skits, such as the planting of trees, the bringing of "first fruits", and others. During these presentations they would sing the songs: Shalom Aleichem Jews, Tell Me Dear Maiden, Tu B'Shvat, To the Bird, and alike.

The shipment of the Jewish National Fund parcels of fruit as presents would be quite poignant. It would look somewhat like this: Many bags filled with the fruit of the Land were placed on a large table in the middle of the auditorium. At the table sat a committee of five of the older students, and two "couriers" stood by, ready to serve.... The parcels could be bought for a pre-set minimum price. But a lot more than the agreed upon charge was usual paid, because the money was a donation to the Jewish National Fund. No one would purchase the parcels for themselves, but they would send them as gifts to somebody else. For example: "Sarahle" ordered five bags, paid for them, and on a slip wrote the names of those to whom she wanted them to be delivered. The "couriers", or as they would jokingly be called, the "Voyazshorn", used to announce loudly the name of the person receiving the offering, and then carry it to the "address". Those who would receive the gifts would not be bashful and they would send them back. In this way, everyone would be drawn into the activity. The parcels would find their way back and forth many times, and then be auctioned off anew. In this way the same bag made the rounds again and again, and each time it would bring in a contribution for the Jewish National Fund.

[Page 24]

The Tu B'Shvat evenings of the Glubokie Jewish School were popular, not only in Glubokie, but also in the Warsaw Jewish National Fund, where they were noted as a unique tradition. Such an evening, would have, besides the large income for the JNF, colossal educational value for the entire Jewish establishment. It would do more for the building of the Jewish Homeland than all of the usual commotion, sermons, declarations and discussions. In time, this Tu B'Shvat Holiday became a tradition. Village merchants would watch the calendar, and two weeks before they would present their wares and request that they be given a stall to lease, to sell their carob and figs, which they claimed were truly from the Holy Land.

The school had a large choir, which was directed in the early years by Melech Bielinske. The choir would perform during these school celebrations with a plentiful repertoire. We must mention here, albeit with but a few words, the children's' club. They would fill the rooms of the school, when they would gather, not only on holidays, but also on Friday evenings in the winter and Shabat afternoons in the summer. Not only school children, but also with other youngsters and parents, who used to come to spend a few hours with the students. They were not able to tear themselves away from the spiritual pleasure which they found there. The melodic singing of the choir would bring tears to their eyes. The discussions between teachers and older students of various topics made them proud. the declamations and recitations by students, the different plays, in which both old and young would take part, were so intense, that it seemed that the spiritual life was elevated and seemed eternal. It felt as if their Jewish spirit Would never be extinguished.

[Page 25]

The ambience sparkled like the Sabbath, and the frame of mind so joyful, not at all artificial, but with an authentic flavor of the "world to come." Those who experienced the children's' club in those days will never forget the experience. They won't forget the true spiritual thrill, which seized all of the bystanders, the thrill which pinched the soul, and would blow into the workaday week, the genuine supplementary soul. (Based on a traditional Jewish belief, that a Jew who observes the Sabbath is endowed with an additional soul for the entire Sabbath day.)

Members of Hashomer Hatzair

The extensive, diverse, many faceted and unique activities of the Glubokie School received publicity, at the time, in the daily Jewish press in Vilna, and also in many pedagogic periodicals and journals. Through various officials, school activists, and public relations people, the outstanding events in the life of the school, would be brought to the public's attention. In the columns of the Vilna "Tzeit" (Time) and "Tag" (The Day, which was a Yiddishist paper), would be found from time to time, articles and notices about the

Glubokie School. One such notice, under the headline: "The First Commencement of the Glubokie Jewish School", which appeared on the 27th of August 1925 (7th of Elul, 5685) no. 174, was found in the Vilna Museum, after the War, in 1946. We quote: "On the 16th of August, at a festive assemblage, in the presence of Dr. Vigodsky, who came especially from Vilna for the Commencement. There were also present the Mayor (Burgomeister) of Glubokie, and representatives of all local institutions, and also delegations of all of the groups in the Jewish population. The Commencement took place in the beautifully decorated auditorium of the Jewish Folks-Bank. It was the first Commencement Exercise of the Jewish School.

[Page 26]

After the opening ceremony and greetings from the Director of the school, M. Rajak, Dr. Vigodsky, who was chosen as Honorary Chairman, gave a warm speech, greeting the children and also the general audience. There were also greetings from the Glubokie community, the teachers, and from various institutions and persons. Many written greetings, letters and dispatches were read. Separate mention must be made of the warm and helpful words of greeting from the local Mayor, who, in a fiery speech promised to support the Jewish School. At the end of the proceedings, several works of students were read, and the outstanding one among them was the work of the student, Aaron Veitzkin, who wrote about the characteristics of the prophets, Amos and Hosea.

Then there was the distribution of the diplomas to the graduates: 1) Aaron Veitzkin; 2) Hirsh Chaves; 3) Pesach Mindlin; 4) Devorah Katz; 5) Zalman Shaynkman; 6) Michael Shapira; 7) Baruch Shapira; 8) Slave Shparber; and 9) Geshe Shulheifer. The affair was so impressive that one of the parents called out, in a trembling voice: 'Fortunate are the eyes which behold all of this!' After the official program was over, there was a reception at prepared tables, which lasted well past midnight. Then began the most spirited and festive part of the proceedings. The youngsters, together with the honorable and dear Dr. Vigodsky, sang, recited, and then, together with the entire audience, enjoyed themselves immensely. For a long, long time, Glubokie will remember the First Commencement Exercise of the Jewish School."

The above-mentioned students were almost all victims of the Germans, may their names be blotted out, except for Aaron Veitzkin and Baruch Shapira, may they have a long life, who now live in Israel. In the early years, there also existed in Glubokie a Yiddishist School and a very orthodox school, "T'ushia"_ All of these were filled with students, with

"Moishelech" and "Shloimelech", and everywhere there pulsated a vigorous Jewish life. All has disappeared!

ALL LOST! THERE IS NO MORE YOUTH, NO PARENTS, NO TEACHERS! ONE GREAT DESOLATION! GRAVES UPON GRAVES!....

The greatest portion of the school youth, to our great misfortune, remained in the graves in the fields and woods around Glubokie. A small proportion which was already in Palestine and other countries during the German occupation, where the German boot had not trod, remained alive. This small remnant of living youth is a memorial and tribute to the former beautiful and distinguished educational establishment in Glubokie.

[Page 27]

Wedding of Moshe Leib Rodstein
(well-known communal worked of the Chasidim of Chabad)

Glubokie also had a very fine Yeshiva. Tens of Yeshiva Bachurim (young men) learned Torah there. The Glubokie Jews supported them, almost on their shoulders. The prominent supporters, with Rabbi Katz, of blessed memory, at the head, were the Shochet (ritual slaughterer) R' Benzion Chanovitsh, of blessed memory, R' Shalom Weinstein and his son-in-law, R' Shachnovitsh, of blessed memory, and others. All were righteous, without blame and upright. Of the heads of the Yeshiva there was the present Warsaw Rabbi, Rabbi Katz (not so well known), R' Mordecai Yeshurun, of blessed memory, and the last one before the war, R' Reuven Moses, of blessed memory. He perished in the Holocaust. He had been a disciple of the famed and holy, "Chafetz Chaim", may the Zaddik's memory be a blessing. He had strongly hoped that the Jews of Glubokie would peacefully overcome the catastrophe of the German occupation. I am reminded of his great faith and trust, and how, with certainty, he expressed himself once during the month of Adar in 1942. (The month in which the Holiday of Purim falls): "During these months of salvation - Adar and Nissan (the month in which Passover occurs) - the Jews must get rid of the Germans. Just like in those days - a miracle will also take place now!" Glubokie also had Jewish religious elementary schools called Cheders. The old One, "Yosheh Tishes", of blessed memory, had shaped several generations of students. Some of his students must still be around somewhere. He was considered the best teacher....most able and competent. In addition, there were R' Eliakum, a typical teacher from a White Russian or Lithuanian town; R' Koppel Feigelman; Levitanos and others, were more modern.

[Page 28]

In the town there were 10 Houses of Study, Hassidic and non-Hassidic. The larger ones were the Staroselier, the Lubavitch and the "House of Study". The separate congregation in the upper school consisted of over 1000 people. In all of the Houses of Study there were daily prayers and learning sessions. How solemn the town appeared on the holidays, especially Rosh Hashanah, when, after the services, thousands of Jews streamed out of the Houses of Study and Synagogues; men, women and children. All were dressed in their holiday finery, and would deafen all passers-by, with their traditional greetings: "Gut Yom T'ov!" (Have a Good Holiday!).

The town had 3 Rabbis: two Hassidic and one who wasn't Hassid. Of these, Harav Yosef Halevi Katz, may the memory of the righteous be blessed, was a Rabbi in Glubokie for about forty years. He called himself "The Vishinter", since he came from the small Lithuanian town of Vishint. He could trace his ancestry back through a long chain of rabbis spanning many generations. He was a member of the Mizrachi Religious Zionist Party, and actively engaged in communal affairs. Of the Hassidic rabbis, there was the well-known, brilliant R' Avrohom, may the memory of the righteous be blessed. After his death Glubokie was without a Hassidic rabbi for a long time, since no arrangement could be made with a rabbi. Later there came R' Zundel Rabinzon from Radashkovitsh (see Radoshkovich Yizkor book for information and pictures of the family), and after him, R' Menachem Mendel Koopershtok. They were distinguished rabbis. The latter left for the Land of Israel quite a while before the war. Then R' Menachem Mendel of Lubavitch came and the non-Hassidim took R' Hillel Zalmanovitsh, the son-in-law of rav Katz, as their rabbi. All of them together with their families perished at the hands of the Germans. R' Katz on the 4th of Tammuz, 5702; R' Menachem Mendel Mandelbaum, the Lubavitcher, -on the 19th of Av, 5703 and R' Zalmanovitsh in Vilna, when the Germans entered the city.

The Jewish doctors were Mrs./ Dr. Vilkamerska Rajak, the wife of M. Raiyak. She was the administrator of the Jewish Childrens' Consultation Service, and had great satisfaction from her work, which involved helping the sick and the poor. She herself was an enlightened woman, and a true saint in her generation, in the full meaning of the word "saint"! Being a good doctor, she was very popular, also among the Christian population. When she was already in the ghetto, they would come to her to seek out ways to receive her help and her advice for their sick. (Jewish doctors had been forbidden by the Nazis to heal sick Christians.)

[Page 29]

Dr. Britanistisky, the head doctor of "Toz", an eminent gynecologist, renowned in the entire area, was also the vice-mayor of Glubokie. Dr. Kasriel Kalmanovitch of Germanovitch, a young doctor of very prominent lineage, was orthodox, and is now lives in Riga. Towards the end of the war, Dr. Nachum Lekach, a son of Shimon Lekach from Disne, settled in Glubokie. Later he became one of the most popular surgeons.

Professional school – Women seamstresses

Very popular here was the barber-surgeon, Yehoshua Geller, Israel the barber-surgeon's son. Also Christians held him in high esteem. He was one of the first victims of the German murderers. (Exact details will be given in the account of events during the Holocaust.) Glubokie had a considerable number of Jewish dentists. These included the two Faigelson sisters, Sarah Shulovitch, who was Michael Alperovitch's daughter; Moshe Katzovitch's daughter-in-law; Friedman-Yash from Yatke Street; Ginsberg and others.

There were also several ritual-slaughterers (Shochets). The chief of them was R' Benzion Kanovitch, of blessed memory, a son of the old ritual slaughterer, R' Israel, who bred a chain of ritual-slaughterers here in Glubokie. He was a fervent Lubavitcher Hassid. His wife, Elke, may she rest in peace, was a God-fearing woman, a sister of R' Maier German from Lieplie, the author of "Bais Rabi". Of this many branched family, only four children survived. One came to Israel and three others to America, at the start of the German-Polish War (1939).

[Page 30]

All of the town's organizations, institutions, and alike would often sponsor varied activities of one or another of the institutions. The local communal undertakings were very active. Very popular were the balls arranged by the women's auxiliary of the "Toz", the bazaars of the Jewish National Fund and others. How cheerfully and passionately would the young people run about with the flowers on "Flower Day"! The local youth also had a drama circle and quite often a troupe from a center in Warsaw or Vilna would come. Various distinguished personalities, eminent Zionist activists and guests from the Land of Israel would appear. And also so many others!

In town Jewish life moved along noisily. Everyone jointly, the religious and secular; the old and the young; grandchildren and grandfathers were acquainted as family. One locked tight, closely knit, joyous unification that made Jewish life spicy, juicy, spirited and absolutely delightful. It is difficult, in retrospect, to paint a faithful picture of all of the influences. Much more could be written about the Yiddish school, about the Yeshivah, the library and other institutions that the Jews created there. Not to mention the dedicated civic and public employees.

In listing the organizations in Glubokie, mention must be made of the Jewish sports organization: "Maccabi", which numbered several hundred youth. One's heart would quiver with joy, witnessing these young healthy boys and girls, in their sports outfits, marching to the sound of music, through the town on a holiday, on a Lag B'Omer outing, or going to the stadium for a match or gymnastics. Thousands of people would stream from all over town, and the site would assemble with onlookers. The Firemen's' Organization, which consisted mostly of Jews must also be spoken of. During celebrations, both Jews and the general populace would come to watch them marching through the streets, as they captivated their attention.

[Page 31]

The town's orchestra consisted entirely and exclusively of Jews under the direction of Bertchik Lekach, who is now in Valbzshik, Poland. Glubokie was a provincial center and part of the Vilna Military District. It was the seat of government for the local parliament and magistrate. It also housed a provincial hospital and bank, and other state and communal institutions. There were also two Polish elementary schools, a Polish high school, a big library, a vocational school, and a nursery.

Glubokie is destroyed! No Jews are there! Not even a memory remains of our past there! Just naked walls of several synagogues protrude, as the only witnesses of a former Jewish settlement. The murderers also destroyed the Jewish cemetery. They chopped down the trees. With the headstones they paved sidewalks and built a theatre. And there, where the bones of entire generations of noted great scholars and rabbis rested, on the hallowed ground of the Jewish graveyard, cattle and horses graze today. However, this consecrated place was mostly tarnished by the two-legged beasts!

[Page 32]

The Outbreak of World War II

By the Rajak brothers (sons of Ytzhak and Sara- Rachel bat Shimon and Guta)

Translation supplied by the Kotz family
in memory of Ephraim Dov and Ethel, Frada, Arkie, and Label Kotz, all of whom perished in the Holocaust

Edited by Eilat Gordin Levitan

On Friday, the 1st of September 1939, Glubokie was stunned by the German assault on Poland. Although the town was sufficiently distant from the German frontier and was located all the way in the extreme northeast corner of Poland of that time, the imprint in the first few hours was horrendous; the extent of the blood-bath was felt immediately. Many young men were mobilized and had to leave instantly. People ran to the banks and savings associations to remove their assets and the last to arrive could not be paid since the bank ran out of cash. The Polish officials began to confiscate textile products, shoes, and alike for the military use. The population began to search for ways to provide themselves with the necessities, and the prices skyrocketed. One encountered numerous women and children with tear-stained faces in the streets. You could also hear some wailing and cries of distress coming from inside the homes. Since the men were drafted, that Sabbath was spoiled for Jews… Around the public radios at the two ends of the town (3rd of May Place and Mark Place) people were crammed and did not leave the spots. They listen to the news that got progressively worse and increasingly disturbing. In the very first hours of the War, many Polish cities were heavily bombarded, and the number of causalities was high. We weren't used to it yet!

Correspondingly, at the railroad terminal, there was much chaos. It was swarming with people. Those to be recruited were being sent to war. Women and children, who had come to say farewell to their husbands and fathers, burst out crying. Even the "valiant" men were yammering. Their expressions hinted at; "Who knows if this isn't an eternal farewell?" There were no trains accessible for civilians. The only trains passing through were those brimming with military personal and ammunition. Kinfolk were extremely nervous about relatives who were stuck somewhere far from home. The War unexpectedly trapped them and they couldn't return home to their dearest.

[Page 33]

When I, Zvi Rajak, the writer of these lines, had to travel on August 31, 1939, from Vilna to my home, we still held on to the hope that maybe a war would somehow be averted. However, I by that time, needed a special pass issued by the military, since the railroad lines were at present under military jurisdiction. Thanks to my documents from the Vilna Board of Education, which indicated that I had to travel on their behalf, I was able to obtain a special pass at midnight. At headquarters, on Zsheligovski Street in Vilna, where a senior military official issued such passes, many tragic scenes unfolded in front of my eyes. People who found themselves torn away from their homes, far from their families, were suddenly engulfed by the War and couldn't return to their relatives. Mothers, with tears in their eyes, pleaded for mercy, to be allowed to return to their children, who had been left unattended. Here was a bridegroom, traveling to his own wedding, which was set for tomorrow, the eve of the Sabbath, and he was stuck on the way. He couldn't proceed, and they didn't allow him return home to the town or village that he had come from. There were also businessmen, who were cut off and couldn't contact anyone concerning their affairs. The Headquarters was besieged by hordes of people neglecting the fact that it was already after midnight. In the streets of Vilna, there were no means of transportation available. All taxis, trucks and even "droshkes" had already by noon- time, been procured by the military. If someone, by chance, happened to find some sort of mechanical vehicle or "droshke", he would have to pay an unbelievable amount of money to be transported only a few kilometers!

Also, the railroad itself, had been put on a war footing. The civilian authorities were replaced by well-manned military patrols, who checked everyone carefully. The railroad cars and train stations dimmed their lights. On the city streets the lights were extinguished and the windows of homes were blacked out. It was incomprehensible. At first it made a very strange impression. The city looked dead! And even the optimists, who still hoped that the wild German beast would forestall the worldwide tragedy, quickly saw their mistake.

The schools, which should have begun the normal school year on this day, postponed their opening until the 11th of September. On the second day of the War, tragic news arrived, informing the citizens of the destruction of many cities in Poland, especially the capital city, Warsaw! Civilian war casualties had already reached the thousands. The Germans advanced and occupied massive areas of Polish territory. The Polish Army fought valiantly opposing the foe, and in a few places they were victorious. However, this was insignificance as far as the bigger picture. The situation steadily worsened, and the tension grew by the minute!

[Page 34]

Sunday, the 3rd day of the War, the radio announced some cheerful news: England and France had declared war on Germany! National flags were hung, and people presumed that our rescue was forthcoming! In fact, the report at that moment didn't deserve our trust. The Germans were able to damage and dissolve Poland, almost without any opposition!

In a few days there began to arrive in Glubokie, refugees from the central Polish provinces, and even from the eastern parts, such as Grodno, Vilna and others. It could be immediately mastered that the frenzy heightened expeditiously.

We anticipated shelling and sudden bombardment. On Kopanitze, in the city park, and in many other locations, shelters were dug, for hiding in the event of bombing. In the gardens, and empty spaces around many homes, private shelters were dug. Shelters were also dug in public places, such as the Polish churches, the marketplace, small parks and the like. Through notices and printed flyers, posted in the streets, the public was instructed on how to behave in the event of a bombardment On top of a high tower, above the fire station, those guards who stood watching and listening for enemy planes, could be seen from the ground. As soon as the slightest sound was heard, the sirens were sounded. This was the signal to the populace of some impending peril. The sirens would cause great panic, and there were many cases of false alarms.

In the courtyard of every house, water and fire fighting equipment had to be arranged. Garrets had to be filled with sand. (How much effort was expended on this!) Many people walked around wearing gas masks. For months before the War, people were taught how to behave in the event of a poison gas attack; how to use the masks; how to save oneself, and how to administer first aid in case of gas poisoning. On the first day of Rosh Hashanah, at the time of the afternoon prayer - on the 12th day of the War - while the Jews were in their prayer houses, passionately praying, a powerful barrage of sirens pierced the air. It was unmistakably a bombard raid and hysteria reigned. People began to hide in the nearest shelters, or wherever one could find a hole. The flight from the bustling streets was hurried and confused. In a few moments deathly silence spread through the streets. Not one human being was to be found walking the streets. The majority fled to the fields outside of the city., where the Germans would not drop their bombs. At the end, after half an hour passed the "all clear" was sounded. The German planes were actually not far from the city, but they had veered away and the city dwellers escaped with only a fright.

[Page 35]

The next day, Friday, the 2nd day of Rosh Hashanah, at 6:00 A.M. the same thing occurred again. The entire scene repeated itself, and once again the city escaped with only a fright. It is true that the Holiday Prayers lost their flavor. They were, to a great extent, spoiled. People were afraid. They rushed through and did not extend their prayers. Afterward, during the Sabbath of Repentance, a large number of refugees from Vilna, Kovno, Grodno and other places arrived. Previously, many displaced people arrived. They told us of the great damage and atrocities in the above-mentioned places. About Warsaw, there was nothing good they had to say! Complete sections had been laid ruined. A large portion of the city had been demolished. There were thousands of civilian casualties. People were buried alive under the huge piles of rubble. The enemy was formidable and his war-making capabilities were frightening. They conduct the War not only at the battlefront, but also against unarmed and helpless civilians.

Sunday, the Fast of Gedalia (Day after Rosh Hashanah), before dawn, we were again awakened by an air raid warning. We ran, undressed, to the shelters and dugouts. Our family went down to the basement. This sort of hiding place was truly self-deceiving. The smallest bomb would have destroyed it completely. Also, R' Katz and his family, of blessed memory, came there since they lived in the same house. The family of Shalom Weinstein, the owner of our house, and Dr. Britanishsky and his family, who were our neighbors in Meir Hadash's house, came down. We stayed there for long hours, not knowing what had transpired outside. We didn't hear planes, and the "all clear" wasn't sounded either. I'm reminded of R' Katz's, of blessed memory, joke at the time: "It's a pity to live these few hours like this. Life is so short!" We could not yet, at that time evaluate our situation and had no inkling of what awaited us ... Dr. Britanishsky went out to "reconnoiter" and he soon returned with provoking news: The Soviet Army crossed the Polish border a few hours ago and was approaching us. They are occupying our area. This news had been conveyed by phone from the border. No one knew what this meant. Did it mean there is a war between

Russia and Germany or was it a peace settlement? At last we found ourselves in a more favorable situation. All were astonished by the news and Dr. Britanishsky was summoned - after all - he was the Vice Mayor of Glubokie...

[Page 36]

Immediately after we heard the humming of planes. We didn't know whether they were German or Soviet planes. We also heard a weak explosion and afterwards a few more explosions, which were a bit stronger. The railroad station was lightly bombed. A few people were killed and then it was quiet again.

We found out that the Polish civil government and officials are fleeing in panic; some on foot and others on horseback. They said that the provincial governor was seen fleeing in his underwear. He was so frightened of the unexpected news that he received, that being awaken from his sleep he failed to get dressed... or maybe this was just another of the fantasies that people invented at that time. In the offices of the Secret Police they saw to it that communiques, documents and other such things were destroyed and burned. This was also the case in other offices.

We received false rumors that all young men would be mobilized immediately and be given arms to fight off the Bolshevik invader. As it was proven later, there was little basis for this rumor. There were really some young Polish hotheads, who had no understanding, and as in Krilov's fable: "The elephant and the little dog, Moska", they ran to attack, with handguns, the huge might of the powerful Soviet Army. A number of these foolish "heroes" perished.

[Page 37]

The Soviet Army advanced from the border almost all the way without opposition, and Sunday, the 17th of September 1939, at midday, they occupied Glubokie. Some of the populace breathed a sigh of relief. They were mostly Jews who feared German occupation. A large portion of the non- Jewish population were understandably not happy with the Soviet control, but they had little choice, and against their will had to accept it.

Molotov immediately announced over the radio that the Soviet Union realized that the Germans force was about to occupy Poland in its entirety. The Polish Government had fled overseas on Saturday eve, the 16th of September, and left the country in a state of chaos. in order to liberate White Russia and also Western Ukraine from the German claws, the

Soviets decided to invade the area and, in effect, end the War on that day for Western White Russia.

Soviet forces did not cease advancing for three days on end, day and night they drove through town, Their might appeared extremely formidable. There were diversified motorized units utilizing the most modern technology, and a long row of cavalry units proceeded. There were almost no infantry units. The units were all on motorized vehicles. For us, civilians, The terror of war passed. There was no longer danger to life and limb. The sword no longer hung by a thread before our eyes. It was peace time in our area. The war continued far from the outskirts of Glubokie, far outside what used to be east Poland province for nineteen years. Our area is now occupied by the Russian military, with its Soviet might, with whom the Germans are now living, so to speak, at peace.

With the change in the situation, the Jews now faced new problems, and a new perspective. With the establishment of the Soviet system and its concepts of "new order", the Jewish element who were mostly engaged in business and trade for many generations, must now, comply with the Soviet system and break with their past and establish itself on a fresh foundation, with different employment. The Jews would no longer be storekeepers, or merchants. They must engage in labor, and alike. The majority of Jews did indeed make the adjustment quickly and found themselves in organized labor groups. The fortunes of the wealthy were nationalized (confiscated), as well as the large houses, but they (the former well to do) also adjusted and it wasn't so terrible. Life normalized. Some moved away to other cities and established themselves there. The winter of 1939-40 was a very cold and difficult one The elderly did not remember such a hard winter. Certain elements of the population were deported by the Soviets to Siberia., mostly the Poles, but also some Jews. Among them: Dr. Britanishsky and his family, Meir Gittleman, Arke Sherzon, Zalman Levitan, Novick and others. Some people, who previously worked for the Polish regime, were arrested. Some wandering Jewish refugees, who came from German occupied Polish cities, arrived to our area. The German boot was already treading upon the Jews. They risked their lives crossing the border in order to save themselves in the Soviet territory. The turmoil the refugees endured became especially grim when the Soviets recognized an independent Lithuania and returned Vilna to Lithuania. Some Glubokie Jews and even entire families moved to Vilna. Vice versa Refugees from Vilna, who did not want to remain in Lithuania came to Glubokie. When the Lithuanians were granted their independence by the Russians, they began to persecute Jews. Glubokie, at the time, became terribly crowded. The refugees had to be settled. The local Jews welcomed them with open arms. My wife, Dr. Rajak, gave up her medical offices for the sake of the displaced.

[Page 38]

In the winter of 1939-40, a German Commission came to arrange the exchange of war refugees and prisoners. The Russians free Folks-Germans from their districts, and the Germans freed Soviet citizens from their occupied territories. Among others who were freed and given to the Germans was their spy, Vitvitski, may his name be blotted out, who had worked there during Polish times and who has to his credit quite a bit of Jewish blood from the entire region. (More about this in a separate chapter.) Also, Jews displaced ones from Poland, registered to be returned to their "homes" in the area occupied by Germany! ... The life of wanderers was not for them. They couldn't imagine, what was in store for them at the hands of the Germans. But, to what turned to be their good fortune, the Russians, instead of sending them to German-occupied Poland, sent them deeper into Russia, and saved them from a cruel death at the hands of the German murderers.

[Page 39]

If only that had happened to more Jews at the time, even though, at the time they felt most unfortunate.

From Vilna, which was under Lithuanian rule, there came news that with a mighty effort, the Jews there are making arrangements to go, either to Eretz Yisrael or America. In the atmosphere you could sense the impending war, which could break out at any moment, a war between Russia and Germany. Among the non-Jewish populace there were elements that were impatient for that moment and they purposely spread all sorts of provocative reports.

Large military convoys passed through Glubokie from time to time. they were all going westward. Also, the Russian military occupation of the Baltic States did not bode well for peace. It seemed as if the appetite of the Germans was set on devouring Russia....

June 22nd, 1941 arrived., Sunday morning was a tranquil and dignified as usual. Christians in a holiday mood went to church, and the church bells with their pealing rang through the air. Jewish housewives were preparing breakfast and making "plans" for lunch. The youngsters were preparing for sports activities, which usually took place on holidays and Sundays, and life went on its merry way according to plan. Suddenly, at about midday, the radio announced came.... ...During the morning of that day the Soviet Union was attacked by Germany. A number of large Russian cities were bombarded. Among them: Kiev, Zhitomer, Bialostok and others. They had been badly damaged, and there were many casualties.

This news greatly upset most of the populace. Even the authorities displayed exceptional nervousness. It was received as being extremely critical. We understood what it meant. We stayed by the radio, wet listened to Molotov's speech. We swallowed the words of the Jew; Illya Ehrenberg, who in a speech on the radio lasting for hours, decried the treachery and the nefarious act of the German bandits.

In town everything was topsy-turvy. Strange, in a moment everything changed. The chaos among the populace was such that it cannot be described. Essential commodities immediately disappeared. Contact with the outside world was cut off for civilians, and there was no way of communication. Technically Post offices still accepted letters during the first day, dispatches still went through, but this was only a show. They didn't really go anywhere. People who were on the road, suddenly were cut off from their homes, and from their families. It is easy to hypothesize the precarious situation that those families faced. Husbands were far from their homes and were stuck in a strange place far from their wives, children, parents, and alike Especially tragic was the condition of those whose relatives were in one of the above-mentioned cities that the radio said had been heavily bombed. Among the latter was the family of M. Rajak, who was at the time in Bialystok.. He was working as a teacher in the Bialystok Middle School No. 12. He planned to shortly move his wife, Dr. Helena Rajak, who worked as a doctor in Glubokie, and also the rest of his family, to Bialystok The War shattered his plans, and M. Rajak was separated from his mother, wife, child and brother. They, upon hearing on the radio that the city of Bialystok was amongst the first victims of the German blitzkrieg, became so unhinged that nothing else engaged them. They didn't eat or sleep or concerned themselves with the calamities that are about to come right here to Glubokie. They did not notice the events of the day... The impending disaster was of great concern to all others Pandemonium magnified from moment to moment. The queues in front of the stores stretched for kilometers. People stood there to obtain produce and baked goods, Their feet swelled standing in line and most received nothing. People greatly feared hunger. The days to come appeared very harrowing. Citizens ran to all directions wishing to obtain whatever commodities possible. They even prepared medicines... Monday, the 23rd of June, there was a mobilization order for all reservists. people besieged the military commissarat. They were volunteering to fight "the bloodiest foe in human history." Everyone was ready to throw himself into the fray! On the same day, in the morning, there appeared vehicles carrying refugees from the furthest distances: Kovno, Shavell, cities on the Baltic, and so on. These were evacuated families of ranking military men and officials, who, already yesterday, on the first day of the War, barely managed to flee. They told terrible things about the frenzy that had seized everyone, and about destruction and ruin. Many Soviet officials had not even managed to escape or be evacuated from those areas. The enemy advanced swiftly. Nothing can stop him! Before he occupies some city or other, he wreaks havoc and destruction on it from the sky.

[Page 41]

There are also many casualties as a result of the bombardment. In many cases, the displaced were seized on roads. the enemy, who either caught up with them, or surprised them by coming from an entirely different direction, captured them. Other refugees who attempted to flee east- deep into the Soviet Union- would often be stuck on the way, not knowing what to do next. If someone was able to disguise himself in such a way as to appear to be neither a fugitive nor a Red Army soldier, he would have a chance to save himself and return to his city. If not, many, who were on their way, lost their lives. The appearance of the refugees bore witness to the hurried way in which they had fled. In the vehicles, their belongings were scattered, not packed with any order. The passengers, especially women and children, were tired, depressed, frightened with disturbed faces, and couldn't answer questions. They were physically drained and psychologically broken. Some would lie, continually sleeping among the disorder in the vehicles. It appeared as if what was happening to and all about them, just didn't concern them at all! Others, on the other hand, looked frightened, they searched to see that they weren't being chased. They were in a great hurry and inquired about the way to Polotsk and Minsk. They didn't know which of the two was safer. They were right. Any delay was fatal. The reports of the enemy's advance followed one upon the heels of the previous one. The later refugees did not even pause to stop. They ran wildly and swiftly. They trembled at the prospect of being caught. So, it went on for the entire day.

Here in the city some began to construct shelters or refurbish those that that had been constructed 21 months earlier, when the Germans invaded Poland. We were certain that sooner or later, the German bombs would not overlook Glubokie. Tuesday, the 24th, the third day of the War, The Soviet officials, and their families, began to evacuate Glubokie. This magnified the panic. People became so confused that they just didn't know what to do. All wanted to flee. The Soviet officials and followers were even more terrified. But where and how to flee? There were no trains for civilians. Rides couldn't be obtained for any sum of money. The only remaining alternative was to flee on foot. This could be done only by healthy, well-built adults, who had no family. (Most of them had already been mobilized, previously.) To flee on foot was an even greater risk, since the enemy could easily overtake you. Others, with gold and jewelry, were speedily able to purchase horses and harness from the farmers.

[Page 42]

They received much higher prices than they had ever imagined asking. Later, it became known that the retreating Red Army, had taken the horses and wagons from the fleeing civilian population. From our courtyard, on 25 Warsaw Street, on the 25th of June, at dawn, the teacher, Shaul Yididovitsh, (the well known Bundist in Vilna) left quietly on foot, with his wife, Manya and his son, Vove. Some turned back, discarding their modest possessions, which they had taken along. (Adler, his wife and child, and others.) Our family members could not think of fleeing, since M. Rajak was in Bialystok, which was the first city to be bombed. We did not think of the future, the days to come, since we were tormented by the present. For the moment our only concern was to receive at least some live regards from him. At the time it seemed like a childish fantasy. But the emotions did not want to deal with logical conclusions. We imagined that perhaps, from somewhere, would come our salvation. How fortunate it seemed were the "unfortunate ones", whom the Soviet regime had deported east a few days before the War began.

The Soviet force did not completely abandon the town. On Wednesday the 25th, in the morning, they only partly withdrew. Joy reigned among Jews. They assumed that the soviet had an astute strategic plan. They commented that probably the German enemy was forced to retreat. Some were overjoyed that they hadn't fled the previous day and ruined it for themselves. Several days passed normally. The civilian force left town and in the morning return. It was the same in other towns. Therefore, knowing that the force had not completely abandoned the town, made everyone optimistic and reassured. During the stay of the Red Army one could be more certain of prevention of attacks and pogroms carried out by the darker elements of the local Christian population, who would, if the force left, surely rob and murder the Jews.

Red Army soldiers started appearing, they were separated from their units. They were exhausted, demoralized, half naked, and wandered aimlessly. This made a harsh impression. The enemy was on the attack, both in the air, and on the ground. Meanwhile the local populace, except for the Jews, began snatching products from the Soviet Base.

They "shlepped" flour, sugar, fuel, salt, tobacco, leather and other things. Poor peasants became well-to-do overnight.

[Page 43]

Shabbos, June 27th, enemy planes appeared. They circled over the town, and in the section east of Glubokie, Lavrivnov, they dropped several small caliber bombs. There were several casualties among the civilian population. From then on, planes began appearing often but did not drop bombs. They were probably reconnaissance planes. The people would run at each appearance, not knowing where to go and how to protect themselves. The noise of the planes would drive away the people who were standing in line for supplies, at the bakery and grocery. Later they got used to it and ceased running away. The air raids were especially terrible when the Germans were chasing the soldiers who separated from the Red Army and wandered into our town by accident.

It was Sunday the 29th, when an extraordinary joyous event took place. I, M. Rajak, after wandering for a week and undergoing a most horrendous journey, arrived home from Bialystok. The family became delirious with joy. My wife Helena (born in Wilno in 1904 to Bentzion and Breina Vilkomirski) noticed my arrival through the window and shouted: "Michael arrived!". This seemed so unbelievable that she began blessing and making vows… and from great enthusiasm did not know what to do; whether to run towards me or to run to tell mother, who was in her room. I cannot forget the joy that enveloped us at that moment. Soon our very good friends and acquaintances came running. In spite of the general calamity, we drank a L'Chaim and recited the blessing of thanksgiving. The joy was so great that the German danger lurking from without, the planes and the bombings were all forgotten for the moment. My son, Aaron Itzakel (the pain of his loss…) was 6 years old at the time. He did not know what to do, he was glowing with immense delight.

I will digress a moment from the general course of events and briefly relate how, during such a time, I made the terrible journey on foot, practically, from Bialostok to Glubokie, a distance of almost 500 kilometers.

When on Sunday, the 21st of June at 4:00 in the morning, the enemy began bombing Bialystok, no one could imagine that it was real, an attack by an enemy? A war. Throughout? it was thought that these were only war maneuvers that were taking place in Bialystok. When entire walls started collapsing, and people covered with blood ran, we realized and absorbed that it was not a joke.…

[Page 44]

The realization came that Germany, according to her well-known methods, had unjustly attacked the Soviet Union. Its difficult to accurately describe the chaos and the dismay that enveloped the town. People were running about confused, like madmen. The evacuation of offices and families of the military took on a very disordered characteristic. Everyone wanted to save himself but did not know where to go or how to get there. The authorities arranged for evacuation of the higher echelons, also for some of the civilian population, but traveling by train was perilous. The Germans especially bombarded the trains. They did not even consider who was traveling by train. They also targeted defenseless women and children. Even approaching the train stations was fraught with great danger. Bombs were falling on all sides. There was utter confusion. The populace, however, would not be deterred. They ran to the trains which became the symbol of deliverance from this hell! I was among the last. I would have paid any price for a way to get to my family in Glubokie. At the time it seemed infeasible; like traveling to Mars!

After a bitter day, I caught a train, at 10:00 o'clock at night, which went through Volkovisk and Baranovitch to Minsk. Though this was not the direction I wanted to go (I needed a Grodno to Lida or Grodno to Vilna train), I decided to take it to Minsk. The night was as if non-existent. When it began to dawn, the planes began chasing our train. During each raid the train had to halt and the passengers ran out and hid in the corn and high grass. This happened so frequently that we only covered a small distance during the course of the day. By the time we reached Baranovitch, we already had 16 dead. A separate railroad car was reserved for the casualties, and the train officials made an effort, as much as was possible, to keep passengers away from the car carrying the dead, since the nerves of the passengers were already very stressed.

Tuesday the 24th, in the morning, we arrived at the Ratomke Station, 7 kilometers from Minsk. Minsk had was heavily bombed. From afar, it looked as if the city was entirely engulfed by flames. Thick pillars of smoke were seen, covering a large expanse of sky. Wherever one's gaze fell, people could be seen fleeing. Leaving all of my possessions in the railroad car, I got of the train. What happened to my fellow passengers, I do not know! I went by foot to the shtetl Rakov about twenty kilometers west from Minsk. Arriving there, I again encountered a bombing. At night I left for the shtetl Radashkovitch (father west), where I arrived on Wednesday morning, the 25th. Generally, the road was safer at night. In Radashkovitch all offices were already evacuated. I went to our friends there, to the family of Yoel Lippman. They kept me there so that I was able to rest a bit, and on the same day, at dusk, the Germans came in. I saw their swastikas for the first time. They entered immediately after the Red Army units abandoned the town. In Radashkovitch there were refugees from Vilna and other places. Among them, I met the eminent Vilna community leader, Yevzerov, who, in fleeing from Vilna, like many others, was stuck midway, and didn't know where to hide himself. I, too, remained in Radoshkovitch overnight. In the morning of Thursday, I was again kept from continuing on my way. German troops appeared in droves and I was frightened to continue.

[Page 45]

On Friday, the 27th, the Soviets bombarded the Germans, who were entrenched in the town, and half of the town burned down. The large House of Study also burned. That day, I left, going north towards Dolhinov through the woods,

[Page 46]

and the woods were being steadily bombed and strafed by German planes. They were pursuing the retreating divisions of the Red Army. Not far from the shtetlk Ilya, a truck with people freed from captivity, approached. They wanted to give me a lift, but I declined. I didn't know who, or what they were. As the car moved on, one of the passengers began shouting from a distance: "Comrad Rajak, come ride!" Several times the call was repeated. But the car was going too fast, and I couldn't catch up! I was so disappointed. Near the village of Ilye, the car stopped, it was out of gas, and could not continue on its way. There, I met the tailor from Glubokie, Aarons, who was riding in the car. He had recognized me and was the one who had been calling me. He was fleeing from Molodetchno. I was as delighted to see him as he was to see me. In Ilya, we met many refugees from Smorgon and other towns. The Jews of Ilya received us very cordially. Especially our student, Brida, who was concluding a vocational school term in Glubokie, he couldn't do enough for me. Friday evening, we wanted to continue on our way, but we were strongly advised not to, because, in the woods, 'there were Red Army patrols, who did not let anyone through.

Shabbos morning, we left for Dolhinov. On the roads and in the woods were many Red Army soldiers. They checked out everyone. We, too, were detained by a patrol who led us to staff headquarters, in the woods. My documents were in order. They were very reliable. By the same token, Aarons, who accompanied me, had no documents at all, and his situation was most grave. He could have been taken for a deserter and with them (deserters) they made short shrift. They would be sentenced on the spot. With a mighty effort, I was able to save him from death. I argued with the staff officer. Thanks to my papers, which identified me as a prominent and upright person, the officer warmly bade us farewell and told us to be careful to avoid Germans on the way, since their attitude to Jews need not be spell out for us.

In Dolhinov also, there was no reigning regime. We stayed there overnight with one of our students, Shayne Shapiro. Sunday morning we arrived in Dockshitz. There, a refugee from Lodz, Leib Shnayerson joined us. Together we arrived in Glubokie on Sunday during the day. Aarons was afraid to enter the town, since he might be perceived as a deserter. He hid in an unfinished building, and I informed his relatives of his arrival. He had arrived safely, and I felt happy that, during such a calamity, I was instrumental in bringing him through it all.

The journey took its toll on my health. I could not heal for a long time. It was very difficult for me to talk, and I lay as if I was paralyzed. But subsequent events did not permit me to repose for any length of time.

Monday, June 30th, the morning after I arrived, an air attack, and not a light one, was directed against Glubokie. The roofs of many buildings were blown off. The windows of most of the houses were blown out. There were deaths among both the military and civilian population. The enemy had targeted two areas: the district of the city garden and Senkevitch Street (Kaptziker), where units of the retreating Red Army were concentrated. The sirens, the warnings of an imminent air raid would begin wailing hours before. And has previously mentioned, there would be air raids without bombings, designed to disorient and demoralize the populace. Just then, when the bombings did occur, the people had, just a short while before, crept out of their hiding places thinking that nothing more would happen. Thus, for example, a bomber would suddenly appear and fly over our courtyard, at a time when a long line of people was standing by Sholem Vienstein's bakery, for bread. Luckily, everyone would manage to flee when the plane swooped low, firing its machine guns, so that no one was harmed. Only the windows of the nearby houses fell out, and the walls of the bakery were damaged. Bombs also fell in the lake, resulting in unusually strong and high waves. It seemed as if the entire lake would spill over, onto the dry land.

[Page 47]

On Tuesday, July 1st, during the course of the day, there were repeated long wailing of the sirens. Heavy bombings followed. In the city garden, there were encamped many Red Army soldiers, with their supplies and ammunition. The fright was great. In the evening one did not see a living soul on the streets. It was as quiet and as empty as if in a graveyard.

From time to time the stillness was disturbed by a Red Army vehicle racing through the town. No one slept! They waited... and actually, at 4:00 A. M., at dawn, just as it was getting light, a strong humming sound could be heard. On the horizon there appeared many planes. There was such a roar, that one could not hear what was being said by others. The bombing encompassed almost the entire town. The explosions, at times became stronger and more frequent. We all lay stretched out on the floor. (Neighbors came running, each one thinking that perhaps it would be better to hide oneself by someone else.) The men began reciting chapters of the Psalms, reading the Sh'ma prayer aloud, and so forth. Also, the women were praying, pleading, with tears. The panes of the windows were pouring out like hail. The walls were shaking, and buildings were falling like balls. The little children, who were with us, huddled close to their mothers. Near our house a bomb exploded, with such force, and we became so confused, that we just didn't know what was happening to us. We picked ourselves up and began running about aimlessly. The planes circled about for a long time, even though they were no longer dropping bombs. It seems that they were observing the Red Army. The populace

[Page 48]

was terror-stricken the entire time. After the planes flew off, and disappeared beyond the Glubokie horizon, we all calmed down a bit.

The bombardment had fatal results. There were many casualties: Friedman, Maier-Mordechai, a tinsmith, 8-year-old Nechamele Gordon and her 16-year-old sister, Gita, (who was seriously wounded, but pulled through). Both were our students, very wonderful children. Also, there was the little boy, Mentkowitch, Mordechai Schulheifer's grandson, and many more whose names we no longer remember. Harav Katz, who hid in Kishelaike, outside of the city, believing it to be safe there, was buried alive. He was completely covered with earth for a long time but survived this time. Many Christians were also killed at that time.

The general appearance of the town, for us who were not used yet to devastation, was terrible. Many buildings were completely destroyed, and others partially ruined. (Among them: the homes of Lazar Gittelzon, Mendel-Leib Fliskin, Maier-Mordecai Friedman, Binyamin Gittelzon, Shmuel-Ryder, and others.) In Ryder's house, Yaakov-Leib Asmans, a boy, the grandson of Chaim Kevlin, was killed. Other houses had halfway hanging roofs arid pieces of walls sticking out. The windows of practically all of the houses and of the post office in town, had fallen out. Dark holes looked out, seeming to be hidden, mystical and secretly concealed.... The streets were strewn, and spread with fragments from the collapsed houses, with glass, with uprooted trees, with telegraph and telephone lines, and so on. the torn telegraph, telephone and electric wires were so entangled that one couldn't walk through. Very often we got hurt because of deep holes in the very center of town, and on the side streets. Bombs fell there, tearing out large chunks of earth. No sort of Soviet vehicle that had survived, was able to penetrate through the streets, and had to seek a side passage somewhere else. It was not a time to be wandering about for any length. Any moment could bring annihilation.

After the bombing people came to the bakery in our courtyard and began grabbing bread and flour from there. The owner wasn't there to guard it. Others, however, were fearful. Also, a Soviet vehicle arrived

[Page 49]

and loaded up with bread. At that time one of the ranking Soviet military men, a colonel, came running in, drinking. He confronted us and gave us hope that the German assault would be pushed back.... During the time that the Soviet vehicle was parked in the courtyard, we were filled with a great terror that the German spy plane would notice that in our courtyard there are Red Army troops, and that they would rain down death-dealing bombs.... And The results of the bombings were fatal. There were many victims: indeed, so it happened! As soon as the automobile drove out of the courtyard, the bombers appeared immediately and began circling over our houses. Neither dead nor alive, we sought to hide ourselves in the pits, in the cellars. Suddenly, it became completely still, a stillness that - was even more disturbing.... There was no bombing this time, but the mood continued to be a very nervous one, and no one could foretell what sort of a surprise might be forthcoming at any moment. It is interesting to note that the Christians, during the period of uncertainty, ran to grab products from the Soviet base which had not yet been emptied; not taking into account the fact that the danger to them was no less than it was for the Jews. At the time, the German bombs did not make a distinction between Ayran and non-Aryan, but there was quite a distinction in that they (non- Jews) did not fear the arrival of the Germans, and so, their mood was quite different.

At 2:00 in the afternoon, on July 2nd, the deathly stillness was shattered by quick, heavy treads on the stone sidewalk. We stuck our heads out to take a look. We saw the first German soldier from the arrival-depot, running with his gun pointing, as if to shoot. We looked all about. Luckily, he didn't notice us. He was dressed in a green uniform. On his head he wore a protective head covering. On his sleeve was a "swastika". Right behind him, there streamed Germans and more Germans and the frogs came up and covered the earth!" (Exodus 8:2).

And the Germans occupied Glubokie. They appeared to be strong and healthy. Their manner of speaking and laughing was deafening to our ears. They displayed not a bit of apprehension or discomfiture. They rode in on their machines, and their arrival gave the impression that it was a scientific experiment and not the commencement of war. "Not one was tired, and none faltered!" (Isaiah 27:29)

[Page 50]

The bombardment was over, and we assembled in our dwellings. Terrible nights ensued for us. Exposed before our eyes were floors strewn with glass and shattered utensils, plaster from the walls and so on. The doors were twisted out of shape, and no windows remained. The ceiling curved, giving the impression that it was suspended in air, and would fall at any moment. With great effort and hardship, we succeeded in making a little order. Momentarily the main concern was how to manage without windows. (At the time that seemed like a calamity!) To install new ones was out of the question. We covered the windows with blankets, sheets, tablecloths, various rags and so forth. The adversity to later come, understandably, by comparison would pale all of our previous discomforts....

In the street, civilians from the local population began to surface. Jews, as much as was possible, tried to avoid being seen outdoors. During the initial days, the Germans did not bother most Jews. They only shot several people who had dragged themselves out of the Soviet base. As soon as the Germans arrived, the streets in town emptied and the German massive armed forces took control.

The Jews under the first German influx

By Zvi and Michael Rajak

Translated by Eilat Gordin Levitan

Everyone sensed that there is nothing that could be done to prevent the Arrival of the Germans. All comprehended that the German boots would most certainly tread upon the ground of Glubokie. Still, not until the very last moment, did they really want to believe it. They shun such contemplation, hoping that perhaps the terrible impending plague would not extend to this place, perhaps by the help of god, the menacing force would be vanquished.

However, the calamity occurred, and immediately the German claw was felt by the Jews. A claw which was about to start to strangle us. During the initial stage the ruling rights on the local level were at the hands of the commanders of the military divisions who first arrived marching through our region. The last to march to town and stop there did as they pleased with to us Jews. The oppression and their caprices behavior were instantly felt upon the Jewish neck. Here is an example: During the first days after occupying the town, some Germans went to Rabbi Katz, of blessed memory, and under death threats demanded that within 20 minutes he supply them with several bicycles. The unfortunate old and weak Rabbi, suspended in life/ death state of mind,

[Page 51]

began running around town looking for bicycles. Clearly, they were not to be found. The Germans had already confiscated all of the bicycles, a few days earlier. After 20 minutes the Germans returned for their merchandise. When they realized that their demand could not be fulfilled, they began to avenge themselves on the Rav. For a certainty, they would have shot him right then and there. However, by trickery he managed to twist himself away from them and hide. They had no time to search for him since they had orders to leave the town forthwith. And only thanks to this coincidence was the Rav saved from a tragic death for a time… A year later the German murderers were able to carry out their evil design upon him. There were many such instances. Constantly we received new demands from the German officers and soldiers. Demands that were many times impossible to comply with, any time Jews were liable to be shot, and the murderers need not supply a reason for the killing.

Thus, the entire Jewish population, from the first day of the German occupation, was geared to comply with German demands and caprices. Strained, and in a state of great fear and confusion, they Jewish community members ran from one Jewish house to another gathering and taking from wherever and whoever they could, any merchandise so that they would be able to adequately satisfy the illogical demands of the Germans. On top of it, often, the German soldiers themselves entered Jewish homes, robbing and stealing the most precious possessions of the owner and before they left they beat the homeowners with a vengeance.

The First German Provocation

Translated by Eilat Gordin Levitan

One of the principal tasks of the Germans was to torment and disjoin the local population by inciting one segment of people against the other. The Aryans were pitted against the Jews. The Jews had not only the Germans enemy to contend with, but also the local Christians population was encouraged, incited and galvanized to no longer tolerate the Jews. Just like everywhere else, here too, there was a core of sinister element among the local population, who happily assisted and served the Germans.

False rumors were spread amongst the local population; … the Jews, together with the Soviets, took revenge upon those arrested by the Soviet regime prior to the war. The prisoners were held in the Berezvetcher Prison, about 2 kilometers from Glubokie. There (the rumors said) they shot 2,000 men and 500 were bricked-in, alive, in the thick walls of the Berezvetcher Monastery. They were punished because they deserted the Red Army. Fear and terror fell upon the Jews as they found out of the rumors being spread. The local Black Shirts (assistants to the Nazis) utilized the frenzy for their own personal intends. Just like their bosses, undisturbed, they went to Jewish homes, stealing whatsoever their hearts desired. Guardianship by elements sympathetic to the Jews could not be counted upon at all. The Jews were too frightened to react, and not a mouth was opened to complain. Some amongst the Christians made their looting "honorable" by being well mannered. They would introduce themselves to the Jews as "good friends", who, in time of trouble and stress, would strive to protect the Jews, and for this they should be paid a good price in advance….

[Page 52]

Levandovski, the baker, Yaremek and others, brought a unit of German soldiers to the home of old, highly respected, Sholem Weinstein, of 25 Warsaw Street. They took their revenge upon him by screaming to the soldiers, that he was responsible for imprisoning 500 people behind the walls of the Berezvetcher Dungeon. Therefore, they then pulled out of closets, from beds and chests, whatever they could and bestowed these "offerings" upon the soldiers.... Later, the Germans established "order", and declared that the entire Jewish holdings belonged only to them, the Germans. The local thieving element could no longer take any belongings or exchange any wares from the Jews.

Sholem Weinstein was a pious Jew, with curly gray hair and a beard. He devoted most of his time to Torah studies and performing good deeds. He only partook in matters pertaining to the House of Study, Yeshivah and charity. Just his patriarchal appearance bore obvious witness to the fact that he did not concern himself neither with politics nor with secular affairs of the outside the Jewish community. The naive, innocent and God-fearing Weinstein did not grasp what the hoodlums wanted from him. He stood paralyzed, not comprehending what they said. He looked on helplessly as they dragged away his hard-earned possessions, he was afraid to resist. The same thing happened to Chaveson, and to many other Jews.

For several days the Jewish community lived in deathly fear. They awaited the consequences of such a blood-libel, terror-stricken that it would provoke further destruction, or a terrifying pogrom by the local population. Fortunately, the provocation was not accredited by most of the local Christian population. They

[Page 53]

knew well that among those arrested and thrown into Berezvetcher Prison, at the time of the Soviet occupation, there were also many Jews. Jews such as: Dr. Britanishsky; Dr. Kahn; Hannah Safra; Miakinin and others.

Here we must allude to the local council, which was responsible for illuminating to the Christian mob, the absurdity of such rumors and the senseless "Jew- baiting" and the distortion being spread. They called upon the population of all faiths and allegiance, to unite and make peace among themselves. They strove to enlighten the community so that they should not be influenced to do evil, and not be led astray and drawn into a web of crimes and horrible deeds. This failed provocation undertaking in order to unite the locals under the flag of hate, was very enlightening. There, where the local population did not let themselves be easily inflamed, the Germans were not able to carry out their extermination policy against the Jews as effortlessly.

Russian Prisoners of War

Translated by Eilat Gordin Levitan

It is doubtful that with words alone we would be able to accurately convey the absolutely tragic state of the prisoners of war. The P.O.Ws that met their horrible deaths here in Glubokie. We speak of the fate of 47,000 soldiers and officers of the Red Army who fell under German captivity. At the beginning there were a lot more. However, on the forced walk from the battlefield to Glubokie, 60% of them perished. Using various misleading tricks along the way, the Germans would torture and shoot them. If, for example, an exhausted soldier could not keep up with the quick moving column or convoy; or if one of the prisoners would cast a wrong glance; they would be shot. If a crust of bread was thrown to one of them by the women who stood by the road crying, without a doubt, if he stooped to pick up the bread, he was immediately shot.

Transporting them by military conveyors, they were crammed in and pressed so tightly in the boxcars, that they perished not only from starvation and thirst, but from suffocation. It was impossible to breathe in these improvised conveyances. The unconscious and dead were not even removed, they were taken, together with the living, to the designated destination. Consequently, the number of dead steadily increased. These inhuman circumstances were not accidental. The aim of the Germans was to deliver as few living prisoners as possible to the prison camps.

[Page 54]

As a result of the tortures, the sufferings and deaths of prisoners, along the way, a "remnant" of 47,000 living men was brought to Glubokie. They were driven from the train station to Berezvetch, to the prison barracks. The youth of yesterday, which days before was full of energy, who were only weeks before appeared as strong courageous fighters, heroes of the Soviet Union, were now famished, feeble and wounded, broken shadows of their old selves, with pale drawn faces. They were cruelly beaten for all to see. Openly tortured by tile Germans! Hunched over, they dragged themselves along the road like very old people; their dull gaze from their deeply sunken eyes was begging for food and drink.

They languished to be free, to survive.... verbally begging for a piece of bread, or a little water, was forbidden. It was also forbidden for the civilian population to offer them any food or drink. And those, who upon seeing the unfortunate prisoners, were bold enough to throw them a crust of bread, were severely punished by the Germans for their "impertinence".

At the beginning, people didn't know that giving a prisoner a piece of bread or a little water to drink, was a crime. People were gallant enough to throw bread, vegetables and other food items to the passing prisoners. Immediately, announcements were posted; "anyone caught giving bread to a prisoner, would be shot to death" Understandably, such an announcement frightened people off, and so they restrained themselves from helping the prisoners. There were some, whose pity for the wretched prisoners weighed so heavily upon them, that they could not keep themselves from secretly throwing the bread, thereby putting their lives in jeopardy. The extent of the length of the Germans' cruelty, is exemplified by the fact that when my seven-year-old son, in compliance with his mother's instructions, gave a piece of bread to a prisoner, the Germans noticed it and chased after the child. By a miracle of God, the child was able to hide in a closet, and the Germans were unable to find him. Incidentally, the Germans could not search for him too long, since they were accompanying the prisoners, and thus the child was saved!

[Page 55]

The Germans brought the prisoners to Berezvetch and here they were "lodged" in specially arranged pits, which were "so-called" barracks. These barracks-pits were not covered on top, and when autumn arrived, followed by a cold winter, the prisoners, who suffered from hunger, thirst and German torture. In addition, that winter of 1941/1942, suffered from the bitter cold. After such a terrible journey, experiencing so much torment along the way, a new order of suffering began for the prisoners, a new chapter of tortures. In order to protect themselves from the cold, to warm themselves somewhat, they would huddle together, pressed tightly among themselves, to alleviate their suffering somewhat.

The barracks-pits were in such unsanitary condition, that it is hard to describe. There was no private place for the prisoners to relieve themselves. The filth was so great, and the lice had reached such proportions that the gaunt, emaciated bodies of the prisoners, were devoured by the vermin. It was told that when a prisoner would take off his shirt, the shirt actually moved, because of the quantity of lice.... The stench, the malodorous air, was carried from the barracks-pits to a great distance enveloping the camp. Not a word was ever said by the "German master race" about taking the prisoners to a bath-house or providing them with a change of clothing.

The prisoners in Berezvetch were fed "bread" - a mixture of some ground-up straw and "sawdust" (30% according to the testimony of the baker, Elihu Gordon). This was given in such a small portion that the prisoners would become swollen from hunger. When the Germans, on rare occasions, would bring into the camp some frozen rotten potatoes, and the prisoners would fall upon them, grabbing and clutching, the Germans would shoot into them for "failing to keep order!" The hunger was so oppressive that death punishment was not a deterrent. The shooting did not frighten the prisoners. Better death by a bullet, than the slow death by hunger. They grabbed the rotten, raw potatoes as though they were the best of delicacies. It is clear that such a "life-style" in the camp, gave rise to disease. The strongest human being would succumb to it here! There was not even a talk of healing the sick. They either died of disease or were shot by their guards. Every morning, dozens, and even hundreds of bodies were scattered about. Bodies of those who died during the night.

[Page 56]

The Germans, by their cruelty, brought the prisoners to a state of inhumanity. When the portions of bread would be scattered, the prisoners would lift up their dead comrades, supporting them as if they were only sick, so as to get their portion of bread for themselves. When a German wanted to have fun, he would bring the prisoners a dead horse. The unfortunates would throw themselves upon the animal like beasts, tearing the putrid horse flesh. The stronger ones would grab the portions of the weaker ones.... At that the Germans would amuse themselves and shoot several tens of prisoners for their "bad manners" and for not "restraining themselves"!

The hunger in the camp reached such a degree, that there were cases where the prisoners permitted themselves to eat the flesh of their dead comrades. Some of Yesterday's Heroes, normal thinking human beings, were transformed by the German's murderous actions, into cannibals!

Every evening, the sounds of gun shots or machine guns reverberated throughout Berezvetch. The Germans shot the prisoners during the night. The issue of escape was a difficult one for the prisoners. Not because of the guards, but because of their own physical weakness and the injuries which they suffered from regular beatings by the Germans. There were some cases of prisoners fleeing from the camp. After escaping they would come running into town in small groups, where they would be given civilian clothing to change into, and in this way they would be saved. One of the prisoners, Ivanov, fled to the Ghetto, and there, in due time, he organized a group of 18 youths, who went into the forest as partisans.

Special commendation was earned by a truly small proportion of the populace, they were ready to sacrifice themselves for the fate of the imprisoned. People would "innocently" bring wood to a point not far from the camp, and when the patrols failed to notice them, they would throw food, clothing and other things over the fence. Whoever was lucky enough to catch the clothing, would immediately change and flee. They would thus save themselves. There were cases of peasants, from nearby villages, who would remove prisoners from the camp, under bales of hay and straw. They would then provide them with food, clothing and even weapons. These prisoners later joined the partisans. However, such cases were extremely rare.

[Page 57]

Among the prisoners there were also traitors, which made it even more difficult to flee and to receive any help in one form or another. The Germans appointed these traitors as the "seniors" in the camp! They were supposed to be a sort of police who would watch the other prisoners. These traitors, who sold their souls, took revenge upon the prisoners, as much as the Germans did. They informed on them, and in front of the eyes of their "lovely bosses" the Germans, they would beat their fellow prisoners "black and blue"! The Germans derived great pleasure from this, and they would laugh and make merry. The traitors won the trust of the Germans to such an extent that they were even given weapons with which they themselves killed prisoners.

Of the 47,000 Red Army prisoners brought to Berezvetch, almost none were left alive, except for the few who had managed to flee. The Germans annihilated them in Berezvetch's Concentration Camp, where over 50 pits remain, a testament to German brutality and barbarism! Many of those who perished were true heroes, who till their very last breath did not forsake their humanity. Here it is worthwhile mentioning one of the Jewish prisoners, Captain Raskin, whom the Germans, for some unfathomable reason, wanted to keep alive. He was wounded at the time that there was a shooting of the prisoners. When a German officer brought a doctor to him to give him medical aid, Raskin refused. The German officer turned to him with the following words: "Herr Captain! Your wound must be bandaged. You are losing blood and you will die!"

The Captain straightened himself, his vigorous face became even more serious, and with an angry, almost shouting voice, he answered him: "Herr Officer, better to die than to be bandaged by the hands of a German doctor!" Trembling from head to toe, he added: "The Germans have put the world into enough bandages! They've tied her up so that she has ceased breathing. The day is not far off when the world will free herself from your chains and the gruesome hour of reckoning will come when you will pay!" Thereby the noble countenance of the Captain became very distorted, for it was apparent that he was in great pain! He collapsed, blood gushing all over him. Several hours later he died!

This sight so affected those present, that many of them swore revenge for the blood that had been shed! And indeed, that night a group of prisoners choked the German sentry to death and fled. The Germans hunted them all down and murdered every last one of them. The fields were covered with dead bodies. Only the above-mentioned Ivanov, who came to the Ghetto and from there went to the partisans, managed to save himself. Near the pits of the prisoners in Berezvech, a grave draws a special attention. It is the common grave of the eight members of the prominent family of Chaim Kozliner of Berezvech, who through the cruelty of the German murderers, perished at the start of the occupation. They were killed because they were "guilty" of giving food and water to the war prisoners. May their souls be entwined in the vine of everlasting life!

[Page 58]

The Agreement Between the Magistrate and the Mayor

Translated by Eilat Gordin Levitan

Shortly after the invasion, the Germans appointed a new Mayor in Glubokie. The appointed person was someone by the name of Naumov, and a representative of his, Ostashevski, a Pole, a local resident. Naumov came to Glubokie in September of 1939, as a refugee from Grodno. In Grodno, where he lived until the outbreak of the War, he was the Director of the Polish Government Bank. When Naumov first arrived he worked in Glubokie as a bookkeeper in the Soviet-Government Bank. After some time the Soviets removed his family from Glubokie. Soon Naumov disappeared and nobody knew where he was to be found. He showed up again when the Germans arrived_ Naumov and Ostashevski won the confidence of the Germans. The German Commandant immediately announced that everyone must obey the decrees of the new Mayor, and those who would not fulfill his orders or demands, would be sentenced to death.

Bread Rationing

The first edict of the newly appointed Mayor pertained to bread rationing. He announced to the population that every family, regardless of size, would be entitled from now on to no more then 20 kilo of bread (taking into account the supply of flour, grain and the like). The surplus was to be handed over to the Magistrate within several hours time. The decree did not apply to farmers.

[Page 59]

It actuality applied mainly to Jews. The second decree was that all inhabitants must obtain personal identification documents at the City Hall. The color of the documents was different for the various nationalities. Under the threat of punishment by death the decrees of the city administration had to be carried out with the greatest exactness. And the masses who prepared their bread for the War emergency, turned it over to the City Hall. Along Zamkover Street, there a queue of hundreds of people, waiting for their supplies to be taken away from them, stretched through the town. People stood waiting with their sacks and packages an entire day and night arrived. They waited because according to the decree, everything had to be handed over in a matter of hours. Aside from that, acquiring the "treasure" was most nerve wracking, and was done at the risk of one's life. In addition to the fear of a dreary future the terror of hunger was great, so people were happy that their bread was taken away without any pretensions, and without prior claims. At this point, terror of death by a bullet, was much stronger than the fear of hunger that was in the morrow for them. In a short time, it became self-evident in comparison with the troubles Jews were to suffer later on such decrees were a mere trifle!

How pitiful these poor people appeared. They stood in line to give up their "luxuries", which consisted of 3 kilos of flour, corn or oats. Many people, after turning in their excess bread, did not themselves believe that, heaven forbid, they had retained something more than the norm, 20 kilo. They exercised strict self-control, weighing and measuring, and if there was a half kilo over, they destroyed it, pouring the excess flour or grain into the lake, into the mud, grass or some other place. One had to be very cautious that no trace was left, so no suspicions would be aroused. The population's fear and terror mounted! But, so to speak, these were just the first buds of the later blossoms and flowers!

Death Sentence for having Extra portion of Flour

A horrible imprint was made upon the public, by the murder of the family of Asher Hoffman. The local police controlled the surplus bread supply of the Jewish population. In the home of the above-mentioned Hoffman, there was found a bit of extra flour. Over and above the allotted amount. The explanation that this luxury had been left over by mistake was of no avail! His entire family: wife, parents and children were taken to the outskirts of town, where they were forced to dig their own graves, and then shot.

[Page 60]

This was the first case of shooting, by the local police. An entire family Was murdered for such a minor incident, threw such a fright into everyone; that one could not find a repose for oneself. At first, no one wanted to believe what had taken place, did not want to think about it since they couldn't imagine that such a thing could really happen. But when Christian witnesses appeared and told how they themselves had seen what had happened, how the family had been led out and tortured even before they were shot; then, the unbelievable became a fact and the Jews realized what an abyss they had fallen into!

The families of Yaakov Olmer, Wolf Drotz, Kantrovitz, Pliskin and others, where there were even larger amounts of bread products at the time, were threatened with a similar punishment. At the home of Drotz the police found an "excess" of just a little glue that he completely forgot he had. It had not even entered his mind that a little bit of glue was in the category of "bread" and had to be turned in! The "criminals" were arrested and within three days they and their families were sentenced to death. However, they suffered only torture. This time, with the aid of a huge bribe, they were fortunate enough to escape a terrible death.

[Page 60]

Forced Labor

Translated by Eilat Gordin Levitan

As soon as the Germans entered Glubokie, they immediately impelled the Jews to work for them. Men, women and even children were forced to labor like slaves. During their work, for no reason whatsoever, the Germans would torment and torture the Jews. There were cases that people returned home so beaten and mutilated that they lost consciousness upon arriving. Among such people were the Advocate, Slonimsky, Buchhalter, Nalanzokn, Pintzov, Aztinsky, Kravitz and others. During hours of hard labor, The Jews also had to fulfill all kinds of whims of their guards or employers. The Germans would want to be entertained during work hours, and would force the Jews to sing songs, imitate various animals, creep on all fours, dance, jump, kiss their boots and so on.

[Page 61]

Here is an image that was repeated almost every day: During hot summer day the Jews stand all hunched over on the road, digging a deep sewer channel. They've been digging like this already for many hours, laboring with fading strength, drenched in their sweat. Their oppressors do not permit even a little rest. If someone faints, he is rolled aside and no one is permitted to go to him or bring him a sip of water. In the midst of this, a German overseer with a puffed out red face, wants to make fun of his Jews, who are completely wretched. With a sarcastic smile, he picks out several Jews, but only the intellectuals amongst them, such as lawyers, engineers, teachers, etc. The German already knows the professions of his Jews. He tells them "sing, dance, do gymnastics" and then he tells them to make all kinds of expression, line up to kiss his boots, undress, and while naked, do their wild tricks. In order to give a greater effect to these scenes, and to make the Jews do their tricks in a livelier manner, he beat the Jews with his whip. The Germans and the local Christians who are standing about, laugh, enjoying the beautiful entertainment and praised the "lovely" German for his clever themes.

The outcome of the arduous labor above and beyond their strength, the overwhelming weariness and because of physical exhaustion and the debilitation of their bodies from the beatings, and the tremendous moral degradation, the consciousness of the Jews was greatly weakened, to some degree they became anesthetized. The Jews of Glubokie were also taken by the Germans to work in Krolevshtzine, a central train station, about 14 kilometers from the town. There, very often, the Germans and their local helpers would during work hours, make the Jews stand under the water pump and even though they (the Jews) were fully clothed, would turn a stream of cold water on them. Very often, they would also drive the exhausted, sweaty fully clothed Jews, into the lake "to bathe themselves". Afterwards they would force them to lie down in their wet clothes on the "sand beach". The Germans would often tease the Jews, telling them that Germany already occupied Moscow and the Red Army was completely beaten. As a result, they said "the Jews would never get help from anywhere or anyone!"

[Page 62]

The Isolation of the Jews

Translated by Eilat Gordin Levitan

Approximately two to three weeks after entering Glubokie, the Germans issued an order that the Jews must put white armbands on the sleeves of their shirts, to detect them from the rest of the citizenry. At the same time announcements were posted. They were signed by the German Governor of the District of White Russia. The posters announced the Restrictions concerning Jews. It was stated in the announcement: "Jews are not allowed to be greeted, and they are not to be answered by anyone who is greeted by them. No business at all is to be conducted with Jews. Jews are forbidden to walk on the sidewalks, and so forth!....." Also included in the same ordinances were Jewish converts to Christianity going back as far as four generations. They were without any rights, the same as all other Jews.

The military divisions that were stationed in town replaced very often. Each division had its own commandant, who would issue new orders to the inhabitants. The more orders, the harsher it was for the Jews. At the beginning during market day the Jews were permitted to go to the market for two hours. This was until the decree, and then it was entirely forbidden. To use butter, eggs, milk, meat, fruits, etc. was also forbidden for Jews. Bread was rationed - 125 grams a day per person. All the restrictions, the isolation of the Jews from the outside world (they were not to take any form of transportation or leave town), made the Jewish community despondent and severely depressed. Anti-Semitic slogans in Russian and Polished were posted on the streets: "Beat the Jews! Annihilate the Jews! Death to the Jews! Cleanse the town of Jews and Communists!" And so forth! The sanctions brought immediate results. Local hooligans attacked and beat Jews. Christian children ran after Jews in the street, cursing them and throwing rocks at them. At the beginning, when the Jews did not completely grasp what their situation was, they would run, bloodied and beaten, to the German Commandant for protection. However, there they were laughed at and immediately thrown out. As time passed the Jews realized how forsaken and defenseless they were!

The Police

Translated by Eilat Gordin Levitan

The regional police was composed of native inhabitants of Christian background, who organized themselves during the first days of the occupation. They were very scrupulous about carrying out the orders of the Germans. Many times, the police were no less vengeful than the Germans. They robbed, beat, tortured and murdered without any pity! The following people served as policemen: Levandovski (Commandant), Pobalski, Zablotzki, Lenkevitch, Vaitzechovski, Yaramek, Yotzkevitch, Berniakovitch, Bok, Baravak, Targanski, Volov, Krivitchanin, Sergei Lavanak, Sodenkovitch, Zakrevski, Dubrovski, Kolie the shoemaker (family name no known), Toimkovitch, Butchko (later sentenced by the Soviet authorities to 10 years) Dambrovski and Kozlovski. The police became quite polished and insidious, in carrying out their tasks. They endeared themselves to the Germans, winning their complete sympathy. As a result, they would seek out enemies of the nazis, skillfully luring them into a "trap". They would dress in civilian clothing and send their agents to win the confidence of the inhabitants. People would drop their guard and speak ill of the German occupier. In this way the victim fell into their hands. They would attribute to their victims, anti-government activities, hostility towards the Germans, and so forth. With this they (the police) found favor in the eyes of their "bosses", the Nazi beast. Besides this the police would kill victims accused of robbery. The police would carry of these murders and take everything they confiscated for themselves: money, watches, jewelry, from the women they would take earrings, rings, and strip them of their clothing, shoes, etc. Most of the members of the police force started their job as poor Christians. In a short time, they became quite rich. They became so cruel and greedy that they would also remove gold and platinum teeth, in order to torture their victims. It would never have occurred to anyone, that local inhabitants, with whom we had lived together for many, many years, would be capable of such behavior. We didn't know, and for all of those years, we couldn't imagine among what kind of people we lived. Who are our "devoted good friends?" It is therefore no wonder that the Germans trusted them so much!

[Page 63]

The Judenrat

Translated by Eilat Gordin Levitan

The method that Jews were seized for forced labor, from the very first days, brought about a terrible pandemonium. It caused Jews to tremble.

[Page 64]

People were grabbed from the streets, from courtyards from their houses, from the houses of study, (during the early days Jews still went to worship in the houses of study.) and from any place they would be found. The police and the Germans didn't take into consideration whether the person was elderly, a child, sick, weak or even a pregnant woman. They snatched anyone who was available. They would take a doctor visiting an ill person, a sick person on the way to the infirmary, a midwife rushing to a pregnant woman, a mother going to the pharmacy for medicine for her sick child, whom she had left alone at home. In the case of the mother, the father had already been seized long before by the Germans - all these and others were captured on the ghetto streets for forced labor. To protest, speak up or plead was to no avail. As soon as a German would see a Jew from a distance he would motion with his finger and in his brutal voice call out: "Jew, come over here!". Then you were lost! Frightened and disturbed the Jew would run towards this wild animal, not knowing what else he could do and disregarding all else. He only wanted to escape with his life, to return home and once again see his loved ones. Even hiding at home was not a better solution. Before dawn the police would invade Jewish homes, and brutally remove men, women and even children, from their beds. They would beat and slap their faces and drive them away to God knows where. If they encountered a very sick person who could not be dragged out of bed, he would be beaten and left to die.

The circumstances became unbearable, much below par to slavery, worse than horses that would at list be fed and would be allowed some rest from their toil. Jews began to think of ways and means to improve the situation and alleviate conditions, to find a way to negotiate with the Germans. They knew they had to let the forced labor continue, but in an organized fashion. Jews were "ready" to serve, to do everything, but they want that the matter at least be "normalized" and done in an orderly fashion. The Jews were willing and ready to assign people, as many as necessary and whereever they were needed, at any time and for all kinds of work, provided that the seizures of people would come to an end. Towards this end, all men, up to age 60, and all women to age 50 were registered in the city. (This was at first. Later on, age didn't matter at all.) The Jews chose from among their own ranks a number of people. Some of the people were: Rabbi Katz, of blessed memory, Max Ostrovsky, Moshe Shulheiser, Gershon Lederman, David Yechiltzik, Zalman Sparber, Zalman Rubashkin, David Munbaz, Yaakov Almer, Yosef Meyerovitch Chana Pintzov, Zundel Musiz and others, who were responsible for providing Jewish labor to the Germans. They saw to it that all Jews except the sick should go out to work. They would be punctual, go to whereever they were assigned, be devoted and diligent workers no matter how arduous the task was. They attempted to accomplish the above-mentioned tasks, precisely. The Jews thought that by behaving in this way they could appease the beast. By "petting" it, they figured it might be less inclined to torture them. maybe they would not resort to beating and torturing Jews if they taken to heart that the Jews were good workers. The chaos brought by seizing Jews for forced labor was now somewhat stall. Nevertheless, it did not lessen the beatings and tortures. The cruelty was immense, and as time passed the Jews were tortured even more.

[Page 65]

In addition to assigning people to workplaces, the so-called committee had to "regulate" issues like stealing. This meant that instead of Germans and police going to Jewish homes and upsetting everyone, the Jews now provided things on their own. The demands for bribes did not cease. Every passing German unit had to be provided with the nicest and best things the Jews had to offer. The committee couldn't refuse to provide anything that was requested, because if they did not provide it, or even if they didn't provide it time to the exact minute, their lives were in danger. How much misery, agitation and blood all of this cost! Jewish homes were successively empty by the hour. Insufficiency and destituteness grew; the abyss became ever deeper… After a set period of time, one of the commanders appointed the above-mentioned persons as the official Jewish governing body. It was called the "Judenrat" Two Jews from every street as well as the above-mentioned individuals had to assemble and a gendarme would read the instructions for the "Judenrat", which bore the responsibility for carrying out all kinds of demands that the Germans made upon the Jews.

It is interesting to note that the gendarme ordered that a stool be brought for the Rabbi, and as a sign of respect he requested that the "Herr Rabbi" be seated. Everyone else stood! He indicated that if the Jews would work and be loyal the Germans, carry out exactly the demands placed on them, go to where they would be sent, then no harm would befall upon the Jews. For a time, the Jews breathed a bit easier. They still didn't "recognize" the German mentality, and their hypocritical nature.

Sometime after installation of the "Judenrat", the predicament became most terrible.

[Page 66]

The demands exceedingly increased; very often it became unfeasible to carry them out. They demanded such precious articles, that the Jews did not even have, and could not possibly get anywhere, even for huge sums of money. These included such things as special furniture, large amount of silk lingerie, musical instruments and other rare things. In many instances, the Jews bought things secretly from Christians (the very things that had earlier were stolen from Jews). There was no price to large for such purchases in these circumstances. They paid what the sellers' fantasy would come up with. And their fantasies did not miscalculate, because they knew that the Jews had to have that particular in order to save themselves from death at the hand of the Germans. For a diamond that the Jews had to have for the provincial commandant, Hochmann, the "Judenraat" paid a railroad official 72,000 Ruble, when the price was actually between 15,000 a 30,000 Ruble. Every demand had to be met in order to see to it that there were fewer victims.

The plight of the Jews became irremediable, and the entire community absorbed what a deep, dark Inferno they had fallen into.

The Gestapo in Glubokie

Translated by Eilat Gordin Levitan

The German Gestapo became active in Glubokie during the month of August of 1941. As soon as they took over, they instilled an entirely new approach. Almost immediately this particular "institution" became quite prevalent. The Jews felt its rule in all their limbs.

At first the Gestapo, with the help of the local police and some other local Christians, began to search for communists and their cohorts who had worked for the Soviet occupation forces, or served them in some capacity. Almost immediately, 42 persons were arrested. Among them: Yehoshua Geller - a barber-surgeon, who had dozens of years of practice in his profession. He had healed non-Jews as well as Jews; Shimon Budov - a baker; Levi-Yitzhak Drizenshtok - who had a large crockery business; Merim Vant - iron-monger; Rachel Glass, Malka Kozliner and others. There were also a few Christians amongst the arrested: Chachalka, Sivka and Korolenka. All of those arrested, except for the above-mentioned merchants, were officials of the Communist regime during the Soviet occupation.

What became of those who were accused, we didn't know for a long time. All sorts of stories were told. It was said that they were taken "somewhere" for forced labor.

[Page 67]

Others had seen them in the vicinity of Plotsk, Vitebsk, and alike… Others "knew" that they would soon return, and so forth. Later we found out that on the very same day that they were apprehended, they were shot to death without a trial or any investigation.

When the wives and close relatives of the victims turned to the German authorities and pleaded to at least release to them the bodies for burial, the Germans laughed, and mockingly added that they should "wait" till the War ends…

Approximately in November, after two months wait, a few families with the aid of a huge bribe, were able to recover the bodies and bring them to Jewish burial. At the time the entire city gathered at the Jewish cemetery. There was no funeral at the time. The bodies were brought on a cart. The living sneaked to the cemetery by various secret routes, and little-known streets and byways.

During the burial there were heart-breaking scenes. We choked back our tears. Some were seized with spasms and tore their clothing. Some even fainted, and so on. We were afraid to cry out loud, fearing that the Germans would detect our presence in the cemetery. Those gathered, the mourners and undertakers, did not comprehend yet that the fate of those being buried at the moment was a better one than their own fate…. They at least received a Jewish burial. But what was in store for those participating in this unofficial funeral? What will happen to them? Where will they end up?

For a long time, the community members found themselves affected by those events. The deeds of the Germans were not yet fathomed; the inexplicable murder of innocent victims was new to us still. It is easy to imagine with what terror and fear the Jews strained themselves to carry out all of the whims of the Gestapo. They provided them with all sorts of things and also people to serve them. This was in addition to the demands of passing military units, about which we've already wrote. And the demands were not for simple things. We had to provide items that were truly great luxuries. Death was constantly before our eyes. The sword hovered over us, and under this great fear all of their demands were met.

How tragic for us was the feat of providing these bandits with everything that they ordered! It seemed just like entering a lion's den. We could never be sure we would ever come out. We would cast lots to determine who would bring the items to the Gestapo. The wives and children of those men whose turn it was to go to the Gestapo to bring them the "gifts", cried bitterly and bade them farewell... Also, the "Judenrat" members would bid them farewell and wished them a safe return.

[Page 68]

And how great the joy, when the messengers returned alive and well from Gestapo headquarters. Expressing their thanks that this time they escaped with no more then a "beating"... Once the messengers were so "honored" (with a beating) that they had to be brought home in cart but at least they survived. (They were Zack, Almer and Meierovitch.) This was the state of affair after the first Gestapo visits.

The German Civil Administration

Translated by Eilat Gordin Levitan

There were clear differences of opinion Amongst the Jews. Some said that with the arrival of a civil administration the situation would improve. They rationalized that with the stabilization of the administration, the anarchy would cease and every individual German or a German unit would not be able to do as they pleased. The pillage would come to an end. At least there would be only one official body to answer to and to provide with what they would demand. Even the physical abuse would abate. The Jews toil with all their might and are enslaved to their German masters just like the black slaves of former times. Maybe they'll no longer be beaten. It will be an administration that will maintain order in its German tradition...

Others had just the opposite opinion. They maintained that with the arrival of a civil administration, Hitler's program would be carried out to the letter. Exactly what Hitler's program consisted of? No one knew as yet. But they maintained that it wouldn't get better. Hopefully it wouldn't get any worse. But even the most pessimistic amongst us, could not conceive that the monstrous German program for the Jews, however horrible, included the complete annihilation of the Jewish people. That in other places, thousands and tens of thousands of Jews had already been slaughtered, we didn't know any of that as yet. We didn't even know what was happening in neighboring villages and shtetls (interaction with others was not permitted). We thought that they killed only who they conceive as "criminals" (and the bar was low). They are punishing who ever was not carrying out German orders or demands in regard to the rationing of food items.

[Page 69]

But innocent Jews who hadn't transgressed any of the rules of the Hitler program?! Jews who wouldn't eat or go or stand without being told to do so? Such Jews could not and would not be harmed by the Germans, they told us so..... But even most extreme pessimists were, unfortunately, greatly disappoint With the arrival of the civil administration there began, for the Jews, a new page of troubles - new in every sense. The civil administration begins to incorporate in our lives the "German program". A very deliberate and definite program for new world order.

A district commandant arrived, accompanied by a large staff. For the Jews who had already been relieved of most of their possessions, a new sequence of supplying the officials with nicely furnished and comfortable apartments began. Good furniture, luxury items, jewelry and alike., had to be obtained. Everything had to be of regal quality and appear elegant. Jews ran to and from home to home. They became disturbed and upset. Where is all of this to be satisfied? How can it be assembled? From Jewish homes there were dragged out and loaded on carts mirrored vanities, buffets, divans, beds, tables, chairs, good wall clocks, pianos, violins, mandolins, all sorts of cutlery sets, dishes of all kinds, window door draperies and other items that could be found. Also, they chose the very best suits, dresses, footwear, lingerie and all kinds of ladies' wear. They ran secretly to Christians to buy at inflated prices, because among the Jews everything was just about gone. A few would hide their things and preferred to give money instead. The families of the German officials were also provided with household help, and the fine, modest Jewish maidens, the genteel Jewish daughters became maids, simple servants in the German and police homes. They did the simplest and lowliest jobs. How superior they were to their German mistresses! But their fate was unfortunately a lowly one.

The civil administration announced that Jewish obligations in all matters must be fulfilled. All the demands placed upon Jews must be consign only to one person, the "Jewish Elder". They're to report to him about everything that involves Jews. No Jew may cross the threshold of any German official except him. They may not speak to any German, not come in contact with any German under any circumstances. The Jews are obligated to take off their caps before every German that they meet, and only replace the cap after the German has already passed by, leaving the Jew at least 5 meters behind. To greet a German with words or pleasant demeanor was forbidden!

[Page 70]

In this matter too, there were great sufferings inflicted on the Jews. Jews were only permitted to walk in the middle of the roadway. Only Germans and other "kosher" Aryans walked on the sidewalk. Many times, the tired Jews did not notice the fast-walking Germans on the sidewalk. They would not tip off their caps. Suddenly e a hail of blows would fall upon the Jew who had transgressed in this way and he couldn't even fathom from where or why they came. Jews became bloodied because they hadn't "doffed their caps". The more "humanitarian" Germans would simply reprimand the Jew for his "chutzpah" and not beat him. But these were few in number!

A Jew passing through a street, did not know what to look out for first - a passing vehicle which might run him down (since they would not blow their horns for a Jew, and there were cases in which Jews were run over - see further on) or whether or not he should look out for a German official, running along, to whom he must doff his cap, and then replace it on his head at the proper time.

Prior to the time that the Jews became totally acclimated to the German instituted customs and regulations, they attempted to bring their problems to some regarding the new rules to some of the public offices. They would, under the best of circumstances, be driven out by being mocked. But very often the German officials got themselves involved in "debates" with the Jews and they would bombard them with any object that was handy. Once the local lady, Dr. Helena Rajak, had to tend to a Christian patient, whom she had always taken care of. Even though she was in doubt about whether or not a Jewish doctor has the right, under Hitler's decree, to continue caring for her Christian patient, and being fearful of taking the responsibility upon herself, she wanted to refer the matter the local commissioner. When the duty guard at the entrance referred the matter to the one in charge of Jewish affairs, Gebell, indicating that a Jewish female doctor was making an inquiry, she was given entrance. As soon as she entered and crossed the threshold, Gebell (who later conducted all of the slaughter in the neighborhood), grabbed an inkwell from his desk and threw it at the doctor's face. She stood stunned for a moment, not understanding what had occurred. Her face and clothes were covered with ink and when she exited into the corridor there was an outburst of joyful laughter from the Germans, who were pleased with the clever act of their chief! This welcome which was accorded to the best-known doctor in the area made a fearful impression on everyone, including Christians. It was sensed that Jews had become the object of humiliation and mockery, the lowest of all beings. But what was to come later, the surprises in store, were to make us forget these earlier events. Further German acts paled previous ones.

[Page 71]

As the Jewish elder, the Germans appointed the former local businessman, Gershon Lederman. He became the "go-between" the enslaved Jews of the entire area, and the Germans. All the German demands were put to Lederman, and then, the members of the "Judenrat", at his bequest, would track all the Jewish homes and literally suck the marrow from their Jewish bones. All of the capricious demands of the civil authorities had to be met, and the military authorities, for their part, sucked Jewish blood on their own.

The unbearable situation was meant to oppress and demeaned the Jews. There was no escape. The "Judenrat", for its part, tried to demonstrate to Jews that with dutiful labor, with carrying out all of the demands made, the Germans would soften their attitude towards Jews, and tame their bestiality towards them. But the facts, the daily torture and the torment, the beatings for no excuse, the organized murder of individuals and groups, did not allow the hapless Jews to overlook with whom they were dealing. They were too conscious of the horrible Abyss into which they had fallen.

The Jewish Police

Translated by Eilat Gordin Levitan

The Jewish Police represented a peculiar chapter in the Ghetto story. The setting up of such a sinister "power device", made up exclusively of Jews, was yet another shrewd

German ploy by which to demoralize and extract all things from Jews. Design to suck out the last bit of juice and completely demean and shatter the destitute souls, physically and spiritually. Set against and rule, who could better accomplish the looting of Jewish wealth, either willingly or by force (of death punishment), than Jews themselves? Who could know better than other Jews where Jewish treasures were hidden?

[Page 72]

And by the sinister ploy, Jewish young men of respectable Jewish homes, who only yesterday were dignified and composed, overnight turned into co- oppressors and persecutors assisting the Germans. Unfortunately, the members of the Jewish Police suffered from the same delusional thinking that prevailed in the ghetto. "The more we satisfy the Germans, the more we give them their way, the better they would insure our own lives, and in particular the lives of our families". Some were drawn into the police because of the privileges that were accorded them. They didn't have to report for forced labor and had a source of income... They were in contact with the local Christian Police and local Christian population. It must also be pointed out that a definite proportion of those who enlisted did so with the best of intentions, thinking that in this way they could do some good by preventing even greater atrocities and blood-letting against Jews. There is no doubt about this. But, to our great misfortune, they were mistaken in their assessment of the situation. They did not understand the political background of the Germans who meant only to "milk the cow" as long as it could be milked and then to slaughter it. The Germans knew that the Jews had hidden assets, buried fortunes, and they looked for ways to obtain these treasures before they murdered them, they assumed that after the killings the treasures would remain hidden and be lost to them.

The Police helped the Jewish Elder, Lederman, carry out all of the German demands. The Jewish Police saw to it that Jews went out to their forced labor assignments on time. That they gave to the athurities everything that they possessed, and even when it came to choosing those who were to be murdered, the Police came to the moral conclusion that by sacrificing certain individuals they could somehow save the masses... They didn't understand (some did not want to understand), the lowly, evil intentions of the Germans, that after extorting everything from the Jews, they will finally exterminate them all... One of the greatest errors of the Jewish Elder and the Jewish Police must be pointed out. It was that in this most unfortunate and critical situation they did everything on their own, not consulting or soliciting any advice. The old Rabbi and communal activist, who was a more of a practical thinker, Rabbi Katz, of blessed memory, Lederman called him "senile". When the Rabbi's young daughter, Shprintze, with her astute and efficient expression, attempted to tell the Jews that "they should not let everything be taken from them, but better that they should keep some possessions. As long as they still had something they should flee to the forest, where maybe there would be some chance to save oneself. Why should they give everything to the German, and then die?" The Jewish Elder wanted simply to ostracize her… They did not ask anyone's advice, nor did they listen to anybody who came to them with a suggestion even when he was in dire straits.

[Page 73]

While assembling Jews for forced labor, or when carrying out changes in homes, the Police learned from their German masters, they would quite often beat Jews. In the Ghetto it was rumored that there were Jewish policemen who personally benefited from confiscated Jewish fortunes.

It must be pointed out here that a portion of the original Jewish Police force recognizing immidiatly that they couldn't relieve Jewish suffering by serving the Germans. In order to carry out the German demands, on the contrary, they are causing Jews even more pain and suffering. They soon left the Police force. Some of them later fled to the forest, joined the partisan groups and distinguished themselves in the struggle against the Germans. Among the latter were Yitzhak Blatt, Lyusye Pintzov (both of whom died a heroes death), Israel Shparber, Zalman-Ber Kotz and others.

Utilizing such evil methods as setting their victims one against the others, the German degraded the Jews into the lowest depths and placed them in a persistent pall of gloom and despondency. The formation of the Jewish Police in the Glubokie Ghetto was as follows (including people who later resigned from the force): Yude Blant, Commandant; Chaim-Ber Gordon; Yude Gilevitch; Arke Sheindlin (Leibe Toibe'son); Chaim Sheinkman; Isaac Weinstein; David Friedman; Ziske Kotz; Lusye Pintzov (who later perished as a partisan in the struggle against the Germans); Zalman Yungelman; Michael Shapira; Israel Shparber (later an outstanding partisan); Shloimke Zimmer (from Sharkavshtsizne); Israel Ichiltsik; Abba Sragavitch (who perished as a partisan); Leibl Shapiro; Budniov (a brother-in-law of Zatsepitzke); Zalman-Ber Kotz (later distinguished himself in the Red Army); and Yitzhak Blatt (a heroic partisan who fell in the struggle against the Germans).

Confiscation of all the Jewish Property

Translated by Eilat Gordin Levitan

Until that time the plunder of Jews occurred "unofficially", without the benefit of a governmental decree. The Germans and their assistants simply came and took or ordered the Judenrat to bring it to them certain items. With the arrival of the civil administration, there came an official letter from the ministry in which it stated that, according to German law, Jews were no longer permitted to possess any personal property whatsoever. Accordingly, everything that the Jews owned; from a thread to a shoelace, is to be confiscated, and within a 24-hour period the Jews are obligated to turn in everything of value, be it gold, silver, earnings, diamonds, candelabra, cups, watches, sets of dinnerware and so forth. Also, all paper made money of any label and sort.

[Page 74]

In a long line at the ministry, stood hundreds of Jews, holding their most precious possessions. Items they inherited from their parents, grandfathers, great grandfathers, and who knows how many generations' back. They now came and waited for the evil enemy to take their possessions, believing the promise that there would be no charges or beatings if they complied. They turned over the beautiful Passover goblets, the silverware, which used to enhance the Passover Seder table only once a year. And who knows how many Seders these precious utensils remembered, how many memories we engraved in the minds of the owners of these most fine items. Even engagement rings were brought. The fear was indescribable. People arrived to a state of mind that they only desired to remain alive. They thought that these gifts, together with the forced labor for the Germans, would help to show the Germans that the Jews are needed to be kept alive…

On the second day came a fresh decree. All Jews must bring all their linens, quilts covers, etc. as well as materials no yet sewn. The previous day's shameful exhibition wass repeated once more. Once more Jews stood in long lines with the nicest of linens, apparel, outer garments, and alike. They waited for the hangmen to take these. People worried, cried, and even fainted. The arduous winter was soon to come and they would remain bare and naked. The fright of the Jews of their new masters reached the point where they brought children's clothing, not thinking about the morrow. Certain manufacturers, who had hidden supplies of merchandise, now brought them in wagons.

Others reconsidered what is best and speedily brought their things to Christian acquaintances. Among the latter there were later to be found some good people that restored some of the items to their original owners, or at least gave a small sum, in produce, to the Jews. But there were more then a few criminal elements, which remained full "inheritors" of Jewish merchandise, and fearing that perhaps someday the Jew will claim his fortune, they made sure to bring about the speedy demise of the particular Jew.

[Page 75]

There were also those who during the night buried their valuables. Everything of course had to be done very carefully. The Germans, and even more so, the local police, investigated and sniffed out whether or not the Jews were turning everything in. They staked out all places where Jews went, what they did, and so forth. It's clear that without victims this did not pass. (Berl Zeldin, Berkowitz and others)

Confiscation-Money Action

Translated by Eilat Gordin Levitan

Ignoring the fact that the Jews had already turned over their entire fortunes - gold, jewelry, precious things, clothing, etc. - the Judenrat, at the end of September 1941, once again received an urgent decree to provide a large sum of money. If they don't carry out the terms of the decree immediately and exactly, the decree stated that all Jews would be shot. The Germans and the police clearly understood that a number of Jews had riot yet turned over their entire fortunes.

The Judenrat began calling emergency meetings, speaking and influencing those who might still have something hidden away, to come forward with it, because the entire Glubokie Jewish population was in terrible danger. The Judenrat especially approached those elements who were suspected of having some hidden money or possessions.

Not all were able to withstand the torture and suffering of the demands and there were some victims of suicide. The 60-year-old Mendl Kliot hanged himself, because he couldn't raise the sum that the Judenrat had assessed upon him.

Finally, a solid sum was raised, and it was presented to the Commissar. It clearly demonstrated that the Jews had not yet been completely cleaned out. They obviously have even more... And the actions to confiscate even more clothes, underwear, shoes, utensils and cash, did not cease.

The Jews, as time passed were much less able to fulfil the beastly demands of the Germans. From this point of time every subsequent action carried out by the Germans transpired with casualties.

Village population under Terror

Translated by Eilat Gordin Levitan

At the beginning of the occupation, they would bring Christians from the villages to the city. They were arrested. These people belonged to elements, exposed through German espionage as having participated in underground, anti-German activities. The Christians were brought to town either in smaller or larger groups, mostly at 4:00 A.-M. when the local population was still asleep. Large masses were not eyewitnesses to the phenomenon but it could not remain hidden from the citizenry for long. People would silently sneak about very early in the morning, and from corner houses, behind fences and through the open cracks of doors and windows, they would peek out and see how through Bialistoker and Lomzsher Streets they are leading men, women and children in the direction of the Boroker Forest, about half a kilometer from the city where they were all shot. In the early days this had a horrible effect on the Jews. They couldn't get over it. They couldn't eat, drink or sleep. They couldn't reconcile themselves to the idea that people could be taken out and shot without any recourse to justice or a trial. The women and children were certainly innocent! Afterwards they became used to it. They became indifferent! They would simply tell about it, passing it on from mouth to mouth, that before dawn so many and so many people were taken into the Borok to be shot. Quite often they would lead Christians, who were familiar to us, through the streets. It depressed the Jews greatly, and eventually the apathy in which they viewed life greatly increased.

[Page 76]

The Gypsies' Chase

Translated by Eilat Gordin Levitan

If some of the village peasants were punished for "specific crimes" the neighboring gypsies, just like the Jews, suffered simply because of the fact that they were gypsies, and not for any crimes. It was because their skin color did not suit the "super race". They were also exterminated wholesale in the closing months of 1941. The local police would find them in the surrounding area, in the neighboring woods and villages, bring them into the city, and murder them.

Once, in December 1941, they brought in a group of more than 100 gypsy men. Before shooting them, they were stripped naked and kept that way for a long while in the bitter winter cold. Their children were seated naked on the ice. They turned blue. Their faces froze so they couldn't cry. The cold froze them, and they stiffened. Soon thereafter most died. Other children held on longer but that only prolonged their suffering.

[Page 77]

The parents of the children, especially the mothers, cried, screamed, wailed, tore their hair from their heads, fell in a faint and pleaded with the executioners to shoot the children rather than make them watch the suffering of their children, who were expiring from cold lying naked in the snow! One gypsy mother became insane from the torture and began laughing, singing, dancing and doing other odd things.

A chill passed through the body and the blood froze in the veins as we watched the horrors, the terrible scenes. Also, those onlookers murmured and pleaded. It was beyond human strength to endure. Those who were more mild-mannered were ill for a long time afterwards. It just didn't seem to affect at all the Aryan light complexion, so-called "noble, civilized European race ", who made merry with the dark complexion gypsies.

After mocking the victims, and filling themselves with satisfaction, the Germans drove the gypsies into the Borok. They were naked, forced to drag along their frozen, dead children. There, at the open pits near their dead children, the murderers ordered them to sing, dance, jump, clap and so on. As they performed, they were beaten with whips to make them dance better, sing louder and the young gypsies were forced to laugh...

The strains of the original, sad gypsy songs, combined with their crying, yammering, and screaming cut through the air and were carried through the entire forest and rolled far beyond the forest to the peasants of the villages and farms. The peasants shuddered in their small, impoverished homes, listening to what was taking place in the nearby forest.

The Germans photographed this macabre sight. When they completed the "entreating" part of the scene, the murderers pushed the unfortunate gypsies into the pits, where they had previously thrown their dead children, and there, they shot them. It is characteristic that not only the Germans could satiate themselves with pleasure from the horrible pictures, but also the policemen,

[Page 78]

local Christians, and German lackeys such as Levendovski, Dombrovski, Krivitshanin, Yaremek, Zakravski, Targonski, Sudinkovitsh and others. They stood by joyfully and had a good time. They carried on an animated conversation, joked, laughed, and with great satisfaction observed it all. Their faces weren't any less inflamed than the faces of the Germans. They all looked like those beasts of prey who steal a carcass from some other animal and devour it after tearing it to pieces.

The Ghetto

Translated by Eilat Gordin Levitan

The story of the Jewish Ghetto is well covered, when one studies the History of the Middle Ages, as well as that of later times. We have some idea of what life there was like. We know of the servitude of the Jews, the dread they felt toward the immoral political system, and so forth. Before the German-Russian War began, we heard that the Jews under German occupation in Poland, became segregated in special peripheral sealed quarters in cities and villages, which were named "Ghettos" But the true taste of "Ghetto" we only knew, when we found ourselves encased in one. When we experienced the daily living in such place. We are certain that those prior generations which experienced Ghetto life in the Middle Ages, with all of the restrictions, with all the strife, with the suffering and pain, could not possibly imagined the despicable Ghetto of the 20th century. Ghettos packed with millions of Jews, which the Germans expelled and drove there. Those Jews of the middle ages, suffering so much at the time, could not have imagined the Purgatory of the modern Ghetto. Such Hades mankind never experienced or witnessed yet.

After civilian rule was reestablished in Glubokie (in the summer of 1941), all sorts of commissions headed by the Burgomeister, Naumov and other members of the Council started to go around the city and began inspecting the neighborhoods, especially the section of back streets, making all sorts of plans, combinations and so forth.

At first no one knew what it was all about. We thought of different things and commented about them. The governing body kept it a secret from us. Later on, we became aware of the fact that the Germans set up a separate area at the edge of the city, which was to be a Ghetto for the Jews. The Christian families who resided in those Streets, will have to move to the center of the city, in order to vacate their homes for the Jews.

[Page 79]

A good portion of the peasants did not want to make the exchange. They would prefer to remain in their own homes, near their fields, their gardens, orchards, barns and stables. To live where they were born, grew up and lived their lives, rather than go into the more expensive, beautiful apartments in the center of the city. On the other hand, some were pleased at the prospect of living "the good city life" in the Jewish homes. Whatever people felt, neither the Christians nor the Jews knew of the true harmful intentions of the Germans. The Nazis objectives were to gather all of the Jews into one isolated place, cram them all into a "cage", weaken them and squeeze the last bit of juice out of them and lead them to a state of despair and resignation. Subsequently, when time comes to exterminate them, it would Be done with out any resistance. The Jews all along thought that the Ghetto would be no worse than the Ghettos of the Middle Ages, where Jews had suffered greatly, but were not subjected to planed mass murders.

On the 22nd of October 1941, the Minister of Information ordered that all Jews must, within an hour, move into their new "dwelling places". At the same time, they were told that they weren't to take any of their better things out of their homes. (You can imagine what kind of "better things" still remained in their homes!) And for some things which they wanted to take they had to have special permits from the Magistrate.

A number of Jews had cleverly foreseen what was about to be taken place. They found out in various ways where the Ghetto was going to be located, and they secretly transported some of their things. They were able to transfer clothing, utensils and even bigger things.

The more courageous ones were even able to transfer furniture. It was all done during the evening or before dawn. Some even carried possessions over in the middle of the night, when it was truly a danger to be outdoors (curfew time). They knew which policemen would be the easiest to bribe, they would watch to see when these "good" police were on duty at their posts.

On that 22nd of October, the resettling of the Jews in the Ghetto, set the city boiling like a noisy kettle. The police chased the Jews from their homes similarly to livestock being chased from their barns and stables. The streets were filled with large masses of unnerved, frightened people, carrying heavy packs on their backs. Pandemonium of the old, children, women and the handicapped who were just pulled out of their homes. People, who couldn't move on their own, were pulled along by others. Women with suckling babes in their arms, could barely move along sighing. Infants cry and scream. When they heard their children, the mothers also cried. The noise was enormous. They were shouting and pushing each other. Others fall under the weight of their bundles and were trampled by the masses of people, pushing and being pushed. The police were "keeping order". They were beating people mercilessly with their whips, with their clubs and guns - on peoples' heads and wherever else they could reach. People were moving along bleeding profusely. Long trails of blood Were visible on the streets mixed with broken, battered furniture, valises, broken utensils, footwear, torn lingerie and bed linens. The air was filled with feathers. From afar they appeared like small white snowflakes floating in space.

[Page 80]

People left their homes, the rooms where they had first seen the light of day, where they grew up, loved and lived. Homes where they had moments satiated with joy and moments of suffering. Children were born here, children were raised and married off here. There, in those homes, they became grandparents. Now they must leave it all in one hour, in the time it takes to blink the eyes, they must go, go to unknown barren places. No one knows if they will ever return...

Of the possessions and fortunes that were accumulated with sweat and blood over the generations, their inheritances, there only remains the backpack, which the enemy allowed them to take along. The exceptions were only those Jews, who had secretly stashed earlier a number of things in the Ghetto, as was mentioned above.

Like black crows, when they sense the smell of death, the aroma of blood, so, in the same fashion, during the above-mentioned commotion, did the defiled, undeserving, low life individuals throw themselves upon the Jewish homes. Old men and good-looking young Christians, their faces flaming and eyes bulging, ran with outstretched arms to seize Jewish loot. A strange sort of frankness and largesse could be seen in their demeanor: "Today we may take everything from the "Dzid" (Jew). They cannot prevent it!" The Police only allowed the young and good-looking Christian girls to drag thing from Jewish homes. Maybe these were their sweethearts! The Christian men were not permitted by the Police to go near Jewish possessions.

Even earlier, before the Jews knew that they would have to leave their homes with everything in them behind, it was typical that Christian acquaintances, would come to the Jews and ask that they would give to them, their "old good friends", their possessions and fortunes, "in any case you, the Jews would no longer need these things..." These Christians, the "old good friends", could not hide their impatience concerning the removal of Jews. They wanted to "inherit" promptly. They competed with each other to grab the last bite from the mouths of the Jews and they knew that he who would be the "early bird, would catch the worm"!

[Page 81]

A number of Jews, out of disappointment and despair, secretly took their possessions and destroyed them. They would break them, tear them, burn them and so forth; as long as they didn't fall into the hands of the Germans, their lackeys, or even into the hands of "our own good old friends".

The Ghetto was laid out in the side and out of the way streets of the city: Lomzher, old and new Kishelike, Dubrove, Polne and one side of Vilna Street. Nobody could imagine where and how in these few crowded and narrow streets everyone could be accommodated. The fact that we were being isolated, torn away from the free world, set into a prison, robbed of all our humanity, our elementary rights, no one thought about any longer. We didn't indulge in deep thought. The will to live was being dulled. Everything was done mechanically, without will, without understanding, without sensations... No desire or strong will was displayed by anybody. Just getting some corner to lay one's head! was on our mind. In one small peasants' cottage a number of families would have to be "accommodated". In a low ceiling, small "hut" dozens of souls, men, women, old folks and small children, resided all together. It was a blessing that the Germans and the Police did not allow any possessions to be taken into the Ghetto, because those that had been brought in were scattered in the streets, on roofs, in stalls, in gardens and so on. It took a long time before everyone found some place for themselves.

In order to sleep we had to spread ourselves out on the floor by families. We pressed one against the other. If one had the good fortune of finding a bed, 5 or 6 people would lie on its width. Cooking in the Ghetto was extremely hard. One stove would accommodate 8 to 10 housewives. The curse mentioned in the Bible, that "10 women would cook on one stove", actually came to pass. Men and women would have to leave for their forced labor very early each morning, so there really wasn't a problem of cooking something. People would leave without having eaten anything, or anything to drink. In the evening, when they returned from their labor, they were thoroughly exhausted, broken in spirit, and often beaten, so that there was no energy to occupy oneself with cooking.

[Page 82]

Those, who still "in their homes" had left someone elderly (This was only in the early days before all of the old folks were murdered.), who did not go out to forced labor, would, during the day prepare something warm. The food was entirely pareve (non-meat). Jews couldn't use any meat products, or any dairy product, no fish, no eggs, no fruit, berries and so forth. The domestic animals had long since been taken away, and not a bit of milk was available, even for the little ones.

The heating problem caused a huge amount of bitterness for the Jews in the Ghetto. To buy wood was forbidden to Jews and getting wood from the forest was out of the question. If someone, returning home in the evening from labor, was carrying a stick of wood that he had somehow obtained, it was usually taken from him and he would be badly beaten. On occasion, when a kinder guard, who had been bribed by the Judenrat, stood at the Ghetto gate, he would permit a Jew carrying some wood on his back, to pass through. Whoever had brought furniture into the Ghetto used it for firewood. Others would take the risk and during the night tear planks from roofs and stalls, which they would use for heating. With all of this the Jews still froze in their houses. There was also no lighting in the Ghetto. The electricity had been turned off. There was no kerosene available either and Jews sat mostly in the dark. Quite tragic was the situation in those homes where there were ailing people.

The sanitary situation was bearable., except for the extreme crowding and atrocious conditions in general. The Jewish inhabitants were extremely alert about keeping the Ghetto clean and maintaining the health standards of the Jews. In this effort the following were most active and self-sacrificing: Dr. Helena Rajack, Dr. Moshe Chaves, Dr. Haradishz,

Dr. Schwartz, and also the nurses, Rachel Rappaport, Mire Zinger and others. Almost every day they would go through the Ghetto, through the all the houses, and carry on among the Jews active propaganda about the importance of cleanliness in the Ghetto. They would emphasize the fact of the danger posed by the Germans to everyone in case someone came down with a contagious disease. (The Germans used to murder entire communities if it became known that someone there had come down with a contagious disease.) This was done to keep the enemy from having a pretext to shoot Jews.

[Page 83]

In the homes where elderly men and women still remained, they would (when the younger ones were away at labor) wash the floors, clean up around the houses and dig deep pits in which they dumped the filth. There were more outhouses than apartments in the Ghetto, and everyone was very concerned about keeping them clean.

Medical help for the Jews in the Ghetto was provided by the above mentioned four doctors. But the situation with medicines was a lot worse, because they couldn't be obtained from the city pharmacists with the prescriptions written by the Jewish doctors. It was forbidden to the Christian doctors to treat the Jewish sick, just as it was forbidden to Jewish doctors to treat the Christians who were ill. The only fortunate thing was that the Jewish doctors and pharmacists had smuggled a supply of medicines into the Ghetto at the time that we were moved into the Ghetto. It is obviously understandable that these did not suffice for any length of time to satisfy the demand placed upon them by the Jews of the Ghetto.

In a set period of time, when the Jews had "settled in and accustomed themselves to the new living conditions, a hospital with an out-patient infirmary was organized in the Ghetto. This undertaking was also done thanks to the self-sacrifice of the doctors and nurses. It must be mentioned here that even the Germans and their Police used to secretly seek medical advice from the Jewish doctors.

The restrictions on seeking medical help from Jews, imposed hardships on the Christians. They trusted the Jewish doctors and wanted desperately to be healed by them. A specific category of Christians, who were used to their Jewish doctors over a period of many years, suffered greatly after the decree that forbade them from using Jewish doctors. At first there were those ill Christians who, in individual cases with a great deal of effort and trouble, managed to get a permit from the Germans to continue being treated by Jewish doctors. Later, such permits were not given under any circumstances. And in spite of all of this the Jewish doctors would secretly continue to serve their old Christian patients with advice as much as was possible. This was accompanied by great risk, and involved a great deal of care, alertness and agility.

The Christians couldn't appear in the pharmacies with prescriptions written by Jewish doctors. With a substantial bribe the pharmacists would give the medicine without taking the prescription. This could only happen if the patient was well acquainted with the pharmacist.

In the city hospital there worked, during the early days of the occupation, the young Jewish surgeon, Dr. Nachum Lekach. He was an excellent specialist, and there was no one who could substitute for him. He suffered there a great deal, because the attitude towards him was exactly as it was towards all Jews. The Christian populace loved him dearly and the village peasants used to bring him food products, which he could not use, according to the German decrees. In spite of the fact that no one else was appointed in his place he was fired two months later. The hospital remained without a surgeon. The Germans sent Dr. Lekach later to a hospital in Luzshki and from there he escaped and joined the Partisans.

[Page 84]

Jews were forbidden to leave the Ghetto. At first, they could go freely to their forced labor. Each one had only to report to his designated place of work every morning. the Judenrat and the Jewish Police supervised the labor force. Later there came an order that Jews could not report for labor individually. They must appear in large groups, staying close together, not talking while walking and not looking to the sides, and other such "regulations"! If someone transgressed and went alone, either to work or from work, he was detained, brought to a barrack and, like a "criminal", shot.

Each day, at 6:00 A. M., all Jews had to assemble at the Judenrat, from where they were, under Police guard, taken to their set work places. The German Police also guarded diligently to see to it that no products of any kind were brought into the Ghetto. At night, when the Jews returned from their labor, the Police at the Ghetto gate would search everyone. If they would discover someone with a bottle of milk, a slab of butter, a few eggs, fish, a bit of flour, berries, and so forth, the "criminal" was immediately taken to the Police Station, from where he would never be seen again.

The number of victims accused of such crimes was quite large. It was indeed rare when someone could save himself with a bribe of a gold watch, a diamond or a large amount of cash. This was only possible if only one Policeman had been involved in the incident and it was worth his while, because if the guilty Jew was caught and shot, he would have to share his loot with other comrades. It paid for him to take everything from the Jew and let him go alive and well. (By David Hazan, of Szarkowszczyzna; when he was entering the Ghetto, they found, in his trousers two beets and a radish. He saved himself with a bribe, a large sum of money, and at that moment they let him go.)

[Page 85]

Those who had nothing for a bribe, a precious object, or money, had no chance to remain alive. This was an opportunity for the Police to turn over even more Jews to be shot. Other Policemen figured that everything the Jews had would eventually be theirs anyway, so why let them live? In spite of all of the vexations, these restrictions, and the victims, there was no great starvation in the Ghetto. People took risks, and products were brought in at any price. Also, the village peasants used to bring in products such as: Potatoes, milk, flour, chick-peas, barley and more. In the workshops, which were located outside of the Ghetto, and where only Jews worked, the products would be left. There was also an incident, whereby an Aryan woman put on the Jewish badge (the yellow star of David), went into the Ghetto and brought products to one of her Jewish friends. (Botvinick from Dokshitz)

Up to the time that the Ghetto was sealed off, many Christians would provide products for a good price. Naturally, everything had to be done secretly and very carefully. The Christian neighbors would set up during the night, on the grass in a set corner, a bottle of milk, a piece of butter and so forth. The Jew would come quietly to take it away. We, for example, living in neighborly terms with the Christian family Shebeka near by-, (from the other side of the Ghetto fence) every day we would obtain a bottle of milk for our sick mother. there would also be transferred through us products from someone named Grishkevitsh to the family of Leizer Gitelzon and for the tailor, Shamash. That Christian would either at dawn, or in the evening, throw over the fence into our yard; potatoes, cabbage and other things, which would later be picked up from us by the others.

Albeit the Christians in many cases would take from the Jews their possessions which were to pay for food products and would deceive them. These Christians would give the Jews nothing. Jews were later even afraid to remind these Christians of what they had done. They were afraid that because of these stolen things the Christians would want to get rid of them even sooner. This was, at the time, one of the easiest things... The Jewish fortunes were the frequent cause of a speedy death to their rightful owners. Because the local Christians knew who were the prosperous Jews, in most cases, they would always seek ways in which to obtain their possessions

[Page 86]

and their fortunes, promising that they would help and save them in their time of trouble. But, in most cases it brought tragedy upon these Jews even sooner. The majority of these thieves approached the unfortunate and unprotected Jews in a sly way, and as they drank together, they would reach for their knives. The Jews had no choice. Maybe! Maybe Ivan, Stephan, or Frank be honest and not want them dead in order to obtain their fortunes.

But in vain! The atrocity of those local Christians was immense. They would try with all their might to eliminate those Jews who had left any possessions with them. In this way, Labanak inherited the engineer, Max Ostrovsky, who was shot, thanks to Labanak's denunciation, Philipak inherited Treister's things, and so on.

Occasionally, Jews would return to the Ghetto without their outer garments and barefoot without their shoes. It would occur that during their labor or at the gate of the Ghetto, the Police would remove their clothes, and if someone had money in his possession or some other object, it would certainly be stolen, and the result would almost always result in the Jews being shot. It became clear that Jewish life was altogether worthless. It had nothing to do anymore with clothing, food or possessions. The problem became much more serious: How to prevent physical extermination, a complete annihilation, a final solution? The Glubokie Jews thought that maybe they could prevent it by becoming a needed element, by being productive so that the enemy could utilize them and, in this way, leave them alive.

The Jews began to establish in Glubokie various enterprises and workshops to help the Germans. They established a large leather factory, mechanical workshops, knitting mills, fur factory, shoe shops, tailor shops, joiner's workshops, brush factory, chimney factory, wheel factory, sweater factory, sock and handkerchief factory, hat factories, boot factory, shoe polish workshops, spinning workshops, wool cleaning workshops, a candy factory, a marmalade factory, quilt factories and others. In a short time, the Jews turned Glubokie into an industrial city

The Jews would rush off every morning to the above-mentioned enterprises, to the "holy" work. Every morning there would march off from the Judenrat large groups of workers, under police guard, as if they were arrested. In the evening they would return tired, hungry, overheated and dispirited to their cold, dark homes.

[Page 87]

Quite often there used to wait at the Ghetto entrance a German who would take the tired, tortured Jews to some new, fresh work, where they were kept until late at night. At home the family would be beside itself, not knowing what had happened. They would think that they would never see him again. It was not at all unusual for someone not to return home after work.

There were occurrences where people were held at the Ghetto entrance for no reason at all, when they came back from their labor. The fate of those who were held in this way was well known. - They would no longer be found among the living…

There was no trial, no investigation for Jews. A group of Jews would be rounded up and shipped off to the barracks.

[Page 87]

Bemma, Commandant of the Glubokie Slaughter-House

Translated by Eilat Gordin Levitan

In order to clearly comprehend the magnitude of the Jews' enslavement and the abyssmal pit they had fallen into, the extent that they were prey with which every German could do as he pleased, we will dedicate several lines to a specific German officer who was named Bemma, to whom we must ill-repute many Jewish victims.

His exterior demeanor, the way he strutted and his gestures were enough to instill fright in everyone. He was a person of military build, his facial expression beastly, his nose turned upward, blond hair, sharp cunning eyes, and with a piercing look that would devour you up. His gait and his conduct, his casting of quick glances to all sides from under his heavy brows could be compared to a wild animal that is seeking its prey. On top of it all he would constantly twirl and snap his whip, play with his revolver and run, run like he was doped.

To his slaves, the Jews, he never spoke softly or peacefully. He would constantly shout, bellow, and revile brutally, in the

[Page 88]

most obscene language and expressions of hate. As he spoke, he would point his revolver and make you feel that he is the one and only ruler, the "Fuhrer" with unlimited power even to the extent of shooting someone to death just for fun. It is understandable then that everyone was stricken with fear at the prospect of meeting this wild creature. Such a breed, such a depraved individual could only be created by the Nazi schools in Germany, who "were liberating mankind of conscience and morality."

The first "accomplishment" of this officer was the shooting of 35-year-old Isaac Gordon - a Jew and a family man, - who worked with him in the slaughterhouse.

On an early morning of a December day in 1941 - Bemma approached Gordon, and, in the presence of many Jewish laborers - drew his revolver, without any provocation, and shot Gordon twice, killing him on the spot. He did this only to satisfy his own pleasure. Looking at the dead man he smiled and told the older son of Eli Blach to say Kaddish for the deceased. With expression of contentment on his face, he went to eat his breakfast

The news of this murder spread like wildfire throughout the city. It made a frightening impression on everyone. In an instance Bemma became infamous... the Entire area knew about this cannibal, who sucks human blood and lusts after fresh mortal victims.

It was no longer a shock to anyone when he tortured Jews at their work place. He beat them, whipped them, and shot them without any provocation or reason.

Galinska, daughter of the postman Martzinkevitsh, a Christian woman from Glubokie, told that she herself saw how the wild German, Bemma, once grabbed the 18-year-old boy, Y. Gitelzon, threw him to the ground, kicked him with his boot and stomped him. Gitelzon screamed, pleaded that he would do anything for him if he would only leave him be. He only let him go when the boy fainted from the blows. Badly bruised, Gitelzon was carried home, his arm was broken. He remained lying in bed until the liquidation of the Glubokie Ghetto in August of 1943.

Bemma was the main subject of "terror" for the Jews. His name cast fear in everyone. "Bemma is in the ghetto", - "Bemma is seizing Jews" - children would cry in horror and run to tell their parents to hide. Neighbors would run to tell that "the serpent was crawling through the Ghetto", and all would flee to hide. Mostly he would come into the Ghetto to "circulate" during the evening hours. The Jews he would come upon, he would chase in his car. Indiscriminately he would snatch anyone he encountered. He would harm men, women, the elderly and children, supposedly for labor, which in reality did not exist at all. He needed this only for his own amusement, some one to play with… He used to demand that the Jews sing, dance, roll, make all sorts of faces and so on. He would force older people to jump from his car as it was moving, and if the weak and elderly refused to jump from the car, it meant a certain death for them. There was always some bodily injury involved in his perverse games - Bemma would beat them on their feet with a stick, or whip them with a thick rubber whip and be overjoyed at his new discovery… The elderly men and women would cry so bitterly that a stone would melt, but this German satrap was not touched by their cries at all. Later on Bemma turned the Jews into a very nice source of income for himself. These Jews who were seized by him for "labor", he would not release until their relatives would bring him a substantial ransom. And being released from such bloody hands, from such a bandit, was not such a common good fortune which all were privileged to enjoy The murderer Bemma - the educated and cultured German - remained in the memory of all of the survivors of the Glubokie Ghetto, as the most villainous image of a creature in the form of a man!

[Page 89]

The Abuse of the Jews from Krulevshchizna

Translated by Eilat Gordin Levitan

Suddenly on an early morning hour at the end of December 1941, the Police ordered the Jews of Krulevshchizna (14 kilometers from Glubokie) "to gather their belongings and in one hour arrive to some peasants' carts and load them on the carts and leave town". The Krulevshchizna Jews had to bid farewell to their homes, where they had been born, brought up and lived their entire life. Not only they lived in those homes, but also their parents, grandparents and great-grandparents. Who can tell how many generations had lived there, worked there and created there!

Whereto and why they were being taken they weren't told and the unexpected "surprise" pounded their minds. They were disturbed, not knowing what was happening. These Jews, at that time, did not know yet the horror of the Germans, even though they had already heard "something" about what was being done to Jews in many other cities and towns.

[Page 90]

Some thought that they were captured to be shot. They had heard that in some places Jews were deceived in this way only to be murdered. Fortunately, In this case it did not happen. They were just being taken to the Glubokie Ghetto. (Later they were murdered there together with the Jews of Glubokie.)

On the way they were disturbed, tortured and beaten. In Glubokie they with their belongings were taken to the Police barracks. There the Police took away from them their better items, and the remaining ones were shaken and spread out as they searched for hidden gold and other valuables. If they found anything, it was too bad for that person.

Finally, they were all thrown into the Ghetto where they suffered together with the Glubokie Jews. At first, they considered themselves fortunate, they escaped from the murderers' hands with their lives. Soon they realized that the vast majority of them had no place to sleep. It was so crowded in the Ghetto that taking in new people even with the greatest strain, was impossible. There wasn't enough room to insert a button. Days on end they would run around with the members of the Judenrat looking for a place under some roof. Families had to be divided up, splintered - the husband in one place, the wife in another, one child separated from his sibling and so forth. To settle a family all together in one place was absolutely unattainable. At the time these Jews accepted all of this lovingly. They had expected much worse, and therefore they were pleased. This was an unusual occurrence that in the enslavement of Ghetto life, in the deep darkness of existence there appeared a ray of joy. However, their optimistic spirit did not last for long. The Germans would not permit the "joy" to endure among the Jews in the Ghetto of Glubokie. Bloody episodes began to follow one another. The sword dangled right over the Jewish heads!

The Murder of Forty Souls

Translated by Eilat Gordin Levitan

On an early morning, during the last days of December of 1941, rumors spread throughout the Ghetto that during the night the Police removed from the ghetto 40 people and

[Page 91]

murdered them. The reason for this was, supposedly, their "evil behavior". They displayed insobriety, had charges brought against them in the past, and so forth. And since Jews mattered not to the Germans anyway, they were condemned without any of the legal processes of investigation, indictment or trial. Here also, as in all other murders, the small, innocent children were the victims of the "transgressions" of their parents and grandparents - for the "crimes" of sons and grandsons...

It happened in this way:

At 4:00 A. M. the Police arrived, with great commotion they broke down doors, woke the people, dragged them from their beds and ordered them to take along their little children, even the suckling infants, and go. Where and what, they weren't told. The mothers who wanted to take something along for their small children to eat or drink, were not permitted by the Police to do so. They weren't even allowed to dress themselves properly. They were taken to the Police Station, and an hour later the commandant read a decree issued by the German civil authority, "those who had been arrested, as a "useless" element, are sentenced to death." At first these unfortunates could not orient themselves; they couldn't comprehend what was taking place here. What was wanted of them? Why do they deserve to be shot?! Soon, however, they understood their situation. They began pleading, crying, screaming, but there was no one with whom to speak or to argue. Their questions were answered with blows. They were beaten with whips, with sticks and with the butts of guns. Only then did the familiar scenes begin, such as the tearing of one's clothing banging their heads against the walls, tearing out their hair, throwing themselves to the floor and crawling on all fours, etc. Also, the little children, imitating their parents, and not knowing what was occurring burst out crying and screaming. They were allowed to continue this way for a long time. They were later taken to the barracks, where they were murdered. A certain woman and her children lay themselves down in the middle of the road on the snow and screamed that they would not move from that spot. They were beaten senseless and the others were told to carry them on their shoulders into the forest. The small children were thrown into the pit while still alive. Afterwards the Police came to the homes of the murdered, took their possessions and forced the neighbors to tell them where they could find the better possessions of those who were killed, such as gold, silver, etc.

The effect in the city of the first mass murder is not easy to imagine, but earth-shattering events followed one after the other, and each one was more dreadful than the preceding one.

[Page 92]

The Great Exodus from the Vilna Ghetto

Translated by Eilat Gordin Levitan

During the winter months of 1941-2 rumors were spread that in Vilna, Jews are being murdered by the thousands and tens of thousands. Consequently, a portion of the Vilna Jews, seeing that they have nothing to lose anyway, started fleeing from the Vilna ghetto to the forests and small towns (shtetls), wherever they could. A few of the Vilna Jews arrived also in Glubokie. They conveyed terrifying details of the tortures and persecution which the Jews in Vilna had to endure and spoke of the mass murders. They told us that this action were mainly being carried out by the Lithuanians and the Lithuanian Police. The policemen were going through the Ghetto, into the houses seeking Jews who were in hiding, dragging them out and murdering them. Only those who were needed by the Germans for forced labor, or for some other useful purpose, were left alive. Also, they told us about people who are in hiding in the ghetto. Those hiding places not yet discovered, were spared for the meantime.

At the beginning the Lithuanians would discover the hiding places of the Jews in a refined way. When then entered a Jewish dwelling place and found no one at home, the Lithuanians would remain sitting quietly listening intently for every movement and sound. The Jews, hiding behind the false wall or in some other place, hearing that all was quiet in the house, would think that no one was there, and would begin to talk softly among themselves. This was enough for the murderers to discover their hiding places. The Lithuanians would often sit all night in the Jewish homes, silently, motionless, in order to trap the Jews in their nets.

Quite often, small children with their crying, sneezing or coughing. The sounds would give away the hiding place of the Jews. They would be discovered by the Lithuanians and could not save themselves. There were tragedies whereby children were strangled to death to keep them from crying. In some cases, this was done by their mothers with their own hands.

The Vilna refugees fled to us to save themselves. This notion was but an illusion. They met their deaths here only a bit later.

[Page 93]

Hitler's hangmen did not do any less butchering here than they did in Vilna. The refugees were all alone. They had already lost their families in Vilna. Men had fled after losing their wives and children, and sons and daughters ran after they had seen their parents shot. They also brought from Vilna to us, the granddaughter of Rabbi Katz, after her parents were murdered in Vilna. (Rabbi Hillel Zalmanovitsh and his wife, the daughter and son-in-law of Rabbi Katz. At about that time Jews also fled from Sventzian, which was in Lithuania.They told us that also there the Lithuanians raged against the Jews was strong. Soon after the Germans entered, (the Sventzian refugees relatedto us), 100 Jews were seized. Saying that they were being taken for forced labor, they were in reality taken outside the city and there they were shot. this event was repeated on a daily basis where were ever Jews were held.

Three months after occupying Sventzian, the Germans gathered all of the Jews from both the old and the new city, from Haidotzishek, Tzaiatzishek, Ignaline, Padbradz and others. Altogether, about 8,000 souls were taken to Poligon, 15 kilometers from the city, where they established for them a camp. On the way they bullied and jeered these exiles: The elderly, women and small children dragged along with the bundles on their shoulders, and if someone would even pause momentarily, the Police would hit them over the head, tear the bundle from them and sneak away.

The Poligon camp was dense and surrounded with barbed wire, heavily guarded by armed Lithuanians, so that it was impossible to rescue anyone from there. No food was given to them, and there was also no water to drink. The 8,000 Jews who were there were tortured for 12 days. Afterwards they took them all out, supposedly for forced labor, and shot them. This took place on the 9th of October 1941. A few amongst them saved themselves. Among those was the family of Nachum Zinger of Glubokie. Of all the Jews in Sventzian, the Lithuanians left only 15 necessary skilled laborers: shoemakers, tailors, mechanics, etc. More precise details about the martyrdom of the Jews of Sventzian is to be found in the yizkor book "The Destruction of Sventzian".

In Glubokie they still thought at the time, that mass murders on such a broad scale were taking place only in Vilna because of the Lithuanians, who were known to be such great anti-Semites. Here in White Russia, where the anti-Semitism was "milder", people thought that it wouldn't go so far.

[Page 94]

Mass Murders in the Surrounding Shtetls and villages

Translated by Eilat Gordin Levitan

In January of 1942, or a bit later, rumors began to spread that in the surrounding villages, such as Prazarak, Pliste, Yad, Germanavitsh, Halvitsh, the hamlet of Shipi (where Jews lived) and other places, the Jews are being slaughtered in mass murders. Rarely, someone would succeed in saving themselves.

it was clear that the situation of the Jews in White Russia was no better than the situation of the Jews in Lithuania, Were the White Russians no better than the Lithuanians? here also theGermans were able to find enough local anti-Semites who would actively help the Germans in their discriminatory policies towards Jews. The few refugees who escaped from those villages, would relate the horrible details about what the Germans, together with their helpers, did to the Jews. They did not only shoot them, but they tortured them with awful tortures. They would cut off hands, feet, fingers, poke out eyes, pull teeth, etc. The victims would bleed profusely, and they would struggle for a long time before the welcomed death would come. Other refugees were so disturbed, and in such a beaten physical condition, that with their mute, wandering looks they would constantly look about them not knowing where they were and what they were doing here. They just simply couldn't remember what had happened to them. They were chased and shot at. Many fell on the way, and as if by a miracle, they weren't hit by the bullets. Among those who fled there were some that crawled out of the pits, where they had been lying among the corpses, saved because they had played dead. Before the pits were covered over, they manage in some way to crawl out. The children, in most cases, were tossed into the pits alive, and the earth that covered them would move for a long while until they suffocated!

There are no words to describe the German bestiality. It is a disgrace for all of humanity, for the image of God, when we recall that something like this could have taken place during a period of advanced civilization, in the 20th century, in the heart of cultured Europe!

The Murder of One Hundred and Ten Jews

Translated by Eilat Gordin Levitan

The Glubokie Jews didn't bemoan the fate of the Jews of the provinces for a long period of time. Soon a fresh shock; a mass murder on a greater scale. It happened on the 25th of March in 1942, (7th of Nissan, 5702). During one of those beautiful early spring days. The Police broke into Ghetto homes, whole families were dragged from their beds and chased into the street. At the outset the Jews couldn't orient themselves to the situation and were unable to figure out what was happening. They were under the impression that during the night, a demand for some unexpected essential labor arose, some chore had to be done at once. But when they were forced to leave (by cars) together with their children, in the direction of the barracks, they understood to what kind of "labor" they were being driven to!

[Page 95]

Terrible heartrending scenes took place on the way there. The grumbling, crying and screams filled the air. The victims tore off their clothing (in most cases, underclothes, because they hadn't gotten the chance to get dressed), tore their hair from their heads and embraced each other. They tried to protect parents, children, husbands, wives. The cries were mixed with the brutal shouts and jeers of the policemen, who beat the Jews mercilessly and drove them like cattle, hurrying them along, so that they wouldn't have to spend too much time with them...

On Lomzsher and Kishelike Streets, other Jews trembling with terror, were looking on through the cracks of doors and windows, as they were driving their relatives, their brothers, sisters, parents, children and other Jews, towards the barracks to their slaughter. They saw how the Police beat them, clubbed them with sticks on the heads of women and little children. They stood paralyzed, numbed, not knowing what to do, how to rescue them, how to tear them from the clutches of the wild beast. They knew that if they crawled out of their homes, they themselves would fall into the jaws of the beast. With their glances from the cracks of their doors and attics, they were bidding farewell to their friends... In barely an hour the policemen were already riding on several sleds away from the barracks. They were transporting the possessions that they had just torn from those murdered. They were sitting around drinking... Right after the tragedy that occurred, they began playing music in the marketplace. Even the Christians, who still had some human feelings, this massacre of the Jews made a terrifying impression. The sounds of the music did not have any less of an effect than had the cries and pleas of the victims. They could see as it happened, so it seems, how death spread its wings

[Page 96]

and flew unhindered through the air. The bandits immediately arranged orgies, noisy feasts, in honor of the "victory" over the 110 souls of Glubokie' Jews.

This massacre was an occasion that the local Police found the opportune moment to avenge themselves on Jews with whom they still had "old scores" to settle. In this way, for example, Kolye, a former shoemaker, who had become a policeman, revenged himself on the family of N. Reichl (who had been a leather merchant), with whom during the times of peace, he could obtain no credit. The same thing also happened with the families of Shaike Shapiro, Zalman Gitelzon, Eli Kurkudiansky, Zalman Shparber (from-whose family a son and daughter survived), Lazar Gitelzon, Dr. Moshe Chaves {* whom they searched for a long time and couldn't find, and instead of him, they took his father, Israel Chaves and his wife, and others.} Esther-Shayne, the wife of Lazar Gitelzon, who was a god-fearing, intelligent woman, even during that dark time she did not cease to teach her children. She was optimistic and believed in a bright tomorrow, and in a quick end to our troubles. Tuesday, the 6th of Nissan, March 24th, she sat with the writer of these lines, in the house where we were dealing with and "debating" about the coming Passover; how to organize it in such circumstances. Where do we get Matza and the other necessities? Our mother, may she rest in peace, was lying ill from the events, and pessimism reigned. there was no inclination to concern ourselves too much with Passover. We felt that at least with the food we would somehow manage. If only we would remain alive! ...But Mrs. Gitelzon assured us that she takes upon herself the burden of providing Matza of high quality. On the morrow, the 7th of Nissan, quite early in the morning, Esther-Shayne Gitelzon was no longer among the living. She, her husband and three sons were among the 110 murdered victims. For a long while The Ghetto could not regain a presence of mind in regard to the bestial murders. The Jews didn't know what to do. They couldn't make peace with the thought, that innocent people could be murdered, without any "reason". Many, due to the aggravation of having lost relatives, became ill. There was no lack of attacks of rage and hysteria among the women and other such ailments. As it was later related in the city, the 110 Jewish souls had fallen victim because of a… love affair. A certain German Lieutenant Shultz had fallen head over heels in love with the Jewish maiden, Gite Gordon, who worked in the Gendarmerie. This German Lieutenant, the burning patriot, and "pupil" of Nazism, could not resist the charms of the Jewish maiden, and Gordon had a strong influence on him. Thanks to her, the teacher Fisher, Pupko, Kasher and others were saved. (Later they were all exterminated in the mass murders.)

[Page 97]

The infatuation of a German with a Jewish girl was in open opposition to Hitler's theory of racism and discredited the local German administration. When nothing, no reprimands or threats of punishment, could dissuade the Lieutenant, the Gordon girl had occupied a more important place in his heart than Hitler's teachings, the civil administration decided to carry out "Operation Without Pain" on behalf of the Germans. In other words: when the infatuated Lieutenant wasn't in the city, the Police "innocently and courteously" called out Gite Gordon, not telling her what or when is taking place, and shot her.

When Shultz returned and learned what had happened, he was beside himself. He quite simply went crazy, but he couldn't tell anybody, and couldn't complain to anyone. Everything had been done "legally" for his own good, removing the blot from his name…

Being helpless, and not having anyone on whom to vent his anger, there appeared the wild beast in this Hitlerite. In order to calm his impure blood, this lover of a Jewish girl took part in the murder of the 110 Jews. As a result of the tragic love affair, there perished the innocents: Drisviatskes, Koenigsbergs, Hidekels, Gitelzons, Reichles and others, together with their wives and infant children, who cried and did not know why this was happening. And not only the small minds of the little children could not understand the "wherefore", but also the adults, the practical, educated, cultured people, could find no answer to the queries of the small children. The "clever, cultured" Germans had however, indeed found a reason. The German Minister of Justice declared that some Jews had been engaged in "speculation", which meant that they had disobeyed the law and bought food products for themselves and their children, from Christians (in actuality nobody was caught in this "offense") and for this they received proper punishment.

[Page 98]

Concerning reactions and protests against such trepidation, in those dark times and circumstances there was nothing that could be even discussed. The only option was to listen to the wild German cynicism and remain quiet...

There soon came fresh shock, new frightening episodes, horors which will be related in later on chapters. The sighs and cries in the Ghetto constantly grew. The result was that Jews fell into even deeper apathy, which bordered on complete resignation, and all things were treated alike. The situation became even more complicated there was no way out. There was no reaction to anything...This resignation was perhaps the greatest disaster!...

The Ghetto Space Allowance Decreases

Translated by Eilat Gordin Levitan

Since the number of Jews was constantly decreasing, the German administration was concerned with the problem that maybe the remaining Jews had too much room in the Ghetto. They therefore decided to reduce the Ghetto-area. A few days after the slaughter of the 110 Jewish souls there came a decree from the Germans to reduce the Ghetto-area. From the Ghetto boundaries they cut off the ends of Lomzsher and new Kishelike Streets, and also cut away the entire old Kishelike Street. In these areas the biggest and nicest houses were located.

the Jews had to leave their homes in those areas of the Ghetto in thirty minutes. They were allowed to remain in the meantime on the street, if they couldn't find a roof to put over their heads. In the Ghetto it had been overcrowded anyway due to the "new refugees" about 800 souls, who also hadn't found places for themselves. But there was nothing to be overly concerned about, since this was a matter of life and death, no matter what kind of life it was, places had to be found...

They began throwing things out of the homes and the things began hitting the street with an impact. They threw things through doors and windows, broke them, tore them, and ruined everything. Underfoot one felt broken dishes, and glass utensils, also pieces of broken furniture. Bedding came apart and the air became filled with feathers. The streets and courtyards were spread with pages from torn books, and religious books, Bibles, Talmuds, and others. We, the writers of these lines, had a rich library (also an important collection of medical literature), our own as well as those from the schools, which we kept in the Ghetto. A portion of the library had been given to us in October of 1941, when we had moved into the Ghetto. Now, on the eve of the Passover, 1942, almost all of the books, hundreds of them, roamed the streets, torn and flicked. Also, there were photographs scattered all over, as well as pictures and pages of manuscripts in Hebrew, Yiddish, etc. Mothers were wandering about with their crying little children, who trembled from fear and the cold. The mothers tried to calm them. The children were influenced by the nervousness of the adults. The sick were carried in their beds into the street. There they remained unattended. On top of it all, that Passover was an especially cold one with biting cold weather.

[Page 99]

Since the best houses of the cut-down Ghetto were now going to be occupied by Police and German officials, they stood over the Jews and drove them on to evacuate their homes quickly. They cruelly beat the Jews, threatened to shoot them if anyone remained even a minute after the allowed time in their homes. The Jews ran from the houses and left them as they were with everything in them for the murderers. And then they were outside! On Lomzsher Street, one of the policemen wanted to take over Slidzevskes house, where our family was located. This particular house was the nicest one in the Ghetto. The policeman did not permit the things to be taken from the house. He jeered and harassed and in this way he showed off his "Police authority". He related how he walked around wide awake and slept very little because every morning at 4:00 A. M. he already finds himself in the barracks. He was reciting his pedigree, one of the most diligent participants in the early morning actions... While relating this, he used a kerchief to clean his bloody boots, that had not yet dried after the morning's action...

Telling us about his "heroism", he was able to cast upon us an even greater fear, which was already quite substantial. He let us know that in the coming days they are preparing an even greater blood action, but he is willing to let us know about it a few hours before it will take place, so that we'll have time to hide ourselves. For this information, understandably, he must be well rewarded... Under the threat of being shot, he told us that this must remain a strict secret, no one should be made aware of it. We were very reserved in our reaction to this. We knew that the local Police would use this in order to extract large ransoms from Jews, and that when the danger was really great, they never helped. On the contrary, most of the time their redeemers would trap them in their nets even faster. Also, in this case it was clear to us that he is attempting to squeeze as much as he can from us.

[Page 100]

On the eve of the Passover, together with others, we threw a portion of our things out of the door and the windows, onto the street. We also took our sick mother outside. All day we ran around searching for a place under a roof for her and 7-year-old Aharon-Yitzhakl. The Judenrat was helpless. All attempts to bribe the Police, so that they would be less brutal, were of no avail. The murderers did their thing, even though they were satiated with goodies. Some Jews from the houses that had been cut away from the Ghetto, became so depressed that they were unable to rescue from among their possessions even those things that they would be able to save. They thought that anyway it was no use... It was clear to all that the lessening of the Ghetto area was not being done because there weren't enough apartments in the city for the Christian population. In the city there stood houses that were empty, and no one needed the Ghetto apartments. The magistrate was selling Jewish houses for 100-150 guilders in order to get rid of them. Village peasants jumped on the wild bargains and every day there were carried out of the city, on tens of carts, the materials that had been taken from dismantled Jewish houses. It was clear that the reduction of the Ghetto area was done solely to crowd the Jews into a narrower box.

During the dismantling of Chaim-Meir Freidkins estate (The Centralke) there were many casualties. The roof fell in on the workers and in the wreckage, Chodosh, Haberman and others were found dead. Also, many wounded were dragged out. When the injured were brought to the city hospital (which was near the site of the catastrophe), they were denied first-aid, with the excuse - "They are Jews"!... Only late in the evening, on the first night of Passover, were we able to squeeze ourselves into the apartment of Zalman the miller. This was in the court of Shimon Lekach on Vilne Street. Several families lived there, and the crowded conditions were indescribable. There, the "Seder" was conducted. We also participated by standing (it was impossible to sit). The eyes were dimmed, the head dizzy. In place of wine - tears. No symbol of bitter herb was necessary.

[Page 101]

But at the same time, we considered ourselves fortunate, that we had succeeded in arranging a place for our sick mother, who had suffered so much during the day. We ourselves had to be satisfied with a bare floor, but fortunately there was a roof over our heads. We had nothing to eat. The wife of Zalman the miller gave us a bit of potato.

Right after Passover, I, Zvi Rajak, became sick. I was walking around with a high fever, and large rashes over my entire body. I had no place to lie down. No one could know anything about it. The Germans would not tolerate any sick Jews. Finally, On the Judenrat's "horse" they took me to the Ghetto Hospital. There were many sick Jews in the hospital – Jews who shortly before were quite well. In about 10 days I was "cured". I returned "home" and again slept on the floor. I was very weak and could not fully recover. On top of it all, that spring was a very cold one.

In the midst of all this there came the rumor, that in the distant shtetl, Dalhinov, on the eve of Passover, there was a pogrom against the Jews. 1,000 souls were burned alive. This news only aggravated our own anguish. We have forgotten what normal life is. We only anticipated the worse. The hopes for anything good disappeared from almost everyone's thoughts. Unfortunately, our intuition did not deceive us, as we will see in the following chapters.

The "Black Students"

Translated by Eilat Gordin Levitan

For a long time, we had already heard of them, but we could not imagine what an accursed breed they were. We knew that there was a German organization, which was called the S. D. (Security Forces) or as we called them here, the "Black Students", who carry with them destruction and liquidation, death and elimination.

Until May of 1942 they hadn't shown up in Glubokie. On an early morning of the aforementioned May, there spread as fast as lightening, throughout the city, the rumor that they had arrived here. It is impossible to convey the terror which fell upon the Jews. People gathered in groups to discuss and consider how they could save their lives. No one had any concrete thoughts about what to do. A few attempted to deal secretly with Christians, to be rescued by them, or hidden by them, if not the adults, at least the little children. Unfortunately, there were to be found very few among them who wanted to help Jews in their tragedy. Quickly people began to "build" hiding places in attics, in cellars, under the floors, in the gardens, in pits, etc. They made "fake" rooms in the walls, disguised staircases in pits through closets, ovens and cupboards. They made deep holes in cellars - worse than graves - and carrying out the work was very complicated, not only because of the exhaustion and strain. Time was short. The angel of death was already sitting in the city, waving his sword. Also, the work could only be done at night, because, during the day, everyone had to be at forced labor for the Germans. In addition to all of this, the work had to be done secretly, hidden from all human eyes. The will to save oneself from death was in itself considered a great offense. There was no place at all to dispose of the earth and sand which was dug out of the pits and cellars. It couldn't be dumped on the street - this would be noticed and raise suspicions... There was no way out. They remained dependent on their own luck.

[Page 102]

In just those terrible moments of despair, we attempted to console ourselves, and calm ourselves. We wanted to hope, "believe" in the promises of the German civil administration that the visit of the S. D. to Glubokie will pass without any bloodshed, because "the Jews of Glubokie are exceptional". They are "necessary Jews" as they would often put it. The Jews will get away with only material losses. Therefore, the Minister of Justice suggests that the Judenrat should, as fast as possible, assemble a greater amount of gold, jewelry, clothing, footwear, and just plain money, so that it can be given over, and the S. D. will leave the place more quickly.

Everyone was recruited... they ran from house to house. They gathered together and everybody pulled out from his hiding place whatsoever he possessed. The exceptions were only those, who had previously turned over their fortunes to Christians for safekeeping, and now they couldn't take it back.

[Page 103]

They brought and carried everything, valises filled with things, briefcases filled with money, and with incredible patience, waited for the fortunate moment when the German bandits will finally leave the city. They were, or wanted to be, naive and believing that their calm was justified.

From the attics and through crevices in cellars, and from cupboards, with bated-breath they watched. The hangmen, loaded down with Jewish wealth and goods, left the city. The Jews breathed more freely... This time the murderers left, leaving behind almost no victims. I say "almost" because there actually were 20 victims. (In those circumstances this was considered a small matter)

At the time they murdered the family Melamed-Koenigsberg (David Melamed's daughter, Rivke, her husband and children, Leib Krivitzky, the Birzsh girl, Gershon Isaiah Igeses' granddaughter), Sarah Fronovitsh and others... When the panic at the coming of the S. D. had taken place, the aforementioned had fled the Ghetto to hide. They had hidden themselves in unfinished buildings, stalls, sheds, ditches, etc. Local Christians noticed them and informed the Police, who came and murdered them on the spot. These tragic murders made no impression in the Ghetto. The psyche of the Jews had already accustomed itself to such events, and they just didn't react to anything so "insignificant". It left no lasting impression because the lives of all hung by a thread.

As was mentioned after the S. D. left, the Jews were able to breathe more freely. They did not understand and could not imagine, that the "good fortune" of the S. D leaving at the time, was really a tragedy. The disoriented minds of the Jews did not understand that the Germans sensing the nervousness and unease of Glubokie's Jews, had left momentarily to carry out their devilish designs inthe surrounding villages. No one thought that their leaving was intentional, in order to rid the Jews of their dark thoughts, so that later they could carry out their extermination plans more easily. They wanted the Jews to be completely calm, so that they won't look for ways in which to save themselves.

As it later became clear, that the S. D., before leaving Glubokie, left a secret plan with the civil administration, a plan about how to prepare the blood action against the Jews. They only left, in order to return in three weeks, and carry out the slaughter with greater success and ease than would have been possible earlier.

[Page 104]

Step by step the Germans succeeded in drugging the Jews of Glubokie and making them numb. Later, with much greater success, they were able to trap the Jews in their nets.

As it later appeared, the S. D., before they left Glubokie, made had a secret agreement with the Judenrat, whom they deceived. Glubokie was truly "privileged", they told the Judenrat, but without the shedding of some Jewish blood, they could not proceed. The privilege that Glubokie enjoys, is that they will be satisfied with "only six hundred" s owls (the elderly and the weak), who are to be found in the second Ghetto. More than this number, the mothers and the fathers, they will not murder...

The Judenrat, for understandable reasons, kept this massage from the S. D. a deep dark secret. Therefore, they were able to carry out the terms of the "agreement" to the letter. They prepared the second Ghetto for the slaughter.

How the Germans kept their promise to the Judenrat, that they will satisfy themselves with just that portion of Jewish blood, from only the "unfortunate Jews", we will see later on.

The condition and situation, into which the Jews of Glubokie had fallen, we can see from the fact that the representative body of the Jews had "agreed" to the murder of more than 600 people, thinking that with this gesture they would save the remaining thousands of Jews.

The Extermination of the Jews of Surrounding Shtetls

Translated by Eilat Gordin Levitan

After these events, after the Jews had "released" themselves a bit from the dark nightmare, regular news of terrifying mass murders on a much larger scale began to arrive. Reports came from the surrounding villages and shtetls that the Germans were murdering all of the Jews. They were "sweeping the Jews clean with an exterminating broom", and no survivor or remnant remained.

Those were bloody days, which had their epilogue in Glubokie, where the Jews, according to the assurances of the Germans, "were in a special privileged and safe situation".

The month of June 1942, the bloody month, will forever remain infamous in the memory of the few Jewish survivors of Glubokie and the surrounding area. In that gloomy month, the Germans and their local helpers obliterated them from the face of the earth: hundreds of communities, entire Jewish shtetls. In a matter of a few days the Jews of Braslaw, Mir, Disna, Luzshky, Szarkowszczyzna, Druya, Flisa, Dokshitz, Ziavky, Parapianov, Padsvilie and others, were annihilated. It is worthwhile emphasizing a few points.

[Page 105]

In Szarkowszczyzna, for example, for the time of the summer of 1942, over 50% of the Jews were saved. This was thanks to the Judenrat, which during the entire time stood on guard, and with special alertness watched and spied out the deeds and intentions of the Germans and the local Police. That particular Judenrat must be mentioned favorably, it was just about the only one in that area that evaluated the situation accurately. They did not deceive either themselves or the population, doing all in its power to rescue when and where it was only possible. They did just the opposite of what was done by other Judenrats and did not calm the Jews with promises that all would be well or filled their heads with empty assurances to ease their pain. They didn't tell Jews that they were the Germans' "darlings" who would allow them to live. On the contrary, - they kept on warning that the situation was serious and the Germans will kill them; that a slaughter of Sharakovshtzina Jews is imminent, and so forth. Therefore, everyone must be on his guard. The Germans, with all of their assurances are out to deceive, and no one can depend on them. One must be ready to flee at a moment's notice, since that moment might arrive unexpectedly.

During those days, when the S. D. was in Glubokie and the surrounding area, the Sharkavshtziner Judenrat intensified its spying on the German Police and Gendarmarie. Here we must mention with praise, the Jewish Elder, Hirsh Berman, who with an extraordinary intense inquisition, and keen observation, noticed the preparations being made by the murderers. On the eve of the bloody day during an "intimate-friendly" conversation with the Oberwachsmeister, Hite, he understood the real reasons why Hite came from Glubokie to Szarkowszczyzna. Hite told Berman that he had come there to carry out "maneuvers", which will take place on the day after tomorrow, in the morning, and he is informing him that the Jews have nothing to fear, since no harm will befall upon them.

This was already a sufficient signal, and the Judenrat quickly informed everyone to be ready... That night no one slept.

[Page 106]

From the attics and other hiding places, they kept a constant watch to see what was taking place on the street. When in the morning they noticed that the Gendarmes and Police had risen earlier than usual and are dressed more elaborately, running to and from the Gendarmerie well armed while conversing secretly and so on, the Judenrat pronounce the situation to be terrible and ordered all Jews to flee forthwith.

The murderers were late. When they surrounded the Ghetto, almost two-thirds of the Jews were already beyond the town. Thirty minutes later the S. D. arrived on their motor vehicles, they found only the elderly, the sick and children in the Ghetto. The Jews had fooled them this time...

For the infuriated, German beast there remained too small a portion of Jewish blood. They were incensed at Jewish "Chutzpah". The "charlatan like" psyche in them flamed more shrewdly. They were jumping out of their skins. To be so humiliated! Can it be? The Jews have outwitted them, fooled them! Their action in Szarkowszczyzna failed. Too small a dose of Jewish blood had remained for them to swallow!

They still did not consider that they had lost out completely. They had vehicles, they were armed and are strong enough so that they will find a way to avenge themselves on the gloomy and dejected Jews of the small town.

After murdering the old men, old women and children they found on the spot, murders which naturally did not take too long for these German creatures to carry out, they sat themselves in their vehicles and chased the fleeing Jews.

Unfortunately, they caught quite a few, and the "criminals" were severely punished. One death wasn't enough for them. They devised such tortures and torments for the escaped victims, that only the Germans are capable of devising. And how advanced German wisdom was in murder and killing was already well known. They poked out the eyes of the unfortunates with red hot rods, skinned them alive, broke the fingers, pulled out the teeth (especially if they were gold teeth), cut out tongues and more!

On that day they exterminated about 700 Sharkavshtziner Jews, a sum of those who had been left in the town together with those captured on the roads.

This success - it must be told - was in a large measure due to the help that the Germans received from the local peasants, who were able to catch the fleeing Jews on the road and give them into the murderous hands of the Germans. Especially diligent in this were the local policemen. But it didn't end with only the 700 victims. The Police did not tire. For days and weeks on end they continued searching for the hidden and fleeing Jews. They were lying in the bushes, in the woods, in corn planted by the roadsides, and from these places lurked for the Jewish refugees. a peasant would find a watch, a ring, earrings, or some money on a murdered Jew. The murderers had a special appetite for a Jew with gold teeth.

[Page 107]

The Jews knew that they were being hunted and that they are lurking for them. They would lie in the corn and under bushes, not moving from that spot. They were even afraid to breathe deeply; they didn't eat or drink and lay in the rain and cold (June of 1942 was, to Jewish misfortune, a wet and cold one).

How far the local Police would go, can be seen from this fact: 5 weeks after the slaughter, a Sharkovshtziner Jew, Leib Chazan, unable to withstand the suffering of his children, who were prostrate from hunger, defied all dangers and crawled out from the corn, and went to find a bowl of water. When he kneeled in the mud to fill a broken utensil with water, there sprang out from behind a bush, a policeman who demanded money from him, promising him that he will let him live... Afterwards, when Chazan gave him part of his money, the policeman shot him and critically wounded him. With his waning strength, Chazan took out the rest of the money and quickly tore it to shreds, so that the murderer will not benefit from it. The policeman immediately shot Chazan a second time and ended his life.

This was all witnessed by Chazan's wife and children, who were hiding nearby. They couldn't even assuage their terrible pain by crying out, by moaning. They had to choke back their tears, because sobbing, crying or any other sound would give away their hiding place. Although at that moment they had protected themselves, the cruel hand would later also seize them.

As was mentioned, many of the local Christians were the best detectors of those Jews who were in hiding. The peasants were especially well acquainted with the highways and byways and forests and fields in theis region. Some would themselves kill the captured Jews in various ways: by axes, shovels, crow-bars, pick and other such implements. Others turned them to the Police or Germans. In this way the peasants would receive recognition from the occupation forces, and they would also be materially rewarded with a few kilos of salt, matches, soap, etc.

[Page 108]

In this way, for example, Makar, from the village of Palilyek, captured Zerach Krapivnik and murdered him. He also killed Motke Budov; the family of Lazar Radaskovitsh he drove into the river and drowned them there. An inhabitant of the hamlet of Bedi came upon three Jewish refugees. He fooled them into going with him, promising to protect them, and afterwards turned them over to the Germans.

David Vashtai fooled the family of D. Pildas, into coming with him, promising to conceal them, and later turned them over. He had also fooled a little boy, Estrin, the same way, and murdered him with an axe.

In the midst of so much cruelty, we must mention the goodness of the brothers Stankevitsh, Marian and Adolf, from Barsutshine, who aided Jews in their time of trouble.

They helped them hide from the German murderers, fed them, and showed them where to hide and flee.

With great praise, someone named Statzevitsh, must be mentioned. He lived in that neighborhood, and simply sacrificed himself in order to rescue Jews. Knowing that at Statzevitsh they could find a refuge, Jews came to him from all over. He hid them wherever he was able to- in the shops, in the barns, in the attics and even with his acquaintances, which he was able to trust. He would feed not only those who turned to him, but he would also carry food into the forest into the corn fields, any place he knew where they were hiding. Many Jews, thanks to him, were saved at the time.

This most generous man, savior of Jews, Statzevitsh, became too popular in the region as a protector of Jews, and that wasn't good. As was mentioned, the vast majority of peasants in the region, helped the Germans in their extermination of Jews. And because of this, the local well-known peasants, decided to get Statzevitsh out of the way. These "good neighbors" found out that seven Jews are hidden in Statzevitsh's bath, and two more in his attic. They traveled to Szarkowszczyzna and told the Police there. The Police, accompanied by the Gendarmes, immediately came to the scene of the "crime", and set fire to the bathhouse on all sides. The seven hidden Jews were burned alive, it was so horrible, no one was able to identify their bones. They also went to Statzevitsh's house, looking for Jews. Statzevitsh, whose name must truly be engraved in the memoirs of our bloody pages with golden letters, displayed an extraordinary moral character and self-sacrifice. Instead of fleeing from the murderers, to save himself, he occupied himself with saving those Jews whom he had hidden. He speedily let them out of the windows, and he himself, unfortunately, was captured by the bandits. They led him away to Glubokie, where he was shot.

[Page 109]

These were rare oases in the huge empty desert. If there had been such luminous figures as Statzevitsh in a greater number, the German beast would not be able to so thoroughly carry out his devilish acts of eradicating the Jews. The Jewish tragedy would have been much smaller.

The Sharkavshtziner Ghetto numbered about 1,200 Jews.

Something especially bizarre occurred in Disna, a city on the west bank of the Dvine River. During the extermination action, the Jews themselves, set fire to the Ghetto, in order to keep the enemy from enjoying the Jewish loot that he would have gotten. The Judenrat, seeing that the Ghetto was suddenly surrounded by German Gendarmes and Police, immediately poured gasoline and set fire to several houses. Quickly the entire Ghetto was in flames. The Germans opened fire from all sides, with guns, flame-throwers, grenades, etc.

It was impossible to save oneself, because they were thickly surrounded, and it wasn't long before the entire area was spread with the dead and the badly wounded. Jewish blood flowed in the streets, like water after a heavy rain. The air was filled with groaning and the cries of the wounded. Smoke and fumes from burning bodies spread, not only over the Ghetto, but also throughout the entire city. The tongues of fire licked the beams of the old Jewish houses and cottages and caught the bodies which quickly turned to ashes. And the Germans were beaming with pride as they observed their great victory, their accomplishment...

[Page 110]

In the Disna (Dzisna) Ghetto there were about 3,000 Jews. Just a few survived.

In Braslaw (Braslau) the S. D., as usual, arrived in their motor vehicle very early in the morning and with the help of Police and Gendarmes took over the Ghetto and carried out their bloody work. In the course of a couple of hours they murdered nearly 3,000 souls, leaving alive only a few scores, mostly skilled workers. Some were able to hide in cellars, in pits and in other underground places. The majority never came out alive of their hide outs. The Police did not let up searching for those who had hidden themselves.

Here there must also be mentioned the beautiful humanitarian deeds performed by the former governor under the Polish regime, of the local Natshalnik Region, named Kiselevski. Wanting to save the hiding Jews, he personally went to the Justice Commissioner and requested that the Police guards around the Jewish homes are removed, and the hidden Jews not killed. He justified his request by stating that all of the work in the uniform factories had come to a halt since there is no labor force with which to continue it. The Commissioner of Justice agreed and promised to honor his request forthwith. This pleader for Jews went home, feeling completely certain that no harm would befall the remaining Jews of Braslaw. But as soon as Kiselevs left the Justice Ministry, The Commissioner phoned the Gendarmes in Braslaw, that they should carry out the slaughter of the Jews till not one remained alive. By the time Kiselevski got back to Braslaw, the 300 remaining Jews had already been murdered.

During these dark days, these fearful days, the S. D. carried out a slaughter of the Jews of Mir, where very few survived. Among the survivors there was Lipe Landau, of blessed memory, a man of great knowledge and deep intelligence. He managed to actually escape from a pit, where he, together with his wife and children, and all of the Jews of Mir, had been thrown to be killed. In Mir, at that time, there were about 2,000 Jews murdered by the German murderers and their local helpers.

During this same period the following Jewish communities were liquidated: Pliste (Plisa), Luzshki (Luzki), New-Pohast (Novy Pahost), Prazarak (Prazaroki), Ziavki, Halubits and others. In Druja about 2,000 Jews were killed. The murderers carried out their extermination work in the towns very quickly, at the rate of two towns a day. Very few Jews managed to save themselves in the above-mentioned communities. The bloody work was carried out in this way: The S. D. would arrive in a town, carry out the slaughter during a couple of hours and leave. The local Police would then complete the unfinished work. The local White-Russians and Poles, in their black "Police-crow" uniforms, would diligently search for the hidden Jews over a period of days and weeks and then murder them where ever they were found. They searched for the unfortunate hidden Jews in the houses, in the attics, ditches, the surrounding fields and woods, and other such places. Those who distinguished themselves in catching Jews, the Germans rewarded handsomely with gifts.

[Page 111]

The Second Ghetto

Translated by Eilat Gordin Levitan

In addition to the inclusive extermination plans of the Germans, a supplementary concept developed. The clear distinction that was made between the "useful" Jews, and the "useless" Jews. For the "useless" Jews, such as the weak, sick, elderly, cripples and in general, those unable to perform arduous physical labor, the Germans set up the so-called "Second Ghetto". For the second Ghetto zone, they divided the street from the old Kisheleike (Legyonove) and the small streets: Nave, Glere, Mostove and others. And to that area they began transferring the "useless Jews". Germans also utilized The transfer action for their thieving purposes. Parents who did not want to part from their children in the second Ghetto, or children who didn't want to part from their parents, would buy their way out of the second Ghetto with money, jewels, clothing, etc. The truth is that the Jews, in general, just didn't know the real reason for setting up a second Ghetto. It was explained in diverse ways. There were rumors spread that the "useless Jews" in the second Ghetto would not receive any bread, and that for them a special regimen would be established.

The were also contrary rumors that the inhabitants of the second Ghetto, such as the sick, weak, etc. would definitely be treated better in their designated area. There also spread a terrible rumor that the second Ghetto was established with the "useless" Jewish element in order to provide the Germans, when they desire it, a definite portion of Jewish blood...

This was discussed in whispers and certainly with great fear, but nobody wanted to really believe it. In actuality, the very fact of the second Ghetto created a terrific commotion among the Jewish population, and they viewed it with great suspicion, and the robbers used this to their advantage.

[Page 112]

The previous inhabitants of the old Kisheleike gave their last bit of treasure for permission to move into the first Ghetto, and the elderly, and weak did all in their power to buy their way so that they wouldn't fall into the second Ghetto.

In this tragedy those who were able to get out of old Kisheleike, and also those whose lot had been to remain, but somehow got out, felt lucky. Those who had to remain there considered themselves most unfortunate. And there remained there, not only the designated "useless", but also those who did not have the means to buy their way out. There remained some carpenters, tailors and other skilled workers, even though they belonged in the category of "useful Jews". There were there, among others, healthy and young, the carpenter, Shulman, the tailor, Ettingoff and others who happened to reside there from the start.

The bafflement among the Jews about the particular event was a unique one. This establishment of two distinct types of Jews; two categories, this separation of Jew from Jew, Shook everyone to their very core. They could clearly see that the Jew had become a very cheap article and weighed by the Germans and their helpers as a silly toy in their hands, with which they can do anything they please. The Jews of Glubokie, like all Jews everywhere else under the German occupation, were absolutely helpless. At the time they couldn't think of anything constrictive. In their mind there was no way out of the bitter, uncertain situation.

There was no salvation from this misfortune.

There were still no established Partisan groups in that area at the time. On top of it all no one had even heard of Glubokie in the resistance movement.

The Second Ghetto is about to be liquidated

Translated by Eilat Gordin Levitan

"..the voice of the daughter of Zion groans… woe unto me for my soul is weary of the murderers." (Jeremiah 4:31)

"…the faces of elders were not honored.(Lamentations 5:12)

The elders have ceased from the gate…" (Lamentations 5:14)

After the departure of the S. D. from Glubokie (see the section before; "THE S.D"), the Judenrat energetically began to transfer Jews from the First Ghetto to the Second. For the most part, the elderly, weak, cripples and even whole families of healthy and young people were transferred. The old folks who happened to be related to the Jewish Police and the Judenrat were not transferred, and also a few who were able to bribe their way out. On the contrary direction, a few of those who inhabited the streets of the Second Ghetto, were permitted to go to the First Ghetto Why this transfer of people assumed such an energetic and urgently speedy character, no one knew for sure! At first it was thought that this was "merely" another ruse to pressure Jews to give up their money, jewels etc.

[Page 113]

For a bribe, they did permit a select few to remain in the First Ghetto. The inhabitants of that Ghetto, whose houses were to be found there, such as M. Shulheifer, A. Cohen, the Faigelson sisters (who were dentists), Y. Shulevitsh convinced the local wealthy Jews, that they should not be taken away. They should remain where they were, where they had always lived. As an example, they declared that to the Germans there was no difference between the First and the Second Ghettos. As one could seen by the fact that when the slaughter of the 110 Jews occurred, in April of 1942, they murdered more Jews who resided in the First Ghetto area, than they had from the Second.

The action of transferring Jews grew from hour to hour. Old folks, women and men were separated from their families. Even the critically ill were not spared. The mother of those who are writing these lines was lying ill, and the police, ignoring all of our efforts, our pleas cries and screams, they took her together with the bed on which she was lying, to the Second Ghetto. The policemen David Freeman (who was nicknamed "David the Righteous"), Arke Shaindlin (Arke Liebe Toibes) and Yungelson (a son of Fishl Pines; it seems it was Zalman) brought with them a peasant's cart. I, and my wife, Dr. Helena Raiak, of blessed memory, strongly struggled with the Jewish policemen, and did not want them to take our mother, who was so sick. They pushed us, beat us and in the end the physical prowess was to their advantage and they overcame us, tearing our ill mother from our hands and throwing her and her bed up onto the cart and rode away. It is most difficult to express in words our frame of mind as we followed the wagon in which they were taking our mother to the Second Ghetto. The policemen themselves whipped the horse, hurrying him along. On the way, in exactly the same fashion, they loaded onto the cart another old, weak lady (it seems that it was the mother of the lawyer, Frucht).

The transfer into the Second Ghetto looked something like this: There goes one, two or more old folks, surrounded by Jewish policemen. With a trembling, almost tearful voice, one of them tries to ask: "Where are we being taken?" - "Go where You're told!" comes the brutal answer of the policeman. If someone had the "chutzpah" to refuse to go, he was pushed, hit or prodded, or the policemen would grab him under the arms from both sides and forcefully pulled him.

[Page 114]

Even a more terrifying sight were the carts on which they transported the weak ones who couldn't move under their own power. 4 or 5 old men and old women were in each peasants' wagon, half lying and half sitting, their heads bent down, some crying and others quiet and gazing, with their eyes popping, benumbed, in one direction as if they recognized nothing and felt nothing. One policeman drives the horse, a second one walks alongside and a third behind the cart. The "criminals" were securely guarded. Following the cart are other members of the household, wringing their hands, talking among themselves and crying and pleading. It looked just like a funeral procession, and certainly not less sad and tragic, because they are accompanying the living… living, like calves in the slaughterhouse…

The entire Second Ghetto was filled with crying, with wailing, with groaning and with sighing. The elderly continually asked where and why they were being taken. For what transgressions were they being separated from their children, from the remainder of their families. How will they, alone, be able to live and subsist on their own, and so on. The young relatives tried again to move worlds because they were deeply concerned about the fate of their elderly parents, who would be without protection and care (about murder, no one seriously thought, since they did not want to believe that such a thing could happen).

The street scenes of Jews being dragged into the Second Ghetto, by Jewish Police at the order of the Germans, took about 2 weeks, from the 20th of May until the early days of June 1942. During these 2 weeks it was "joyful" in the Ghetto streets. The Police, actually our own Jewish Police, to our great shame and even greater tragedy, treated these old men and old women in a most rude way.

The action of transporting the "useless Jews" to the Second Ghetto ended. All of old Kisheleike (Legyonove) and the nearby streets such as: Gluche, Mostove, Nave and others, were filled with crying and sighing of the embittered Jews. The old men, as well as well as some old women, continuously recite the Psalms, and pray with great pleading and tears that God, Blessed be He, should rescue them from their great trouble. Several times during the night the Jewish Police patrol the Second Ghetto, to make sure that no one had, God forbid, "deserted" back to the First Ghetto to their own family, to their children, and to make sure that the children had not "stolen" their ill father of ill mother. If the Police, even during the night, found out that someone old was missing, they quickly ran to the First Ghetto, to the family, looking for the "deserter" and in the middle of the night, with great violence, screaming and beatings they would return him to the Second Ghetto.

[Page 115]

At times someone of the immediate family members wanted to remain overnight in the Second Ghetto, near the bed of his sick father or mother in order to be of help the old, weak person. The Police, under no circumstances would permit it (by day it was possible). A special bitterness was aroused by the fact that certain parents of policeman as well as of the Judenrat, were allowed to remain with them. Amongst them were Zalman Gordon and his wife - the parents of the policeman Chaim-Ber Gordon, and others. They remained at home... This also roused many suspicions and all sorts of ironic comments.

The embittered, despondent Jews turned to the Jewish Elder, Gershon Lederman. They request that he reveal the secret of; "why certain families had been torn asunder?"

He declared that the German Civil Administration is carrying this out in order to save on the distribution of products to the non-productive (those who performed no labor). The truth, the dark reality, though, was, as we shall later see, was entirely different. This truth was already known to Lederman at the time.

* * *

Meanwhile they began, quickly and energetically, to draw up lists of the Jews who were in the First Ghetto. They listed all laborers, their wives and children. Laborers, naturally, meant Jews who were useful to the Germans; Jews, whom the German recognized that they have a right to live, who have a right to walk the earth and breathe the air for now. To be among these people who are listed as 'useful" was of course something that everyone wanted. the Rabbi, the teacher, the beadle of the synagogue, the lawyer, the accountant, the doctor, the secular teacher, the Yeshiva Bachur, the student - all looked for ways to be registered as tailors, shoemakers, furriers, sack makers, weavers, mechanics, locksmiths, joiners, chimneysweeps and blacksmiths. All "wanted to be" useful to their terrible oppressor, the German, and be registered as laborers, in order to be assigned to work which (they were under the illusion) would guarantee their lives...

At the time we were still naive and we trusted the promises of the Germans, that a Jew, a laborer would be privileged and would be assured of life. Therefore, it is no wonder that everyone was exceptionally tense; everyone searched for all sorts of ways to obtain for himself this type of work permit. In the shoemakers' workshops there sat, mixed in among the real shoemakers, Rabbis, teachers, Yeshivah boys (Rabbi Lipa Landau, R' Kasriel Schneiderman and others).

[Page 116]

They used shoemakers' thread, hammered nails, lifted the hammers... In the streets, lawyers, teachers and accountants dug pits, cleaned toilets, sawed wood and so forth. At the same time, the Germans used the situation for material gain. They squeezed the marrow out of the bones of the Jews for these little pieces of paper (work permits). They issued the permits to those with whom they were able to reach an acceptable price... Not all were able to be so "fortunate", not all had the opportunity to come up with the required sum, because from many, everything had already been taken away. And actually those who were unable to purchase the permits went around as if they were already condemned and looked with great envy upon the "fortunate ones", who were supposedly "assured" of living...

We place the words "fortunate" ones, who were supposedly "assured" of living..... in quotation marks, since it later turned out that those who were saved from the slaughter were indeed those, who did not have these "life-assuring documents". How come this whole procedure with lists, with the privilege of labor, with permits, with all of the commotion surrounding it? It was all a German ploy, a hateful deception to squeeze from the Jews everything that still remained in their possession, and later to trap them in a terrible way in their net. This was the generally acceptable German system, to first win the confidence of the unfortunates, despondent Glubokie Jews, and later to exterminate them unexpectedly and without any opposition since they were not suspecting a ploy.....

At that time no one could imagine that a government, a regime, a "cultivated" European regime, would have the ability to commit such lowly acts of deceit and falsehood, a deceit concluding with a savage act of such magnitude which has never even occurred among the" unrefined "ancient peoples.

The Germans strove for a means to deceive the Jews of Glubokie, thinking that, since they had already fooled the Jews in the surrounding shtetls the action against the Jews of Glubokie might not be crowned with suitable success. On the one hand they had a secret agreement with the Judenrat, that they will "satisfy" themselves with that portion of Jewish blood, namely, the killing of "only" the 600-700 elderly who were in the Second Ghetto. On the other hand, in order to calm the tumult of the Jews, so they won't notice what was happening, they gave out to a portion of the Jews in the First Ghetto, work permits. All was done in order to seize the entire population in their hands in a period of two weeks. Unfortunately, they were indeed able to achieve their goal, just as they had planned it (see following chapter). When the well-known hangman, Kapfenval, on the 11th of June, came into the Judenrat for some things, such as money and jewelry, someone close to the Judenrat, who knew about the agreement, told him that there are upsetting rumors being spread about a slaughter of Jews. The murderer categorically denied these, and as an official of the civil authority he assured, on his "word of honor", that such a thing would not occur in Glubokie. Such rumors, he argued, are spread for various reasons by the local Poles, who will be severely punished for such provocation...

[Page 117]

* * *

For the next two weeks, entire days we would find ourselves in the Second Ghetto by our mother's side. Sometimes, all of us together, with my wife, Dr. Raiack, and with our child, Aaron-Yitzhakl (both of whom later perished tragically), who didn't want to part from his grandmother. Sometimes we would alternate. We made an effort not to leave our mother alone, at least during the day, even for a moment, (at night we weren't permitted to stay with her), attempting to occupy her so that she wouldn't think of the dreadful circumstance. We carried food to her and strove to provide her with the best of everything. She was a very clever and prudent woman, a woman of valor in the full sense of that expression, and she understood everything. She evaluated the true situation, and for the most part kept quiet. But this silence said a great deal... She was very concerned about us, her children - always inquiring: Do we have enough to eat, and requesting of us not to worry about the possessions that were stolen from us- but only to live and be healthy...

We shouldn't concern ourselves about her, and so on. On the 18th of June, a day before the great tragedy, the Judenrat sold wood. It was another trick to divert the attention of the Jews from that which was being prepared for the old Jews and make them feel that they won't be touched. She sent us away so that we could provide ourselves with wood. We had to obey her, even though agreeing made us quite nervous. The German bandits, members of the S. D. were in the neighborhood, and we didn't know how their visit to Glubokie would end up.

[Page 118]

On Thursday afternoon we bought a meter of firewood from Reuven Ratnitzky, and barely were able to smuggle it from the railroad station to our home in the Ghetto, on Peretz Street. Our mother was very pleased with this, because to obtain firewood in the Ghetto was a very complicated thing. Also, it partially pleased us. We hadn't yet evaluated correctly the true predicament.

In the same house with Motte Shulheifer, there lived Zalman Veitzkin and his wife (the parents of David Veitzkin) and a few other women who had been brought from somewhere else. Z. Veitzkin was confused, he did not understand what people would say to him. The women would always question us, the so called "knowledgeable, clever ones" about the purpose of keeping the elderly separated from the young people. Not paying attention to the fact that we ourselves were desperate enough, we had to calm them, telling them that it means nothing... And, in truth, we really couldn't imagine the imminence of the tragedy. We didn't want to believe the version, that they had separated the elderly, in order for them to serve as a sacrifice for the young.

The argument of Motte Shulheifer was an interesting one. He was a religious Jew, a man well versed in Torah learning. "I want to have", -he would argue,- "a Din Torah (religious court case) with the Judenrat. Namely: - for example: Jewish law states that if a mother is having great difficulty during labor, while giving birth, and her life is threatened, it is permissible in order to save her, to kill the baby. But this is only if the baby has not been exposed to the air of the world. But if the baby's head had already been exposed, then it is considered a living human and it cannot be sacrificed in order to save the mother. (Later my wife told me that the same rule also holds in modern medicine.) According to this we must ask what right the Judenrat has to set up the parents as a sacrifice for their children?" But, in truth though, the same Jews, who argued in this way, did not believe that it was really going to turn so.... With these sorts of questions they only wanted to expose the Judenrat's secrets, to know what was actually true. On Thursday, the 3rd of Tammuz, a public fast was called. We fasted, recited Psalms, and the Selichos (Penitential prayers). In the evening we parted from our mother, as we did every day, not having even the slightest inkling that this parting was the last one and that we would never see her again... She kissed our child very passionately at the time of parting, her grandchild, her beloved Yatzhakl. But none of us even thought that this would be the last time, even though the situation in general was very oppressive...

We went "home". Soon it was curfew time, and we were to be off the streets. It was a rainy evening, quite cold. The stillness of the night was broken from time to time by the screams, shouts and cries of those who had run away from the Second Ghetto, and whom the Police had caught and with force brought back in the middle of the night.

[Page 119]

And indeed, there were more such incidents on that night than at any other time. (Later, it turned out, that a few had been forewarned about what was going to happen, and they ran from the Second Ghetto, without any regard for the consequences). The work of dragging the elderly back into the Second Ghetto was not an easy job for the Jewish Police and the Judenrat. Among those who had been placed in the Second Ghetto, by the Judenrat, were to be found quite a few who were swift on their feet, both men and women, and the Jewish Police had to wrangle and fight with them. It very much upset the street when Sarah Kraut, who had run away from Vilna Street, would not under any circumstances, allow herself to be taken back, and she even beat up a few policemen. Alas, they beat her up good, and threw her into the Second Ghetto, to be devoured on the morrow, together with everyone else by the German beast. A like incident occurred that night with Motte Shulheifer, who had also fled the Second Ghetto, and hid by David Muncaz in Schron together with many others. The Jewish Police discovered him at night and dragged him back into the Second Ghetto. There were other such incidents, which we cannot concretely remember.

This, of course, threw a great scare into everyone, and even though we still didn't know the horrible truth, nervousness grew from hour to hour. This June night dragged, and we began to sense that something terrible is awaiting us on this June early morning. Unfortunately, we were not deceiving ourselves...

The Liquidation of the Second Ghetto;
2,500 Jews are Killed in One Day

Translated by Eilat Gordin Levitan

The sun rose, the acacia tree blossomed and the slaughterer slaughtered...

(From "The City of Slaughter" by Chaim Nachman Bialik

And the accursed day of trouble, the terrible bloody day... arrived. It was the eve of the Shabbat, the 4th day of Tammuz (19th of June 1942). Before dawn the Jewish policeman, Abba Sragavitsh, banged on our window and told us not to attempt to leave our home until we received a very specific order. Today, he told us, Jews would not go out to labor.

[Page 120]

The Police informed everyone in all of the houses in the same way, in the entire Ghetto - "No one is to step out of the door of his home"! That was a strict order. Meanwhile we discovered that the Second Ghetto had been encircled since midnight by armed Germans and non-Jewish Police. That which we didn't want to believe, had occurred. The terrible news opened everyone's eyes, and it became clear to all what the intent had been by the transferring the old and the weak so speedily two weeks before, into the Second Ghetto. Everyone already absorbed that the unfortunate parents and relatives were turned over to the bloodthirsty beast, the German S. D, members - for liquidation. But all felt helpless, nothing could be done to save them now.

Almost everyone had a portion in the Second Ghetto: Parents, a grandfather, a grandmother, a sister, a brother and other relatives. Some, in great desperation, ignoring the strict edict not to leave their homes, ran to the Second Ghetto "to save", in some way their relatives. They didn't know that the German Angel of Death hovers over them no less than over the 600-700 Jews of the Second Ghetto, that he won't be content with just "the few Jews", which the Judenrat "agreed" to give him... They let them - those who had 'run there to save their parents and relatives - into the Second Ghetto, but the way back they didn't find. they were no longer to be seen amongst the living. Molye Zinger had run to the second ghetto to save his parents, former Vilna forest merchants, and he remained there. Also, I, Zvi Raiack, in great confusion and disappointment, wanted to run from Peretz Street into the Second Ghetto on old Kisheleike to our mother. However, they didn't let me, because it was clear that I would be going to a certain death. All of us, together with a larger group - the entire family of Eli Gordon, Libe Chodosh and the children and others - went up into the attic of Eli Gordon's bakery, in order to hide. From there they did not let me go, - arguing with me, that I will perish and not help my mother. Naturally they were right. Even I understood that, but I was being carried along against my will... I felt better when I broke out into a spasmodic crying and I was left exhausted... What was happening in the city we didn't know. We all heard from the attic how the Germans were shouting something at the peasants. It could have been that they weren't letting the village folk into the city, or something else.

[Page 121]

We also heard the shouts and cries of Jewish women, who were pleading with the murderers, but we couldn't understand exactly what and on what occasion. We were lying and trembling. The small children - our Aaron-Yitzhakl and Edye Chodosh's child - who were with us, also understood the situation. They lay still and didn't utter a sound.

A few hours later, exactly what time it was we don't remember, but it was still during the early morning hours, the Jewish Police issued a second edict: All Jews, together with their entire families, wives and children, must immediately gather in the Sports Plaza. They must be there in order to regulate the handing out of labor permits, and to see if it actually matches up with the members of each family, etc. Only permits that had been checked and properly stamped on the spot will be valid. Those permits, which do not have the official stamp of the Germans on the spot, will be null and void. - And after the inspection, the Judenrat and Jewish Police assured everyone that they would be permitted to return peacefully to their homes with certificates as "useful" Jews, who cannot be touched.

Almost all who had such "life permits", appeared with their wives and children on the Plaza. In one moment the street became black with Jews, with Jewish children, whom the parents were escorting by the hands and carrying in their arms. They were even moving sprightly, they believed... For the moment they had even forgotten the tragedy of the Second

Ghetto. Everyone endeavored to take to the Plaza all of their children, sisters, brothers, who did not have permits. To show that they belonged to the family of one who was privileged by being a member in a family of one who was useful, and should be registered on his permit and be saved...

How terribly pitiful and tragic was the situation, at that moment, of those who did not receive the-certificates at the time! How unfortunate they felt at the time and with what great envy they looked upon those with their "papers". Those who went clear and free with their families to the Plaza, where they will have the papers stamped as "useful" and be assured that no harm will befall them! The others began to hide in various places, in pits, ditches, in the attics, in the cellars - into the thickets they came, into the trees they climbed. They thought that since they didn't have certificates, they were useless, and that the German would certainly kill them. The true fate, on the other hand, of the Jews of Glubokie, was different.

[Page 122]

On the Sports Plaza there gathered, from the First Ghetto, thousands of souls, the young, the healthy, the skilled - the flower of Jewish Glubokie. The intelligentsia came - doctors, teachers, dentists, accountants, religious teachers, former merchants, etc. All with their wives and children, with relations, whom they thought they could possibly save. Even Rabbi Katz and his wife, together with his daughter, Shprintze and grandchild came, at the suggestion of the Jewish elder, Gershon Lederman, to the Plaza. (His daughter, Devorah, was not at home at the time and didn't come.) According to what we were told, Rabbi Katz had been hidden, but Lederman convinced him to be the first to go and seeing him, the mass of people would not be afraid and would follow his example. (Rabbi Katz, in spite of his advanced age, was not in the Second Ghetto.)

Before the assembled could orient themselves, at the blink of an eyelash, the Plaza was thickly surrounded by armed S. D., Gendarmes, Police and other evil doers. All streets were shut off with a stringent guard, so that no one, who had not yet arrived at the Plaza, could possibly enter it. One Jacob Almer, who noticed from afar what was taking place on the Plaza, took the opportunity to sneak into a courtyard and hide himself. The Germans did not allow others, who had already oriented themselves to the situation and wanted to withdraw, out of the street. The orientation came too late. The great tragedy became unavoidable. The victim had sprung into the mouth of the wild beast...

In order to calm the terribly upset Jews, who were on the Plaza, the liaison person for Jewish Affairs in the Justice Ministry, Hebelish, came out and made a speech. , Declaring that the Jews have nothing to fear, that nothing bad would happen to them. They will simply be sent for labor to other cities such as Smolensk, Warsaw, Borisov and others, and because of this they had begun a selection of Jews. They were sorted and lined up, partly on the right and partly on the left. It meant that a portion of the Jews were to remain in Glubokie, and that the greater portion will be sent out to labor in other cities. And so, as a result of this, the largest portion, during the selection, was sent to the left.

[Page 123]

According to the way the Germans treated those Jews who were sent to the left, it was obvious that their fate was already sealed. They were immediately ordered to kneel with their heads down. For the slightest movement, for lifting the eyes to look to the side to see what was happening, they were severely beaten. The Germans beat the Jews over the head with clubs, sticks, bricks that had been torn from the cemetery fence near the Sports Plaza, and so forth. And from the kneeling Jews with the lowered heads there already immediately began to pour out streams of blood. Also, the Jews who stood on the right could not avoid blows and violence, but not quite so severe as those received by the Jews on the left.

After separating the Jews, the Germans suddenly realized that "too many" are to be found on the right. too few had been left "to send for labor in different cities". They immediately began to choose another 500 persons from among those who were at hand, and those who were seized were driven to the left. The ones who weren't fast enough in going to the left, they already understood what was taking place, , with bestiality Germans murdered them on the spot. In this way, with a brick torn from the cemetery fence, they beat the teacher, Zalman Kravietz and Shlomo Verachavsky over the heads until their brains were exposed. In front of everyone, undergoing terrible suffering, they expired. Some Jews were brought from the city where they had been caught hiding. Among the latter were the dentist, Yash, from Yatkove Street. With an open skull they dragged him through the Plaza and his brains spurted onto the ground. This was observed by the thousands of unfortunates who were in the Plaza, who felt that the same fate would soon befall them.

During the time of the selection, terrifying and heartrending scenes took place. They split families, tore husbands from their wives, children from their parents, brothers from sisters. Many of those who were granted life by the German Angel of Death, those on the right, refused the "gift" and went by themselves to the left, choosing to die together with their own relatives, rather than remain alone in sadness and suffering with the terrifying visions in their souls. This happened to Yoshke Mirlin and his daughter, to Tzertl Zeldin and her parents, to Dora Gitelzon and her parents, to Roza Kraut and her daughter, Lisa, and others. By themselves they chose their fate and went to the left.

After completing the selection, the Germans and the Police began to lead the Jews.

[Page 124]

Women, men and children – walked from the Plaza, in-groups to the barracks in a wood, about a kilometer from the Plaza. There in the woods, there had already been prepared some long, deep pits for the Jewish victims. On this short journey some ran. The convoy around them was so thick that there was no way in which one could save himself, but they preferred dying on the way, rather than in the woods at the pits. And that's how it turned out. The Germans immediately opened fire on those who ran, and the way into the woods was strewn with dead and wounded in a matter of a few minutes. Some had fled to the nearby Lake Berezvetsher and were shot there or drowned themselves in the lake. On the third day after the slaughter the body of young Zelda Gordon, who was a student in our school, the daughter of Yoel Gordon (also known as Yoel Cantor) was floating on the overrun of the lake.

Ending with one group, they brought a second, then a third, a fourth, etc. Till they brought everyone from the Plaza to the barracks where they murdered them. The unfortunate victims who were left for last, were envious of those who had already been murdered earlier and did not have to live through the dreadful moments of waiting for certain death Inside the wood itself, the Germans, before killing the Jews, tortured them in various ways. Firstly, they ordered them to undress completely, and the murderers, right before their very eyes, divided up their better possessions, their clothes, underwear, footwear and other things. The young maidens were forced to dance naked before the open pits. And only after the Germans had satiated themselves with all of this, did the drive the victims into the pits ordering them to lie with their faces down in the earth. They then opened fire and sprayed them with their bullets. The wounded and small children were not murdered by shooting but were buried alive. Neighboring Christians later told that the earth of the barely covered pits shook for a long while and from under the earth, for a long while there spurted blood...

The 70-year-old Rabbi Katz, before being murdered by the Germans, was lain in the pit between two young girls, the 24-year-old Dora Gitelzon, and a refugee from Vilna, in order to cause him some extra suffering. The Germans photographed all of this, in order to show the blood-thirsty German officialdom their diligence in spilling blood and torturing Jews.

[Page 125]

"Because of all of this my loins filled with terror, cramps seized me, my hearing became distorted, the sight of my eyes blurred, my heart went astray, a quaking hit me."

To this day it is difficult to recall what the Jews went through in those moments before they came to their deaths… To accurately describe the scenes, and convey it fitly with words, it seems that there is no such virtuoso in the entire world who has language skills to do it.

"All hands weaken and all the hearts of men dissolve "

The hearts simply succumb.

The few Jews who had been sent to the right during the selection the Germans left alone and they walked, orphaned and shattered, back the Ghetto to bewail and mourn their tragedyfor the rest of their days…

* * *

The Epilog of this bloody Friday ended with the Jews of the second ghetto.

They had held the victims of the Second Ghetto, naked under the sky for the entire cold and rainy night of June 18th and day of June 19th (4th of Tammuz) in Moshe Chana's garden.

At 5 pm, after the Germans finished with the young and the strong, only then took the old to Barok and murder them.

The action against the old and the weak of the Second Ghetto took place on the 18th of June at midnight. The Polish encircled old Kisheleike and the surrounding smaller streets. The elderly men and women, and the ill were dragged naked and sleepy from their beds, they drove them in such state into Moshe Chana's garden. The night was chilly and drizzly. Naked, the unfortunates from the Second Ghetto stood shivering in the cold and became drenched to their bones. In the afternoon the Polish started mocking them and making amusement of them in the characteristic German manner during such massacre events. Crying, sighing or screaming was totally prohibited. For any of such conduct the old were severely beaten.

Some could not hold out. Their hearts burst and they remained lying in their spot even before they were shot. This was the fate of the wife of Yitzhak Verch (a coachman from Varshever Street) and others. Shimon Vitanus, the son-in-law of Hirshl Paliak began to recite the memorial prayer, "Lord Filled With Mercy" for himself and for all who stood in the garden (for the meanwhile still living corpses…). The listeners broke into spasmodic crying, which cut through the air and carried far beyond the boundaries of the Second Ghetto, combining with the cries of the inhabitants of the First Ghetto, who had returned "fortunate" from the Sports Plaza. The Police quieted them by beating them with the butts of their guns and sticks. The elderly tore the hair from their heads, fell to the ground, rolled in the dirt, banged themselves against the ground, etc. Those who stood paralyzed with fear did not look any better. Their eyes were open but unseeing, their blank stares in only one direction, not speaking and not answering any inquiries made to them. These were the "living dead" in the full sense of the word. Stones could have melted – "Because the stone of the wall will cry out and hands of wood will answer"… This didn't disturb nor had any significance affect on the Germans and their local helpers.

[Page 126]

After this night of depravity and pitch blackness and after this disheartening day, at 5:00 in the evening, they took all of the elderly and weak from Moshe Chana's garden into the above mentioned Barok Woods. They were driven through the new Kisheleike and there, in the houses, through the cracks, there peeked out those who a few hours earlier had returned "in peace" from the bloody Sports Plaza, where they were taking their parents, brothers and sisters, naked and bloody, to the Barok.… The sick, the crippled, who couldn't make it on their own, were being carried on peasants' carts, thrown one on top another along the way like logs of wood. They had to watch as their parents were being beaten in order to make them keep up along the way. Hearts burst, seeing it all, and to react was impossible. This was, perhaps, a lot more difficult than death itself.

As it was told, the mother of Benjamin Zack, who had been the Director of the Folks-Bank, went crazy along the way, and the Germans shot her on the spot and threw her body into a wagon that was loaded with the living.

In the woods the Germans first ordered everyone to sing and dance. Afterwards the healthy ones had to carry the weaker ones the elderly to the pits and lay them out. The carriers themselves had to lie on top of them and the Germans murdered them.

Among the martyrs in the Second Ghetto, there perished our dearly beloved, remarkable mother, who had suffered so much during her lifetime. Having been left a young widow, she, with her own toil and strain managed to give to us, the writers of these lines, not only excellent Jewish education, but also a superior worldly (secular) one. Learning which under the regime of the Czar, was extremely difficult to obtain for Jews (we were born at the turn of the century when the area was part of the Russian empire).

Who could believe, such a god-fearing matriarch,

[Page 127]

a righteous woman of her generation, who during her lifetime, never harmed a fly on the wall. She should be torn away from us in such a cruel, horrible fashion and perish at the hand of murderers. When she was already ill in the Ghetto and thought, that she would no longer get up from her sick bed.

She used to often console us by saying "I have already lived my life…. a person must dance the dance…"

She said that therefor we should not be upset about her well being for no reason…. Except, it never occurred to her or neither to us that the last dance would be such a terrible one…

Sometime later we were informed that the reporters on the German radio announced the day after the slaughter; "The German S. D. uncovered a large resistance cell containing 3,000 men, headed by a seventy-year-old Rabbi. The cell was liquidated on the spot" Such stories also appeared in the German newspapers a few days later.

* * *

A few days later the Germans entered the First Ghetto and tore open all the locked doors of the homes of the fallen victims. People who had left their homes that Friday with clear thought of returning. The Germans gathered all the items they could find and took it to the second ghetto. There they put it in orderly fashion and mixed it with items they found and confiscated from their victims in the second ghetto.

Then they divided all the items amongst themselves. Some items were left for the authorities. Later on they announced in near by towns and villages that a public sale of furniture that once belonged to the Jews will occur the next day. The Majority of the local population, to their great shame, utilized the "golden opportunity" They came in droves and masses to "buy" the Jewish wealth. More about it later.

After the Slaughter

Translated by Eilat Gordin Levitan

Friday evening

The Ghetto looks like a cemetery. Everything is barren, asphyxiated; the homes look like mausoleums, and it is horrifying to stare upon them. The greatest portion of the buildings stand with closed shutters and locks on the doors, which the householders had put in the morning before leaving for the Plaza. The music that was played all day in the city, on Kostiushki Plaza, proclaimed the triumphant victory

[Page 128]

of the Germans over the Glubokie Jews, had finally stopped. It is peculiarly quiet, composed. The Jews are no longer crying, no more wailing is heard, the screams are as if they remained suspended in the air, torn asunder by the murderous hands right in the middle. The few Jews who did not go to the Plaza in the morning, still lay hidden in their holes. They are trembling and afraid to come out of their hiding places. The remnant that had returned from the Plaza gathered in the corners of their empty houses and constrict their restrained sobbing and moaning. The lonely, orphaned children, parents, men, women, brothers, sisters only now begin to retrace what had befallen upon them. The scenes of horror of the past day, as well as the last days and weeks, begin to reawake their memory.

It is Friday night

There is no sign of the Shabbat, no sign of the holiness. There are prevailing signs of death, of killings, of stoning, of burning, of terror, of unending fear and desperation…At night we didn't sleep. Several men attempted to go out on the street, in the stillness of the Tammuz (Hebrew month that usually falls in late June and July) summer night, they listen to what is taking place outside the Ghetto, and interpret each sound, each whisper. They commented about that which the frightened ear had grasped, or what they thought they heard… They wait for the murderers of their relatives and dear ones, to soon come and take their souls. Life for the vast majority, had now become so cheap, that the additional news of any burden, Germans being close and surrounding the Ghetto, no longer made any impression whatsoever upon them.

If anyone under the burden of suffering and sorrow became sleepy, he saw in his dream how his relatives plead, in the hands of the murderers, that someone should save them. How those drowning in the Berezvetsher Lake stretch out their hands for help; how those stuck in the pits under the earth go through convulsions, and wrestle with death.

Saturday

On the morrow, after the bloody day and the muffled deathly night, the streets in the Ghetto were empty. Only the doctors could be seen running around to the sick and the wounded. A few wounded from the slaughter remained, they had somehow managed to sneak out of the bloody Sports Plaza.

During the evening they crawled into the Ghetto. Some of the critically wounded were carried by hand during the night, from gardens arid fields into the Ghetto. Among the latter were Chashe Becker from Varapayeva and Feige Plavin, a daughter of the miller, Zalman Plavin, who were carried into the Ghetto by Tsilye Zinger.

[Page 129]

At about 11:00 A. M. a few Polish policemen came into the Ghetto. They assembled about 50 Jews and took them for labor - the clearing of the corpses from the roads, the fields, the gardens, and carried them to the Barok for burial.

During Friday eve the Jews slowly began to reappear on the streets of the Ghetto. They began to tell many tales about yesterday's slaughter. They told how Israel Ichiltsik had bribed a German to save his sister from the death Plaza and promised him a watch for this. The German had taken Ichiltsik's sister from the Plaza, but a second German took her from him and brought her back, where she was murdered. 'This did not keep the first German from coming to demand the watch from Ichiltsik. Ichiltsik, now fearing for his own life, gave him a watch made by the firm of "Tsima". The thief took the watch, and soon thereafter returned demanding a second watch from Ichiltsik, for himself, saying that he had given the watch to his friend, whose name was Tsima, as was engraved on the watch. Ichilitsik had to give the German a second watch, because, otherwise, he would have been taken to the Barok…

They also told how Shimon Hirshl Polyak (born in 1864 per Yad Vashem testimony by Ester Vachstman of Belarus. His cousin, Binyamin Shneir [son of Gershon] of Ramat Hacovesh gives the date of 1888), who had been in the Second Ghetto, got into a conversation with a German guard. He convinced him to let him go for a set amount of gold, which Polyak had hidden away in his home in the First Ghetto, where his children had remained. The German took Polyak to his home to get the gold. Shimon Hirshl Polyak had forgotten where he had put the gold, and when he looked for it he couldn't find it. No one was in the house at the time. All had gone to the Plaza. One son hadn't gone to the Plaza, he was hidden in the attic and he heard how his father was searching for the gold. He heard how his father was calling all of the children by name, thinking that they were lying somewhere in the house hidden away, and could tell him where the gold was hidden so that he could buy his life with it. Polyak's son was lying in the attic and was afraid to reveal himself. Polyak didn't find the gold, and the German took him back to Moshe Chana's garden, from where he was taken to be murdered in the Barok.

Recounting the various murders, they told about the bloody deeds of the Folk-German woman, Ida Aditska from Psuye, who took very active part in the Killing action in Glubokie. On her own she searched for hidden Jews in the city and brought them to the Sports Plaza. "Thanks to her", Gershon Mirman and Lea nee Drutzs' son (Yosef or Faybush) and daughter Henia, among others, were killed. She found them hiding. When Mirman's daughter tore herself out of Aditska's hands, and ran into the Judenrat to hide, this German woman ran in and threatened that if the girl did not give herself up, she would kill 50 Jews in her place. She found the Mirman girl (Henia from Yad Vashem report by her cousin, Yizhak Mirman of Kibbutz Shfaim) and dragged her to the Plaza.

[Page 130]

They also told about how several Jews still remained in the Second Ghetto. They were hidden under beds, on ovens or somewhere else. It turned out that the Police had not searched the Second Ghetto vigorously, because, as is well known, the Germans did not think too much about the Second Ghetto. They had set up the Second Ghetto in order to easily and without any difficulties liquidate the strong and healthy elements among the Jews. From the Second Ghetto there survived the old Meir Bagin, Yosef Mindel (the vintner), Moshe Fishers, the teacher's mother, Moshe Shmuel Shulman (the Rebele).

They told about how Shmuel Gordon, the Dvilavitsher (the black hen), fled from the Ghetto. The Germans caught him on Wilner Street, threw him down, tied a thick rope attached to a stick around his neck and dragged him through the Barok until he perished.

In the evening a few went into the Second Ghetto to take pillows and other things that remained from their deceased parents and relatives. The Police detained them with the things. Among them were Abba Feigelson (a tailor), and Shulevitsh (a dentist). Everyone thought that they would surely be shot. But contrary to all expectations, they were set free.

Among the Glubokie Jews who escaped the slaughter were a group of fishermen, who on that particular day had gone to the lake to catch fish for the Germans. Quite a while earlier they had organized themselves in such a fashion, so that they would find themselves in the city much less, and "enjoy themselves" on the lake... These were Mulye Salavaitshik, Shalom Yungelman, Arke Levitan and his son, Avremke and others.

Sunday, the 21st of June (6th of Tammuz) there came a decree that all of those who remained alive were to go out to labor because "life must go on"... All those who remained alive in the Ghetto recited the Kaddish. Prayer quorums (minyanim) were organized in several houses. All rushed to participate in a minyan.

[Page 131]

All wanted to say a Kaddish. We had a minyan in our house. We said Kaddish for our mother. On Sunday we sat "Shiva" (the seven days of mourning). Yosef Baudin came to console us. He was once a teacher in our school. He taught Jewish religious subjects, and he told us that on Friday he watched our mother as she was taken on a wagon together with many other Jews. She was sitting like a statue without any expression or feeling... We also listened as if we were statues; the sources of our tears had been all dried up, but we were not allay...

As was previously mentioned, a few days later the German civil administration began to gather the possessions of the Jews in one place. They brought loaded wagons with furniture, bedding, china, and all sorts of pots and pans. They took the Jewish precious china for Passover and all sorts of things... Everything was gathered on old Kisheleike, on the area of the Second Ghetto. The furniture was thrown together on the street.

After the liquidation the old Kisheleike and side streets (the former Second Ghetto) was cut off from the Ghetto area. It was forbidden for Jews to go there. On Thursday the 18th of June, in the morning, I had prayed at my mother's place in the Ghetto. I left my Tephillin there, with the thought that the next morning, I would come early to be with her again... I wasn't allowed into the Ghetto anymore. Some of the city Christians thought how to use something of all this misfortune that befalls on their neighbors for themselves. They knew that such "miracles" only occur once in a lifetime and not even that, because not their fathers, nor their grandfathers, or even their great or great, great grandfathers couldn't tell of anything like it. They knew how to take advantage of the situation. They arrived and really took advantage. They helped themselves to all of the goodies. Understandably, the best things, such as jewelry, good clothing, underwear and valuable things in general, the Germans did not give to the local Christians. These they kept for themselves. For their killings they acted as if they deserve the best of their victims' possessions. But after what the Germans, the Police, their friends and acquaintances had satiated themselves, there still remained quite enough to satisfy almost everyone. Besides Glubokie owned possessions, they steadily brought fresh furniture, new items and other things from the nearby Jewish shtetls, from villages where the Jews of that dark period, were killed. Whole days they would bring loaded wagons to Gluboke. They were filled with all kinds of Jewish possessions. In the wagons there were mixed in Talesim with pots, bedding, clothes and so forth. There were scattered Tephillin with the small talesim splattered with blood; torn books, talmuds, chumashim, Bibles and other valuable books which were found in the homes of enlightened Jews in the small villages. (The writer of these lines had unpacked glass items which were wrapped in pages of the Talmud, Bibles, Maimonides "Guide for the Perplexed" and others. Some of these pages there were spotted with blood stains and we could imagine that the murderers must have killed the Jews, when they were sitting and learning a page of the Talmud. All of this they brought here in special boxes and they even turned them over to the Jews, to take care of - to put them in order and repair them, etc. Furniture was thrown on the street and it was all guarded by a policeman.

[Page 132]

The Germans announced a general sale of everything. There were plenty of takers. They bizzed like bees around flowers. The Christians gathered from neighboring villages and towns and the sale went ahead full blast.

Everything was dirt cheap, so that everyone could buy. A bureau was 3-5 mark (the money had no backing and was therefore worthless). 1 Mark for a good chair, 2 mark for a table and one could "bargain". If a Christian pleaded about his poor circumstances, he didn't pay at all. Peasants took from the city to their homes wagons heavily loaded with bureaus, beds, tables, desks, buffets, etc as if it were from a regular market. It was all taken from old Kisheleike, from the former Second Ghetto. Very few Christians refused to procure and enjoy the bloodied Jewish possessions.

When all had already satiated themselves with everything without end, the Germans "lowered the prices" and they gave everything away to any who wanted and would just carry it off. As was mentioned, the furniture lay in the street, and in the rain became so soaked that there were no longer any takers, even for free. Later, the Jews had to clean up the Plaza and the streets and remove the rotting and broken furniture. From the clothing and soft goods, the Germans, with the help of Jewish hands and labor, established the so-called "German Warehouse" in Glubokie.

[Page 133]

They ordered the Jews to bring to headquarters the bedding, the filling and feathers. The location was in the storerooms of Meir Gitelzon on Wilner Street. There, the Jews cleaned the feathers, sorted them, selected the clean from the soiled, packed them up, and they were shipped to Germany, to the addresses provided by the Germans. In the long summer days, from early morn until evening, the girls and women sat immersed in the fillings and feathers and worked on them. They were simply choked by the work. There were many cases of fainting during this work. They were sorting their own bedding for the use of the murderers of their relatives, for the bloodiest enemies of all humanity. But they wanted to live, and not working and not giving in, meant, at the time, the end of life…

The Reduction of the Ghetto Size

Translated by Eilat Gordin Levitan

During the days after the slaughter of the 19th of June (4th of Tammuz) approximately two thousand Jews remained in the Glubokie Ghetto. The mood among the survivors is easy to imagine, but they couldn't complain or bemoan their fate. They were contiguously and harshly driven to labor, labor filled with sadness and suffering. And anyone who came late, even if illness couldn't appear at work, was brutally beaten, Mottke Bagin once didn't come to work. Not able to find a doctor at the time, which could confirm his illness, the Jewish Police (at the order of the Germans) came to him and beat him so badly in his ill condition that he had to lie in bed for a full month afterwards. For three days the Ghetto doctors had to apply compresses and change his bandages on his wounds.

And perhaps there was a bit of an advantage in all of this horror. The struggle and the fear of the German Devil, the worries about the hunger pangs, did not permit the luxury of thinking or meditating. The persecutions were, perhaps, at that moment in time a consolation. the Jews couldn't correctly evaluate the situation. Like a hurricane at about 12 noon, 2nd of July (17 of Tammuz) there tore into a part of the ghetto the destructive angels, who brought with them new fears of death. The Polish policemen unexpectedly banged on the windows of the homes on Wilner Street, Peretz Street and a part of Dubrove St. and announced that the area of these streets will be cut off from the Ghetto according to a decree. Because of that the inhabitants of the houses there must, in 15 minutes, move themselves into the remaining area of the Ghetto. Each one may take with him only those things, which he can carry in his arms. They won't be allowed to go back a second time...

[Page 134]

We saw that the streets were black with Germans, Police as we looked through the windows. Vlosovtses (Military groups formed by the Germans and composed of those Russian Fascists who had fled Soviet Russia) were also there. A Russian Fascist General named Vlosov had organized them. This reminded us of the slaughter that had taken place 13 days earlier and we were all certain that this was but a maneuver to entrap the remaining Jews. Just as they had used the certificates on June 19th in order to kill the Jews with ease. Now they want to assemble all of us again in one place and enclose us in a tight ring. There was nothing to be done, we had nowhere to go. There was no time to even think. But still we began to gather up things in our hands. We did not think about what would be more worthwhile to take. Some grabbed food items - potatoes, flour, bread; others took clothes. We dressed ourselves in warm clothing, ignoring the fact that it was a hot day; underclothes, bed linens, cooking utensils, tools and so forth..... And we ran. There were also those who took nothing, being certain that they were being led to their deaths and that they wouldn't need anything... In general, almost everything was left behind and ran in panic and deathly fear... Cooked food was left the ovens, bread, which was being baked. In the home of the writers of these lines milk was boiling for the child and we were very much afraid that this would be noticed, since milk was forbidden for Jews. We were afraid to pour it out, and we were in great despair, not knowing what to do with it. We couldn't drink it, because we simply couldn't swallow... We poured it out into the oven, which was still warm, and it dried quickly. Out in the street there was panic. People rushed and ran. No one knew what the next moment would bring, and each one wanted to take yet more things… But how much can a person take in his arms? On top o it all in such circumstances? Those few who remained in the Second Ghetto area came running to help carry things. It was useful. On the contrary, a few Jews came from the tannery, to their great shame, they refused to help us in this critical moment. (I don't want to mention their names, since they are no longer to be found among the living, they later perished.)

[Page 135]

There wasn't even anyone left alive from many of the houses, their inhabitants had left on the 19th of June and never returned. a few homes still hung locks and their shutters stood closed since that bloody Friday. The Germans had not managed yet to remove the remaining things belonging to those they had killed. Among those houses still shut were the homes of the dentist Katzovitsh (the daughter-in-law of Moshe Katzovitsh), the dentist, Yash, the watchmakers, Shutav, Chidekel, Zalkind, Mirman, Sverdlin and others.

You had to go through a narrow path to pass through the new homes of the second part of the Ghetto. which It crossed from Peretz Street to Dobrave, behind the houses of Vilna Street. 'through other streets or alley-ways it was forbidden to go. On that narrow Street, there stood a German commission with Vitvitzken (Tzirkavetz) at the head, and let those who had been chased out, through. They would first check what everyone was carrying, and the better things, such as carpets, linens, clothes, clocks, etc., they took away. During the evacuation some people were slow and were therefore able to take with them some of their better things, now they were naked and without anything. It was actually better predicament for those who had only taken rags. They passed through "peacefully". Also we had to move ourselves from Viebninske (Peretz) Street into the permitted area of the Ghetto, and on the way, they took from us a good carpet and a few pairs of shoes. I tried to get the carpet back by claiming that I had nothing to cover myself with. As an answer I was beaten by a Polish policeman. Suddenly shooting was heard. at the check point. Yerachmiel Mazovetzky, the son-in-law of Yerachmiel Alperovitsh, dragged a bed. The bed caught the eye of a policeman, and he told him to leave it. Mazovetzky did not hear the command, so the policeman drew his gun and fired into the air. The Jews panicked and started to run like an arrow shot from a bow and threw away everything that they were holding in their hands. At the time it seemed as if the Germans were firing at the Jews. They didn't even think of anything. They were satisfied That they had gotten away "only" with fright. Dr. Helena Rayak, (wife of M. Rayak), a pediatrician, when going into the Ghetto, managed to smuggle in a children's scale, among other medical appliances. Now Vitvitzki came to us to pick through our things, and he forbade her to take the children's scale, and also some other medical things, which she had. We were all almost indifferent to everything. He also forbade our taking the Sabbath candelabra. (Vitvitzki knew us quite well from before the war. He used to make decorations for our school when there were special evening activities for the children.)

[Page 136]

The following sights greeted our eyes in that part of the Ghetto where they deposited us: men, women and children, darkened and dirtied, dressed in rags with torn shoes, or partly barefoot, one shoe on and one off, wandering through the streets, the yards and the gardens with nowhere to go. Everyone was loaded with piles of whole "things" (in other words: Rags) - dishes, footwear, torn clothes and linens, flicked bedding without matresses, broken beds and benches, bread, spilled potatoes, broken carriages, thermos bottles, valises, etc. A few of the more agile Jews managed in some way to scamper into stalls, attics, and other accommodations. Many simply remained under the open sky. Shmuel Leib Kurenitz took us in, he had a small cottage at the end of Bialastotzke St., on the very boundary of the Ghetto.

Jews fasted, it was the 17th of Tammuz., and in spite of everything there was a Minyan for the afternoon service. The portion "Vayechal", for the fast day, was read. Also I was there and I was honored with the Maftir, which was difficult for me to read, not so much physically as emotionally. (I was drained).

My heart was clamped by the words:

"Because my salvation is near, and my righteousness to be revealed. He Who chose Israel as his nation"

And so forth… Jews sensed that I was crying and they cried out loud with me…

———————

[Page 136]

The German Spy Vitvitzki

Translated by Eilat Gordin Levitan

Vitvitzki showed up in Glubokie in the fall of 1941, together with the German Civil Administration. He was not a brand-new figure in the town. Almost everyone here knew him. He was nick named the "Tzirkovetz" and this is the reason why:

A circus passed through Glubokie in the summer of 1933. It gave several performances. A performer, who had been part of the circus, remained in Glubokie when the circus left. No one knew, and no one was interested in asking, why this performer remained behind. People surmised that the management of the circus fired him because of some misdemeanor or whatever….

[Page 137]

The "Tzirkovetz" (one who is part of a circus) was very poor, wore old, ill-fitted and torn clothing. The general impression that he made was that of a drunkard who had no resources to imbibe…

He sustained himself by preparing decorations for performances, doing make-up for the performers, or playing in the string orchestra of the firemen. From time-to-time he would arrange evening dances for the local youth and would appear in the marketplaces for the village peasants as a "Fokusnik" (trickster or magician). He tried very hard to obtain a position as an official worker.

Understandably it was necessary for him, for his activity, to be near the correspondence, the telephone, the telegraph, and alike. But since he couldn't provide any moral references, he was unable to obtain such a position. He was a guard in a school near Glubokie for a period of time, and he was also active in the Polish youth organization "Streletz", and others. His outward appearance did not make any special impression; his height slightly above average, thin, Grey, cunning eyes, pales, gaunt face, with a pointed chin – dog like expression, and light hair. He would darken his face and his eyebrows. He spoke softly and he went about with a downcast look. He would tell that he was the son of simple Polish folks, and that he was thrown out of the 6th grade in the Gymnasia (elementary school) because he acted up. He lived on Krakower Street near Shalom Tzentziper, the butcher. He had a room, which wasn't good, and as the landlords used to tell, he lived very inadequately. He would not feed himself properly. His landlords would often help him out. Especially Shepsel, the youngest son, who would give him a piece of meat, bread and other things. Also, the Jewish storekeepers would help support him, because they felt compassion for him. When he would buy a herring in a store for 10-20 groschen, the storekeepers wouldn't take any money from him. Later on, he married a poor Polish girl.

No one could imagine that this poor, dejected, outcast "Tzirkovetz" could possibly be a German spy. The results of his undercover work became apparent at the end of the summer of 1939. Before the German attack on Poland, numerous fires broke out in Glubokie and the surrounding region, seemingly for reasons that no one could fathom. A huge fire started in the home of Moshe Mirman and Dr. Britanishske on Vilna Street, which spread to Dubrove, where dozens of buildings were destroyed. A few days later a fire broke out at the home of Chaim Chevlin and Moshe Shulheifer on Zamkove Street. An exceptionally large fire erupted a few days later in the town of Luzshki, 30 kilometers from Glubokie, and at the time almost the entire town was destroyed. It became clear, that all of this was the work of a concealed, devilish hand. In spite of all efforts, it was not possible to uncover the one liable...

[Page 138]

After the arrival of the German civil-administration to Glubokie, the former poor, melancholy "Tzirkovetz", was to be found among them, as an active worker. He who had earlier served the Polish authorities, was now serving the Germans. It became clear that the arsonist, who had caused all of the summer fires in 1939, was none other than the "Tzirkovetz" who had aimed to create panic among the local population.

In September of 1939, after the arrival of the Red Army, the above mentioned "trickster" played in the string orchestra. Later the Soviet authorities found him a suspicious character and arrested him. He sat in prison until there came the exchange of Soviet and German citizens between the Soviet Union and Germany. The Soviet administration at the time at the suggestion of the German commission freed the "Tzirkovetz" and he left Glubokie. Only after the intervention of the German might did it become clear, that this was riot simply a circus performer, who by chance remained in Glubokie in 1933, and also on the Glubokie horizon he was not to play a usual role...

After the arrival of the German Civil Administration in Glubokie at the end of September 1941, Vitvitzki, the German spy, also arrived. But he was no longer the downcast, pitiful, lonely character, but outfitted in genuine German, sparkling new Fascist uniform. He now looked like a authentic Hitlerite hangman. Those who had formerly helped him, now looked to him as a protector, but... in vain! He "knew nobody" and concerning help from him to save oneself from death, there was no one to talk to. On the contrary, he would pick on them even more. He would look for their "transgressions", and one would have to search for ways how to avert his scrutiny, how to avoid him. Under no circumstances could one recognize the former quiet, easy-going, poverty-stricken "trickster", who had always spoken in a barely discernible vociferation. Removing the mask revealed the actual beast, the bona fide man-eater. He walked erect now, with his head uplifted as if he had suddenly grown tall... When he would walk with hasty steps, with his severe, penetrating stare. Walking through the street, he would always swing his rubber whip, with which he would beat Jewish passers-by. A special fear would be evoked when he went near us playing with his revolver... In short, he would have nothing to distinguish him form the other "nice friends" of his (the Nazis).

[Page 139]

He actively participated in all of the murders and especially during the mass murders. Of course, he was able to carry out these activities better than the others, thanks to his many years of espionage here. The surrounding villages also suffered from him. He would utilize the actions Very skillfully for himself while the Christians were being sent off to forced labor in Germany. For a "knot" of gold 10 Ruble pieces, he would free them of the obligation. Such "knots" he would accumulate in the hundreds and thousands, and, in a short while, the poor "Tzirkovetz" became a solidly rich man. 1t is interesting to note that at the terminal in Glubokie, before the young people were sent off to Germany, in order to quiet the cries as people were parting from their loved ones, Vitvitzki would play the harmonica and perform tricks, working like a true artist... But in relation to the troubles that the Jews suffered at his hands, this was nothing. In the local oppressions and blood actions against Jews, Vitvitzki was always first. He knew better than his comrades did what to find where, and how to work at it. Following his instructions, the exact spot where the Ghetto was to be located was set in Glubokie. After the slaughters, he would carry out the cutting down of the Ghetto area. Ultimately, this bloody artist played a major role in August of 1943, setting the liquidation of the Glubokie Ghetto

The beast was also very active during the liquidations of the Ghettoes of Dokshitz and other surrounding towns.

Besides murders he was like a vampire that would suck out the last bit of juice. Once he came to his former landlords, the Tzentzpriers and demanded that they bring him within two hours, 5000 Rubles and a gold watch. They ran like crazy through the entire city - since the alternative might have meant death - and making a truly mighty effort, they were only able to raise 3000 Rubles. When they came to him with this sum, he fell upon them like an angry snake, hit them with his whip, yelled, taunted them with words and avenged himself upon them to his heart's desire. After a long period of cries and pleading on the part of the Tzentzipers, he tore the money from them and slid it into his pockets, pushing them out the door so hard that they rolled over several times. this time they were fortunate, they escaped the bullet.

[Page 140]

During the contraction of the Ghetto, 17th of Tammuz, 5702 - 2nd of July, 1942, the "Tzirkovetz" Vitvitzki, stood on the road and took from the Jews their possessions. He turned over to the underworld of the Christian population whatever he didn't like His appetite grew so large, that from Dr Henia Raiak he even took medicines, medical preparations, a medical scale and other such things. His greed knew no bounds!

He was also very involved in persecution-actions against the Partisans. Expeditions into the forest often happened under his direction. There would be searches for the Partisans. It was rarely that they returned from these expeditions without causing damage. Mostly they would bring back many dead, and wounded Germans and policemen. The bandit would constantly praise himself for his "ability and heroism". He would often point out the bullet holes in his cap and indicate that it was "done by Partisans" and show his friends how bold and self-confident he goes into the thick of battle against the Partisans. It was clear that he had shot up his cap on his on, in order to show how dedicated he was to his work.

With his stage trickery he would draw people into his net. He would dress in civilian dress or Partisans' clothing and come into the Ghetto disguised (naturally, until the bird was recognized), and convince young people to join up with the Partisans. The fate of those who were convinced by him could easily be imagined. They would not be denied any troubles or torture. Quick death, in this case was a fortunate ending. The hair stands on its edge when we remind ourselves of how because of this provocateur the young brothers, Chazan, Ginzberg and others were tortured.

This Hitlerite hangman had great skill in catching escapees and discovering those in hiding. It was not difficult for this German to travel, even all the way to Vilna, to search for the former county Doctor, Dr. Zashtoft. He put him in his car and then murders him along the way. With this "number" he would constantly boast about how cleverly he had carried this out. After finding out the address of Dr. Zashtoft, he purposely circled the house a few times in order to make it appear as if it happened "by chance". Upon meeting him he proposed to him, as an old friend to ride back to Glubokie with him, by promising that he would later give him a ride back to Vilna…

[Page 141]

He organized "Samochovtzes" - a Hitlerite youth organization- in Glubokie and the surrounding area, for which he arranged courses, during which he would provoke one part of the populace against the other, so that the Glubokie area was soaked with blood and tears because of this frightening brute.

His fortune grew from day to day Because of it all. He had already accumulated quite a bit in Zalesie, near Glubokie, where he obviously planned to remain forever. However, in December of 1943, Partisans from "TZukov-Otriad", Rokosovskes Brigade, interfered with his estate. They let loose the horses, cattle and sheep, and the rest they burned to the ground. It is interesting to note that they left a message, which a Glubokie Jewish Partisan gave after this act, to the manager of the estate for his boss. This is the translation from Polish:

"Herr Vitvitzki! - Don't be angry. All this was done by your well-known acquaintance, with whom you served in the Glubokie Fire Department. After the War we will settle all scores. All!...

Your comrade, Zalman Samuilovitsh Rappaport"

What happened to the "Tzirkovetz" after the Germans were driven out of Glubokie, at the beginning of July 1944, we do not know. We can imagine that this "artist" walks around somewhere, in disguise, with a false passport in his pocket. Possibly even with a Jewish one, which he confiscated from one of his victims, having been aware that the German downfall is soon approaching. And maybe he put himself into the shoes of that German, who was captured by the Russians and declared that his father had been one of the original communists, and a "loyal subject of 'General' Karl Marx"! Who is now in Vienna… (See the War memoirs of Ilya Ehrenberg!).

[Page 142]

Whatever happened to him, this bloody German spy will remain in the memory of the few surviving Jews of Glubokie and the surrounding area, as a symbol of the hateful, freakish reptile, who carried with him death, destruction and annihilation...

"Warehouse"

Translated by Eilat Gordin Levitan

As was already mentioned, after the slaughter in Glubokie and the surrounding the Germans gathered the possessions of the Jewish victims and put it in special storehouses. After the decrease of the Ghetto on the 2nd of July They also took items belonging to the Jews who had been transferred, to these storehouses. the things were sorted there and set up as "merchandise houses" or as the Germans referred to them "Varenhaus".

They opened stores selling linens, footwear, haberdashery, clothing and others on Vilna Street. For a low price, the Germans and their friends purchased good quality apparel for ladies and gentlemen. Stores for porcelain, glass, dishes and a furniture opened. . In the house of Yehoshua Geller (a barber-surgeon), There was to be found the Varenhaus of haberdashery and clothing, with which Henie Raise Lederman dealt. In the house of Shmuel Mote Tzirlin (corner of Vilna and New Kisheleike) was the porcelain store, under the supervision of someone named Gurvitsh (an elderly person, a refugee from Vilejka). In the house of Moshe-Hannah (corner of Vilna and Old Kisheleike) was the furniture store.

There were established special workshops and procedures in order to sort the things first and put them in order, managed by and worked by Jews... a large laundry was established, where everything was washed and cleaned of the blood of the victims, because they hadn't managed to remove their clothes before they murdered them. The manager of the laundry was Kulbis, who had been the proprietor of a chemical cleaning establishment in Vilna.

During the sorting and washing some people would recognize the clothing and other things belonging to their relatives. Manye Freydkin recognized the shirt of her recently murdered husband, Shimon. With her own hands she had to wash the blood off her husband's shirt for the Varenhaus. And wailing and tearing the hair from their heads, the women washed and cleaned and pressed the things that belonged to their dearest, washing off the blood and turning the things over to their murderers. There were incidents when the laborers fell faint during their work, losing consciousness, and they had to be carried off to the Ghetto, in the midst of their work.

[Page 143]

There were also workshops where thins were pressed, repaired and restored. In one such workshop, Raye, the wife of the teacher, Wolf Michelman, had to with her own hands, repair the suit of her murdered husband. During the work she fell faint and with great difficulty she was placed on a stretcher and carried home. After they were repaired, the things were displayed in the stores. The Germans bought them and sent them home as gifts for their wives, children and relatives!

The same was for the store that sold dishes and porcelain. The merchandise was first removed from Jewish homes, and afterwards brought from the surrounding towns, such as Dokshitz, Parafianov, Mir, Luzshki, Plissa, Ziavki, Germanovitsh, Brasluv, lialuvitsh, Druya, Pohost, Sharkovshtzizna, Prazaraki and others. From these towns there were brought whole wagons loaded with crates of utensils and dishes, packed in the pages of holy books. The wagons with these things were covered with bloody torn clothing, often with torn taleisim and bloody prayer shawls..... When the merchandise would diminish in the stores, the Germans would order the Judenrat to provide certain articles. During the months of August and September of 1943, almost every day orders would come to the Judenrat for suits, underwear, socks, shoes, pajamas, children's clothing, and even toys. A situation was created In the Ghetto that not a single perfect item could be left to be seen, because such items had to be sent to the "Varenhaus".

They would consider themselves lucky if they could save themselves by providing some substitute item when it was impossible to fulfill a demand for some article, when it wasn't possible to provide some item or another or substitute item were gold, jewelry, etc.

Selling the Jewish possessions involved a procedure as follows:

The buyers - Germans or police, also officials of German establishments - used to come to the "Varenhaus" with orders from the Justice-minister. one of the Jewish "salespeople", Mashe Bagin, Chaya-Rachel Rabinowitz or someone else would permit the buyer to choose what he liked, and it was lucky when the buyer, after finding and getting what he wanted, delicately wrapped, did not berate the one who gave him the merchandise. It became a thing of amazement if a German, in a rare moment, would greet the salespeople when he entered the store. This would be talked about for a long while. A decent German!...

[Page 144]

Workshops and the Office of the GEBIT Komisar (the Justice-Commissioner)

Translated by Eilat Gordin Levitan

When the Jews of Glubokie realized what a dismal destitute they had fallen into, they began to search for ways in which to save themselves from coming annihilation. Since it was impossible to flee Glubokie, and there was nowhere to flee at that time, the Judenrat began to establish all kinds of undertakings and workshops, where Jews would be able to work and to be "useful". The Germans gave their assurance; Jews who work and prove their usefulness with the work, will not be harmed. At the beginning of 1942 Glubokie became, thanks to the Jews, a truly industrialized factory-city:

1. On Vilna Street, in the home of Shimon Lekach, there was a stamp press, under the supervision of Mendel Galberstein. In that place, there worked about 20 stitchers, among whom there were: Hirsh Izraelov, Yitzhak Shuchman and his brother, Shimon Lekach, Gurevitsh, a young man from Dokshitz, Avraham Budav and others. They would stamp out the heels of shoes and boots, and also leather portfolios, holsters for revolvers, satchels and so forth. They would also stamp out for the German women, bolsters and all sorts of slippers. The work would turn out very nice and artistic. The Jews did it in good taste, and the Germans were pleased with the work.

2. Neighboring the leather stamp press, the shoemakers-workshop was to be found in the house of Mrs.Linushkin, sister-in-law of Shimon Lekach. David Drutz from Hoifisher Street, who was the son-in-law of Eli the Shamash (Beadle), supervised this enterprise. There, there worked: Chanan Meltzer, David Weiman, Zalman Shitzkin and others. Also, fictious "shoemakers" worked there. The former teacher, Kasriel Shneidman used to make wooden slippers. And Lipa Landau, (son of the Rabbi of Droisk, and also ordained), learned to sew a pair of boots there. The shoemakers were flooded with work, always had orders from the Germans, who would send shoes to Germany for their relatives, and also use them for trade. The stitchers and shoemakers provided for the Germans and were very necessary. Once the Gendarmes arrested the shoemaker, Zalman Shitzkin, for bartering some things in exchange for bread with a local peasant. Kern, the chief of the Gendarmes, freed him. This was one of the rare cases in which an arrested Jew was freed. At that time, they detained Motke Pildas at the Ghetto entrance, when he returned from work. And they shot him immediately. In the Ghetto they said that Beryl Pildas' son was a surrogate for Shitzkin and therefore fell victim, because the German tactic was such that if they

freed one Jew, because he was necessary to them, they would kill another Jew, or more than one in exchange.

3. There was to be found the men's tailor and furrier in Sarah Kremer's home (the wife of the teacher, Zalman Kravietz) This workshop was directed by Miakinin. There worked there some dozens of tailors, among them: Zelick Glazman, Zalman Feigelson, husband of Feitze, Arke, the shamash of the blue Minyan, Shlomo-David Pren, Ettingaff and others. They would skillfully make fine warm fur gloves and so forth...

4. Ladies tailoring establishment run by Hannah Knel operated at Kasriel Kotz's home on Vilna Street. They sewed for the German women. The seamstresses used to have to go measure the garments for the German women, and this was dangerous. The first worry was whether or not the German woman would approve of the work and not feel that the Jewish seamstress had not put her heart and soul into the work on her dress, or slip... It was not less dangerous to pass through, to and from, the entire city, outside of the Ghetto. The manager, Hannah Knel, whose duty it was to go and do the measuring or bring the finished garment, would, bid farewell to her fellow workers every time she left, and they would wish her a safe return...

5. A knitwear establishment opened at the Shulvitsh's home. many women would knit sweaters, gloves, socks, hoods and other things There. Girls, as young as 8, also worked there. All told there were about 60 to 70 women who worked there.

6. the workshop for wooden shoes was at Meitshik Rabinowitz's home. Laizer Kotz from Varapaieve ran it. There they produced quite a few wooden shoes. The Germans provided these for the Jews and other manual laborers – Poles and White Russians from the entire area. Those who wore these shoes walked like true cripples, with bloody feet.

7. the broom workshop, run by Friedman from Yatkave Street At Meir 's, was found on the courtyard, in a back house. This workshop was set up to employ the elderly, weaker Jews. The goal was constanly; every Jew should be gainfully employed. There were the following who were employed there: Shimon Lekach, from Disna, the father of Dr. Nachum Lekach; Mendl Pak, Chaim-Simcha Shpier (who had been the Gabbai of the Staraselyer Synagogue), Zalman Gordon Shlomo- Meir Shapiro, Yisrael Alperovitsh and others. The old Jews would often sit in the workshop with the Psalms or another holy books and secretly study them. On Shabbatot they would sit dressed in their aprons, but they wouldn't work. They would come early, pray with a minyan, and read from a Torah. It was also like this on the Shabbatot for the Mincha (afternoon) Service. There they made clothes brushes, shoe brushes, brushes for grooming horses and others.

8. A large factory for the manufacture of marmelade was to be found at the edge of Warsaw Street, in the house of Natarius. It was organized and directed by Moshe Abramowitz (the former proprietor of the firm "Motzni Boot"). This factory was very important to the Germans, because the marmelade produced there was very good, and the Germans liked it very much. Many young people were employed there. Later in this factory they produced sugar products.

9. At the home of Moshe, the blacksmith (Kreines) on 75 Vilna Street was the wagon factory, which was supervised by a Motl Berchov from Luzshki. they assembled wagons, wheels, sleds and alike for the Wehrmacht (German Army). In this "wagonbau" the Jews suffered greatly from the White Russian, Valakevitsh, a

member of the "Council of White Russia" of Astravskes clique in Minsk. Valakevitsh was the steward of the "wagonbau" and by his torture of Jews and incitement to pogroms was very pleasing to the Germans.

10. The Judenrat also organized an ale factory, run by Moshke Katz (son of Tuvia) and Zundel Musin. Most of the ale produced was exported. Ale was also given to the officials in Glubokie and the surrounding area. From time to time, ale was also surreptitiously given to Jews in small quantities. Jews considered this a better place of employment and would chase after jobs there.

11. Many Jews were employed in the local tannery, which was run by A. Kurak and sons, from Dolhinov and also Mendl Katz (the son-in law of Abraham Palant). In this establishment Jews Also strove to obtain jobs, because one could more readily obtain footwear here. Besides this, the tannery would secretly produce hides for Christians and for this the Jews received enough for food for themselves and also to sell other products in the Ghetto. All of this was dangerous and there were victims. The tannery was located outside of the Ghetto at the edge of the city on Wilner Tract, and when the SS would arrive in the city, or other German murderers, and the Ghetto would be seized by panic, the workers of the tannery would remain overnight in the tannery. Some individual Jews would even steal their families out of the Ghetto and bring them to the tannery overnight.

12. They also produced in the Ghetto, under the direction of Zalman Levis, mattresses. The mattresses were sent to Germany, and also distributed to the Germans who were to be found in Glubokie and the surrounding area.

13. Very highly refined furniture factory under the supervision of Tishler Feigelman of Vilna Street was here. The Jews put all of their industry and talent into it and produced very fine and beautiful furniture. Also, here, most of what was produced was sent to Germany.

14. The cap makers organized a workshop in the Ghetto to make hats. Eli Alai, Reuven Gordon, Chaim-David Rothenberg - a Hassidic Jew from Lomzsher Street and others worked there.

15. Run by Reuven Haberman and his sons from Zamkove Street, the tinsmiths also organized a workshop. Reuven, his sons and other tinsmiths crafted all sorts of metal utensils.

16. A sign-making establishment was located on Vilna Street. The following worked there: Eli Podnos, his brother-in-law, Shrira (the former manager of the cinema "Karsa"), Yosef Budin, a former religious teacher and others. They made signs, placards and other such items for the Germans.

17. Also, the print shop, which had previously belonged to Moshe Katzavitsh, Sheinbaum and Goldberg, was taken over by the Germans. There, like everywhere else, Jews worked. Among them were: Haberkorn, former teacher in the Jewish Business School. Mulye Zeldin, Yoske Zeldin, Zalye Milchman, Yitzhak Freidkin, the son of the comb maker (named "Kasar"), Shmerke Katsherginsky (the poet from Vilna) and others. There, the Jews secretly printed blanks for all sorts of false documents, and a few, thanks to this fact, were able to remain on the "Aryan Side". Even the very young children worked. For them, the infants, a workshop was organized. They made cartons, so that the Germans would be able to pack the things that Jews made, and send them to Germany. The 11-year-old cripple, Yashe Mazavetzky, the grandson of

Yerachmiel Alperovitsh, supervised this workshop. In that place there also worked the 7-year-old Zinke (Aaron-Yitzhak) Raiak, a son of M. Raiak.

Furthermore, shoe polish was made in the Ghetto. the teacher Rivke Sragavitsh the daughter of Abraham-Shlomo Rabinowitz and others worked there. They also made combs and twine. Gloves were sewn. There was also a vulcanizing workshop.

As was mentioned, Glubokie became a factory city, where no industry was omitted.

Entire plantations were established in the Jewish gardens. All sorts of hops were planted as well as other growing things. Someone named Katz, from the town of New-Svientzian supervised this. About 40 Jews worked the plantations. Later they were bit by bit eased out of this work, and Poles and White Russians replaced them. The Germans exploited the talents of Moshe Mirman, and therefore let his wife continue to work there. Also, Leib Krivitzky, Sharke Sragavitsh, Tzilye Mirman and others worked there.

Jews also worked in the "headquarters", beside this, in the Justice Ministry, in the Gendarmerie, in the magistrates building, the community center, Police headquarters, and for the Germans in their homes. They also worked on the roads, on the railroad, as street cleaners, at the market, in the gardens, and so on. Every day Jews were sent to the nearby railroad stations around Glubokie. In general, the Germans supported themselves with Jewish labor, and sucked the lifeblood from them right up to the end, and afterwards annihilated them. A special office was set up at 19 Vilna Street - in the house of Meir Gitelson, which was outside the Ghetto. In order to carry on the various enterprises and industries in Glubokie, there which was actually run by the Judenrat. Officially though this Office was called the "Office of the Regime's Kommisarat".

This Office took care of the Jewish workers and made sure that they would get to work on time, controlled production, and distribution. This Office took care mostly of the orders of various items for German officials and personalities. Those who regularly ordered were the Justice-Commissioner, Hochman, the representative of the commerce department, Heberling, Chief of the Glubokie Gendarmerie Kern. The one in charge of Jewish Affairs Hebel, the adjutant of the Gendarmes Hait, Vitvitzki (former spy), Goldberg, Heinliat, Vildt, Shpeer, Tzimer, Becker, Kapenvald, Zemf, Schultz, the Burgomeister, Naumov, Germans from the Labor Department and others. Also, there were often German guests from other cities, who would come here with empty valises and leave loaded with all the best, provided by Jews.

[Page 149]

The Germans would send for the Jewish Elder Constantly, or would themselves, order various things in the Office. Steadily footwear, clothing, linens, produce (butter, honey, hog fat, sausage, meat and so forth) would be packed there, and these were sent to provided addresses in various places in Germany. Heberling would send footwear and suits of clothing to various places in Germany. He would send these items also to a friend of his in Warsaw, a German who was a senior official in the administration there. The Jews had to provide all of the things requested in the required time, in order to be able to fulfill all demands. In the Office it was always lively, there ran around the Jewish Police, who were members of the Judenrat and other Jews to all Jewish the Jewish homes, and would bring to the office clothing, footwear, household utensils, food etc. In the courtyard of the Office there was a warehouse for leather, run by Alter Cohen, a warehouse for linen, furs and other things, run by Yaakov Almer. To the warehouses the peasants would bring from their villages their produce and grain, where it was packed on wagons and entire wagon loads of leather, linen, furs and grain were every week sent off to Germany. There was also a separate warehouse for sewing machines, stocking machines, hat making machines, which were taken away from the murdered Jews of Glubokie and the surrounding area.

There was also a metal warehouse. There they stored samovars, pots, primus stoves, trays, meat grinders, baking pans, mortars, hinges of doors, ladles, candlesticks and others. The Jews packed onto the wagons these items also, and they were taken to Germany.

There was also a warehouse for feathers. The entire summer and fall of 1942, they gathered the bedclothes from all of the towns around and also from Glubokie itself. It belonged to the families of Jews who perished. The heavy quilts and the cushions were opened and the Jews cleaned the feathers, sorted and entire wagons full were sent to bloody Germany. Our blood still freezes in our veins when we remind ourselves that still even today, the evil, unclean creatures sleep on the quilts and cushions of our mothers, fathers, wives, sisters and little children. Who got anything back from them even after the war and after the surrender? In the Office at number 19 Vilna Street, worked: Moshe Shulheifer, Michael Azshinsky (bookeeper), Nathan Gelvan, Sonia Gurvitsh of Vileike, Salye Natanson and Sonia Bagin. Later on - Ire Botvinick of Dokshitz and others.

[Page 150]

Glubokie Ghetto; A Concentration camp for the Remaining Jews of the surrounding liquidated Shtetls

Translated by Eilat Gordin Levitan

After the slaughters of April, May and June 1942, in the towns of Dokshitz, Dolhinov, Sharkovshtzizna, Bruslav, Germanavitsh, Druya, Miory, Luzki, Haluvitsh, Pliste, Ziavki Prazarak, Yadi, Pohost and others in the Glubokie area, and the huge slaughter of 2,500 Jews in Glubokie, the situation among the remaining Jews was one of such despair such despondency, that it cannot be described in words. The Jews were tortured and not permitted even to mourn their great tragedy. They were driven to labor as they had before. The remaining Jews of the surrounding towns who escaped the killers wandered, hungry and naked in the woods, in the mud, in the standing grain fields and hid themselves from death, which threatened them from all sides. In many cases the merciless angel of death appeared in their hiding places.

Partisans began to appear in various places. They would partially hinder the Germans from freely carrying out their plans. For the murderers it did not pay to have Jews wandering in the woods, in the bushes and in the mud. In July 1942 an order was issued by the German authorities that all of the survivors of the annihilated towns should gather in the Glubokie Ghetto. They were assured that no one would be killed. Permits were given to the members of the Judenrat to freely ride around in the places where these Jews were hiding and tell them about the German amnesty, and to gather them into the Glubokie Ghetto. (Officially it was forbidden for Jews to even go out of the Ghetto into the city.)

The Jewish Elder, Gershon Lederman, undertook this task vigorously. He organized a few energetic people, gave them permits, and with the blessing of the Judenrat sent them out to the fields, woods, mud swamps, bushes etc. They were sent to the environs of the annihilated towns to seek out the wanderers, the refugees, and to gather them here into the Ghetto. The unfortunate, orphaned, broken Jews reacted in various ways. Those, who were completely broken, grabbed at this opportunity like a drowning man would grasp the sharp edge of a knife to save himself. They were immediately brought into the Glubokie Ghetto.

Some fought with themselves and didn't know what to do. Good sense, which still served some of them, told them that this was a new German ploy, a deceit to fool them into a new trap, in the Glubokie Ghetto. In order to have them all together and then dispose of them. But for some, the situation in the forest; hunger, weariness and the fear of death at the hands of the peasants, put them into such a bind, that they imagined they had nothing to lose. After a short period of deliberation, they let themselves be persuaded, and against their better judgement, went back to the Ghetto. After saving themselves from the slaughter, they again placed themselves inside the German box The first ones who showed themselves in the Glubokie Ghetto, from the forests, were many of the Jews of Szarkowszczyzna. Because, as is known, the Police and civilian Christians of that town, searched for the Jews in the fields and woods, and killed them when they were found. And if they could hide from the Germans, from the local bandits, who knew all of the highways and byways, all of the caves and hiding places, it was impossible to hide. Therefore, these Jews immediately responded the call of the Judenrat. In a similar situation were the Jews of Dokshitz, and they also capitulated immediately. Later there also came Jews from the other destroyed towns such as: Miary, Druya, Holuvitsh, Disna, Plisse Ziavki, Braslaw, Prazarak and others.

[Page 151]

Men and women, mostly young would come into the Ghetto each day. They were barely able to drag themselves along from the fields around Germanavitsh, Luzshki, Hadutziski, Varapayeva, Parafianov, Dolhinov, Droisk, Braslaw, Zahatye, Bildiyugi, Shipi, Skuntshiki, Parplishtze, Svientzyan, Padbradz and others. Only a few of those in hiding, those who were physically strong, would not be influenced by the Judenrat appeals to give themselves up, and chose instead the dangerous life in the field, rather than give in again to the German.

[Page 152]

The echoes, though, about the safety for Jews in the Glubokie Ghetto, kept on spreading, and to there would stray refugees from the German sword from far away places: Dvinsk, Kovno, Bialistok, Grodno, Brisk, Baranovitsh and others. All of the Jews who arrived were in tatters, with growths of beard, and blackened with dirt. Most of them had swollen feet, hands and faces bitten by flies, bees, etc. There were also some that had been seriously wounded, because in running through gunfire during the slaughters, they were hit by bullets and in the forests they bandaged themselves with rags, and held out…

We would always encounter in the Ghetto, those who limped, those who leaned on branches cut in the forest, with bandaged heads, faces, hands and feet. Swollen "people", or better yet, shadows, who did not have the strength to tell what had happened to them, and who couldn't even mourn their most near and dear ones whom they had lost during the slaughters.

Here were cases where family members lost each other, running from the slaughter in their communities, thinking that the others had already perished by German bullets, and suddenly they would meet again. It is impossible to describe such a meeting. Not all were capable of enduring the joy, just as many couldn't endure the tragedy in its completeness because of the inhuman experiences. They also brought suckling babies into the Ghetto, who had been found hidden under bushes, because the parents had been murdered. No one knew whose children they were.

In August of 1942, the Germans transferred the Jews of Kazian and Nei-Pohost into the Glubokie Ghetto. They were brought in on peasant's carts together with their "possessions"., Jews, refugees from 42 Jewish communities gathered into the Glubokie Ghetto - all told, several thousand people.

Those, who were lucky and hurried into shops, stalls, attics and a variety of "dwelling places", were privileged Those who arrived later did not have a roof over their heads. A large number were homeless on the street. Those who had been brought from Kazian and Nie-Pohost remained with their bedding lying in gardens no way could they find a place for themselves.

The Judenrat did not know how to solve the housing problem of the refugees. On the one hand they had to try dealing with the authorities to persuade them to enlarge the boundaries of the Ghetto. But on the other hand, they were afraid to talk to the Germans about the overcrowded conditions in the Ghetto. So that it would not seem to them as if there were too many Jews in the Ghetto, which might lead to a new series of murders, to a new slaughter. But there was no alternative. The overcrowding in the Ghetto was unbearable and Lederman went to the officials and convinced them (for a very nice bribe, understandably) to extend the Ghetto area. Those sections that had previously been cut off were now attached to the Ghetto: Dubrove, Palne and also one side of Vilna Street near Dubrove. The Christians, who had already settled themselves in those houses, had to (what a pity) move again. The sick and the wounded were placed in the Ghetto hospital and the "healthy" ones (Jews) were driven to work. During their labor the Germans, as we have already told, took revenge on the Jews. Their wild vexations are difficult to understand by a sane mind.

[Page 153]

In the summer and fall of 1942 there was no hunger in the Ghetto as far as nourishment is concerned. The Germans themselves made all kinds of combined "businesses" and would secretly provide products: potatoes and flour and for them they would be paid in cash. The same applied to shoes and other items. The refugees though, as was mentioned, had arrived completely naked and did not have the wherewithal to buy anything. The Judenrat opened for them a soup kitchen in the hospital. Also, the Glubokie Jews fed the refugees on a daily basis, and very often for a number of weeks.

In this time of trouble and calamities each one searched for hope and the promise of redemption. Redemption, at that time, meant a victory of the Red Army over our oppressors - the Germans.

In the Ghetto, when the sounds of planes were heard, moods would become very lively. Jews wouldn't sleep entire nights in order to listen to the hum of motors in the air. What a great joy it was for the Jews, when, in July 1943, a month before the extermination of all the Jews, when a large Soviet squadron of planes bombed the German garrison in Berezvetsh, 2 kilometers from the city. Unfortunately, the bombing did not damage the Germans. The bombs fell in a field on soft ground and did not explode. After the attack the Germans ordered the Jews to remove those bombs that had been buried and hadn't exploded. The "heroes" themselves, fled from that dangerous place, fearing an explosion.

After assembling all of the Jews from the fields and forests in the Ghetto, they began to bring at the end of the summer of 1942, boards, barbed wire and posts in order to enclose the Ghetto. This put even more pressure upon the already choking Jews. Since they were already imprisoned and except for the forced labor couldn't leave the Ghetto anyway, this upset everyone. This was "a favor to the Jews" in the words of the official, Hebel. It did not calm anyone, even though he assured the Jews that it was meant for the various Germans and policemen who previously were able to enter the Ghetto at will. Now they would no longer have free access to the Ghetto. The Jews knew it was a lie but there was nothing that could be done about it anyway. The Jews themselves had to carry out the work. With their own hands they had to build the "box" for themselves.

[Page 154]

For a full two months the Jews worked on it, and in November 1942 a high, thick fence, topped by several rolls of barbed wire encircled the entire Ghetto. The Ghetto now consisted of the north side of Vilna Street, the east half of Dubrove, the east half of Palne, Nei-Legianav (Kisheleike), Druyer, (Lomzsher) Street and the south side of Bialistaker (lower) Street. You could enter and leave the Ghetto by only one gate, which was set up at the boundary of Nei-Kisheleike and Vilna Streets. a policeman stood on guard at the gate day and night...he was attached to the German auxiliary Police. When the Jews returned from their labor at night, the policeman, to make sure that they weren't carrying any products into the Ghetto searched them. If they would find a bit of milk in a bottle, a couple of eggs, a piece of cheese, or even some green vegetable, that person's fate was already sealed. He was no longer allowed into the Ghetto. He was taken to the Police where he was shot.

The Germans also desecrated the Jewish Cemetery. They forced the Jews to break down the fence with their own hands, to cut down all of the trees, to tear up and break the tombstones. With these tombstones the Germans built a theatre in Glubokie. Velvel Leibl, the son of Maznik from Senkevitsh Street would often tell, with great bitterness about this desecration of the cemetery...He was a religious Jew, together with other Jews, he was forced to carry the destruction of the cemetery....

A portion of the youth escaped into the forest to tie up with Partisan groups, but these were only individuals. A mass exodus could not even be talked about. Larger groups could not even exit the Ghetto. The Germans and the Police hovered on all sides, and if one managed to escape from the Hell, his relatives were killed. Here for example is such an incident: In December., 1942, someone named Motke Berchan (who worked in the "Vagenbau" at 75 Vilna Street) heard (in the Judenrat), that the family of Eli Gordon (Becker) is in danger of being killed, because their son, Hirshke Gordon, fled to the forest. Berchan told this secret to Gordon and his wife; they, and their two younger daughters and a small son, Mishal, stole out of the Ghetto, without anything, naked, barely with their souls, in the middle of the night and disappeared. Immediately the Gordon's older daughter was arrested (Hinde), together with her husband, Shabbtai Catkin, (from Kisheleike) and were shot, leaving two infants without care. The impression that this made on the Ghetto is easy to imagine... If someone were merely suspected of harboring the thought of fleeing the Ghetto, he was immediately placed in the basement of the Judenrat, which was in the house of Yaakov Olmer. (This was done for protection) In the winter of 1942-43 the situation became such that everyone in the Ghetto found himself under the supervision of the Judenrat. The Jewish Police and Jews in general, looked out for each other, to see to it that no one should flee the Ghetto. It had been proven that "all are responsible for each other", and that the community is responsible for the individual. In the big, long dark fall and winter nights, the Jews, according to the orders of the Judenrat, would patrol the entire perimeter of the Ghetto (from the inside, naturally)

[Page 155]

They carefully watched that under the cover of might, no one should steal himself out of the Ghetto and flee into the woods.

There were cases when the "night-watch" would catch someone who was fleeing the Ghetto, and on the morrow he was taken to the Judenrat where he was installed in the cellar together with his entire family, and the watch was reinforced in general. In this way, the Judenrat once caught, on the Jewish cemetery, a group of 30 people. They had already managed to escape from the Ghetto, and they were planning to stealthily flee into the forest. Among them, according to the report, there was Chana Shnell (a seamstress, who was one of the managers of the women's seamstress workshop), Chaim-Leib Shulheifer (pharmacist), Marusye Levin (a daughter-in-law of Yisrael Chaves) and tier brother-in-law, Moshe Chaves (a doctor), Gildin (a pharmacist from Luzshki) and others. The Jewish Police kept the entire group under careful watch and brought them back to the Ghetto. The Judenrat did not make a big deal out of this, because they feared that the Germans might find out about it.

Jews looked out for each other, to make sure that no one left the Ghetto and head for the woods. In March 1943 they came to Shulevitsh's house, where the knitting establishment was located, a peasant, and asked that Deborah Ruderman be called out. She was the mother of the Partisan, Yenkl Ruderman. Immediately the Jewish Police Commissar, Yude Blant, found out about it and came running quickly and tore from the hand of Mrs. Ruderman a slip of paper which the peasant had managed to give her from her son in the forest. Before she had a chance to read it, he wanted to seize and turn over the messenger, the peasant, to the German Gendarmes, but he mounted his horse and fled. And Deborah was deposited in the cellar of the Judenrat. The contents of the note, which her son had sent from the forest, remained a secret. It's possible that this note could have prevented the later death of Mrs. Ruderman herself, and maybe also of others.

[Page 156]

With each passing day the Jews in the Ghetto, became more and more broken. The theme of everyone's conversation was the same: destruction, shooting, when and where they would be annihilated... The more religious Jews would pray during their free time, recite Psalms, and study. Some would fast every Monday and Thursday (Shalom Weinstein and others). They could see that the tragedy was coming, as a punishment from Heaven for sins... Some on the other hand drove out every thought of despair and turned to drink. "It's all the same" they argued. "We will be killed!" There were also to be found naive Jews, who wanted to believe the Germans, that the Jews of Glubokie are "an exception", are useful and therefore no evil would befall upon them.

They choked off the evil thoughts about the eventual genocide within themselves and believed in a miracle. Maybe from somewhere the Red Army will break through, or some powerful partisan group would free them. It is impossible to convey the mood of the Jews, their frame of mind in the sealed off Ghetto, cut off from the entire world, where they sat and waited for death. He, who himself tasted the German Hell, can only grasp it. but he who had the great privilege not to gaze upon the German beast, cannot, under any circumstances, understand it. Because the sufferings endured by those unfortunates in the Ghetto, were beyond human reason, and people in a healthy, normal environment cannot envision it at all.

[Page 157]

The First Glubokie' Partisans

Translated by Eilat Gordin Levitan

It was the spring of 1942, some groups of young people from Glubokie by now began to look for ways to gather arms and flee to the forest. They devoted themselves to the task, being extremely secretive and cautious, even prepared for casualties to achieve it. For instance, a Hadutzishker (Reuven Yachelson) managed to get employed in the Gendarmerie. He was able to steal arms from there. He became attached to a Partisan group "Mastitel" (takers of revenge), to whom he sent the arms. He worked all summer and fall transferring arms to the resistance until a gendarme noticed him and shot him.

The task that Yaakov Friedman took in the matter of acquiring arms, was not any less vital. He would ride through the villages dress in a policeman clothes, and obtain arms there, in various ways, arms which he also sent to the above-mentioned Partisan group. He worked like this until the fall of 1942, when he himself joined up with the resistance group.

He later distinguished himself in the battle against the Germans, until the arrival of the Red Army.

The son-in-law of Moshe Berkan deserves much credit for providing the Partisans with arms. He would buy guns, grenades, revolvers and transferred them to the Partisans in the forest. Eventually he paid for this with his life. The Police found out about it and came to the Ghetto to arrest him. He was not easily arrested. He seized a policeman's gun, removed the firing pin, and fled to the forest. But since they wanted to kill his wife, child and relatives in place of him, he couldn't save himself and let them die. He gave himself up to the murderers, to prevent this. After horrible tortures, they killed him.

Klianer of Lutshaier street also worked intensively for the resistance. During the entire period of the summer and autumn of 1942 he also gathered arms, until he fled from the Ghetto into the forest. Even as he was fleeing, he grabbed the gun from a German who was standing guard, knocked him unconscious, and swiftly disappeared.

In spite of militant and heroic stance, the youth, often did not have the fortuity to oppose the wild German beast They would mostly seek ways in which to hinder the savage murderers in their diabolical plan and revenge the innocent blood that was spilled. Bamke Genichovitsh, the young man from Plisse, sought revenge for the murder of his father in this way. He constantly lie in ambush for the German Kapenberg, who killed his father in the town of Plisse. Kapenberg was alerted to the fact that the son of his victim is hiding somewhere in the forest and wants to take revenge on him. He watched out for him… however, young Genichovitsh was much more refined than the German bandit and searching for him ceaselessly he once encountered him on the road from Plisse to Glubokie, where he killed him on the spot.

[Page 158]

The same Bamke Genichovitsh, also took revenge on the folks-German woman, Ida Aditzka, who was responsible for many Jewish victims. She was also very active in the expeditions against the Partisans. She participated in the slaughter of Jews in Psuye, Prozarok, Plisse, Glubokie and others. She killed dozens of Jewish children. (see the section "The destruction of the Second Ghetto in Glubokie") She had also murdered Rutshakavsky, the former chairman of "Selsovet". Once, when this German woman was found in Koshtziol, Genichovitsh and some of his comrades dressed in German clothes and went cautiously into Koshtziol. There they "made her acquaintance" and invited her to go for a walk. She became quite intrigued with the young cavaliers and went walking with them into a wood.

This was all that they wanted. There, they tied her to a tree, recited to her all of her misdeeds, and then killed her.

The youth began to search for ways to escape to the forest and make contact with the Partisans as soon as it became known in Glubokie that there were Partisans in the forest. Partisans who attack German units, and interfere with their devilish deeds, kill Germans on the roads, cut lines of communication, and alike. Ignoring the arduous and dangerous conditions, which were associated with the resistance, several groups manage to flee to the forest. To do this they had to have boundless courage and heroism, because there were pitfalls at every step of the way.

Local Police and the Germans constantly patrolled the Ghetto. Whoever tried to leave could easily fall into the hands of the German Gestapo. Besides this, according to the rumors from the Judenrat, secret agents were planted in the Ghetto. They reported everything concerning what was going on in the Ghetto to the Germans. Besides which, when the Germans would find out about some that fled, many innocents who stayed behind might pay with their lives. Outside of the Ghetto, Jews who would be met by civilian peasants, might be killed by them, or turned over to the Germans.

[Page 159]

Many such incidents took place. After all, those who fled did not know where to go, where to look for the Partisans, and many times instead of coming to them, it was easy to fall into the "trap" of the German beast. (You couldn't ask anybody, because you didn't know whom to trust. The peasants themselves did not hesitate at times, to inflict troubles on the Jews and even kill them.)

And even so, ignoring all of this, in the summer of 1942, a group of young people, disguised and armed, left the Ghetto and joined up with the Partisans. The first pioneer Partisans of Glubokie were: Avner Feigelman - called Alyasha (before the war he was a flax gatherer for Lederman). He went with an organized group on the morrow after the slaughter of the 2500 Jews, into the forest. 'They were among the first group of young men, who fell upon the bloody enemy with their full impact and fought heroically. In this group there was also Itshke Blatt (son of Leibel Blatt of Gomzsher Street), who became a commander in the Partisan Brigade of Tshapayev. Blatt distinguished himself with his sharp sense, boldness, determination and fleetness. He would cast fear on the peasants in those woods, and they ceased their ill treatment of Jews. Blatt was called the "lion of the forest"… In this first group there was also Barke Shapiro (son of Yashke Shapiro of Senkevitsh Street), a girl from Disne, named Chasia and others.

In September of 1942 an armed group of 17 men left the ghetto, among whom there were Ber Katzavitsh and Iza (Moshe Katzavitsh's grandsons), Zalye Milchman (the teacher Milchman's son), Yachelman, Michael Feigel, Yenki Ruderman, Yerachmiel Milkin, David Glezer and others. This group, while still in the Ghetto, was in contact with the Partisan Brigade, "Mastitel", and sent them arms. In September, they joined them. They were in the forest near the village of Univyer, in the Miadler region. From this village a certain Stefan Samasianek, actively helped in the organization of the Partisans in the region.

[Page 160]

The situation in the Ghetto became very strained after this group of 17 Jews left. The Germans and the Police now guarded even more diligently. It was declared that the families would be personally responsible for those who fled to the forest, which meant that for the "sins" of the children the parents would be held responsible and pay with their life. This frightened the youth very much, but their activities did not cease. They prepared arms and did not stop organizing an escape. Another group of 18 Jews left two months later; among whom were to be found: Yisrael Shparber, Moshe Feigel and Sonye, Hirshl Gordon, Shimon Soloveitshik, Hirsh Israelev and both sons of the Jewish elder, Yerucham and Motke Lederman. In the Ghetto there arose panic. They speculated that this would be costly, and that there would be a bloodbath. Unfortunately, they were right. A few days after the 18 had gone, the Gendarmes and Police encircled the homes of the families of Sane Milkin and Feige Feigelson drove everyone out, took them to the Police where they underwent terrible turtures the entire night, and in the morning they were all shot. Fourteen people in the two families died for that transgression, which their children had perpetrated by going into the forest. The fear that seized everyone cannot be measured. Everyone waited to be taken away... People trembled at their own shadow. They tried to avoid their own homes and would not sleep during the nights.

Because Lederman's sons had gone into the forest the unease increased. If the Jewish Elder's sons flee, then maybe not only their family would suffer, but possibly the entire Ghetto. This could cause a slaughter on a large scale, or the entire Ghetto might be destroyed in one fell swoop! This is how everyone interpreted the situation. These were the comments, and everyone went about depressed. All searched for a place to hide, where to bury oneself. But there was no place where one could save his soul. Whosoever had the smallest safe hiding place outside of the Ghetto, left his home for the night.

Lederman, The Jewish Elder, went to the Minister, Hochman, and told him everything about his great tragedy, asking him to help return his "straying" sons from the Partisans.

[Page 161]

The Minister was so "loveable" and he "involved himself in Lederman's bitter situation. He gave him a permit to ride through the fields in the area and look for his sons. Lederman immediately sent two Jews, Eli Gordon and Mulye Soloveitshik (incidentally, their sons were already in the forest also) to the Miadler region to look for and bring back his sons. Lederman made this matter into one of principle, a serious matter, one in which everybody in the Ghetto must be interested - the fate of everyone, he announced, will hang on whether or not his sons would be brought home. In the Ghetto, Lederman's sons became a matter of life and death. All awaited the messengers impatiently, to see what they would bring. And in about two weeks there was suddenly spread the news that they had returned in peace and brought with them Lederman's two sons. With them there also came Hirshele Israelev - a quilter. The Ghetto breathed more freely, but in spite of it the calm did not last, because everyone waited to see how the authorities would react to the Ledermans in particular and to the public - will there be victims, how many and who will they be?

Fortunately for that time, the Commissar Grod was on leave and his replacement was a bit more humane, so Lederman found him to be a bit softer in accepting bribes and other formalities in order rehabilitate the "bad deed" committed by Lederman's sons. He was ordered that they be beaten, and with this their punishment was complete.

For their punishment, the substitute for Grod, the person in charge of Jewish Affairs, Hebel (a frightening devourer of Jews), Chief of the Gendarmarie, Kern, and other high ranking military and administrative officials, gathered in the Ghetto. All the Ghetto Jews were ordered to the Judenrat, and before this gathering, the "culprits" Lederman's two sons and H. Israelev were beaten. This was only for show because Lederman's sons had been told earlier to put on heavier trousers, and then they were beaten lightly. The Jewish policeman, Michael Shapiro, carried out this function. Then Grod's representative made a speech and said that, thanks to the fact that Lederman himself had reported the incident involving his children, and had carried out activities to bring them back, their lives had been spared. He added that for every Jew who allows himself to escape to the forest, first of all his family would be killed and afterwards the entire Ghetto would suffer. This announcement worked.

The Jews strictly guarded each other. The patrols of the Jews themselves was strengthened in the Ghetto by the Judenrat and twice each night the patrols circling the Ghetto boundary were changed. Jews circled the perimeter on the inside of the fence the entire night and watched to see that no one should sneak out of the Ghetto in the darkness of the night. There was a guard of Germans on the outside, beside the guarding of the Jews on the inside, so that the Ghetto was sealed hermetically, and to be able to get out was practically impossible.

[Page 162]

The Arrest of Moshe Abramovitz

Translated by Eilat Gordin Levitan

Moshe A as was mentioned previously, was the manager of a confectionery factory, which also made marmalade and certain drinks for the Germans. He proved and was "recognized" by the Germans to be an excellent tradesman. They even allowed him to live outside of the ghetto, in the city for a greater length of time..

Suddenly, in February of 1943, the Germans arrested him. Everyone in the Ghetto was very disturbed by the news of his arrest. It became known later the reason for his arrest. It was because he, at the advice of someone named Gebeshn (the son of the Sharkavshtziner, Dr. A. Galitzianer), with the help of a German Officer, Kardiel, attempted to falsify a document, stating that his mother was not Jewish and therefore he was not a born Jew. He thought that in this way he could save himself, as an "Aryan". The Germans found out about this, and they immediately arrested him and the German, Kardiel, they turned over to the court in Minsk. Local Germans, friends of Kardiel, made an effort to keep the matter a local one, and they were successful. This change of venues also benefited Abramovitsh. His family, like all Jews in such predicaments, waited for Abramovitsh to be freed. But to tear oneself from the German claws was something that seldom happened and so it was in this case also. The Germans promised to free him for a large sum of gold. When Mrs. Abramovitsh and his other relatives finally assembled the sum that had been demanded, the Germans still did not release him, using the excuse that the clearing of Kardiel (the clearing of Abramovitz depended on it) still had to be confirmed in Rega. (This, of course, was but an excuse.)

[Page 163]

The end of the matter was that the Germans dragged out the release of Abramovitz from day to day. in that way it dragged on until the 20th of August 1943, until the day of the destruction of the entire Ghetto of Glubokie, together with all other Jews, and with the rest of his family (wife, children and parents), Abramovitsh also was killed.

The Germans Arrest the Judenrat Elder; Gershon Lederman

Translated by Eilat Gordin Levitan

In the disheartening Ghetto nightmare, the Jews constantly tried to figure out and predict what was taking place around them. What the Jewish elder, Gershon Lederman is up to? Each time when he would bring gifts, First, to the German High Command and then to the chief of the Gendarmerie, and then to ail the other bloodsuckers, (this would occur on a daily basis) the Jews would impatiently await his return. They awaited the news he would bring for the Ghetto, whether or not there was some new decree. They would simply look into his eyes and from them they would attempt to fathom the "truth", because he would not always want to divulge the evil, in order to not create panic among the Jews.

At the end of February 1943, Lederman, as a result of such a "visit", did not return home to the Ghetto. Evening came, night fell…. The family and relatives waited with great impatience and Lederman did not show up. The entire Ghetto didn't know yet about this, but those who did know became very despondent: They exchanged secrets; they that something isn't right. No one was permitted to go out of the Ghetto. It is already late at night and Lederman hasn't returned.

In the morning of the next day three Germans, dressed in civilian clothing, came into the Ghetto. Inquiring as to the whereabouts of Lederman's home. The Policeman, Michael Shapiro took them there, and they took away Lederman's wife, Henie Raize, his three children: Yerucham, Motke and Rivke. The Germans calmed the Ledermans. They said that they were taking them to their husband and father and they would all be set free together in a short while. The small daughter, Rivke, they freed on the way, and she returned to the Ghetto. His wife and two sons the Germans took to the park on Senkevitsh Street. The young men immediately understood what was taking place, that the Germans are deceiving them, so they tore themselves away and began to run. The Germans shot at them and the oldest was slightly wounded. Escaping the Germans, the Ledermans came running back into the Ghetto. From Yerucham there flowed a slight stream of blood the entire way. He did not enter by way of the gate, but jumped over the high fence at an out of the wayside. In the Ghetto itself they disappeared, and no one knew where they were.

[Page 164]

From early morn the entire Ghetto, was already "on wheels". Everyone knew that Lederman was arrested, and that his family had also been taken away. Everyone became frightened. This was a Shabbat morning before Purim and the older Jews fled from their prayers and hid. They thought that, after Lederman demise, there would quickly follow the end of the entire Ghetto. Lederman, who according to everyone's reasoning was untouchable, had been arrested! The only Jew, who would meet face to face with the Germans and who would bring with him, into the Ghetto, at least some comfort by telling-in the name of the Germans, that the Glubokie Jews are "privileged". They will not be killed. Now he was taken away. And now the last pillar fell the only support was gone.... What can there be now? The fear was indescribable. People ran about as if fleeing a fire, disturbed, not knowing what to do with themselves, with their little children, whom their mothers led by their hands or clasped in their arms. They ran about as if drugged.

A member of the Judenrat who often accompanied Lederman; Zalman Rubashkin (when the latter would bring to the Germans packages of Jewish belongings and goods - Rubashkin used to help him carry), girded his courage and went to German headquarters to find out what had happened to the Jewish Elder, G. Lederman. He found out, that the S. D. from Vilejka arrested Lederman for the "sins" of his sons, who had earlier run to the "Partisans" but had in fact, already been rehabilitated (see above). Rubashkin was assured that the arrest of Lederman had nothing whatsoever to do with the Ghetto and that the Jews can be completely calm. Even if Lederman will not be released so quickly, in a few days a new Jewish Elder will be appointed in the Glubokie Ghetto. This information had a somewhat calming effect. The Germans kept their word this time. A few days later Zalman Rubashkin was appointed Jewish Elder in place of Lederman. He also carried out as Lederman had, the function of bringing on a daily basis, gifts to German headquarters. Rubashkin would also be awaited impatiently, when he would return from the Germans. They would await for him hoping for some good news, to be consoled, to be given assurance... Regretfully, Rubashkin could not bring them any good news, even though he always tried to create an optimistic attitude... The deeds of the Germans in the Ghetto, the daily tragic reality did not permit, even for a short while, to forget the true situation, in which the Jews found themselves.

[Page 165]

Translator's notes:

Lederman Gershon (Chanoch): Gershon Lederman was born in 1907 to Khava and Meir. He was a merchant and married to Chila. Prior to WWII he lived in Glebokie, Poland. Gershon died in 1943 in the Shoah. This information is based on a Page of Testimony submitted on 02/08/1956 by his nephew; Lebenbaum Avraham

Leiderman Gene/ Chila: Gene Leiderman nee Khvas was born in Glubokie, Poland to Ishrol and Sose. She was married to Gershon. Prior to WWII she lived in Glubokie, Poland. During the war was in Glubokie, Poland. Gene died in 1943 in Glubokie, Poland. This information is based on a Page of Testimony submitted by her sister-in-law Khvas Roza

Leiderman Yerukhem: Yrukhem Leiderman was born in Glubokie, Poland in 1923 to Gershn and Chila/ Gene Khvas. Prior to WWII he lived in Glubokie, Poland. During the war was in Glubokie, Poland. Yrukhem died in 1943 in Glubokie, Poland at the age of 20. This information is based on a Page of Testimony submitted by Khvas Roza

[Page 165]

The Germans Swallow Jewish Victims

Translated by Eilat Gordin Levitan

We are unable to elaborate on the details of each and every carnage that transpired in the Ghetto. We will still make an effort to record a sample of the killings.

- We already mentioned in a prior chapter how according to the Germans, it was a crime to help the suffering prisoners of war, who in our area were brought to Berezvetsh. The Kazliners, who lived not far from the "prisoner of war camp," ignored the decree. They couldn't withstand the temptation to help. The Kazliner family would bring bread for the prisoners. They would do it secretly, thinking that no one would find out about it. The Germans did notice it, and they took all of them into the nearby wood and shot them. The common grave of eight martyrs of the family is
    - found near the graves of the prisoners in Berezvetsh Forest not far from the monastery.
    - Rumors spread that the engineer Max Ostrovsky was arrested. The Jews were already in the Ghetto at that point. His wife and brother in-law, the dentist

Yash, ran about seeking advice and strategies how to rescue him. Nothing helped. A few days later it became known that Ostrovsky is no longer amongst the living. They searched for reasons or some crimes he committed as the reason he was killed, and none could be found. By nature, he was a quiet, calm man. Some tried to explain it by the fact that he had held a position as an engineer with the Soviets and had worked in Berezvetsh, near Glubokie. Only later did we become aware of the fact that a certain Lablanka, a White Russian neighbor, was responsible for his murder. Later Lablanka was a policeman. Lablanka was angry with him, and in this way he got even. This had taken place early on. The Jews were still "naïve," they didn't understand yet that people could kill someone for no reasons whatsoever. To spill innocent human blood was incomprehensible for them. They were very upset by the events, until a new carnage occured and the fresh victims made them forget the "old one".

[Page 166]

- The "Leshnitzi" (forest overseer) Shell rode through the city in April of 1943. He was a tall, healthy looking, broad shouldered German, with a full reddish face, wearing a green hat with long feathers. He was riding along the street and shooting to the right and left and to all sides. This episode of the wild German beast cost some Jewish victims. One of them was the young boy, Mishal Chavkin. He stood in the courtyard of Nathan Gitelson talking to an acquaintance. A stray bullet of Shell's hit and critically wound him. He suffered for six weeks and died with frightful pains. He was an only son to his parents. Also wounded by Shell was Haberkorn, the former teacher in the Jewish Trade School in Glubokie; a Jew from Beldyuke and others.

- During Passover of 1943 the spilling of Jewish blood occurred again. It happened in this way: Zalman Fleisher had served as a guard in the local White Russian compound. He used to meet there with his Christian acquaintances, and with some of them he conducted "business" - exchanging things for food products. The Gendarmerie found out that Fleisher bought a piece of butter from a Christian and wanted to arrest him for it. The chief of the Gendarmes, Kern, sent the Gendarmes into the Ghetto and Fleisher became aware of it and hid. They decided to take three other Jews in his place. This was during one of the Passover nights. According to Drisviatzky, a young man and great scholar, and his 16-year-old son, Chloine, the escapee was being escorted in the evening by Lipa Landau, who had fled from a slaughter pit in June of 1942, when his wife and children were killed. Landau, a Jew who was ordained and had a higher education, was having dinner with Drisviatzky. As mentioned, he was a deep Talmudist, mathematician and linguist. After dinner he left the house with his son to accompany Landau and engaged his guest in Torah conversation and wisdom. At that moment the Gendarmes came into the Ghetto and seized the three of them and took them away. Mrs. Drisviatsky and her other son, Moshe, waited in vain, thinking that they would soon return. They never returned... Feeling that a great tragedy had occurred, all night Moshe quietly watched the ghetto. When it began to dawn a bit, he saw through the fence how the three victims were being escorted by the Germans to the "Barak", a wooded area in which they would regularly carry out their murders. The policemen told how the arrested Jews cried and prayed the entire night, (saying the final confession). Prophetically they were saying goodbye to each other, in such a manner that it even made an impression upon the policemen... the murderers, who bathe themselves in Jewish blood, couldn't come to themselves and talked about it for a long while. (Drisviatzky's oldest son, Yehoshua, was murdered before Passover, 1942.)

[Page 167]

- A large number of people in the Ghetto were executed in the months of April and May 1943, for "speculation". They caught them with products, which they used to bring with them into the Ghetto, when they returned from their labor. Their sentence had been sealed beforehand. In this way, at the beginning of May, there were shot, the butcher, Shalom Tzentziper, by whom they found a hen clutched to his bosom. A few weeks later, his son Shepsel was shot without cause. (In the Ghetto they had already stopped asking for "reasons", because they had become used to such happenings. They became so used to it that they cease looking for excuses....

- Police came into the tricot factory at the end of May 1943. In the middle of the day, they took out Libe Krapivnik, who, naked and barefoot had barely escaped from the slaughters in Vilna in 1942. Her mother and other relatives ran to the Judenrat, to the Jewish Police, crying and pleading, shaking the world, but nothing helped. She and other "criminals" were taken to the "Barak" and shot.

- The bloody German, Heinliat, (a young shkotz) found out in May that the blacksmith, Shlomo Kreines of 71 Vilna Street, had shoed a horse belonging to a peasant he was acquainted with. He ordered that Kreines be immediately arrested, and he was also taken to the "Barak" and shot. He was not the only victim that this Heinliat murdered. During the summer of 1943, he noticed the 10-year-old boy, the son of the tailor Zelik Glassman, carrying in a kerchief some berries. In general berries and green vegetables were forbidden to Jews. Heinliat chased the boy. The boy was swift and managed to escape and hide. Heinliat ordered the Jews to search for the "criminal" threatening that he would shoot dozens of Jews in place of the boy. By a miracle we escaped only with a scare at the time, and with a nice "gift" of beating. There were no victims as a result of this incident.

- At the same time the wife of Zalman-Velvel Ruderman was shot. Once when she returned from her labor, at the Ghetto gate they found that she was carrying two concealed eggs, which she wanted to "smuggle" into the Ghetto.

- At the beginning of June, the coachman Abraham Budav went out in the evening after curfew, to close the shutters of the shoemakers' workshop on Vilna Street (Minushkin's house), where he served as a watchman. By chance a policeman noticed this. Budav wanted to bribe the policeman and gave him his gold watch. The policeman took the gold watch and took Budav to the Police Station, from where he was taken to the grave in the "Barak"... Nathan Kraut, the former official of Bir-Zavod, was carrying a sack with a bit of salt on a day at the end of June, 1943. Goldberg, a German who was responsible for inspections, noticed this and stopped him. Kraut began to run; Goldberg shot and wounded him. Policemen came immediately, dragged him away to the station, where they finished him off. A man named Katz, from Sventzian, was murdered at the same time. He was a chauffeur for the Germans and was close to them. He was envied in the Ghetto, since his family's safety was secure, or so everyone thought. He was a sort of official by the Germans, people deluded themselves that as long as he still kept his family in the Ghetto, then perhaps the situation is not so terrible. or better still, Jews wanted to delude themselves, deep down they knew the gravity of their situation. One day Katz drove into the Ghetto at night and quietly removed his wife, children and mother-in-law. Shultz, a German chauffeur acquaintance of his, , told him secretly that something was going to " happen" in the Ghetto, some mass slaughter. When it was discovered in the morning that he was gone, a terrible fright seized everyone in the Ghetto. This was because Katz was considered an insider and must know what was to happen.

This was a repetition of the Lederman affair, only with greater confusion. Again, people ran to hide, and whosoever was able to, fled from the Ghetto. (True, even outside the Ghetto there was no safe place to go, but that wasn't even considered...). There was no way out. As always, the Judenrat blindly believed in the good promises of the German officials, that there would be no slaughters in Glubokie. Immediately, in the morning they went to Headquarters and told about the fear and the panic which had been created and asked what was going to happened. The messenger was calmed and told to calm all the Jews. "The-rumors are but a provocation, for which those responsible will be pursued". They kept their word. A punishment was carried out. But not against the German, Shultz, who had fabricated the rumor, but against Katz. The latter was immediately arrested. They found where his wife, children and mother-in-law were hidden and took them to the "Barak" to be shot.

- Approximately the same time, they arrested the Genda-Yaakov Krashnevsky, who according to the ploy (see above) would stand guard at night to see to it that no Jew should, God forbid, sneak out of the ghetto. The Judenrat immediately intervened on his behalf and vigorously explained his "important mission" that he carried out, and they freed him. A few days later he was seized again, sent to the "Barak" and shot.

- They also shot Salye Brown, because they had found out that she was on friendly terms with a Christian young man by the name of Vitye Sharaveika.

- Not a single day passed without some victims. On a July day the local Police caught someone named Salye (or Beryl) Sverdlin, who was leading a cow. People who never lived in a "Ghetto world" cannot imagine how great a crime this appeared to be. This wasn't a hen, or a pair of eggs, or a beet. This was a whole cow... The Germans with their great refinement, with their entire "Kultur" of torturingpeople, were unable in the case of Sverdlin, to think up a suitable punishment. Shooting him or hanging him could be done only once. That's what was done for a hen, for a pair of eggs, as had been done to Tzentziper and Ruderman. They tortured him until he lost his senses and afterwards shot him. They couldn't do any more. The impression remained, however, that Sverdlin had not been punished enough for his "crime".

- At the same time, they also murdered the 60-year-old Mote Gurvitsh (Mote Yude-Itshes of Kisheleike). His crime? He was driven out to clean the street, and from the distance he greeted a peasant acquaintance of his.

- At the beginning of July 1943, a Michael Alperovitsh and his wife, Bertha (refugees from Kurenets?) arranged with a railroad official, that he should lead them into the forest to the Partisans. They went to the agreed upon place on the road to Konstantinova. There, awaited them "scouts" to show them the way. They led them into the forest, but instead of taking them to the Partisans they took them to the Germans, who murdered them on the spot.

- At the same time, Shimon Godin, without any reason at all, was taken from his labor at the electric station. The young man was first taken to the Police, and a few days later to the "Barak' where he was shot.

- A few weeks later, Velvel Godin, his father, was killed. His death came about in a completely "original" fashion. In the middle of the day Velvel Godin walked to his labor on Vilna Street (not far from the former synagogue of the Raiak brothers). Yaremek, a local baker, drove up in his truck and on purpose drove fast into Godin and crushed him to death. If Yaremek had done it "playfully" or he had a grudge against Godin - is not known. The fact was that Godin was left lying dead on the road in a puddle of blood and Yaremek rode merrily away with a smile on his lips. The face of that local bandit expressed his true pleasure. A former neighbors of Jews and "friend of Jews" had felt such joys from his deed. (In the city he knew all of the Jews and all of the Jews knew him.)

- Over and above the fact that everyone was already used to the senseless murder of the Glubokie Jews, the incident with Godin made an especially strong impression. First; because of the fact that a local inhabitant committed this, someone who lived together with the Jews for many long years, and secondly because the dead man's crushed body was brought to his home, and his large family began to eulogize him. The cries could be heard over the entire Ghetto, and everyone's bloody wounds were reopened. And the entire Ghetto was engulfed in one great wailing - and the wailing and crying multiplied...

- Yoshke Feigelson (a flour and grain merchant from Rain's family on Vilna Street) was taken away in the middle of June 1943. The Germans took him for the crime that his two sons, Zalman and Don, had joined the Partisans. Their mother and younger brother, Labele, the sons took out of the Ghetto into the forest, but the father refused to go, so he paid for it with his life in the Ghetto. (Later the mother died in the forest. The circumstances aren't known). The Germans were not satisfied with only one victim. At night They took from their beds, his sister, Sarah, and her daughter, Nechama Ram. They kept them overnight in Police Headquarters, and at dawn, took them to the "Barok" and murdered them. A few weeks later, Christians saw the dug-up corpse of Nechama Ram at the grave, that had been attacked by dogs. The brothers, Zalman and Done, were active Partisans in the "Panamarenka" Brigade, in the forests of West-Belarus. They distinguished themselves in their fighting against the Germans.

- Pinye Yungelson and his nephew, Leibl Yungelson had worked for several months for the official in charge of national interests, Habel. At first everything went "well". They served the Germans, worked with all their might, even though their masters tired them as much as possible. In July 1943 one early morning, they were seized at work. Habel's wife thundered that the Jews had stolen butter from her. This was a slander. The truth was entirely different. Leib Yungelson had taken a revolver, with the intention of fleeing at night, from the Ghetto into the woods. Label's wife saw this and tried to hide the truth. When the Gendarmes came to arrest the Yungelsons, Leibl fell upon them with the revolver. The Gendarmes quickly disarmed him and took them both away.

- Hebel's wife wanted the Jews to suffer a horrible death. She wanted them to set up, in the middle of the Ghetto, two posts with hooks in them so that the two be hanged by the neck on the hooks. When this became known in the Ghetto, it made life so unpleasant, that everyone was envious of those who were lying in the "Barok", murdered. These two Jews were relatives of the Commandant of the Jewish Police, Yude Blant, and he turned worlds to assure that they wouldn't be killed in such a way. The Jews gathered up a great deal of gold and jewelry and delivered it to the German, Habel, and barely managed to convince him that the Jews be punished in the "normal fashion". The Yungelsons were taken to the "Barok", where they were murdered, as usual, by being shot... It may sound strange, but as a result of this outcome the Jews of the Ghetto could "breathe easier"...

[Page 172]

- The Germans learned that Fleisher's wife and her two grown daughters were in the Ghetto. Even though, for Fleisher's "crime", there had already been victims (see above), the Germans came into the Ghetto at night. They broke the fence at the point where it was opposite the Fleisher home, and did not come in through the gate. They dragged from their beds the naked Mrs. Fleisher and her two daughters (very beautiful girls), took them to the "Barak" and shot them. On the morrow it was told in the Ghetto how the women had pleaded with their murderers; from their crying stones could have come apart. On these hangmen it made no impression, and they carried on their work calmly and completely.

- A week after murdering the Fleishers, policemen came into the Ghetto at night. They used the same way as they had come, when they came for the Fleishers. They took Chanan Pintzov, his wife, Kayle and their 16-year-old daughter. They were taken to prison, and from there to the "Barak" where all three were shot. Mrs Pintzov had been a cook for the Justice Minister's secretary, Guzava. Guzava considered herself a folks German, her husband had been taken out by the Soviets. To this Guzava would often come the Chief of the Gendarmerie, Kern, to while away time. Later Guzava exchanged "lover". She abandoned Kern for the regional commandant. Seeking to avoid encounters with German, Kern Guzava told her cook, Kayle Pintzov, that in case chief Kern should come, she should tell him that her mistress isn't home. And so it was. Kern came into the kitchen and Kayle Pintzov told him that Guzava isn't at home. The German, however, found out that this wasn't so, and at night he drove his Gendarmes into the Ghetto. They broke a hole in the fence right where the Pintzovs lived and unexpectedly they seized the Pintzovs from their beds, took them to the "Barak" and there murdered them.

[Page 173]

- A German officer gave a Mr. Chadshan, from Krulevshchizna In July 1943, a few cans of sardines to sell in the Ghetto. In general, it was the practice that the Germans would steal products and then "do business" with the Jews. They would give the Jews who worked for them, items to sell in the Ghetto, and have them bring the proceeds to them. The Judenrat was afraid that the higher German officials (the biggest crooks) would catch those Germans, the thieves, and they would indicate that they were disposing of their stolen goods in the Ghetto. This would put the entire Ghetto in great danger. When Chadash began bringing the sardines into the Ghetto, the Jewish Ghetto Police warned him not to do it. The German officer, taking the example from similar incidents between Germans and Jews, forced Chadash to sell his sardines in the Ghetto. The Jewish Police once confiscated from Chadash several cans of sardines. He told his officer that he couldn't sell his merchandise because the Jewish Police are frightened and warned him not to bring products into the Ghetto, contrary to German decrees. The Jewish Police told the Justice Minister and he assured them that because of this officer no harm would befall anyone. This officer came to the Judenrat, and there he met Chaim-Ber Gordon (a member of the Judenrat who was responsible for the Jewish Police) and asked that the policeman, Isaac Weinstein be surrendered, because he was the one who had taken the sardines from Chadash. Weinstein hid and Gordon refused to give him up (He trusted the promise of the Justice Minister). The next day Gordon was arrested and turned over to the S. 1). The Judenrat understood that they had been deceived by the promises of the Justice Minister, who, during the entire time of this disagreement with the German, had promised that the officer did not have the authority to do any harm. Gordon thought that he, as a Police official, was untouchable. The Judenrat began to seek ways to approach this officer in order to appease him and still his anger. They sent community leaders and messengers to him, who gave him gold, in order for him to free Gordon. Naturally he took the money, but he did not free Gordon. He was murdered with horrible tortures. First, they broke his fingers in a door, pulled the teeth out of his mouth, and tore the limbs from his body, until he perished.

[Page 174]

- A few days later, Issac Weinstein was seized by the Germans. Also, here all means were tried to save him from the murderers. Again, the German officer (the merchant of these products) was given money and jewels which he took with the promise that he would free him. Weinstein's fate was the same as that of Gordon. They murdered him in a horrible way, with frightful tortures.

- Rachel Pildas, a daughter of Beryl Pildas (Beryl Makar), had in the time of the Soviet occupation, married a Christian, had children by him, and was sure that she was no longer Jewish and would be free of the German troubles. All of the time she had lived outside of the Ghetto. The Germans had a different opinion about this situation. According to them she was truly Jewish. She was arrested once and her husband managed to ransom her. He would bribe the Police, and they would ignore the facts. This situation continued this way until July. 1943. In July the Police came and arrested Rachel and her children, took them into the "Barok" and shot them.

In general, such murders took place without pause during the time of the German occupation. With these many victims it impossible to make a list of all the deliberate murders which could be estimated in the thousands.

We've only verified a few of the incidents, in order to show how cheap Jewish blood was; that for a bit of salt, for a few eggs, for not properly greeting a German soldier, or for no reason at all, they would immediately murder. We will mention one more characteristic incident of murder for not wearing the "yellow badge". This happened to a 17-year-old boy (we don't remember his name), who worked for the Gendarmes in Moshe Kraut's courtyard on Zamkove Street. On a summer morning in 1943, the boy came to work and was met on the street by a Gendarme, who noticed that his "badge" was not sewn on properly to his overcoat (Germans loved order and neatness...). The Gendarme did not think about it for a long while, but, in cold blood drew his revolver and shot the boy. The victim lay in a puddle of blood in the middle of the street until other Jews came by; who were ordered to carry him off and wash away the puddle of blood, so it would be clean. (This made a strong impression even on the Christians and they avoided that street. They no longer made remarks among themselves about Jews.)

[Page 175]

We also want to mention a few incidents when Jews were released from arrest, because the Germans needed them. One incident - in June, 1943, when Vitvitzki, the "Tzirkovetz" arrested Alte Gelman (previously the manicurist), by whom he had found her instruments. Thanks to the fact that she had served the Folk German, Guzave, she made the effort and they freed her. In this way Gelman's life was extended by two months. (Alte Gelman and her sister Sonye, perished during the liquidation of the Glubokie Ghetto).

It is worthwhile mentioning, that the Germans, who would arrest someone and knew that other Germans needed him for some purpose and would make the effort to free him, would murder themselves the one arrested abruptly. This is what happened to the family of Hanan Pinkov, with Pesye Gordon and others.

Another incident reminds us of the teacher, David Pliskin, who worked for Commandant Rosentreter as a translator. Pliskin was able to court the favor of the German and got along with him quite well. The Commandant would give him food from time to time and treated him somewhat better. The German headquarters, where Pliskin worked, was on Zamkove Street, in the former casino. There in the courtyard there grew several blueberry bushes. Once, in June 1943, Pliskin went over to a bush and picked several blueberries. A German engineer noticed it through a small window of a neighboring house, where he was sitting. He was not too lazy to run down to Pliskin, shout at and taunt him with the worst language. At the questions of the engineer, "how come a Jew, allowed himself to pick blueberries", Pliskin, out of fear, answered that Heit, the orderly of the Commandant, allowed him to do so. Heit really wanted to take the blame upon himself and clear Pliskin. The engineer then fell upon Heit, called him a bad German, a truly cultured and intelligent German would never allow a Jew to eat blueberries, and so forth. The "cultured and intelligent" engineer beat Pliskin severely and in a great fit ran into his house to fetch his revolver. During this time the Commandant ran to the Chief of the Gendarmerie, Kern, told him the entire story, and asked that this time his Jew be forgiven for his transgression, since he was very useful to him. Kern could not forgive such a "crime", but, on the other hand, it was difficult to completely ignore the request of the Commandant, and so he agreed substitute a stiff fine in place of the death penalty.

[Page 176]

Kern, at this time, strictly warned that if it should occur again that a Jew eat blueberries, fruit, fat, vegetables and other such delicacies, he would not escape death, which is the punishment for it. This Germans carried out to the letter of the law.

Many Jewish lives were swallowed up by the graves of the "Barok" because of a bit of strawberries, a bit of milk, cream, for not greeting Germans, or for greeting non Germans, for this and for that... because the destroyer had the right... because the "intelligent" Germans, and their local "cultured" cronies couldn't live without spilling blood.

The Radianovtzes Join the Partisans and Fight the Glubokie' German Gendarmes

Translated by Eilat Gordin Levitan

Daily a portion of the Jews of Glubokie, used to go to Krulevhtzina, for forced labor. In the morning they would go about 14 kilometers from the city and would come back in the evening. This daily parting involved very nerve-wracking experiences for the relatives, because until their near and dear ones returned, they didn't know what to think. They were always at the mercy of the beast, which could at any moment swallow them alive.

On the 17th of August 1943, the regularly employed Jews went off to Krulevshchizna to their labor and did not return at night. The relatives became very worried, they cried and wailed but had to "limit" themselves to hysteria, because going out of the Ghetto to look for them was absolutely forbidden. The reason for the Jews not returning to the Ghetto was as follows:

A specific group of Ukrainians and Russians, who had organized themselves under the leadership of a certain Polkovnik Radianov to help the Germans against the Soviets, finally decided to join up with the Soviet Partisans and take revenge on their former allies, the Germans. The Radanovtzes, well armed, were sent by the Germans to the Dokshitzer Region to clear the Partisans out of the woods, where they (the Partisans) were strongly harassing the Germans. The Radianovtzes, after making their secret agreement to join up with the Partisans, fooled the Glubokie German Garrison into coming to Krulevshchizna on the 17th of August, in order to "jointly clear the woods and once and for all rid themselves of the plague of the Partisans in that region". The Glubokie Germans accepted this happily. On the 17th of August and the Gendarmerie and other Germans, approximately 150-200 men, armed to the teeth in armored vehicles, drove off to Krulevshitzine. The Radianovizes were already waiting for them there. They surrounded the Germans and greeted them with heavy fire with their own weapons, which was given to the Radianovizes. There was an intense battle, which lasted for several hours. The result of the battle was fatal for the Germans. There were dozens of casualties and wounded Germans were left on the battlefield. The Chief of the Radianovizes Gendarmerie, the bloody Kern, may his name be blotted out, was also killed there. They also sabotaged the railroad station (a large hub terminal), the water pump and other installations. After the victory, the Radianovtzis withdrew from Krulevshchizna into the surrounding woods, and took with them the Glubokie Jews, who had been working there for the Germans. Among them was Chaim Hertz, Sragavitsh (a grandson of Itshe Sragavitsh), Siame Shrira (Padnas' son-in-law) and others.

[Page 177]

The next day, the 18th of August, the Germans brought their casualties from Krulevshchizna into Glubokie, where they had to be buried with great honor as heroes who had fallen for the "Fuhrer" and Fatherland.

The task of burying the Germans, who had been killed in Krulevshchizna, had to be carried out also by the Jews. They had to wash the "heroic" corpses, clean off their unclean blood, make coffins for them, dig their graves and so on. We must admit that the Jews carried out this work diligently, quickly and happily as no other work before. The hangman of the Jews, Kern, who had bathed in Jewish blood, the Jews buried with a special satisfaction and wished such a fate upon all murderers, so may they he destroyed. They wished such work for themselves always, even though it was difficult and dirty, but even so they got some justice at last ...unfortunately, these were to be the concluding days of the Glubokie Ghetto, the final Hours of the Jewish community of Glubokie……

[Page 178]

The Criminals liquidate the Glubokie Ghetto

Translated by Eilat Gordin Levitan

...Sheol (Hell) widened her soul and expanded her mouth criminally and the multitude went down with great noise, and she was happy with it...(Isaiah.,V, 14)

The Germans tortured the Jews and murdered them one after another with ferocious bestial cruelty. The tears of mothers had no effect on them. Nither the cries of the little ones, nor the pleading of the old. They did their carnage diligently. With demented passion they scoffed at the unfortunate, the helpless Jews. We still today become excited when we remind ourselves of the frightful scenes.

A woman from whom they had just torn away her children, runs with tousled hair broken hands, and staring eyes and screams, not with her own strength: "My children, children mine, where are you?!"

A man goes to the woman and faints in the middle of the street and there is no one even who can look upon them and so on and so forth.... People in general walked around like shadows, not grasping what was happening to them. One thing they did see; that the sword hovers and is being lowered upon everyone - on one a little sooner, and on another a little later.... They could sense it in the air that this was not yet all ......that the ultimate doom was still to come. They sensed that a most tragic day would soon arrive.... The Germans will gather everyone together and liquidate them all at once, they would erase the entire Jewish community of Glubokie of the face of the earth. And when an S. D. unit settled itself in Glubokie at the beginning of the summer of 1943, they were looked upon as angels of destruction, who had come here for a special mission of eradication, of liquidation, of annihilation.

The frightful day of calamity approached. All sorts of changes, which were previously introduced into Ghetto life, bore witness to this.

There came a strict order from the civil administration during the closing days of July 1943. No Jew may remain outside of the Ghetto after 4:00 P. M.!! Since many Jews worked in various places for the Germans until 7:00 or 8:00 P. M. the Commissar ordered that the Germans for whom the Jews worked, must release their Jews before 4:00 and they must return to and remain in the Ghetto from that hour on. There also came an order to eliminate the evening shifts in the various workshops and enterprises which were outside of the Ghetto, since these Jews had often stayed outside of the Ghetto overnight.

[Page 179]

And a remarkable change occurred: at the beginning of August the individual murders were actually lessened, and almost nonexistent. This temporary relief was perceived by the Jews of Glubokie with even more suspicion, and the nervousness reached the point of categorical insanity. All of this easing of the situation was looked upon as the calm before the earthquake, quietness before the storm. These were all preparations for a general liquidation of the entire Ghetto. The heaven over the Ghetto of Glubokie became blacker from day to day and the Jews simply couldn't see before them any brightening. The so called Sufficiently abbreviated area of the Ghetto, was, during the last few days, cut down even more. They carried (Jews themselves, at the order of the authorities) the barrier which bordered behind Lomzer Street, thereby putting that street out of the Ghetto area, and the Jews from there were shoved into Legianov (Old Kisheleike) and other side streets. All of this was carried out for "strategic" reasons. The more the Jews were pressed together, it would be speedier and easier to murder them. Also, the night-guard around the Ghetto was reinforced. The Jews in the Ghetto did not sleep, and in the dark they would spy on the movements of the Germans on the other side of the Ghetto wall.

When Rubashkin (The Jewish Elder, who had replaced Lederman) told the Justice Minister, who actually considered himself a protector of the Jews of Glubokie, that the Jews are extremely frightened because of the reinforcement of the night-guard, the Justice Minister calmed him down and "assured" him that it had nothing to do with the Jews, but it is simply connected with the "overall war plan". Understandably, no one was so naive, and the assurance did not calm anyone. Almost every one of the August days, the German S. D. men would enter the Ghetto; also, Gendarmes and others, and they would steal, rummage and not be particular. None of the refined items were to be found among Jews for a long while already, so they took whatsoever came into their hands. It is typical to mention how a German Officer, an engineer, took from Manve Friedman old-patched children's clothing. A second officer, who had been a teacher, took from Chana Abramovitsh a patched nightgown.

The method of stealing was also an indication that the days of the Glubokie Ghetto were numbered. There was no way out. Fleeing from the Ghetto was now impossible. (Previously it had also been difficult enough.) The Germans and their lackeys watched every movement.

The Jews, who had prepared bunkers in the Ghetto, carried bread and water into them and prepared themselves to crawl into them at any moment. These had been kept secret, one from the other, since they were afraid that it would become known...

[Page 180]

The situation was a hopeless one. On the 18th of August, in the morning, the day after the battles in Krulevshchizna, when the fear of death among the Jews was indescribable, a few souls fled to the Ghetto boundary. The Germans on the other side of the barrier opened fire, the Jews died in the field. Among those who perished were Yerachmiel Verch, Zud and others. Thursday, the 19th of August, in the evening, the SS men came to the Judenrat and took away everything that was there.... Clothing, footwear, linens and so forth, which the Judenrat had assembled in order to bribe the Germans and the Police. They also took away the safe from the Judenrat.

The Last Night

Translated by Eilat Gordin Levitan

The night of the 19th and 20th of August (18-19th of the Hebrew month of Av, 5703) the Jews noticed that the watch around the Ghetto was intensify even more than it had been the night before. There was a steady stream of all sorts of guards. From midnight on, every 20-30 minutes there came fresh units of green clad soldiers, gendarmes, police and also civilian clad elements. All were armed from head to toe. All of them, as we later found out, were brought from some other place to Glubokie in special trains, and from the train station the came directly to the Ghetto.

All of this was carried out silently, calmly, with unusual security, in order to deceive and cover-up the preparations for the coming mass carnage.

The nervousness among the Jews of the Ghetto grew in the same measure that the enemy's preparations, grew. Almost no one slept that night. The children weren't undressed for their sleep. All were out on the street, just like the Germans were at the perimeter of the Ghetto, so were the Jews inside the Ghetto. All were careful not to disturb the quiet. The situation can be compared to a place where a critically ill person is to be found and everyone is careful about speaking softly, avoiding a creaking door. There hovered in the air the feeling that everything must be quiet, that no sign of being awake was to be revealed to the other side. It was as if everyone's breath was being held, and all heads were filled with lead. People whispered among themselves, consulted about what to do, but there seem to be no way out of the situation. It was all too clear, that it wasn't a matter of days, but one of hours and minutes, which were moving along and bringing the end ever closer.

[Page 181]

Some who possessed stronger nerves, who were capable of keeping their heads even when the slaughterer's knife was already at their throats, attempted under the cover of the night to hurl themselves against the Ghetto barrier. They searched for a hole, a crevice, and some way to sneak out. But no matter where they hurled themselves, they found someone on the alert on the other side. Those on guard were so calm, lay so quietly, sat. stood or patrolled, so that it gave the impression that a blood thirsty animal was lurking and waiting for its victim to come out into the open, in order to easily spring upon it. The Jews at the barrier also moved quietly, on tiptoe, and conversed only with eye movements. The Germans and police outside of the Ghetto noticed that the Jews were moving about near the barrier and are looking for places to get out. They did not react, did not call out, but just waited for the condemned to come through the barrier, that the victim should himself jump into their mouths… It was a situation whereby "He who flees loses his staff, the strong his courage, the hero and fleet of foot cannot escape and he who seizes the bow cannot stand" (Amos, II, 14) - No one here could save himself.

The children shivered like leaves and the parents could find no way to console them. Some mothers tried to convince their little ones that the Germans had encircled the Ghetto only in order to frighten the populance. Large number of mothers had fallen into such apathy, that they couldn't react to the terrible situation of their children - Parents couldn't tend to their children because of their own helplessness. (Jeremiah, XLVII) Death itself was really much easier, than this waiting for it…

Friday, August 20, 1943:
A Day of Pandemonium and Carnage

Translated by Eilat Gordin Levitan

When light arrived we were able to clearly see that the Ghetto was encircled on all sides with armed Police and Germans of all sorts. We could clearly distinguish their brown, black, yellow and green outfits, and also the civilian dressed noxious angels of death. The appearance of the crimson, bloated faces of the murderers with the broad boned rounded bodies were in contrast to the living dead inmates, who by the time of their murder were made into a pile of bones...

[Page 182]

Before dawn, at 4:00 A.M., a German Officer arrived in the Judenrat and announced that in 2 hours all Jews are to assemble at the Judenrat, from where they will be sent to work in Lublin! And the Glubokie Jews at that time did not know the meaning of the word "Lublin". They hadn't heard of the infamous "Maidenek" and its smoking gas-ovens.... They did know perfectly well the meaning of the term "to go to work" when the Germans used it as collective term... But there was no way to save oneself. The Ghetto was all enclosed, one couldn't even speak of escaping. And in place of pondering about saving themselves, the Glubokie Jews all wished that they would quickly he shot and not fall a live into the clutches of the Germans, which was considered more difficult than death. There was a most frightful confusion. Women ran about with bulging eyes, disheveled hair and queer cries. Following them - barefoot children who were naked and confused with frightened faces... The air was quickly filled with sobbing, pleading and the cries of men, women and children: "My child, son, little daughter..." Children, searching for their parents ran about crying wildly: "Father, mother, grandpa" and so on and so forth....

The unfortunates threw themselves towards the Ghetto barrier as if by a special command, in an attempt to break out. As was to be expected the Germans opened a heavy fire. From all sides guns were being fired, grenades were thrown, machineguns firing and bombs exploding. The noise of the shooting mixed in the air with the cries and pleading of the victims. People fell like flies, like grass under a mower and in a very short time the streets of the Ghetto as well as the surrounding area were sown with corpses. The strange cries and groans of the wounded now drowned out the earlier sounds, they were suffering terrible tortures as they expelled their last breath. The bullets of the enemy cut off their calling for their mothers and father the screams and crying of the children who with their fingers and their little hands groveled in the earth, throwing themselves convulsively, and calling for a last time: "Ma-ma, ma-ma!". - A frost envelops the heart as we recall these scenes, as the prophet's cry rings out "My intestines squirm, the walls of my heart pound" (Jeremiah). From this, so it seems, the wildest of animals would bend and shrivel. But this shiver did not reach the European, "cultured" Germans, the "supermen of thinkers and poets", whom we cannot compare to any other strange creature on this earth.

[Page 183]

The fallen were the lucky ones… Those, who were still alive, were envious of them. The wounded who were rolling in the streets, on top of and under the dead, pleaded for mercy from the murderers, requesting that they end their misery so that their suffering would cease. Not all of them had the good fortune to meet up with "good" Germans, who showed pity arid put them out of their misery with a bullet…The vast majority of the murderers, with wild sarcasm, laughed. "It's a pity to waste a bullet" came the abrupt answer, - "In a few hours, you, Jew, will die on your on…"

Sonye Ozshinsky, the wife of the bookkeeper, Michael, who was critically wounded, rolled through the refuse, through the sewage, slid herself in terrible convulsions, and only at night, on the 20th of August, a German displayed "pity" and shot her. This also happened to a woman named Dora, a sister of Shmuel Nissan Gelman, and many others. The bitter words of the prophet: "The martyrs of the Lord stretched from one end of the earth to the other; they weren't eulogized, they were not gathered and not buried; they were as dung on the face of the earth" (Jeremiah, XXV, 33) – were fulfilled here in their broadest meaning. The most unfortunate were those who had fallen into German hands alive. This was much worse than being murdered out in the open.

Those, who had prepared hiding places, bunkers, or any kind of hole, crawled into them. People ran to hide themselves in trenches, in ovens, in furnaces - went up in thick clouds and ascended by the palms of their hands" (Jeremiah, IV, 29). But even this, to our great misfortune, helped very little. "Not one of the fleers could flee, nor any of the escapees escape" (Amos, IX). The fate of those hidden ones was even worse. They "lived" for a few hours and even some for an entire day, but because of it their later death was a lot worse. They were, in their hiding places, in their trenches, cellars, etc. finally choked, or burned alive, or their hiding places were discovered, and they fell into German hands alive. Some remained in their own houses and did not even attempt to hide. The murderers drove them into a courtyard near the former cinema "Karsa" (Podnos' house).

[Page 184]

There they also brought those who had been caught in the streets and those found in their hiding places. They numbered about 1,000 persons. Two of them saved themselves. They were Raphael Levin (a grandson of Hirshel Moosin) and Pesarh Masnavick's brother-in-law. (Levin's father, David Levin, is in Israel.) They had stolen themselves away from the courtyard and crawled into an old dwelling, where they hid in the stove. From the stove they crawled up the chimney and after a great effort they managed to reach the roof. From there they were later able to save themselves. (According to gathered information the two of them later perished in the forest.) It was also told that after them a girl had squeezed herself into the chimney, where she got stuck in the middle, not being able to move either forwards or backwards. It is all too clear what the fate of someone like that was. We later heard that her feet were cut off and she was Left stuck like that...

The 1000 Jews assembled in that courtyard were not shot, but instead, tortured. They were to die all sorts of strange deaths: Stomachs cut open, teeth torn out, ears cut off, noses sliced off, flayed, fingers, hands and feet, chopped off with a hatchet. Women had their hair pulled out and their breasts cut off. Men with beards had the beards pulled out together with the flesh on their faces. (Moshe Abrarnovitsh, Mendel Cohen and others.)

The Ghetto is Burning

Translated by Eilat Gordin Levitan

A storm and a gale and the fire devoured... (Isaiah, XXIX)

Planes began to encircle over the Ghetto during the 20th of August, Sabbath eve. It started at about midday. They approached downward very low, actually right over our head, and began firing. Jews were fired at from all sides as well as from above. From the planes they also released a flaming material upon the buildings and almost instantly several hundred homes, the entire Ghetto, was in flames. Certainly, the residents of Sodom and Gomorrah, who perished in a moment, did not endure so many evils. Hundreds of people, embracing their little children in the bunkers, dugouts, cellars, pits and other such hiding places, were suffocated or burned alive. If some ran from their hiding places and try to flee, they immediately fell into the hands of the enemy.

[Page 185]

This scene reminds us of the terrible depiction of the prophet Amos- "He who fled from the frightful sound fell into the abyss, and he who came up from the abyss, fell into the trap." Or - "As if a man were to flee from a lion, and a bear should meet him; and he enter into the house, and lean his hand against the wall, and a serpent should bite him. Behold, the day of the Lord is one of darkness, and not of light; it is obscure and has no brightness (Amos, V, 19,20). There was no place to hide; there was no escape. The absolutely worse outcome was to fall into the hands of the enemy. The Germans attempted to catch live Jews, to take tortures vengeance upon the Jews, while they were still alive, was an exceptional amusement for them.

Each and every corner of the Ghetto, was carefully patrolled by the Germans and the Police, as soon as the inferno commence to ignite the buildings. They expected that the Jews would flee from their burning homes. Many victims, adults and children, were captured while fleeing from the burning houses. A few of the many hundreds were successful in escaping through the fire and smoke as well as the bullets of the enemy. The pharmacist, Chaim-Leib Shulheifer, Mina Kasovska, Gildin (the Luzshkier pharmacist) and others were hiding in a well camouflaged room in the house of Chaim-Hanan Fidelholtz on Lomza Street. They had hoped to remain there until the danger passed, until the slaughter was over, and then they would flee to the forest. When the flames penetrated into their room, they ran to Kantorovitsh's "dugout" on Vilna Street. The "dugout" was made for 50 people, and there were already over 100 in it, so it was already very suffocating atmosphere. The will to survive was stronger than any reasoning. Those who had fled the fire and found a hiding place, did not consider any of the difficulties involved. They pushed themselves in with their remaining strength.

Not only did they not save themselves; they also brought tragedy upon those who were hidden there from the start. From a distance, the Police watched where they had fled to, and they immediately understood that other Jews were hidden there. But they were still unable to find the "dugout". It was very well camouflaged. They threw bombs, and grenades and did not hit the target. Then they warned the Jews that they had better come out at once. If not, then they'll blow up the entire enclosed area. The warnings did not have to be considered by anyone, because they were already lost. In spite of knowing those facts, instinctively, the majority ran out of the "dugout". All of the people who ran out, perished. Pinye Azshinsky relates that several of them fell upon the Germans and the Police, and that Mottke Lederman killed three Germans.

[Page 186]

This could not be confirmed from any other sources. Thinking that no one else remained in the "dugout", The Germans left that area and lifted the siege around Kantorovitsh's brick house. The few who remained there were safe and some of them survived. (Minne Kasovska, Pinye Azshinsky and others).

Approximately an hour after this (it was already evening), the ones who remained in the "dugout", heard someone using the well, which had been specially built for the "dugout", in order to provide water. They understood that one of the unfortunates must be there, and they let a rope down. From the well they pulled up, on the rope, the 12-year-old Yashe Mazavetzky (Yerachmiel Alperovitsh's grandson). He was searching for the "dugout" and fell into the well

Alter Cohen's nephew, in his undershirt, came running a few hours later. He was looking for a way to commit suicide. He decided to drown himself in the well. He came running to this place from David Munbez's "bunker" on Lomza Street. He fled from there during the time that shop under which the bunker was located, was already in flames. It had also been packed tight with people. He explained that all of them were choking and suffering terribly from the smoke, and that the heat was unbearable. Everyone removed their outer garments and were sitting almost naked. When he had left that "bunker" many were already unconscious. He had undressed and barely managed to get himself over here in his undershirt. He considered drowning to be an easy death, rather than to be burned alive. Those who had fainted there were treated with cold water. The water quickly disappeared and people actually choked. He told us that no water had remained for his father, who passed out, and they had to treat him with urine.

The Germans and the Police searched all of the dwellings, before setting fire to the Ghetto. They looked everywhere, every corner was searched: In the attics, in storerooms, stalls, ovens, woodpiles, closets, and they even looked inside every chimney. Those whom the hangmen couldn't find, lay in their hiding places holding their breath. They could hear the conversations and to their laughter. They heard how they tapped on the ground with their lances, the sounds of searching and barks: "Jew, out, out!" The screams of the

Germans sometimes affected the Jews more than their bullets. Some of the frail women would roll on the ground and became essentially mentally unstable by all of these horrors.

[Page 187]

There were some incidents where little children who cried, were choked with the bare hands of adults in the hideouts, it was feared that their cries would give away the hiding place. (Yehoshua Weinstein, Gordon and others). In the larger, well camouflaged and organized "hideouts", belonging to Yaakov Alter, Yehoshua Teller, David Munkaz, Kantorovitsh and others, hundreds of people were found. From one such "dugout", a policeman pulled out the young beautiful Itkin girl, trembling she pleaded with the policeman to save her life...He demanded a reward, such as gold, diamonds a good watch-, and other such things. The girl took out a large gold ring, which she had specially hidden for this "black unhappy hour" and also all the money she had and gave it all to the policeman. But the girl's "life", it seems, was worth more, as far as the policeman was concerned, and this "modest" ransom, this bribe, did not satisfy him... This shameless, bloodthirsty wild animal, for saving the rife of the girl, wanted something more from her... He wanted her virginity, her modesty... But in this the bandit made a mistake - for this decent, upright Jewish daughter, her virginity came before her life and was more dear to her. Hearing his words, she ran... So fast that neither the policeman, nor his friends, who had quickly come to his aid, were able to overtake her and take her alive. They opened fire on the helpless victim, with automatic weapons, and from a great distance shot her dead. Not everyone in a similar situation was so "lucky". Not too many such decent, kosher, Jewish daughters were successful in not falling live into the clutches of the Germans and their local cronies. Not a few women were tortured by these outcasts with the most dreadful of tortures: the tearing out of their hair, cutting open their stomachs, cutting off their breasts, and so on.

The machine guns did not conclude their rattling the entire day of the 20th of August. Bombs, grenades and other explosives, blasted all over. They threw explosives wherever there was some suspicion that a Jew were hidden. As was mentioned, many dozens and hundreds of people met a terrible death in the "dugouts" and pits, slowly choking under the burning pasture and earth.

The 19th of Av, the eve of the Sabbath, on which the weekly portion was Eykev (In the Book of Deuteronomy), 5703 (20th of August 1943), on this frightening day of misfortune, on this day of trouble and reprehensions, more than 3,000 Jews perished in Glubokie, at the hands of the Germans and their helpers - local Police - They perished in all sorts of unspeakably horrendous ways.

[Page 188]

Several hundred Jews succeeded, in spite of the searches and efforts of the murderers during that bloody Friday, to remain in their hiding places. The fires and smoke did not reach them, and the bombs did not hit their hideouts. But the Germans did not cease looking for them. They carried on with their work for several days without pause...

The Germans incessantly searched they went about poking around and observing and on the days of the 21st, 22nd and 23rd of August they caught many hidden Jews. It was enough if someone just stuck his head up to steal a glance to see what was going on, the lurkers would uncover the entire hiding place.

There were cases when those in hiding couldn't hold out any longer in the pits and "dugouts" for days on end, and they came out of their own accord, choosing death as the lesser of two evils...

Therefore, the obliteration of the last Jews of Glubokie, took several days and in just that short period the streets of the Ghetto became thickly spread with dead bodies and the injured. meanwhile, The Germans and their lackeys - local Christians - marched around with special tools and tore the gold teeth out of the mouths of the corpses, the earrings from their ears, the rings from their fingers and so on and so forth. These wild animals chopped off the fingers with an ax to get the rings, in order to lighten their task, ... Distinguished "in this task" from among the local Christians, were a certain Ivan Niedzieletz, Ivan the cripple - Trilop, and others whose names could not be confirmed.

Everything turned to ashes and dust, the Ghetto burned for several days. Corpses, parts of limbs, hands, feet and other portions of human bodies were found in the fields and meadows, in a perimeter of dozen kilometers around the city, there were to be seen severed bodies. Their efficiency in the carnage of Jews was not limited to the city alone. They searched for Jews in the entire surrounding area. They would set "ambushes" in the bushes, forests or on the roads, riding in their vehicles, lurking for every refugee, who had somehow managed to escape from the city, from the fire, and they would murder him there on the road, in the field, etc.

[Page 189]

From the surrounding villages, the Germans drove peasants with their carts. They were forced to be responsible for picking up the corpses from the fields and bringing them to the pits in the Barok forest. Besides the mass graves in the Barok Forest, there were many smaller graves scattered over the fields and meadows around the city. A significant number of the dead remained unburried and their corpses were found eaten by dogs - they became food for wild animals and birds of prey. (The corpses of your servants are food for birds, the flesh of your followers for the wild animals of the forest...)

The engineer, Russkevitsh - a Pole, an old inhabitant of Glubokie, whom the Germans had ordered to clean up the area of the former Ghetto of the Jewish victims, -later informed us that they had pulled out from the cellars and pits, with stakes and shovels, half and completely burned bodies. The bodies that weren't burned were swollen, and he could recognize only very few of them. By and large, Russekevitsh knew almost every Jew in the city. He only recognized the body of Abraham-Yehoshua Fidelholtz, the son of Chaim Hannah's, who remained sitting in the cellar, embracing his wife and son so tightly, that even in death it was extremely difficult to separate them... He also recognized Moshe Shulheifer and his two daughters. He also recognized a few other Jews, but he had forgotten their names.

All of them had been taken out of the hiding and were buried in a pit in the Barak.

[Page 189]

Before the Final Hour

Translated by Eilat Gordin Levitan

During the August days of 1943, a time of the extermination of the last Jews in Glubokie, after the burning of the Ghetto, the murderers went through of the courtyards and gardens of the former Ghetto, looking for hidden Jews. They knew that there were still some Jews who were hiding somewhere in underground bunkers. It was for these bunkers they searched now.

In the spring of 1943, most of the Jews in Glubokie prepared for themselves pits in which to hide during the impending slaughter. they had made some of these hideouts in the gardens near their homes, and planted potatoes above them in order to camouflage the hiding place. David Munboz had also prepared near his house on Lomzshe Street such a bunker, with potatoes growing over it.

[Page 190]

As was mentioned, The Germans and the local Police, walked through the gardens, searching all of the courtyards and gardens with mowers and choppers. They cut down all of the grass and plants. They also came to Lomzshe Street to the garden of David Munboz. While cutting the green tops of the potatoes in the garden they discovered a tube, which was exposed above the ground from the underground hiding place in order to provide air. Seeing the tube, the hangmen threw grenades at the spot, and killed the Jews in that hiding place. Moshe Disvitsky and his mother, Groyne, David Munboz and his wife, the family of Chaim-Hirsh Gilevitsh, Moshe Soloveitshik and his son, Tuviah, the electrical technician, Pulke Metler, the gaiter maker, Israel-Abraham Kliyupt, his wife Tzile and three daughters, all of them perished. From that bunker there survived only two nieces of David Munboz. Their clothing was completely riddled with bullet holes, and their faces completely unrecognizable.

Tzilye Kiupt, was not dead yet. She was lying there badly wounded. The survivors wanted to remove the dress from her body. But she wouldn't let them. At night they went out of the death pit almost naked. They crawled on all fours in the grass. By a miracle they managed to leave the city unnoticed. They went in the direction of the Barok Forest; going past the cemetery the Germans noticed them and fired mortars at them. The girls fell to the ground and lay among the corpses. The Germans came to search for them among the corpses. One German took one of them by the hand, looked at her with a flashlight pointed at her face, but didn't discern any signs of life in her, and left her lying there…

The girls got up and walked further after the Germans left. On the way they met the 9-year-old boy, Nachurn Berkan (the son of Mashke Berkan), leaning against a tree. He was wounded in his private parts. The girls tore a piece of cloth from their torn dresses and bandaged him. Before dawn they managed to drag themselves up to the Barok Forest. From afar they saw the Germans leading a group of about 200 Jews - men, women, old people and children. The girls hid themselves in the bushes, not far from the pit to which the Jews were being led, they heard the shots. They watched the Germans grab children by their feet, swing their heads against a tree and threw them into the pit.

Afterwards the Germans threw a few grenades into the pit. When the Germans left the pit, the girls went deeper into the forest and in a short time came upon a Partisan unit, in which they found some other Glubokie survivors of the slaughter.

[Page 191]

The Glubokie Jewish community, which florished over hundreds of years, was completely annihilated, completely wiped out...We, the writers of these bloody pages, remained safe., after the murder of our mother on the 4th of Tammuz, 5702 (see The Slaughter of 2500 Jews in Gluboke). After the cutting down of the Ghetto in the summer of 1942, we were thrown from one place to another, until a few weeks before Rosh Hashanah, we were taken into a house on Polne Street, near the perimeter of the Ghetto.

Like so many other Jews, we prepared a pit - a sort of "dugout". The dugout was made in partnership with two other families: Yosl Kozshdans' family of Glubokie and Geidenzon from Krulevshchizna.

During the last months before the liquidation of the Ghetto, we heard about the Partisan organization. We considered fleeing into the forest, but the ghetto was strictly guarded on all sides. We were very disheartened by the recurring incidents in the Ghetto. We wanted desprtly to flee but didn't know where and how to go, not having anyone who would stretch out a hand to us. And so, we remained where we were until the liquidation of Glubokie.

Us four and the two abovementioned families, altogether 11 souls, went into the dugout on Friday, the 19th of August, in the morning. In the confusion we forgot to -take the bread, which had been prepared in advance. We did not forget to take a barrel of water and also a first aid kit. Our dugout, which led via an exit to the garden, had been constructed in a very primitive fashion. We had done the digging during the winter months. The roof support was weak, and in a short while, the earth fell in various places, so that we could see out into the street. The garden, and also the top of the dugout was overgrown with grass, so that the holes that had been made by the falling 'earth, could be noticed only if one looked very carefully...

Through a camouflaged opening we entered the dugout. It was terribly cramped in the dugout. We sat so pressed together that we couldn't even turn. Through the holes we heard the cries of the Jews who had been caught, the shooting, we heard a policeman who caught a woman and children, requesting money from her and then taunting her about how little money she had. He then took them to a German, who shot them on the spot. Rhoda, the sister of Shmuel Nissan Gelman, was wounded. We heard how she screamed with inhuman strength, that they should shoot her. Her relatives quieted her, so that the hangmen wouldn't hear her screams. She just couldn't calm herself down…

[Page 192]

In the afternoon we heard planes which flew low all over the Ghetto, and we couldn't understand what this signified. Later we smelled a distinct odor in the dugout. We knew that the Ghetto was aflame…Our house stood apart from the surrounding houses and did not catch fire.

In the evening we heard how the Germans entered our house. "Jews, out, out!" they carried on shouting. When they finally left the house they were laughing, they were content, they were talking out loud among themselves, they were full with triumph… there flowed into the dugout a warmth and it became light, about a moment later - our house was burning like a candle. Burning cinders began to fall into our dugout. It seemed as if the "roof" of our "dugout" would catch fire any minute. Fortunately, the wind was blowing in the opposite direction and the smoke did not choke us. The beams of the "roof" began to smoke, and with our hands we dug up the earth and put out the fire. In this way we fought the fire for a few hours without pause. The hole through which we had entered the dugout, opened completely, and we could see passing Germans and Police. Later we were able to somewhat disguise the hole from the inside.

The house of Kalman Moshe Hoichman burned some meters away from us. In the dugout under that house, dodens of people were burned alive, among whom were Hoichman's wife and four of their children. He and a 17-year-old daughter crawled into our "dugout on on Shabbat, the 21st of August, before dawn, they were badly burned. During their crawling to us, we thought that it was the murderers crawling. After they crawled in, there developed a large hole, and with our hands, we dug earth with which to plug it up. It became so crowded that we were actually sitting on one another's heads. It was impossible to move a limb. K. M. Hoichman suffered greatly from his burns, but he exerted great self control arid kept quiet. His daughter, on the other hand, who seemed to be even more seriously hurt than he was, could not keep herself calm. She moaned out loud or snored loudly in her sleep. We were afraid that her snoring would give away our hiding place to the enemy.

[Page 193]

The Germans and Police patrolled our streets during that Shabbat day, they kept tapping around and searching. We could hear them conversing among themselves, with their bayonets they "tapped" the earth. For some reason, it appears, they became suspicious of our hiding place. At about 2:00 in the afternoon, a few Germans came over to our dugout and listened, tapped the earth near the hole which had been formed by the falling earth, and had gotten even bigger with the coming of Kalman-Moshe and his daughter. The Germans, with their bayonets tapped on the dugout; the earth poured down on our heads... With the German Patrol, there was also a baker, by the name of Kolye, who, until the formation of the Ghetto, had lived in the region. (We don't know his family). As it appears, the Germans had brought him along as an "expert", to search for hidden Jews. From their talk it was obvious that they had suspected our "dugout". But because of the caving in and overgrowth they could not imagine that people would be sitting inside. They asked Kolye about this dugout, and how come it was there. We heard Kolye tell them that in the burnt-out house (our house) his brother-in-law, Alexander, had lived, and that he knows for sure that Alexander had a dugout for potatoes. About the holes, Kolye told them that they had been dug by cats... He declared emphatically: "The holes were dug by cats!". The Germans stood, thought a bit, and left.

Kolye, the baker, had obviously known that we were hidden there, and purposely wanted to save us. There had never been a dugout in that spot, and the "potato-dugout" was a figment of his imagination... We are indebted to him and consider it our obligation to mention him favorably because if he had not at that moment, turned his tongue "aside" a bit, we would have certainly fallen into the hands of the Germans.

Approximately during sunset, Germans came to our dugout to inspect the premises again ... We heard how one of the Germans expressed his opinion and stated that a grenade should be thrown. Fortunately, they did not do it at that moment. But for us it became clear that we could no longer remain in that place... To crawl out of that dugout in the light was impossible. With each moment we imagined that our "dugout" would be blown up. Such "waiting" we endured until midnight.

[Page 194]

That midnight, between Saturday and Sunday, we crawled out of the hole in the dugout. 13 souls, in great fear, left one by one. We took nothing with us, except for a kit of medicines, which the wife of M. Rayak, as a doctor, had brought into the dugout and considered it an object which one could not do without on such a dreadful journey.

Before our eyes there appeared an awful sight after crawling out of the dugout. The Ghetto was burning. The air was filled with smoke. From afar we saw vehicles filled with Germans riding in circles. You could hear very furious voices. With flashlights they would light up the area around themselves and searched… shooting of guns, mortars, and also the explosions of bombs could be heard. The groans of the wounded, whom the heartless ones hadn't killed were heard from all directions. They left them to suffer terrible tortures, and struggle until they died on their on… All around there were dismembered, burned corpses with torn limbs. You couldn't move without being noticed. One had to crawl in the grass. We became disoriented and didn't know where we were… This was the moment and place which later led to our greatest misfortune. We became separated due to our disorientation and lost one another. One of us, Tzvi, remained alone, and Michael. his wife and baby, remained with the others, those with whom they had left the "dugout." To pause to think too long, couldn't be done. The Angel of Death hovered over every step we took, and carried with him, death…

I, (Tzvi) headed in the direction of Vilna Street. The fence was burned down and I left the Ghetto… Also, my brother, Michael, and the others came through the same way later. But we didn't know about each other. The twenty minutes that Michael spent near the dugout, looking for me, proved fatal for us - this time became the most frightful misfortune that would hunt us for the rest of our lives.

[Page 195]

Going out of the Ghetto through the burned fence on Vilna Street near Nathan Gitelzon's courtyard and leaving the city at 5:00 A. M. when It was already light, we (Michael, his wife and child and the others) wanted to cross the tracks that led to Dunilovitz 2 kilometers from the city. As soon as we came up on the tracks, we were overtaken by two vehicles filled with Germans, with the spy Vitvitzki (Tzirkovetz) at the head. We already wrote about him in a separate chapter. They stopped their vehicles and attacked us with all of their destructive weapons. Over our heads there poured the bullets of handguns, automatic weapons and machine guns from every direction…

Confused, we ran in every direction. I, Michael, threw off my shirt, jumped off the tracks, and rolled myself into a meadow with high grass. I was joined by Yosl Kazshdan, the butcher, one of the Gadenson sisters and Kalman-Moshe Hoichman. We crawled on all fours and entered a deep canal. The Germans shot at us, the bullets whined from all directions and as it seems.M. Hoichman was hit, because we later heard that he was not to be found among the survivors. My closest were not with me. We were somehow separated. I had parted from my dear wife, Helena (Louise) and my dearest son Aaron-Yitzhak, who was 8 years and four months old (having been born on the 2nd of the intermediate days of Passover, 5695). I had parted from my dearest and most precious, who had taken with them the nicest and best of my life, they have my soul... The beloved and the most pleasant left me forever - no swabs can ever dry my eyes; no word can ever comfort my soul...

We Wander Aimlessly and Come to the Partisans

Translated by Eilat Gordin Levitan

For about 3 hours we lay in the canal and did not move from the spot. The shooting finally concluded, and we heard the German vehicles leaving the area. We crawled out of the canal and left the meadow. We ascended to a small hill and sat in a sparingly bushed area. The Germans rode around in their vehicles along all the roads and by-ways and fired their weapons incessantly. I sat there in a state of a complete daze.

I did not know what had happened to my wife and child - I could not believe that they were gone.

[Page 196]

We didn't know what had happened to all of those, who had been with us. Yosl Kazshdan had noticed that his wife had stopped a bullet on the way and lay in the spot she fell. As I learned later, my wife had also been shot on the way and my son wanted to hide but found no hiding place. H. Gidenson told me after the liberation (I met him in Lodz) that my child ran behind him, when escaping the German. He turned from him at one point out of fear that they would both fall into German hands.

Until it became dark, we sat in the bushes. We wanted to go back to the place where misfortune had overtaken us, in order to find out something about what had happened to our relatives. But this was impossible, because from the rockets which the Germans were firing, we could see that they had patrols in every nook and cranny. We had to abandon our place and go off in a different direction. Of the 12 people who had come out of our dugout, two lonesome orphans were left - we were drifting, two desolated shadows, in the sinister, evil world.

We went in the direction of Krulevishtzina. We constantly had to change our route; the Germans fired rockets at us from all directions. Even so we were able to distance ourselves from Glubokie before nightfall. I was besides myself; I didn't believe that any of my relatives were still alive, and life had lost all interest for me. I dragged myself behind Kazshdan, mechanically. He knew the area well. Several times along the way, we noticed cars, and Kazshdan would run to hide, with me pursuing him. But I was completely indifferent when a German patrol fired rockets and shot at us. I was only frightened at the thought of falling alive into the hands of the Germans.

We hid in thick bushes when day began to dawn. We sat there all day. A heavy rain fell and we became soaking wet. But who would care at that time for such a thing. We were only frightened of being caught alive. We would tremble at the sound of a bird, a falling leaf, which we imagined to be a person who right notice us. Men became for us the greatest terror.

[Page 197]

We went again on our way in the evening. Kazshdan had Christian acquaintances in most of the villages in the area. In a village we arrived, he knocked on the door of one of his acquaintances, and a Christian acquaintance carried out a piece of bread for him. But the Christian acquaintance was afraid to speak to him and only wanted to get rid of him as quickly as possible. We wandered like this for several days - by day we would hide in the woods or in the bushes, and by night we would travel. We came near the Partisan zone in this way. On the way, we found out that the Germans would not enter the Partisan zone, since they were afraid to show themselves there. We really did not rush in our traveling, because after what had happened to us, we were completely indifferent to life.

We arrived at the village of Yuziche, some twenty or more kilometers from Glubokie, a week later. There we found some of the escapees from the Glubokie slaughter: Kalman Rabinovitsh, Ruvke Kotz, Zalman Rappaport, Benjamin Gitelzon, his wife and little daughter, Abraham Shub, Eli Podnos, Rashe Weiman, Pipik the shoemakers 8 year old son, one of the Gidenson sisters, who had been in the dugout with us, Mrs. Kurak with a young daughter, who was seriously wounded, Arke Birzsn, Itshke Mind and a few others. Near the village of Yuziche there was a small Partisan group, and a few of the escapees, who had arrived armed, immediately joined the group. All were filled with a spirit of revenge towards the murderers who spilled so much innocent blood. This became their only reason for living.

Feeling a bit calmer from the German dangers, we remained here for a few days. We couldn't come back to our old selves. I would go about completely traumatized, as if after a dark terrible nightmare, from which one would not be freed for eternity

Suddenly "courier" from the Partisans came running toward us. They told us that a large German unit was approaching Yuziche and was intent upon blockading the Partisan zone. The group immediately left the village. They went off in different directions. I, together with Yosl Kazshdan, the Gidenson woman, Mina from Dolhinov (a relative of Chaim-Leib Shulheifer) went in the direction of the Miadyaler region, where there was a strong Partisan Brigade. We were also accompanied by Leibl Chasash of Dunilovitz. We would travel only by night. By day we used to hide either in the forest or the bushes.

We came to the village of Misouni, not far from Miadyal, after about 5 days.

[Page 198]

There we met Shalom Yungelson and Chaya Zinger, with her son, they had fled from Glubokie before the slaughter. In Misouni there was a Partisan group, which had arrived from Moscow by plane. The Commandant of the group engaged me in conversation, saw how broken up and confused I was, and requested that I write up the experiences that we had gone through. He gave me paper, pen and ink, and I began to write. This assignment lent some meaning to my days and instilled in me a desire to remain alive, I became engrossed in the task. The memories, though, did not give me any peace of mind. The pains became more severe with each passing hour and I couldn't exert any self control. Also, the writing did not calm me. I just couldn't find a place for myself.

There were different Partisan units around the village of Misouni, and various groups would often cross the village. A unit of Tshapaiev's regiment of Voroshilov's Brigade, under the command of our former student, Itshke Blatt drove through Misouni a few days after my arrival here. Ytzhak Blatt, who was the Commandant of the regiment. gave me a letter from my brother Tzvi and told me that he was coming for me and in a few days would arrive here. This news was as if it had fallen upon me from heaven. I burst out crying. Blatt calmed me down. He told me that the general situation was a critical one. The Germans are preparing a strong offensive against the Partisans and we must be prepared for anything. I recovered completely and awaited the coming of my brother. Not only the hours dragged for me, but even the minutes seemed endless. A few days later I was told that my brother had arrived on the "High island" and is preparing to come to Misouni to be with me. The Island was about 5 kilometers from Misouni., I decided to go to him. Eli Gordon and his family as well as some other inhabitants of Glubokie were on the "High Island. They brought me to my brother. He was dressed in tattered clothing, was terribly pale and unshaven, and so changed, that it was difficult for me to recognize him. He had become gray, and his face wore such a sad expression, one that I had never seen on anyone's face before. When I approached him, he stood near a booth, reciting the "silent prayer". It was morning. When he finished, we embraced and kissed. It seemed to me that he was silently uttering the "she'echeyanu" prayer of gratitude for my being there. He did not ask me a single question. He already knew that my wife and child were no longer with me, and what had happened to them, so he didn't ask. The anguish and sorrow which plagued both of our hearts, rendered the two of us speechless.

[Page 199]

The Principal Murderers of the Glubokie Jews

The following German assassins and their colleagues, who were saturated with Jewish blood in Glubokie and the surrounding Jewish shtetls, marked themselves with their depraved conduct:

1. Hochman –The German appointed "Justice" Minister in the Glubokie area. He began his bloody work instantly following his arrival, in September of 1941. He was the Chief executive of the Civil Administration. In a refined manner he sucked out the last bit of "juice" from the Jewish population. In order to fulfill the objective of making the Jews give up their possessions and fortunes, they had to terrorize the Jews. There had to be victims so bribes would be paid! "Blood" was needed! And the Justice Minister filled the sewers of Glubokie with spilled Jewish blood. It was thanks to his efficiency in that task, that he constantly sent back to Germany, freight cars loaded with Jewish gold and jewels.

2. Hebel - Supervisor over National Questions. The Jews suffered no less from him than they did from his chief (Hochman). His favorite assignment was his regular "stroll" through the Ghetto. This leisurely walk threw the Jews into a panic every time it occurred. Most of the time Hebel would "stroll" in the Ghetto together with his wife, who would master over the Jews in the identical style as her husband. During their "stroll" through the Ghetto they were always accompanied by a small dog who wore a yellow star (the mark of shame that Jews were forced to wear on their outer garments). This German woman ruled with an iron fist, all the time the Jewish seamstresses had to make new wardrobe for her. She would constantly come up with new styles and fashions. These workers just couldn't satisfy her. She tortured them brutally. The same was true of cobblers and quilt makers, who had to fulfill every one of her wildest caprices by making elegant footwear for her. She warned the workers

they should never make anyone else the same style of clothes, lingerie or shoes as those they made for her. The Jewish workers constantly found themselves between the hammer and the rock, in constant fear that she or some other official wife, would be displeased with the products and send them off to their death, to the Barok…Hebel became very promoted for his pursuit of partisans in later time. He would dispatch entire expeditions to the forest and would very often accompany them. He would also distribute leaflets, addressed to the Partisans, asking them to leave the woods and promising them all sorts of wonderful things. Since he was in charge of all national matters, he was one of the most active perpetrators of the slaughters of Jews in Glubokie and the surrounding area. In various ways he managed to incite the Poles and Belarusians against the Jews, and he persuaded some of them to assist him in his homicidal tasks.

3. Heberling - In charge of commercial and economic matters for the Justice Minister. He ceaselessly robbed the Jews and therefore he would post packages to his family in Germany on a daily basis. This was done besides larger shipments, which he would periodically send by railroad. Quite often he would travel to Germany and Warsaw with huge suitcases loaded with Jewish possessions and goods which he gave to his family and friends.

4. Kern - Chief of the Gendarmerie in Glubokie. From the time of arrival until his death (the 17th of August 1943) he did not cease burglarizing and assassinating.

5. Hait - Captain of the Guard of the Gendarmerie, and a close associate of Kern in all of his evil actions.

6. Bemmo - Chief of the "Service Unit". much has been said about his evil activities in a prior chapter.

7. Voogdman - Bemrno's assistant. Like his chief, diligent participant in the swindle and the manslaughter.

8. Shper - Captain of the Guard of the Gendarmerie - he carried out various killings in the Barok and other places, on his own initiative.

9. Vitvitski (the Tsirkovetz). About his bloody abilities - see a special chapter.

10. Goldberg - In charge of the "Inspections". He robbed the people very vigorously, was a devoted Nazi, who actively participated in the various mass killings in Glubokie and the surrounding area, as well as expeditions against the Partisans, and so forth.

11. Morre - The Supervisor of the leather factory. Took part in mass murders.

The Germans: Tsanger, Kapfenvald, Becker, Krieger, Zeif, Heinliat, Smids, Vildt, Peterson; each and every one of them tortured, robbed and murdered the Jews of Glubokie and the surrounding area. About the wild deeds of each one of them we could tell a great deal. Each outdid the others in bringing fresh cruel acts against Jews. Could we possibly point out a wild animal, who would force its victims to take the head of a living mouse into the open mouth and bite off the head? It seems that the wildest fantasy cannot imagine such a thing. The German Smids did this, at the railroad station of Glubokie. While the

Jews were being squashed together loading hay into the boxcars, he forced Hoichman, to bite off with his teeth the head of a living mouse. This and similar atrocities could be attributed to every one of them. But it is impossible to relate all the evils. The few examples that were cited are characteristic of the so-called bearers of Western European culture!

[Page 201]

With humiliation and anguish, we must also acknowledge that our local Christians quickly learned the "Torah" from the Germans and showed that one need not necessarily be a member of the "super-race of poets and thinkers" in order to torture and murder human beings. The animalistic nature which lies hidden in people, could be awaken. You just have to abide by an immoral and depraved ruler, and evil will flourish.

Of the local murderers, accredited for the assistance that they gave the Germans, there were:

1. Valyukovitch - The supervisor of the wagon building factory. He was a member of the "Belarussian Administration", at the head of which there stood the well-known Belorussian official, Ostrovski (Minsk). Valyukovitsh was also an active member of the "White Russian National Committee", and since he was loyal in his position, he dedicated himself to the task of scoffing at and torturing the Jews.

2. Grinevitsh - T, in sight of everyone he supervisor of the blacksmith's shop. An active member of the "White Russian National Committee".

3. Paulski - Regional Head of the Province of Glubokie.

4. Kozyol - Same as Paulski.

5. Guzava - A folks-German woman, who served as a supervisor in the Provincial Government.

6. Askerka Vladimir; Active member of the "White Russian National Committee"

7. Askerka, Henrich; Same as his brother.

8. Subbatin - Inspector of Schools. An active member of the "White Russian National Committee".

9. Agranat, Lapir - Well-known Jew-hater from a previous era. Now an active member of the "White Russian National Committee".

10. Grudman - The Director of the cinema in Glubokie during the period of German rule. He used to beat Jews indiscriminately. One would try hard to avoid meeting him. He played an active role in murdering Jews during the liquidation of the Ghetto in August of 1943.

11. Smolski, Aleksander - Served in the German Secret Police. This German spy alerted the Germans to the fact that the tailor, Yitzhak Lipshin, had been the Chairman of the Tailors Guild in Glubokie during the soviet occupation. He also reported about the tailor, Aronson, who, during the time when all of the sewing machines of the tailors had been confiscated, had not turned in his machine, and instead hid it. Lipshin and Aronson were arrested for these crimes.

12. Shtshebes, Mietzislav - Served in the German Secret Police. As it was revealed later, it was because of his information to the Germans that 12 men from Glubokie were shot in the Fall of 1941. (This was written about in the early chapters.) Shtshebes brought to the Germans the fact that the barber-surgeon, Yehoshua Geiler, had openly appeared at a Soviet meeting on the 10th of October in 1939. Shtshebes informed that the other 11 prisoners had also been guilty of similar crimes.

13. Kandratin, Pavel - Representative of the Z. T. A. in Glubokie. Thanks to him, Nathan Gitelzon's maid, Vavara Baziki, was arrested and tortured for helping her employers.

14. Spakovski. - Participated vigorously in the search for Jews in hiding, during the period of the liquidation of the Glubokie Ghetto.

15. Niedzieletz, Ivan - Took part in many of the robberies and murders of Jews in Glubokie.

16. Ivan Trilop (the one who limped) - Worked together with the above mentioned Niedzieletz. During the mass slaughters, in June of 1942 and August 1943, both Ivans went about with hatchets in their hands and knocked out the gold and platinum teeth from the mouths of the murdered, tore the rings off fingers, earrings from ears and so forth. (This had already been partially done by the Germans while the victims were still alive. The remainder was left for the two Ivans...)

17. Naumov - Burgomeister of Glubokie.

18. Filipak - Close associate of the Germans. Actively participated in the slaughter and robbery of the Jews.

19. Yaremek - Closest friend of above mentioned Filipak, who, together with him carried on their bloody work.

20. Dubrovski - Former chauffeur of "Pishtzepramtarg" for the Soviets. Was friendly with Abraham Shub before the Germans arrived. When the Germans occupied Glubokie, Dubrovski became a policeman and used his "friendship" with Shub... He robbed him blind. Dubrovski used to come to Shub, demanding from him suits of clothing and other things, telling him that they were going to slaughter the Jews anyway, and that his things would be taken by unknown "strangers ". Shub suffered a great deal from his "good friend", but by a miracle he escaped from his clutches alive.

21. At the end, Shub hid himself. Dubrovski took his revenge on all the Jews and participated in the slaughters.

22. When the Red Army liberated Glubokie from the Germans, in July of 1944, Shub went to work for the N. K. V. D. Dubrovski was arrested and imprisoned in the N. K. V. D. prison in Glubokie. Shub took him into his private office, when we were

there. Dubrovski literally shook with fright and was unable to speak. At our questions about his work as a policeman for the Germans, he would answer that he had never harmed Jews, and had not participated in the murders. When Shub, who was present, asked him why he had robbed him, he remained silent.

23. Kaspzshitzki - Also served in the Police. Like his remaining comrades, he also robbed and murdered. He persecuted also non-Jews. As was later reported, he had at the time murdered three Ksiondzshn in order to rob them. The items that he stole he brought home as a gift for his wife. She was on a different level than her husband and she pushed the "gift" into his face and burst out crying. She just couldn't stand her husbands misdeeds, and one night she murdered him. His friends arrested her and had her shot. They left a little girl, who is being raised in Glubokie by someone named Pomieto, who lives on the 17th of September Place.

The names of the Police members were already listed. All of them, as was mentioned above, actively helped the Germans in their savage homicidal undertaking.

The list does not mention however, all of those who spilled Jewish blood in Glubokie and in the surrounding communities. We were able to list only the names of those murderers, whom we knew in the Ghetto. Could we have possibly listed all of the murderers who participated in the bloody work? There were thousands, and their names were unknown to those who were killed by them and those few who survived also know some of their names.

[Page 204]

How painful it is to think about all of those murderers who remain unpunished, those who will never be brought to Justice by the civilized world, because they are unknown.

We believe in a higher justice, judgement that will eventually uncover all of the war criminals, no matter where they are hiding. Their punishment will reach them, and they will be burdened with the reprisals they deserve to the same degree that they tortured us...

In this conviction lies our bit of consolation.

At Combat Against the Enemy

Previously we told about the first Jewish Partisans of Glubokie. Now we want to provide some details about the activities of various Partisan groups who operated in the Glubokie region.

1. Dr. Nahum Lekach left the Glubokie Ghetto in April of 1942, and settled in the town of Luzshki, whereas he worked as a doctor in the hospital. There he searched for a way to contact the Partisans.

    a. In October he took the surgical instruments from the hospital, and together with his wife and niece, Dora Rozet, join the Partisan group that was called "Pietrushenko". A short while later he joined the "Oktiaber" Brigade, where he remained active until the Red Army liberated the area. During this entire period, he played an active role in various battles. His wife, who worked as a nurse, was killed in the Ushatzer region during a battle against the Germans in May of 1944. At about the same time his niece, Rozet, was also killed.

    b. A Jewish girl from Kalinin, who as a Partisan bore the name Klave, was also active in a specialized Partisan group named "Pietrushienko". She served as a courier between the youth of the Glubokie Ghetto and the Partisan group, which was located in the Ushatzer region. With the Glubokie youth "Klave" was connected through M. Shapiro. Klave was a very heroic Partisan arid died a heroine. This occurred in May of 1943, not far from Ziavki. She met an SS Oberlieutenant, whom she knew carried important documents and plans, which she wanted to obtain from him. "Klave" shot him. He fell and played dead. When "Klave" approached him to empty his pockets of the documents, he attacked her and knocked her down. At that moment other Germans arrived. They took her to Glubokie, where she was tortured to make her tell the location and names of her comrades. "Klave" held out and did not reveal any secrets in spite of all the tortures. The then took her to the "Barok", where she was shot.

2. Shapiro, B. (Borka) son of Yosef and Chasia born c 1920 was an engineer. He actively participated in organizing the youth of the Ghetto and obtaining arms. In June of 1942, he organized a band of young people in the Ghetto and together with them went into the woods of the Liepler region to join the Partisans. There he distinguished himself in several of the battles against the Germans, killing many. He fell during one of the battles in 1943 while putting explosives on the train trucks. His sister-in-law, Sonia Shapiro of Hertzelia wrote about him. As well as his brother, Mordechai + wife and 2 children, and his father Yosef who were killed during the liquidation of the ghetto in 1943.

3. On the 4th of June 1942, Peretz (Zalman) Hershman (born in 1905- killed in 1944) and his family (wife, Lea nee Zipelevitz, daughter Chana and another child) fled the Glubokie Ghetto. He was accompanied by Mishe Kozliner and his brother Chaim, and also Hirsh Berkan. They went into the swamps of "Avzshada" near Luzki (the place of Peretz home before the war). There they organized a group of Jewish youth, numbering about 20, who maintained close contact with the Glubokie Ghetto. They would receive arms from Glubokie, and they were active in various Partisan units.

Mishe Kozliner was during this entire period, In the "Razviedke" of the "October" Brigade and was wounded several times.

- a. His brother was during this entire time a commander of a Vozvod of Sazikin's Brigade, which was active in the Disner and Fliser areas. Peretz Hirshman was a Starshina of "The First October" Otriad. He was very bold and brave in carrying out a number of military actions.

4. Chava (nee Kaminska) Etkin left Glubokie to join the Partisans in the summer of 1943, shortly before the liquidation of the ghetto. She was a nurse. She could not take her 8 years old twin boys with her. She left them with her sister-in-law. She was active in the "October" Brigade and distinguished herself in carrying out various tasks. During a mission that took place two weeks before the liberation, in the summer of 1944, in the Dokshitzer region, she and the rest of the unit were caught by the Germans, taken to Dokshitz, tortured and afterwards hanged.

- a. One of her twin boys survived. When the ghetto was annihilated (8-20-1943) Michael Etkin refused to listen to his aunt. He ran out of the ghetto was shot and wounded, eventually he joined the partisans and now lives in Israel.

5. On the 1st of July 1942 Baruch Ben Shimon Tzimer, of Kazian, joined the Partisans. First, he was with the "Spartak" Brigade.

[Page 206]

- a. In December 1942 he transferred to the "Suvarov" Brigade, where he participated in important missions until the liberation. In April 1943, when the "Suvarov" Brigade had to cross the railway line between Padsvilye and Ziabki, they encountered German soldiers. With grenades they killed several Germans and under artillery fire and mortar fire they managed to seize an artillery piece from the German Garrison "Zabki" and managed to cross through the railway lines without casualties. In this action, the above mentioned, Baruch Tzimer distinguished himself. {Added in by translator: Another Baruch Ben Shimon and Sara (Lifshin) Tzimer of Kazan and brother Yosef Zimer weres killed while fighting in 1942. Testimony given by their sister- Lea Ben Arie of Givataim. Also, a Zalman Tzimer from Glubokie was killed as a partisan in 1943.}

6. Yitzhak Blatt (son of Leibl, born in 1919) - The tranquil young man from Lomzsher Street, who had been one of our senior students, distinguished himself by his heroism as well as his intelligence. He was an officer in Tskhapaiev's Otriad of Voroshilov's Partisan Brigade, and later he became Politruk. Blatt displayed so much courage, so much battle expertise, that he became one of the most important figures in the above-mentioned Partisan command. In February of 1944, Yitzhak Blatt died heroically during battle with the enemy,

- a. In the middle of January 1944, the German Garrison, which consisted of 40 Lithuanians, who served with the Germans, situated not far from Kamai in the village of Petritze, not far from the town of Kobilnik, was destroyed by the Partisans of Tshapaiev's Otriad. The third Vozvod of Tshapaiev's Otriad was supposed to eliminate the Petritzer Lithuanian Garrison. A group of 20 men under the charge of Commander Lenko, encircled the Lithuanians. The Lithuanians hid in a school building. The Lithuanians entrenched themselves in the school, in three prepared bunkers, from where they shot at the Partisans and did not let them come near. After an active exchange of fire which lasted for several hours, the Partisans managed to set fire to the building. The beleaguered Lithuanians ran to the cellar of the school and shot from there. Blatt wanted to take the Lithuanians alive. Together with three armed Partisans, he approached the besieged and demanded their surrender. The Lithuanians opened fire on the Partisans with machine guns, and Blatt was critically wounded. The Partisan, Tuvia Sheres, from Vilna, carried the wounded Yitzhak Blatt to Kamai. Ytzhak Blatt died on the way. The name of Yitzhak Blatt is written in the history of the Partisan movement, arid is on the list of those, who had heroically and selflessly fought against the enemy and died as heroes. The Partisans completely destroyed the Lithuanian Garrison in Petritze.

7. The Glubokie partisan Avner Feigelman of the Voroshilov's Brigade was the main nemesis of the Germans in the Miadler Region. The Germans had a "great deal of respect" for "Alyoshen", who boldly and fearlessly exposed himself to the enemy's fire during battle. Feigelman did not rest, did not remain in the same place for more then a few days. He was constantly seen, in Lipove, in Krizshanavke, Pilkavshtzine, Magduline, Uzle, Univier, on the "high island" and so forth. Often, he would accompany the commander of the Brigade, Hlarkov.

The Germans trembled when "Alyoshe" (Feigelman) used to show up close to one of their occupied points. They would lie in wait for him, but were afraid to encounter him, and thanks to that he managed to survive the war unscathed.

Many heroic deeds could be written about other Jews from the Glubokie area. The credit should go to such heroes as Yaakov Ruderman, Bamke Genichavitsh, Yaakov Friedman, Feigel Michl, Tzipe Soloveitshik, Hirsh Gordon, Menashe Kapeliavitsh, Eli (from Krivitsh), and others. How many quantities of ammunition and arms, and, indeed, German lives the young men and women of Glubokie blew up on the railroad lines; how many garrisons they destroyed and confiscated entire warehouses full of arms, which were as important as to blew up the soldiers of the enemy.

In the struggle against the German enemy, the unassuming Jewish youth of Glubokie displayed a source of prowess capable of exploding mountains. They prepared themselves to destroy the German garrison in Glubokie and release the Jews from the local Ghetto. At the beginning of August of 1943, the Partisan Brigade "Suvorov" decided to free the Glubokie Jews out of the ghetto. The task was supposed to be carried out by the Otriad named "Kaganovitsh". The commander of that Otriad, David Pintzov, sent the Partisans, Baruch Tzimmer and Motke Lederman to Glubokie to prepare the youth of the Ghetto for an armed uprising against the Germans and the Police. A decision was made about the exact moment when the Partisan atriad will attack the German garrison in Glubokie. Tzimmer returned to the Otriad and reported that about 300 of the youth in the Ghetto could be organized. There were also arms in the Ghetto. There were guns, grenades, sawed off shotguns, and even two mortars. But it will take a bit of time to prepare for the planned uprising.

[Page 208]

Tzimmer brought with him from the Ghetto about 20 youths to join the Otriad. Among them were Yitzhak Hidekel, Abraham Peikin, Hirsh Pintzov, Alter Leizer, Moshe Skolnik, Hirsh Levine, Kopl Hoberman, Abraham Shub and others. Motke Lederman returned to the Glubokie Ghetto, in order to help the youth organize the uprising at the time of the Partisan attack. Unfortunately, the plan in its large aim was not carried out. After the defeat of the Glubokie Germans in their battle against the "Radagavtzes" in Krulevshizne, they probably sensed the danger in Glubokie, and decided to speed up the extermination of the Jews of Glubokie.

We've already told about that day that the Germans liquidated the Glubokie Ghetto.

We did not report that during the liquidation, Jews with arms in their hands opened fire at the Germans (Motka Lederman). Others managed to break through the German fire. They fled into the forest, where they were able to avenge themselves upon the enemy. At this opportunity it is necessary to favorably mentioning the "Kombrig" of "Suvorov", Y. A. Chamtzenko, who greatly helped those Jews who were saved from Glubokie and the surrounding area. Even before the liquidation of Glubokie, thanks to his initiative, there was the Jewish "Kaganovitsh" Otriad, organized under the command of David Pintzov. Chamtzenko helped a group of 23 Jews, who during the destruction of the Ghetto, escaped from Glubokie, and crossed the railroad line in the Ushatzer region. This was a difficult and extraordinary accomplishment. Thanks to Chamtzenko's help, David Leiman, Raiye Milchman and others were saved from death, at the time.

[Page 208]

After We Separated

Translated and donated by Anita Frishman Gabbay

Edited by Jerrold Landau

When I, Zvi, got out of the pit, an indescribable image unfolded before my eyes. Remnants of buildings were burning all around me. From a distance, the Germans in their autos and motorcycles lit up the landscape with projectors. Patrols with electric lamps were in certain areas surveying for any escapees. Shots from machine guns and pistols continued for 43 hours during this slaughter, making certain any hidden or escaping Jews were shot as well.

The air was filled with smoke. Next to me was my sister-in-law; my brother and nephew were further away. I thought about what to do with the first aid kit that my sister–in–law had taken into the pit. I took it and crawled out of there.

[Page 209]

I am holding my brother's Tallit. My sister-in-law moves away and I don't see anyone. No one is here? I am confused, I don't know what to do. I don't know where to look for them, and I don't know where to go. Death is lingering on all sides. I must be very careful that no one sees me. The entire area around me is covered with tall grass (former gardens). I crawled out and lay down between the overgrown grass to consider my options. My heart is racing, almost leaving my body! What happened to the others? (As I found out later, they were only two meters from me, and neither knew). I completely lost my orientation. I left behind the first aid kit. I threw off my overcoat, took off my boots, and started crawling on all fours through the "Mashiachs" colony. I crawled like this to Kasriel Katz's house on Wilner Street. Crossing this way, a few hundred meters in fire and smoke, I saw everything on Wilner Street burnt – the houses, the ghetto fence. No patrol was seen. I cut through Wilner Street, came into the garden of Sara Kremer (wife of teacher Zalman Kravietz). My thoughts became clearer. I began to think, the worst is over and a have a chance to survive... Standing there I heard groaning and moaning coming from the grass, the potatoes, and the garden. Perhaps some wounded people were lying there. The shooting hadn't stopped, the rockets were still flying from all sides, I must be decisive... The only thing troubling me and not leaving my mind – where are my loved ones? Oh, how lucky I would now be if they were with me? I can't forget that I left the ghetto. I feel an inner turmoil, what shall I do? Shall I continue? Shall I cross the fields and meadows or return to look for them, my dearest. This would mean I would certainly fall into the hands of the murderers, so I think again, if they saved themselves, they would feel sorry for my unnecessary death. Therefore, I decided to leave the city. I left through the gardens of Wilner Street, walking over dead corpses which lay in the potatoes, cabbages and other such things. Many times, I lost my footing and fell. In the pale light of the moon, I tried to look into the faces of the bodies in the gardens. Perhaps I would recognize someone, but I didn't. I felt like I was going to faint. The instinct to save myself overwhelmed me. I gathered speed, ran through the barbed wire, and leapt over wooden planks. I tore my clothing. My body was wet. I thought it was sweat, but I soon noticed the blood dripping from my body. I didn't feel any pain... I ran without shoes, in my socks. I took off the bloody socks and wanted to use them to bandage the wounds, but I couldn't do so. My thoughts were too preoccupied with using the cover of night to run away as far as possible, to the forests.

[Page 210]

The shooting in town still was continuing – guns, rockets, etc. which even reached close to me as I was running. The shine of the moon scared me a murderous eye should not spot me now! I dragged myself to Glavnitzki's garden, which was very familiar to me, for our school building was located there for 12 years. I glanced at the building from a distance, the place where the children played, and the once–happy memories flashed before my eyes, now disappeared forever...

At number 77 Wilner Street, next to the school building, I noticed a patrol. I was frightened, I didn't want to be seen so I hid in the potatoes. He soon left. As I was lying there, I began to ponder where to go. I was inclined to go south, in the direction of Krulevschchina. I thought perhaps my beloved ones went there, so I got up and set out in that direction. I had to cross the railway about half a kilometer away. After 50 meters I heard machine guns coming from that direction, so I took another route. Meanwhile days dragged by. I decided to go back to the Baraker woods. In a period of two years the Germans learned the area so well, and they murdered thousands of Jews. I needed to pass through the territory that goes from Dunilovitch to Postov. It was frightful. I arrived at the road and I noticed a patrol. I thought everything is now over! I must not run!

[Page 211]

I continued along the road, holding my breath and believing I would be stopped or shot from behind. To my great relief, nothing happened. I turned my head slightly and noticed his rifle was not drawn and he didn't move. I didn't see very well, my soul was blackened not only by the dark sky, but perhaps also by my thoughts, so I increased my speed. Bent over, I continued shuffling by, and he still was not moving. A thought occurred to me, perhaps someone murdered him on this spot. If so, why is his rifle still at his side? I wanted to take the gun... Should I turn back? I stared again and noticed him stirring, getting up from his sleep. I saw that he was still alive and understood that he was drunk or just sleeping. This miracle was a clear sign for me. I crept safely in the northward direction, to the bloody Baraker woods. It was already light when I got there. Now again the question, where shall I go? Where shall I hide during those 16–17 hours until nighttime? I found some bushes and hid. I didn't like this place, but to look for another place was too risky. I heard German voices. The laughter and amusement of the German voices filled the air. I don't know if I was covered by the bush, but I looked through a small opening, and if the enemy would see me, this would be the end.

The terrible pain of not knowing where my beloved ones were weighed heavily on me. My memories, even in these dark moments, didn't leave me. I was paralyzed by fright, this nightmare! I even forgot where I was in this world...

The hell–fire from Glubokie didn't ease. It is now the third day of the slaughter, and there are still people to shoot...

Thirst started to overtake me. I didn't wet my lips for two and a half days, let alone have food. I wanted to get up and lick the dew off the leaves of the bushes, but they were dry. I soon forgot about my thirst...

[Page 212]

I heard the Germans and their Christian helpers making a commotion, shouting orders, and screaming. Trucks were passing by and stopping. Where are they going? Later I found out the corpses were brought not far from me for burial. How many of my fellow Jews are gone? I thought to myself, as a Gluboker, one who has survived, I may be the only one who witnessed these atrocities! It can't be...there must be more saved ones! Where are they wandering? In the fields, in the woods, in the bushes, or in other places? Perhaps they are lying not far from me, perhaps the others from my family, how happy I would be! To look for them is not an option. Even to peek out of my hiding place puts me at risk. Deep in my thoughts about my unfortunate circumstances, when I found out some of our people are still alive, I noticed a young Christian boy running with a shovel. It seems he was not a "black worker" (common labourer). He was here to bury the corpses. Suddenly the unknown Christian cast a glance at me. It was as if an electric shock with great force passed through me! He signalled to me with his hands, no words were spoken, that I am safe (that is what I understood). He continued on his way. I cried for the first time. This went on for about half an hour. A small weight was lifted, my thoughts became clearer. I began to have my doubts about this Christian, can I rely on him? Perhaps he will mislead me, with this false sense of security, regarding what happened to other Jews. Other Christians fooled other fellow Jews and later reported them to the police or murdered them on the spot themselves! Seldom was there a Christian who remained passive and didn't react... I soon changed my hiding place. This wasn't easy, the forest was crawling with German Patrols and police.

I want to stress again, my life was not my most important preoccupation, it was important just so the others could find me and for those who remained alive.

After an hour in this new hiding place, I felt somewhat relieved. The shootings and explosions that were taking place in Glubokie for two and a half days were lessening, it became "normal" and soon there was a moment of silence. I began to get used to it. My thirst bothered me, worse than before. I couldn't continue, I began to lick the leaves, but they were dry. It was a hot day, I was parched, there was no saliva left with which to wet my lips. No food, three days passed like this! Three days ago, I shared my last meal with my loved ones. I didn't want to remember! But to have a drink now, oh God! I will never forget this moment! If there was any place to find a drink, I would sacrifice my safety. This was a heavy weight which I had to endure. I almost forgot about my situation; the day seemed endless. It seemed longer than the entire Jewish exile. I lay close to the place where Germanavitch, the wagon driver who brings peasant men and women from Glubokie to Shtaravtzina in their festive clothing, lived. Usually, one was drunk. It seems odd, as earlier it seemed to me that the entire world has disappeared! As it was sunny, perhaps I made a mistake, the world was alive. It was no more, the world is black for me, for us Jews! I envy them! I bit my lips with great heartache. The sun was slowly setting. That long, black summer day found its end! The forest became still, and nobody could be seen on the roads. I had a wild idea. Across the road I saw the house where the Gluboker Jews came to every summer to vacation. I thought to myself, the Christians who live there now are certainly merciful. They certainly feel bad about the great Jewish misfortune. They lived once amongst us in harmony. My wild thirst brought me quickly to my feet, I looked around, and with the speed of lightning ran across the road to the house. It was locked. They probably saw me running towards them and locked the door. I did not let up and started tearing at the door. I ran to the back door, which I opened. A group of Christians, young and old, descended upon me with sticks, screaming wildly! I couldn't even speak. I couldn't ask them anything. Understandably, the reception I received drove me away, so I sprinted back to my hideout. I don't know how I did not break my neck.

[Page 214]

This picture is exactly such as when wild children pounce upon a homeless and helpless dog. They chase him away with sticks and stones, and he runs for his life, until he runs behind the mountains of darkness. I ran back to the bushes. Somehow another set of strange miracles took place: the Christians let me live (for my head, they would have received rewards from the Germans, money and other concessions) and amongst the group there were no policemen or Germans or any other of the "good" people who wanted to murder me! No one had seen me on the road.

The forest was empty, no talking, no movement, no singing. When a bird flew by, a squirrel sprinted from tree to tree, or the field mice were running around, I instinctively trembled ... even they wanted to know what I am doing here. They understand I am hiding from my species, from my "people", in their forest where they live with other creatures. I knew this territory belonged to them. I knew they meant me no harm; they will not tell anyone. I looked at them with caution ... they also made me feel uncomfortable ... why are they flying and jumping in front of me? I was glad that night arrived. The day was endless, but even such a day comes to an end. It has been three days. Remember, three days of slaughter and burning in Glubokie. The Jews are murdered and burnt. Those three days seemed like a lifetime that I had been separated from my beloved ones – without whom I cannot live! It ended, the night arrived and spread its "wings" over everything. It was easier to endure in the nighttime. Security is more certain, but the pain grows worse. Emotions begin to stir; my insides begin to growl – what happened here? Is my life worth living? It is still not certain that I will continue to live. Is it a joke that I still want to live? Why am I better than the others? What will I do all alone in the world? Soon my thoughts change. The night is short. I must do something. Last night I survived by some miracle.

[Page 215]

And after that day I can endure everything... except, why do I have to wait here? Yes, I must continue my flight. In which direction shall I go? The world has four corners, which one is safer? The main question, where can I meet up with the other survivors from Glubokie? It is clear, I have to continue "blind" and have luck. There is no amount of calculating, no logic remains. I was drawn to the west. But where is the west? I knew where Glubokie was situated and orientated myself accordingly. I crept out of the forest to the field. It was lighter in the field, but one could still not see far. The moon hadn't appeared yet (it was the 22nd of Av), I needed to distance myself from Glubokie during those four hours. My thirst bogged me down, I cannot control it any longer. Food was of no importance to me, although I hadn't eaten in three days. Like the bushes, the fields and meadows were dried up, there was no stream, no well, no leaves to contain any water. I moved in a westward direction through the fields and meadows. I became frightened when I approached the main road as it was dangerous. As I was walking and thinking, it grew lighter outside. A rocket came in my direction followed by shooting. It was bright outside and they were still looking for escaped Jews from the ghetto. I lay down again and soon the shooting stopped. I began my journey with great fear, my fate was not a certain one. Patrols were everywhere. Shall I continue my journey? What shall I do? I am in the open field and cannot see the forest. It's been awhile since I left the Baraker forest and to turn back could be risky. A second rocket falls, then a third and a fourth and so on. If someone saw me, I would have "no way out". I continued while looking back in the direction of the rockets, I lay down again waiting. The rockets "chased" me like this for three quarter of an hour. One rocket fell close by where there was no grass, no flower, no hill, and miraculously on the other side I noticed a well.

[Page 216]

I jumped into this well. I was completely immersed, except for my nose, so I could breathe. Even here they could spot me. I trembled from fear. Finally, when it got dark, I pulled out my head. The shooting stopped so I got out of the well (careful not to make any noise). The water poured off my body, I felt the pain from my wounds. My soaked, torn clothing made it difficult to walk, but the momentum spurred me on. Lying in this water, being so thirsty, I don't know why I didn't satisfy my thirst. I realized this much later when I had left the well. The rockets stopped, and I calmed down. Along the way I came across some troughs with water. I drank from here...this was the first time in four days. I drank and drank this swampy water. I continued with my soaked clothes, rubbing and swishing, making noise; I was afraid someone might hear the sounds. What shall I do? Undress? Go naked? I don't allow myself to undress, take off these torn "schmates" (rags) which were falling apart, at least they covered my body! I sat down to rest. I got very cold. I started to convulse and again my thoughts began. Why am I struggling to survive? But perhaps someone saved the others. How happy will they be if I survive as well! And for this reason, for them alone, I must struggle to survive. I went further, I ran, to distance myself a bit. Days passed. I had to again figure out how to endure the days.

Another night passed wandering around aimlessly, until I first arrived at the Zawisker Forest – four or five kilometers from Glubokie. I cannot understand to this day how I made the journey so quickly. I do not even sense the entire night as I wandered about or was delayed for kilometers; but, thank God, I was kilometers further away from the hell of Glubokie.

Another terrifying night was behind me. I had more chances of surviving. I went into the forest. I do not know how I found my direction.

[Page 217]

It is better and "homier" here than in the Baraker forest. I wandered for an hour; the sun had already set. Everything around me was quiet, still! Birds were chirping, frogs were croaking, flies buzzing; the water must be close by. Oh, I feel at home here! Not a single voice, no ridicule, no laughter! I can breathe normally here. The taste of "solitude" ... I find an open space, not blocked by the sun, where I undressed and spread my clothes to dry. I noticed the marks on my body from the barbed wire, not only on my hands and feet, also on my chest, stomach and neck. They were somewhat dried up. I now saw my watch, the prized possession that I carefully tied around my arm and hid in the ghetto; amazing, it is still working. After the flight from the rockets and hiding in the well, it was still working, it was now 5 in the morning. It was very dear to me, a friend had exchanged this watch, his whole life! He should be here with my other loved ones. This watch is ticking! Odd! Guns should be "ticking"... all seems quiet here in the forest. What existence lays before me? My clothes dried ... I put them on and begin to pray. I don't remember all the prayers, I will say only part, just the Shema. I was thinking, as I was reciting "and you shall teach them to your children" [Deuteronomy 1:19] that my brother was fulfilling this commandment. He raised his only child Aharon Yitzchak in the spirit of Judaism and studied with him from the age of five years and onward. At the time of the misfortune, he had already systematically studied all the way to the Torah portion of Emor (Leviticus 21–23), and he had studied the books of Joshua, Judges, and Samuel from the Prophets. I recall how once he came to pray with us during the morning service in the ghetto. At that time, we were reciting Kaddish for our deceased mother of blessed memory. The Torah reader made an error during the reading of the Torah. He mixed up the letter *shin* with *sin*. Aharon Yitzchak called out that the Torah reader must be from the tribe of Ephraim [translator's note: see story in Judges 12]. Who else cannot pronounce a *shin*, and says *Sibolet* instead of *Shibolet*. (Judges). All those gathered, especially the Maskil Reb Shalom Weinstein of blessed memory, were charmed by the child's understanding. At that time, I understood that the "*veshinantam*" [and you shall teach] would certainly protect the child with his parents, and they would survive...

[Page 218]

I continued my "walk" in the forest. My watch indicates 7 in the morning. I notice three open pits where farmers hide potatoes in the winter. I understood that some sort of a settlement – a village or hamlet – must be nearby. Instead of being happy with such an understanding, I was uncomfortable. I realized that I was not completely isolated from "people" here. The beast can catch me here as well...

Suddenly... something was not right...how did I get here? I was wandering about in the potato pits. What happened to me? I am confused. Where is everyone? My head is aching like I was wounded, something on my conscience is nagging at me. I felt my head, my hand is covered in blood... I looked at my watch, it is 2 in the afternoon. What happened, first it was 7 a.m., now it is 2? God in heaven, what is happening to me? The watch is working, what did I do in these 7 hours? My wound in the head hurts! Blood was tricking, but not a lot. I touched my head and remembered, where is my hat? I looked but could not find it. Now it is bothering me. Why did I come here? Where are the others? Suddenly, I turn around... there in the ditch is my hat rolled up in the sand. I still don't understand, I am not feeling very well... I am all alone, where are the others? Something was wrong. I lay down on the ground and cried uncontrollably. Two or three hours passed. I think the crying brought me back to reality! It was like a strange dream!

[Page 219]

I started to remember. Friday morning in Glubokie, the slaughter started, we lay in the pit for 2 days and I don't know how I got separated from the others, how I reached this forest alone... I felt somewhat relieved, but the days seemed like long years had passed... A time where the slaughter took place Glubokie! Saving my watch, Leaping into the well, my hat in the sand... I realized that it was Monday, August 23 in the morning... After these few days I must have fallen into this pit and passed out! I probably fainted and hit my head. I must have come to. It is still blurry, crawling out of the pit without help. I don't know how I did it. Fate was on my side. I felt that it was in the merit of my mother of blessed memory. I pulled the hat out with a long stick. I cleaned it a bit, put it on my head, and recited the blessing "He who brings to life the dead"... I cried again, but not as much as before. For the first time, I felt very weak. Perhaps it was from surviving the past few hours, or perhaps it was a reaction to the entire time. Until this time, I was in a daze. I sat down. The clock showed it was after 4. It was a nice day. No human soul was seen or heard. I thought that I must eat something, for in two hours, it will have been an entire day since I drank a bit of dirty water, and my mouth was dry. I felt that if I had survived Hitler's troops to this time, I could continue in the forest. I was so weak that I couldn't move from this spot... My motivation which brought me here will eventually disappear. I have to sustain my body, but how? How do I get a piece of bread? I need companionship... before I thought this solitude would sustain me! It is impossible to find a person who will not demand our blood... If I am near a village, I cannot crawl out of the forest, for appearing in a village would mean certain death. I would have to wander about that day until the next morning. I thought that I would find a stream within 15 hours. Perhaps another miracle would happen. I began to wander aimlessly in the forest. I thought that maybe this time I would meet some of the saved Jews. Am I the only one who survived from the city? There must be somebody else who crawled out... Who knows through which forests and fields they found themselves? I came upon a stream, both sides covered by tall grass and bushes. I stood in the reeds and looked to the other side, without any purpose or aim. Suddenly, not far, I noticed a Christian not completely dressed like a peasant, but a bit city–like. He did not see me. What shall I do? Shall I ask him for food? Who knows, he may inform on me. He may tell his entire village about my hiding in the forest. It was good on the other side, for he was alone, and I would be able to escape if something was out of sorts. I made a sound, mouthed some words and he understood who I was and from where I came. He did not think for a long time. He told me to wait and he will return shortly with some food. I remained apprehensive. I was not sure whether to wait for him or to escape from him. I hid in the bushes and watched to see if he would come alone and whether he indeed had brought bread. I had to risk it... There was no other choice, for dying of hunger is no better than being shot. Half an hour later he returned to the opposite bank. It seemed like a year to me. He was indeed alone, but I didn't notice any bread. He looked for me with his eyes. I came out from the bushes a bit and he noticed me. Like a thief, he pulled some bread from his coat and threw it over. It was a kilo of bread. This moved me greatly, and I cried again. He then muttered something to me, which I did not understand. Was this a warning? Was he frightened not to be seen? Soon he disappeared.

I could not calm myself for a long time. The bread got soaked with my tears which were salty and wet.

It was already 7 p.m., four days since I last ate dinner with my family. I remember my last meal together with my nearest and dearest. I shuddered again and could not calm myself for a long time.

Darkness settled in the forest. Through my tears, I broke off a piece of bread and put it in my mouth. I held it for a long time without being able to swallow. It got stuck in my throat. I took some water and tried to get the bite down. I succeeded, but it was not easy. I swallowed three or four, or perhaps five bites, but could not swallow any more. It was completely dark in the forest. I could see the horizon through the branches of the trees. In the silence of the night, I heard the playing of a harmonica, as well as some shots from the other side. I did not know from where the shots had come. I had lost my orientation after the earlier events. I had the impression that they were still shooting in Glubokie, and the area. As I later found out, I was not mistaken. They were still searching for escaped Jews in their hideouts and in the fields and forests and killing them. The sound of the harmonica tormented me. How can this world be two separate places – ours and theirs?

[Page 222]

I found a spot under a tree and began to pray the Ma'ariv service During the recital of the Shema, I again thought of the section "and you shall teach your children"... I lay down. It is interesting that being alone in the forest at night did not scare me at all. I slept well that night.

Tuesday, August 24: the day was bright and quiet. The forest calmed a bit. I decided to remain here another day. Perhaps I will find some of the escaped Jews. I noticed some gentile youths with fishing rods going to fish. They stopped me. I was not comfortable with this encounter, but they understood what I was doing here and who I was. They questioned me and I answered in a pleasant manner. I excused my appearance, asking them for pity. I was not one of those rich Jews, just a living "corpse" and as they left, I asked, in a broken voice, that they not tell anyone... They gave me their promise... I did not trust them, though, and I moved on from there. I entered another forest. I did not find any Jews there. While wandering about in my new place, I encountered several Christians, young and old. They were well dressed. The younger ones started to run when they saw me. They were probably afraid of my appearance. The older ones went along on their way and did not bother me. The encounter made me even more uncomfortable than the previous one, and I set out in a different direction. The entire time, I looked back to ensure that they were not following me. As it turned out, I did not get away from them completely. The entire day, I hid and searched for saved Jews in the forest. I did not find anyone... I did not know from where I would get my energy. The bread I had saved from yesterday was dry and I couldn't eat it. I wasn't hungry, I only wanted to drink. For once I had a lot of water. I didn't know exactly where I was in the forest, later I found out I was still in the vicinity of Glebokie. I don't remember anything else that happened to me that day. There was only one thing that I remembered: I was beside myself that I had not found any Jews. I hoped greatly to find at least one Jew... I lay down under a tree but did not sleep. I was consumed with my thoughts, which were stronger than every terror, than every fear. They paralyzed me. The fear of death by the Germans during the previous days had the "benefit" that it drove out the nightmare from the survivors, and provided the impetus...

[Page 223]

Wednesday, August 25: I began to think of a "purpose". I did not know what happened with my family. This is what drove my further struggle for life... I did not encounter any Jews. I did not know whether they had "finished off" everyone in Glubokie. I wandered around the edge of the forest. From afar, I could see peasants working in the fields. I did not know whether or not to approach them. I continued to wander around the edge of the forest. More peasants were working, but a distance away from the forest. Approaching them in an open place is risky. I continued a bit and noticed a peasant going back into the forest. I quietly called out to him. He stopped his horse with the plow, looked around to see if anyone was watching, and approached me. I did not have to explain to him who I was and what I was doing there. Everything was clear to him. I did not learn any special things from him. He explained to me that "Zhidkes" had fled through that area on Friday, Saturday, and even Sunday. He saw them. One butcher had dragged a person wounded in the stomach to their village, and he wallowed there in a barn. He did not get any help. He did not know what had happened to him. I could not figure out who that person was. I found out from him further that I am now closer to Glubokie, to the hell, than I had been yesterday. The Christians from his village were not in Glubokie on that bloody day. They were afraid...

[Page 224]

He didn't know of any saved Jews. He only knew that peasants from the neighbouring villages came with their wagons to collect the bodies and bring them to the Baraker forest. It had been a lot of work... There would have been fewer bodies had they been burnt, but there were many more since they had been shot. The Christian left. He refused to give me food, for his village was far and he didn't have anything with him. I went into another nearby forest and asked a second peasant. I felt I could trust him. I asked for some milk, a cucumber, and salt; it was seven days since I last saw these. He brought me a flask of milk and a piece of bread and asked me for a "finferl" (a 5-dollar piece) – a gold "finferl". His appetite for gold left me unsettled. I regretted this encounter, I had some coins in my pocket and would have given him some, but I was afraid to reach into my pocket and show him.... I assured him I didn't have any gold, I had never been a merchant, only a simple teacher, and I lived from the fruits of my labor. I took out 90 Soviet rubles and gave it to him. He wasn't very happy, he thought he encountered something useful – a Jew running away from the knife, how could he not have any gold? Is it possible? Certainly, many of the peasants amassed gold and other valuables from the victims, as well as from those fleeing and giving away all their possessions in order to save themselves. As I was later told, after the slaughter, the Christians in Glubokie, paid for their liquor with gold coins! They carried them in their pockets like small change. He finally took the 90 rubles and left with a sour expression. I was very unsettled. I was afraid to approach a Christian. I began to seek a place to hide in the forest. I sipped a bit of milk, which literally restored my soul. I began to wander further. I reached such a place that seemed to me like a human foot had never trod there. There, I was calmed... I lay down again under a bush in my new place. I again had a difficult night. My thoughts about my dear ones troubled me as usual... The effect of the entire misfortune upon my mind cannot be described...

The next day, Thursday, August 26, I wandered through the forest and thought... there is no trace of Glubokie Jews. What was going on there?

[Page 225]

I did not know anything. I was wandering around like an Arab in the desert. I went in search of another peasant closer to the edge of the forest. Peasants were working in the fields. I called to one in the grove. He stopped to talk to me. When he realized that I had been a teacher, he related to me with a special respect. He opened up to me a bit, and explained that he had already read for a long time about the current terrible times and against the world situation in general. He showed me with signs that everything had taken place exactly as he had read. His "philosophy" did not penetrate my head at all. I consented to everything he said, not caring that I had not even heard what he had said to me. He was no wild beast, from which one must hide. This comforted me. I was happy that a peasant was standing and talking to me for a while, and considered me as a human being... According to his remarks, he considered me to be an intelligent person. Nothing was practical, however; what I was most interested in I did not receive from him; he did not know what was happening in Glubokie, and who had survived. He remarked that he did not belong to the band of robbers who were taking advantage of the misfortune of the Jews to enrich themselves. Just the opposite, he sympathized with the Jews. I had the impression that he was indeed one of the better Christians. He belonged to the few who still possessed a bit of conscience. With a good wish, he parted from me and returned to his hut, to his normal work, to his home, to his family... And me?... Like a fox I went back into the forest, where I must watch out that anyone does not find me.

I could not calm myself. I wanted to find out what was going on in Glubokie, whether anyone had survived, and where were they? Where was I? Is this place safe? The Christian told me that they had heard that the Germans and the police, may their names be blotted out, are wandering around the forests in the vicinity of Glubokie searching for Jews in hiding.

I made contact with another Christian, named Yevgeni. He was about 35–40 years old, with blond hair. He talked calmly for a long time, with sweet talk. He made the impression of someone like Laban the Aramean [i.e. a trickster]. He was talking to me, and at the same time, plotting in the background... He explained to me that young Jews and children had fled through their village (near Zawiski – I do not remember the name) to the fields and meadows. They had attempted to evade the villages and people. He suggested that I go to the neighbors in his village to find out what was happening in Glubokie. Incidentally, he would also be in the city the next day and would try to find out something. I asked if I could spend the night. I wanted to test him, to see whether he was trustworthy or bloody and deceitful. Some showed another side of their unfortunate "friendship", inviting them in and then delivering them to the devil. He told me that taking me in would be a danger for us both. The best he could do would be to leave open the door of the shed, which was located at the edge of the village, and would be dark. I could stay there. However, I must leave the shed in the morning before the villagers awaken from their sleep and the herders go out to the fields with their animals. For him, an open shed is not suspicious, and there is no danger, but couldn't assure me if nosey neighbours or prying eyes might notice me. I must take care that I not be seen by a human eye. It was risky, and I decided to remain in the forest under a bush that night.

[Page 226]

Yevgeni brought me bread, a cucumber and milk at night and told me the aktion in Glubokie was still not finished (it had been over a week). They are still looking for Jews, more murders are taking place. Tomorrow, Friday, he will go to Glubokie to find out more. He parted from me, saying that he would come to me again the next day. He would come riding on a horse, so that the village would not suspect that he has some sort of a contact in the forest. If he rides a horse it would appear that he was returning from foraging for food at night. He would come to me in the evening in the same manner and bring me information about what he had found out and seen in Glubokie during the day.

Yevgeni kept his promise. In my situation, such a contact was a great thing for me. It reassured me a bit, even though I did not trust Yevgeni completely. I had to hide in a certain bush when he came to me in the morning and evening. From there I could see if he was coming alone, or with someone else...

Friday, August 27, a week from when the terrible slaughter in Glubokie started. A week in which the sounds of weapons of destruction did not cease. It has been a week and still no news of my nearest. A week of wandering day and night alone in the forest. A week that was an entire era of exceptional experiences. A week of not more than seven days during which I began to turn grey and older, and aged decades. A week in which each hour, each minute, was an eternity. It continued....time, as bad as it was, it is still passing me by.

[Page 227]

On that very Friday, the "fortunate week–day" of my survival, I got up from under the tree and looked at my watch. It was 4:30 a.m. I couldn't believe my eyes; it was exactly at this time one week ago that the Jews of Glubokie met their final hour – the shooting in the streets of the ghetto and the rioting had begun. The hour in which there had already been several tens and hundreds of Jewish victims. The hour in which I, my sister–in–law, Dr. Vilkomirska–Rajak, my nephew Ahron–Yitzhakl, my brother and our neighbours, ran quickly to our hideout in the pit, not knowing if we would ever crawl out of there and see the sun shine again....

(Incidentally, Dovid and Sonia Hazan (Chazan) lived with us in one house in the ghetto. They saved themselves from the SharkevtzItzke Ghetto as soon as the shooting started, by running away as soon as the shooting in the ghetto started. They chose to run instead of hiding in the pit and being shot by the bullets.) I was deeply immersed in my thoughts about all the events of the past week in Glubokie and hadn't noticed Yevgeni on his white horse. He approached, took me by the hand, and asked "What's up with you? What are you thinking about?"

I was so shaken up that I had no power to answer him. He understood this and was not offended. On the contrary, he tried to figure out my thoughts and cheer me up. He said that today, Friday, he will be in Glubokie. I requested that he find out something about our people. I told him that my sister–in–law, who had been a popular pediatrician, was known not only in Glubokie, but also in the entire area. I asked if he could find out something even from a small gentile boy or girl. He left, and I waited for him the entire day. During the day, I thought about every moment, every event that had taken place in such a such an hour or minute one week earlier, where were still all lying in the pit. They day passed quickly, and Yevgeni came to me riding on a white horse. I was disappointed, for he didn't tell me too much. He only told me that Chaim–Leib Schulheifer, wandered into Mrs. Ortoyav's garden (on Wilner Street) begging for cold water. She turned him over to the police or the Germans, who came and killed him... As per the rumour in the city, Schulheifer was found with a large sum of gold and valuables. This implicated Mrs. Ortoyav, as it was found on her property. He didn't report about my family. I suspected that he was withholding information, but he assured me that he held back nothing.

[Page 228]

I spent Shabbos in the forest. My thoughts lured me to those Sabbaths in my house and so on... We would tell the children stories about "The Sabbath in the Forest" and other such ones. I searched for some meaning to Shabbos in the forest, I didn't find any solace, no "magnificent lit–up palace" with a beautifully arranged Shabbos–table. Neither Abraham our Forefather, Elijah the Prophet, or other such sages appeared to me. I didn't hear any sweet singing, such as "Lechu Neranena." My blood–filled heart did not allow for any fantasies in the dark forest, and a stream of tears poured forth from my eyes. This well–deserved cry calmed me. I recited the Kiddush... was it appropriate in such a dismal situation to bring in the Shabbos? Was I desecrating the Sabbath with my Kiddush? It states explicitly that "one must call the Sabbath a delight." I prepared the first "seudah" (meal) with a piece of bread and some milk.

[Page 229]

I recalled that, at the same time one week previously, when the slaughter in Glubokie had already been gong on for 16–17 hours, I was still together with my dear ones, lying in the pit in the ghetto, and we extinguished the smoldering remains of our bunker...

We did not know how this would end, and whether we would emerge alive.

As the custom after the meal, I lay down under a bush and fell asleep. I slept on the Sabbath night in the forest… It was "a bit" terrifying. Various thoughts were weaving around me…. Finally, I fell asleep. A thunder the next morning awakened me! This time it was not from a wild human beast, but from nature. Dark clouds had been gathering all night. A terrible storm arrived; the trees were swaying from side to side. Some broke and fell. The nature was frightful, the darkness unforgiving. Lightening bolts pierced and lit up the sky, then darkness again. Everything was pouring down on me, as if from a pail over my head. I got up quickly, again thinking that I am all alone, and went under a tree. I don't have any other options… The trees were swaying around and around. I have no other place to go. I tell myself its much better than last week, when my situation was much worse.

The pouring rain, accompanied by strong thunder and lightening, lasted for several hours. I was soaked to my bones. I had very little clothing, a few torn rags. The rain began to let up. Nature took its course. I couldn't sit down, and certainly couldn't lie down. Everything was wet and muddy. I remained standing. I got cold and began to tremble… I anxiously waited for the sun to warm my body. But who knows what type of a day it will be! I am waiting for my Christian. Time passes, and he had not come. During the few days, he would come regularly in the morning and the evening. Perhaps he was delayed due to the weather. Soon the sun rose, and I warmed up a bit. Yevgeni arrived several hours later with news. He said that Germans and the police were preparing to perpetrate searches for Jews in the fields, forests, and village. The nearby region around Glubokie had already been cleansed of Jews. They had captured many Jews on the way, and now wanted to "cleanse" the more distant area… He meant that I must move from the area and seek a further area in which to protect myself. I did not know whether this was the truth, or whether Yevgeni simply did not want me near his village for some reason. Even according to the second hypothesis, it was clear to me that I must leave my "new home." He told me the quicker the better, for every hour could bring more surprises. I told him that it was impossible for me to go during the day, and therefore I must wait until the night to set out on my way… He agreed. Yevgeni came to me again the evening. He brought me food for the journey and showed me the direction in which I should go. First, I should go about 2 kilometers to the Merecki huts. From there, another 5–7 kilometers, to a larger town of Udelo, then another 4–5 kilometers till I meet up with the partisans. The Germans were afraid to venture in this area. According to his calculations, I would be going through forest and fields for 15–18 kilometers in the specified direction. I gave Yevgeni 1,000 Soviet rubles and said my heartfelt goodbye. There were tears in my eyes, and I noticed that the Christian was not indifferent. He wished that I go on my way in peace, find my family, and it will be good. He was afraid to leave the forest together with me, so that we'd not be noticed together. He left, and I remained in the forest with my thoughts about my journey.

[Page 230]

I left when it got dark. I concentrated on my directions, passing villages, huts, horses grazing in the pastures, and young gentile lads building a fire. I overheard them talking about me: "Someone is going to Merecki." It didn't bother me, for they assumed I am a peasant from a village. This spurred me on, and I continued along my way. I passed a hut on a hill. It was festive in his courtyard. Many young people were there, singing and laughing. One was playing a harmonica, there was dancing... I stopped for a few seconds. It was dark outside, and I was stand behind a wall... how far away was this sort of life? How long has it been since I was in my home, in my environment, among my family! Now they are "above" and I am "below". We are in two separate worlds!

[Page 231]

The joyous laughter, singing, and enjoyment of the Christians pained me. I haven't seen the world for over three years; I forgot that such a world still existed. I thought the skies fell down and choked everyone, not only the unfortunate Jews. I wandered through the dark night, and the thoughts tormented me. It has been eight days since I have left the pit and snuck out of the ghetto. It has already been a week since I parted with my dear ones. One week since I left Glubokie – the Glubokie in which I had taught hundreds and thousands of students for over a decade. My thoughts were interrupted. I came to a wide ditch, with young trees and bushes on both sides. How do I cross? I wandered around for an hour and a half, and barely found a way to cross. I lost my orientation and couldn't figure out how to continue. I noticed a hut in the distance. It was calm and quiet. The residents were certainly sleeping. After a bit of thought, I decided to knock at the window to ask directions to Merecki. I saw a woman, then a man. They were polite to me and did not seem to wonder why I had disturbed their sleep. They seemed to know who I was, for it has already been a week that Jews had come knocking at night; some to ask for a bit of bread, a drink of water, directions, etc. The unfortunate Jews were fleeing from Glubokie. I now realized that while wandering around the ditch, I had not gotten farther from Glubokie, but rather closer to it. I was open hearted with them and was not disturbed. They showed me the direction. It took four or five hours until I reached the Merecki huts, which were no more than four kilometers from my place of the previous day. I was very tired, so I lay down to rest. Not far away, I noticed straw under a canopy, and I lay down on the straw. After ten days of being away from my bed, this new night lodging felt like a palace to me. I was no longer in the forest, and for some reason I felt that I was not so alone... Houses in which people live were not far away... In truth, I understood very well that the householders would not be very happy with their "guest" who "set up" his night lodging. However, I felt at home there. I lay in the straw in that manner until day began. I hastened to leave there before people would awaken. I went further along my way. I passed through forests, bushes, and fields. I made sure to avoid being noticed. I succeeded, as it was Sunday, and nobody was working in the fields. I did not have anyone whom I could ask for directions. I stumbled about.

[Page 232]

I felt that there must be partisans somewhere in this region. However, what would I, a broken, oppressed person without a drop of energy, do with the partisans? They require people who are strong, mighty, with a firm spirit, who would be useful... However, maybe some of my relatives were here with the partisans? My sister–in–law is a doctor, and the partisans certainly require doctors! A bit later I encountered simple, village women, and went with them along the way a bit. They knew the region very well. They did not ask me who and what I was. Everyone already knew who we fleeing Jews were, and from whom and for what reason we were fleeing... They told me that the Germans and police were no longer traveling around individually, but rather in large groups, for they were afraid of the partisans. I felt a bit more comfortable... I came to a village (the name of which I do not recall), and the peasants in that village assured me that there is no one in the village of whom we need be afraid. I entered a house. There, it was light, happy, and festive. They had baked "*blines*," cooked and fried. The house was full of adults and children. Everything was normal, as if nothing had happened. Before my eyes the depths of oblivion into which we had rolled again opened up. I entered several other houses. Almost everyone appeared the same.

[Page 233]

I found city furniture: finely constructed beds, closets, Trumo mirrors, tables, stools, wall clocks. In one house there were two fine buffets... This was completely out of character with the poor, peasant huts. It seemed somewhat strange. I did not wonder about it. It was known that a large portion of this was Jewish owned furniture that had been taken to the villages after the murder of their owners.

Near the village of Udele, I had to pass over an area that was fraught with danger, for Germans and police used to traverse that area. Blessed be G–d, I traversed that area securely and peacefully. I must have walked ten kilometers that Sunday, and this was a great thing. I spent the night of Sunday going on to Monday in an open barn near a hut. In general, I did not hurry anywhere... My "day" was anywhere where I was wandered, sat, lay down – the entire land was mine... One only had to hide from the Germans and non-trustworthy Christians devoid of conscience.

I set out on my way again on Monday August 30. I again went only on tortuous routes. There, the journey was less dangerous. I had earlier encountered a Christian there. The Christians were more forthcoming, for they were afraid of the partisans. I wandered about freely through the fields and meadows without a defined objective. Where and to whom must I go... I went through a "*punka*" where Christians arrange hay and lay down there in the middle of a bright day and fell asleep. The owners soon arrived and did not wonder at all about my presence there. They permitted me to remain longer. However, I wanted to go and search for Jews. Everyone had said that Jews had fled through that village.

When I asked anyone if they had noticed a lot of fleeing Jews, I received the answer of "Yes, many Jews were through here." One had seen four, another had seen another two (probably the same ones as the first one). Another Christian had seen two Jews women with a child. In this manner, I counted eight or nine people.... I waited until the Christians got worn out, and I left my "resting place." I wandered further – where and for what, I did not know. I knew only that I was getting further away from Glubokie. A Christian was working in the fields. I approached him. He explained to me that partisans often come to his hut. A few partisans were with him the previous day, including Itzke Blatt (a former student of ours, a very good lad, and an excellent partisan).

[Page 234]

He said that had I come the previous day, I would have met them all in his home. Here I felt free. My heart was heavy, however, and tears flooded my eyes. No words came out. The Christian offered to feed me and let me sleep in his barn. He tried again to reassure me the escaped Jews of Glubokie will pass this way to Ushike, a farm five kilometers from his hut [Barsuki]. There were already many partisans in there in Ushike, and the situation was more secure from the Germans. He talked a great deal about the situation, about the partisans... In truth, this concerned me very little at that moment. I was in a completely different situation. It was very fine with me that the situation was more secure, and I had more chances of survival. I was afraid of becoming completely calm, because then my wounds would open… I ate with my host in Barsuki. His name was Stankevitch. It was the first time during my wanderings that I ate at a table, with a spoon and on a plate, like a human being. I was in no hurry to go to Ushike. I was exhausted, and nothing was urging me on. My thoughts still focused on my nearest and dearest, perhaps I didn't want to confront the truth about them. I returned to Stankevitch's barn and fell asleep there. This was the first time during the entire time that I was able to sleep soundly.

The next morning, Stankevitch again invited me to eat. His son was sick with dysentery, so I was afraid to eat there. I couldn't refuse his hospitality, so I ate with him. Stankevitch showed me how to go to Ushike, and I departed. I felt as if I were in a dream, crossing the fields and meadows, stopping to speak with the peasants who were working in the fields. They were all telling me the same thing, that the escaped Jews were in Ushike. I described my brother, sister–in–law, and their child, asking if anyone had seen them? I could not find out anything, however. I arrived in Zalnitze, two kilometers from Ushike and was informed that a German division had just passed through. This disturbed my false sense of security. I thought no Germans ventured here. I was still a few kilometers from Ushike. I had to pass through deep swamps.

[Page 235]

I wasn't anxious to go, but I had no choice. Who knows what I could find out about my relatives here? I drag myself onwards until I encounter partisans. At first, my encounter with them was not very friendly. I thought, who knew if I would be welcome? Would they not be suspicious of an unknown wanderer…? The first partisans whom I met near Ushike were a group of men and women riding in peasant wagons well disguised. When they saw me, they stopped and inspected me from head to toe. I evidently made the impression that I had suffered greatly. One said something to the other with compassion that I had evidently not eaten. They asked me from where I had come and who was with me and allowed me to continue. I felt more comfortable and somewhat lighter. This encounter with armed people, who meant me no harm, and on the contrary, showed a certain degree of empathy, cheered me up. I did not believe that this could happen…

I finally arrived in Ushike on Tuesday, August 31 at sundown. I arrived at a large house of a small squatter, from which the owners must have fled, or the partisans murdered them on account of their collaboration with the Germans. Here I met three refugees from Glubokie: Feigel from Vilna, more than lightly wounded; and Mrs. Kurak with her 14–year–

old daughter, also seriously wounded in the Glubokie slaughter of August 20, (the mother carried her on her back in this condition all the way to Ushike). Feigel managed to come on his own, and made her own bandages for her wounds, from straw and rags. However, the young Kurak was lying there almost dead. She did not speak. She lay there, groaning, on a floor with a bit of straw, but this was also good.

[Page 236]

There was no news about my sister–in–law and nephew. Perhaps they didn't want me to know.

One kilometer from Ushike was Zukov's Brigade of partisans, with those from Glubokie who fled, who were: Arke Birsh, Itzke the Cukernick, and Mindel–Dina Fidelholtz (a nurse). They came to us in Ushike often and brought help. Dina Fidelholtz brought bandages and medicine for the wounded Kurak and the elderly Feigel. The others brought food. The armed Glubokie youths also told me that Glubokie Jews who had escaped, including my brother, had been in Ushike and had spent several days there.

My situation changed completely. I had two opposite feelings. On the one hand, the good news about my brother evoked great joy. On the other hand, I was pained and unsettled that I did not know anything about my sister–in–law and nephew, who would have been with my brother, but whom nobody had seen. This dampened my joy. I was also pained that my brother knew nothing about me and would be completely broken. I regretted not coming here sooner, wasting time in the potato fields. Had I come earlier, I would have met him here. The partisans brought me potatoes, but I couldn't get anything down my throat. The others wondered why I was so unsettled. They calmed me, saying I should be grateful; they didn't understand my inner feelings. My appearance was terrible. I had turned grey and become unrecognizable. I looked at myself in the mirror for the first time, and could not recognize myself...

After I calmed down a bit, I became involved with the sick people. They told me that they had been wounded on Friday, the first day of the slaughter, as they were fleeing from the ghetto. Mrs. Kurak had left her husband, four sons, and two daughters in the city of slaughter. They had fallen dead before her eyes from the bullets of the murderers. She carried only one daughter, wounded with a bullet in the abdomen, through the fire of the ghetto, and barely managed to get her here. Feigel, more than 50 years old, had also lost everyone as she was escaping from the slaughter. Wounded in a narrow place, she ran through the fire and barely dragged herself here. I gave the woman some money which I had with me. She had left the ghetto completely without anything. She told me that I saved her help with my assistance, and she would never forget this. She set out to the village and purchased eggs, butter, milk, etc. for her sick daughter. I also gave money to the sick Feigel – she did not take it as she did not need it.

[Page 237]

My thoughts consumed me, how to meet up with my brother? Nobody knew when he had left. They only said that one group had left in the direction Mior, another in the direction of Kazian, and some to the Myadel [Myadzel] region. According to their estimation, my brother was in the latter group.

At night, I lay down in a second room on a long table. It was cold and hard, but I did not feel it. I couldn't fall asleep. I felt more nervous energy than before, with simultaneous feelings of joy and agony in my heart. I was weaving plans in my mind how to reach my brother and how to avoid another disaster. Now my life has meaning, not for myself alone... My situation was more secure than before, but the Germans were still lurking. They hadn't disappeared from the face of the earth. Not to mention that I had to set out on an unknown journey. I did not yet know in which direction I must set out to get to my brother. Nobody knows for sure where he went. And what would happen if I set out on the dangerous route, and found that I made an error with the directions? And had I known that he left to the Myadel region, how would I get there – as it is 70 kilometers away, and one would have to cross many railway lines, where the danger is very great. I had nobody to accompany me. As I was sitting there immersed in my thoughts, there suddenly was an explosion, which threw us all in the air. We ran like frightened mice, not knowing to which direction. It was clear that the Germans had attacked us. Then it was quiet, with no more banging. It was dark, and we looked around carefully. A window had fallen and shattered into pieces. No one could sleep after that. We spoke about our survival stories and the entire situation until it got light outside.

[Page 238]

On Wednesday, September 1, I left for Barsuki (or Barsutczyne) to Stankevitch. I hoped to encounter Itzke Blatt or other partisan acquaintances. I was looking for advice on how to contact my brother as quickly as possible and tell him about me. They all discouraged me from travelling alone on such a dangerous journey. I asked if anyone would accompany me on the journey to the Myadel region, but nobody agreed. During the day, Falke Lewin arrived, then a nephew of Zundel Musins (a student of ours), and a brother–in–law of Fishke

Satnowik (I do not remember the family). They told us how they saved themselves from the slaughter in a chimney (see chapter Liquidation of the Ghetto) on that terrible August 20th in the ghetto. At first, they wanted to go with me to Myadel, then changed their minds and left for Kazian.

Not far from our house I met an old woman, Soshe from Glubokie. She came to Ushike and made arrangements with a Christian to work as a seamstress. She gave me news about my brother. She assured me that she had spoken to him, and he was very worried about me, but she wasn't sure where he went. She was saved in a miraculous fashion. On Friday morning when the slaughter started in the ghetto she escaped to the gardens of the "Messianic Colony" and lay in the tall grass. She placed all her hopes on her talisman booklet… She saw how the Germans close to her dragged their victims and beat them. She witnessed the last young girls begging for mercy from the Germans to spare their lives and not kill them. The cruel ones responded with laughter, beatings and abuse. (this was done by our own Christian policemen). She overheard how they were planning to extort gold and other valuables in exchange for their lives, so to speak. Hundreds of bullets flew over her head, but nothing scathed her. She lay motionless in the tall grass. On Friday night, she had great regret that she couldn't light the candles and greet the Shabbat, as she always did. She did so in her thoughts… She witnessed the Germans torching the Jewish houses in the ghetto and people struggling with death. She witnessed before her eyes the horror of the slaughter. She lay the frozen the entire night and the next day. The ghetto was burning from all sides. She saw everything, laying there in the grass. The 75–year–old Soshe, clenching her teeth, didn't break down. Saturday night she crept away from the ghetto and the city and changed into peasant clothing. An old Christian friend gave her a shawl, and she started her journey. No one paid attention to this old village "peasant" woman with the shawl over her shoulders. When she noticed a vehicle with Germans or policeman, she knelt down on the roadside and began to cut grass. She got up and continued her journey when the bandits disappeared. This is how she arrived to Ushike, got work as a village seamstress, and "settled in". She had a house and food to eat.

[Page 239]

She told me she has a son in the partisans, around Dolhinov [Dolginov, Dołhinów] and Plestzhinetz, and that she wanted to go there. But how? She wants to join me, if I want to take her along. Honestly, this 75–year–old Soshe was more heroic than I, the 30 something year old man. She had more strength and was very successful. But I still needed someone else, I told her as soon as I find another person, I would take her along. Indeed, we needed to leave here as well, for the Germans had probably smelled that there was a small nest of Jews here, and they would attack Ushike. For the same reason, the partisans were not happy that Jews were congregating in a single point. I decided to leave there on Sunday, the 5th. I did not want to go on the Sabbath. Itzke the Tzukernik, Arke Birsz, and Dina Fidelholtz came to me. I told them about my plan, and they prepared to look for a Christian who would take us. They went, and I remained waiting until Sunday.

Suddenly on Friday, September 3, Itzke the Tzukernik ran to me, not dead and not alive, and told us that we must flee as soon as possible, for they Germans are attacking that place and the partisan forces here were too weak to drive them out. This confused all our minds… What should we do with the wounded ones? There was shooting from the patrols. We took the wounded out of the house to the bushes, for the hiding place was very poor there. Old Soshe and a wounded 16 or 17–year–old girl from Sharkovshchina came running to us. The girl was wounded in the mouth (the bullet entered her mouth through a cheek). She was able to move freely. She had escaped from Glubokie where she lost her entire family. We brought the wounded Kurak and Feigel from bush to bush. Soon the shooting stopped, but it was not yet clear whether the situation was calm. We didn't know what to do. It was difficult to look after ourselves because of the sick ones. After 5–6 kilometers we stopped for the night. We slept in various huts. We took care of the sick.

[Page 240]

Next morning, Shabbos, September 4, Soshe and the young girl from Sharkovshchina proposed we divide into groups of three. I did not know what to do. I surmised that we must distance ourselves from there, but we couldn't leave behind the sick people, who could not come with us. Feigel and Mrs. Kurak had set themselves up well in the hut and told me to not tarry there. The three of us left. We found out from the peasants in the fields that we were going in the direction of the Kazian forest, another 18 kilometers away. Honestly, this was not where I wanted to go. I wanted to go to Myadel region, where my brother was. However, the situation was that we were going to the Kazian forests, where we might find out something about my sister–in–law and nephew from the escaped Glubokers. Perhaps my brother had changed his plan, and was also there? In general, I wanted to know which of the Glubokie Jews survived. We left the village on Saturday morning and "set ourselves up" in the field… We did not want to travel on the Sabbath… However, we also did not want to remain in the village. We wandered through the fields that day. In the evening, we snuck into a barn near a hut and spent the night there. Very early Sunday morning, when everyone was sleeping, we set out on our "way." We passed by burnt villages with no buildings still standing. The Germans often broke into the partisan zones and burned and destroyed everything, so that the partisans would not have resources. The elderly Soshe helped me a great deal on the way. She found it easy to obtain food from the peasants (I was ashamed to beg...) She often brought me food from a peasant house, whereas I found it difficult to enter a house. I could not lift my eyes or look people in the face. I could not tolerate it when young peasant gentiles looked at us as if we were some sort of curiosity. I have to admit that the elderly Soshe managed far better that I. She wasn't as broken. This amazed me greatly. She wore on her breast her booklet of omens for times of danger, illness, etc. I do not recall the name of the booklet. She told me that it saved her life and that she puts her faith in her survival by wearing this booklet.

[Page 241]

We finally arrived in the Kazian forests on the evening of Tuesday the 7th, after a long journey. A few kilometers away, we met some Glubokers, Brudna and a young girl (I do not recall the family) who lived on kernels of corn that were not yet taken to the barn. Closer to the forest, we met Jews in "lapzies" that they got from the peasants. Some were barefoot. Their gloomy faces and gait left a heavy impression on me! Perhaps I didn't look better, but I couldn't see myself. The woman accompanying us took us into the forests one by one, where we met other Gluboker Jews, as well as from Dokshitz, Mior, Sharkovshchina Lozki and other places. Almost all the people knew who I was, even though I knew only the Glubokers, who came to greet me while looking at me strangely, inspecting me from head to toe. Shrugging my shoulders and wondering, I didn't know what they were looking at. At first, I did not understand what type of portent they saw in me. A girl (Korman), who had studied in our school for a year, quietly asked those around who I was. Now, everything became clear. I asked for a mirror. I looked into the mirror, and it was now clear – my long-time student didn't recognize me, nor did I recognize myself... I had become grey, overgrown, aged by decades, and everything was completely dark... They recognized me only by my voice. My student approached me, and I could not talk then. I was overcome with tears, but I controlled myself so nobody would notice, for we were all in the same predicament.

[Page 242]

Mrs. Pinczow from Pohost, who left to the forest with her family before the slaughter, brought me some dairy farfel, which I ate only for appearances, as I could not eat in this situation. The Jews there were somewhat "in order." They had food, for the partisans brought them. They all looked after me. The older "residents" concerned themselves with a bed for me. They question of a dwelling was very serious there. Cabins were only available for those who built them, but they still provided me with a cabin. Soshe didn't like this way of life in the forest. She left for a nearby village that hadn't been burnt and made arrangements with a peasant.

It was 60–70 kilometers from Kazian to Myadler forest. The roads were difficult and dangerous. There were many railway lines, large open roads, and highways to cross, where it was quite probable to encounter the enemy. What do I do? I need to reach my brother. If I find some one to accompany me...

I spent the night there. In the morning, there was movement. Itzke Blatt arrived with other partisans from the Chapayev Otriad, which was stationed in the Kazian forests. Blatt was an exceptional partisan, and everyone there knew him. He quickly ran to me when he saw me (he had been a student of ours for eight years). There were tears in our eyes, and we could not speak... He said to me: "Enough, enough..." I understood that he did not want the gentile partisans to notice this. I could not control myself, and I turned to a side...

Soon more Jewish partisans came. They were well armed, free, strong, brave, and battle ready. They made an impression on me. They were not the sorrowful figures of bent, beaten, worn out Jews. This brought me satisfaction, and simultaneously my heart jumped. I was encouraged that so many Jews of Glubokie could have saved themselves. There were always ways, true, not always easy, nevertheless easier than being burnt alive or being buried alive in the earth...strange! As if no one saw the warning signs! We had become frozen, hardened, detached, as if it was a natural phenomenon... Itzke Blatt and his group left on a "Zadanie" [task or mission] in the Myadel region and told me he will reunite me with my brother. This calmed me a bit. I felt life here in the forest much like in my own community. Everyone drew closed and comforted me. Yankel the Kazianer, old but steadfast, managed to escape with his family from the Glubokie ghetto in time. He had two sons and a son–in–law in the partisans, so he was quite at home here. He insisted that I eat and drink at his place. The Jews prayed here with a minyan three times a day. Yankel was the only one who put on tallis and tefillin. In the evening, we recited the blessing on the New Moon, as it was the beginning of Elul. Suddenly Berel Shapiro arrived, son of Chavel Shapiro of Vilna Gasse. He had been a ghetto policeman and the Jews didn't receive any favors from him. Now there were several who wanted revenge and turn him over to the Partisan police for his past. He was liable to the death penalty. With great courage I had to intervene to calm the enraged moods and rescue him. In the current situation, I couldn't reconcile with Jews killing Jews, even if they were guilty... (I had never heard of anyone being killed directly by Shapiro in the ghetto.) Shapiro was later killed because of things that he had hidden with a Christian, but I do not know the details.

[Page 243]

Here there were also people who were lightly wounded, whose wounds had been bandaged with straw and rope. Itzke, the son of Chaim Hershel Gilewicz, was among them. Fear overtook me when I saw the tattered, barefoot images in the forest, who were more shadows than people. Later, Yoshke Shapiro from Dokshitz arrived – the kilo of gold (as they called him), for the Germans had paid a kilo of Gold for him when he was arrested in the Glubokie Ghetto. Shlomke the Loszkier, Hershel Slobodkin, and Tzalke Kremer also arrived.

[Page 244]

Thursday, September 9, I decided to embark on my dangerous journey to Myadel forest. With me were: Aidele Shperber (Zalman Shperber's daughter), Chana Kutchak, someone from Gelsan, and a tailor's daughter from Kisheleika, Nechama the tailor from Zamkova Street near the bridge with her young nephew boy Pipik (his father, a shoemaker, lived on Zamkova Street near the bridge), and Hilie the wigmaker (I don't remember his family name). No one knew the way. We had just "crawled out from underneath our mother's apron", but off we went. I felt that our group was too large and easy to be spotted, but it was impossible to split up, since they all wanted to go with me. Soon I became the "leader" of the group. My praying calmed them. They said that it gave them hope and pleasure...

I went barefoot and my feet swelled. They got rags for my feet, and this literally saved me. We wandered aimlessly, and frequently had to retrace our steps, adding many extra kilometers to the journey. We ran into a light German–machine on the way, so we hid under a small hill. We were very afraid, but it passed without incident. The German bandits didn't see us. In the evening, we arrived at a railroad track. We walked along it for several hours, not knowing where to cross in a way that we would not fall encounter a patrol. Finally, we decided to separate. I went first with Aidele, Zalman Shperber's daughter. We noticed a hut on the other side of the tracks. We snuck into a barn and spent the night there, and continued our journey the next morning, Wednesday, very early, before the peasants awoke. At Volazhin we were stopped by a group of "Manachovche" Partisans, who detained us for a half day in an open field. During our "arrest" we were well treated. They brought us food. A Jewish partisan watched us and told us we will soon be released. In our situation, this was a scant comfort. We would have certainly preferred at that time to remain under that "arrest", or, more accurately, under their guard… The young girl was uncomfortable, however, as she could not believe that armed men could mean no harm. Finally, an older partisan with two of his comrades came to question us. After some time, they released us and warned us not to be fall into the hands of the enemy. They sent us to a hut to spend the night under the protection of a partisan, who ordered the peasants to give us food and treat us well. We were calm and felt good. The next morning, a partisan arrived to bring us food and sent us on our way.

[Page 245]

On Thursday, September 9, we travelled the entire day, almost without stop. We often met partisans along the way, who reassured us. We arrived at another village late. A woman peasant called Michlia Feigelson gave us all apples. We spent the night in the village.

The next morning, Friday, September 10, we had the serious problem of crossing a highway through which German automobiles often travel. The highway was guarded by Germans, and it was dangerous to cross it. We were not bold enough to cross it ourselves. We decided to find a scout who knew the side roads, this was difficult since we didn't know who to trust. We were afraid that someone would give us over to the enemy instead of protecting us. Eventually we were approached by a Christian woman who had to go to that region via the highway and offered to take us along. To win our trust, he told us that her husband was a teacher and freedom fighter who was killed by the Germans. Having no choice, we set out on the journey with her. She went so fast that there was no way that any of us could keep up with her. She told us that we must go through that way as fast as possible. Our hearts fell, but we followed her with our last energy. When we came within a half a kilometer of the highway, we started to go slowly and more securely. We noticed the tips of the telegraph poles rising from the highway. Our teeth were chattering, and our hearts were heavy. We were silent, not calling out a word to each other. We all had the same thoughts: Will cross the highway safely? The highway marked the border between one partisan group and another. We hid in bushes. Our leader was running about to "scout out" the region… She told us that she hopes that we could cross safely, however, she didn't want to accompany us. She would go in advance and wait for us on the other side. We weren't convinced, but we didn't have a choice. We waited until the Christian woman was on the other side, and then immediately began to run after her across the highway. She was very unhappy about this, as she was afraid that she might fall into German hands due to this. After running 200 meters, and already on the other side of the highway, we noticed several

German autos hurrying from behind. We quickly fell flat into the fields. They didn't notice us. This was another miracle for us, that we crossed the highway at a fortuitous moment...

[Page 246]

We rested a bit and then continued further. Our scout drove us hard again, and we couldn't keep up. Furthermore, it started to rain, and the roads became slippery, swampy, and difficult to pass. Our bare feet kneaded the wet, cold lime. We didn't eat the whole day. We could not give up. In the evening, we arrived in the village of Kalinovke, in the Univerer region of the Myadel district. Our Christian scout left us about a kilometer from the village, as she didn't want the partisans to find out that she had brought us (why?) She was afraid because she took money from us, even though we paid willingly. On the way, the partisans indeed asked her whether she was taking gold from us to transport us.

We were so exhausted that we were barely able to remain on our feet. Even speaking was beyond our strength. We had one focus, to rest as soon as possible. The local partisans awaited our arrival in Kalinovke. There were anti–Semitic sentiments there so they told us to go another kilometer and a half from the village, where there were some other houses in a hamlet. For us, this was more difficult than the 35 kilometers we had walked during the day. We became desperate. If there was a German blockade around us, we would have been unable to escape. We sat down in the soggy grass near the village, ourselves soaked from the rain and our own sweat. We could not move our feet.

[Page 247]

It got dark and wished for an eleventh miracle from the ten miracles that were created on the eve of the Sabbath at sundown (It was indeed Friday evening) [**Translator's note**: see Pirkei Avot 5:6]. The partisans from Kalinovke would certainly come to us soon... Soon a person arrived from the village with an order from the elder that we couldn't remain there. I don't know where we found the strength to get up and continue, but we did so. Infuriating an unknown partisan was also impossible to do. What should have been a half hour walk took hours. There as well, we received a cold reception from the Christians. This must have stemmed from the bad relations between the partisans and the Jews. We told them that the partisans had sent us there. We had no energy left to plead with them. They were well–rested and sated in their own home, and who were we... We pleaded with them to allow us to spend the night. We were assigned to two in a house. I could not eat due to weariness. I also could not sleep. I lay down like a log of wood. Even the thoughts...

The next morning, Saturday, September 11, most of us couldn't even get up. The exhaustion and hardship from the previous day had not dissipated. Not only me, but all of us lay down that night like blocks of wood and could not even move an eye. Indeed, first thing in the morning, we felt that we were aching, some our hands, some our feet, and some our shoulders. It was a difficult effort to hold our heads up. Our option to remain and rest longer was not good, for, as noted, we had not received a warm welcome... We again had the question, to where? Where should we go from here? Earlier, our destination had been the Myadeler region. We had already come this far, but what was further? After a few hours of collecting our desperate thoughts, we divided into two groups. The larger one went to the Misuner and Uzler region. I, with Nechama the dressmaker (wearing eyeglasses) and her small niece went to Univier, a large group of large huts where partisans are situated, and where individual refugees from various towns have found a bit of refuge. As we said our goodbyes, we cried a bit and wished each other good fortune... Nobody knew where they were going, to whom they were going, and what awaited them in the next hour. My goal was to find my brother, but where? I had given Itzke Blatt a letter when I saw him in the Kazian forest, telling him I was alive. But did he receive it? Nechama and I remained in Kalinovke a while longer. There, partisans lived in almost every house. They ate, drank, and got drunk. A drunk partisan, apparently an elder one, came to our house and questioned us about who we were, what we were doing there, and how we got there. I explained to him all the details in brief, about our experiences and tribulations, and that I want to go to search for my brother in Univier, where there are Jews. He got angry, went on a drunken tirade, and talked about Jews in the most disgusting way, in German style. This frightened us! We wanted to distance ourselves, but we waited for him to end his tirades. He did not leave us alone, and threatened us with his gun... Finally, he told us not to go to Univier. He would soon be setting out in that direction on his bicycle, and if he would find us on the road he will shoot us. He showed us the loaded gun and pointed it at us to show us what he would do... We assured him that we would not be going to Univier, and we quickly rid ourselves of him. Even the Christian from the village couldn't believe what she heard. The peasants behaved better toward the Jews out of fear of the partisans, and if this is how a partisan behaves, what good could come of things here? He and two other drunken friends left on their bicycles in the direction of Univier. We remained in a great dilemma and did not know what to do. It was not possible to remain in the village, for our relations with the villagers were poor. If we went to Univier, where there are Jews, we would be in fear of the partisan. Indeed, we set out in the direction of Univier. We were afraid to ask the Christians about Jews, lest there were Jews hiding there about whom the Christians did not know. We encountered an elderly female peasant, and cautiously asked her if there had been Jews there. She answered, "About Jews you need to ask Stephan." Stephan was a known personality in that region... First, he was the go–between the partisan units. Second, he was involved with the "Jewish question". He even collected a significant sum of "fives" and "tens", but Jews who had such found refuge and salvation with him. As we went along the way to Stepan's, I noticed a Jewish woman and child picking berries in the field. I was happy, as they would certainly know everything. However, the woman, upon noticing us from afar, turned in the opposite direction – that is, she did not want to encounter us. I was pained and confounded. However, I quickly realized that she was probably disguised as an Aryan and was afraid to speak to any Jew. I did not want to cause her any distress, so I decided to leave her alone. But Nechama the seamstress didn't back off. She approached the woman. At first, she did not recognize us and acted like she did not know anything. I barely trusted her. Nechama soon recognized her as a woman from Glubokie, Tzipe Rudstein (I didn't know her from Glubokie, but I later realized her son studied at our school). Then Nechama spoke to her in a "womanly manner", complaining and asking: how can you hide from your own Jews under such circumstances, not being willing to show your face, acting like you do not care? In the middle of that discussion, the aforementioned Stepan's wife came running by. She was no less involved than her husband in the local "Jewish question." She was indeed a driven, intelligent, practical peasant's wife, and certainly valued the satisfaction and income that she received lately from Jews. She strongly scolded Tzipe for wanting to ignore us and not tell us anything. (To this day, I do not understand why Tzipe wanted to hide from us.) Stepan's wife told us the Jews were close by, in the forest, on the "high island", about 3–4 kilometers away. The Jews come to the village from time to time to collect their provisions. She then called for Jurke, a young shepherd who was close by, to lead us to Kriszanevka, a place of a few huts a few kilometers from Uniever, from where it would be easy for us to meet up with the Jews in the forest. Along the way, I found out that Jurke was a young man from Myadel, whose father Yoel (I don't remember his family name) gave him over to Stepan to serve as his shepherd. Stepan adopted him and gave him the name "Jurke". After saving his only surviving child, Yoel went to join the partisans to fight the bloody enemy. He didn't see his son as he was stationed far from Univier and could not meet up with his son. (Later, before the liberation, he returned, and we met him). I was somewhat envious of Jurke, roaming free amongst the cows and pigs in the fields, crossing roads, having what to eat and where to sleep. For me, having where to sleep was an exceptional situation! He also had "steady" employment! Along the way, I learned a few more things about Stepan, how he hid the Jews and other things. He would hold a Jew with him only for a few days and would then direct them to the forest in a "different zone." It was more difficult if someone was poor and did not have the money to pay – however even in such a case, he would not turn anyone over to the Germans or police – and naturally, that was the most important thing...

[Page 250]

We arrived in Kriszanevka on Shabbos, September 11, in the evening. We spent the night there, for, after an exhausting journey, we didn't have the strength to look for the "Jewish settlement" in the dark. We went into a barn and collapsed from exhaustion. I couldn't fall asleep. It was already half dark when I suddenly heard two people sneaking into the barn and speaking. I very badly wanted to find out who they were, but I was afraid to call up. They did not know that someone else was there. Soon, the two started a conversation between themselves, and I recognized the voice of Moishe Mirman! He was Zinger's son–in–law. The Zinger and Mirman families left Glubokie in March 1943 and were all saved. The second was a Jew from Druya, Yankel, who was hiding in the forest with the Zingers. I called out to Mirman, but he didn't recognize my voice, for it had changed. I told him who I was. He was so overwhelmed with joy that it didn't have any boundaries. As veteran "residents" here, they lived in some village and it was too late to return to their "home" from the depths of the forest in "Goloducha" (as their "place of residence" was called). This was not far from the "high island" where the other Jews were living. It was difficult to reach either of those Jewish "settlements", as they were surrounded by large bogs and deep swamps. Therefore, they were more secure from German attacks. The next morning, Sunday, September 12, we left Kriszanevka for the forest. We had to go through difficult bogs and swamps. The entire time, we thought we were lost. We couldn't understand how people lived in such a desolate place. Then we saw some people. We thought they were Germans and got frightened. To our good fortune, they were three partisans. They showed us the way. We found Jews after wandering around in the forest for a few hours: Eli Gordon and his family, Alia Padnos, Yosel Kasdan, who had been with me in the pit, Chaim–Meir Bipkin (a young boy). Later, Motke Genshteyn, Meir Bliachman, Motke Markman, and others arrived. Gordon's wife, Vichne, gave me a shirt. The Jews had built a primitive bath and heated it in honor of the "guests." I washed up and put on my "new" shirt. I felt human again! They were well entrenched in Zemliankes and in Beidelech (primitive huts).

[Page 251]

I found out that my brother was waiting for me in the village of Misun, seven kilometers from the forest. Three days previously, the partisan Itzke Blatt told him I was alive and heading in that direction. My brother thought I was going directly through the village of Misun and was very anxious about why it was taking so long. I had gone through fields and forests in order to avoid human settlements, and thus did I evade the village where my brother was. I found out that Misun had a partisan house and asked around if anyone would accompany me. I didn't want to go on my own as I didn't know the region. Nobody wanted to go, however, and I decided to set out myself the next morning, Monday, September 13. Sunday dragged on for a long time. I spent the night in the bath house, on the "floor" made of cold, rounded stones rather than flat planks. The air was veritable bath air, saturated with sweat and mold. It had recently been used by 30–40 people. Nevertheless, I felt "good."

[Page 252]

It was warmer... I spent the better part of the night sitting up. The pebbles under me were rounded and hard, and it was possible that I was also a burden for them... In the morning, I woke up to nice weather. I was immersed in my thoughts as I set out to go to my brother in Misun. I rose to recite my prayers before leaving when I suddenly saw my brother behind the trees. He came looking for me. He looked like from the other world and made a frightening impression upon me. He had aged and greyed. His eyes were sunken. He walked hunched over with a stick in his hand, barely making his steps. I was very frightened for him.

I finished the *Shmone Esrei* prayer and we kissed, and did not say anything... I didn't even ask about his wife and child. My brother wept a few tears, and I couldn't bear it. I started to utter the Shehecheyanu blessing, and said: may G–d's name be blessed, etc. I should have felt salvation at that moment, when I started to cry. I was happy for my brother, and simultaneously filled with grief that my sister–in–law and nephew, Aharon-Yitzhakl, were no longer with us... I did not want my brother to notice my inner feelings. My immediate task was to support him, so he doesn't go into a depression. I felt guilty that I had not endured the great misfortune. I had left our hideout on August 21. I had left everyone behind, and this brought great agitation upon my brother's thoughts. He thought that I had been killed and that he was therefore completely alone. I was further guilty in that he was not calm at that time, and he set out blindly to Yosel Kazdan, who clumsily wandered about the world. They then encountered the Germans who perpetrated the great misfortune. After remaining for a long time near the bath, we set out for the huts. My brother worried everyone with his appearance. It was had to image that a person could change so much within a few weeks – aging by decades.

We were welcomed by the other Jews. They comforted us that the others had been saved, and we would hear from them quickly… We let them convince us, and we wanted to believe in this miracle. We went about with piqued ears, listening and asking every partisan we encountered whether they had seen so and so… Many of them gave us various innuendoes that they had encountered them in some partisan base. We hoped and waited, for this was our entire aim in life.

[Page 253]

We began our new life in the forest together with the other rescued Jews and partisans. Aside from rifles, we armed ourselves with the pen. We conducted first-hand publicity work among the White Russian villagers regarding the importance of fighting against the bloody Germans. We continued with this work tirelessly until the liberation by the Red Army on April 7, 1944.

After the Liberation

Translated and donated by Anita Frishman Gabbay

Edited by Jerrold Landau

As I said, we were liberated by the Red Army, April 7, 1944. In the village of Univier, in the Myadel district, the few surviving Jews welcomed the first intelligence officers with open arms, calling them saviours, liberators, etc. The tears that had been quelled suddenly opened like a floodgate! I too was among the welcomers. When a major came riding in, he stopped near us. We greeted him with photos and told him about our tribulations. He comforted us, assuring us that the German beast will be defeated its own den until the end… We were informed that an evacuation office was opened in Buguruslan, where we could search for evacuated people and refugees. Through the military post we made our inquiries to find our nearest and dearest.

We left the forest together after a few days, along with the Sverdlin, Dreizin, and Kaplan families with whom we had formed a bond. We set out for their town of, Krivitch, about 150 kilometers from Vilna. Our sole aim was to find out anything about our loved ones. We could not believe that they were no longer alive.

Several days later, we left for the liberated Glubokie. Our town lay completely in ruins. The Germans had burned the town before they retreated. Several tens of surviving Jews, terribly broken, had gathered there. They settled into the less burnt houses at the edge of town and didn't know what to do. The world was indeed freed from the Hitlerite beast, but the lonely, orphaned Jews felt more unfortunate in the free world than in the forest, where they at least had a goal in life – to fight the enemy and avenge the blood of their kin. Now what?

[Page 254]

I started to wander about, still hoping to find someone. A woman doctor, the wife of the Glubokie official of the N.K.V.D., told us that she had heard in the White Russian Health Ministry in Minsk that a doctor Rajak was alive and must be brought back to her former medical position in Glubokie. We left for Minsk and to our great misfortune, no one knew of her in Minsk, even though she had worked in Glubokie until the war.

As former teachers, the representative of the Education committee, Kochanovski, acted very friendly to us. He comforted us and suggested that we remain in Minsk and continue with our teaching professions. However, we were not in a proper frame of mind to continue teaching. Kochanovski then sent us to the White Russian State Museum where they requested that we take a position in scientific work. We were restless and didn't want to remain in one place. We connected with the museum in a position in which we would collect historical material about the events that took place during the occupation in western White Russia.

We were drawn back to destroyed Glubokie. We hoped for miracles… Perhaps our dear ones would come back from somewhere. We wrote endless letters to the various offices in Russia, as well as to friends. To our misfortune, our search was fruitless. No miracles happened…

A short while later, we found out that they were killed by the Germans in the beginning when we were separated on the highway to Dunilovitch.

Now, our motivation to live was to tell the world, the whole world, about the catastrophe that befell the Jewish communities of western White-Russia and Lithuania – what we went through ourselves, and what the survivors would tell us. We understood that this would not be an easy task, as those that did not endure this would not be able to comprehend it. This didn't stop us and we embarked on our task with the full fire of our pain.

[Page 255]

We began to accumulate material about the events in the Jewish communities during the time of the German occupation.

I wish to note that digging amongst bloody ash and ruins, we realized that human language does not have the necessary words to describe everything that happened, just as human comprehension is too small to grasp it. This didn't stop us however. With fortitude and determination, we continued our work, which we considered holy. We absorbed all the inhuman horrors through which the Jewish settlements were annihilated. If the world cannot comprehend this, then at least let them know, so they can transmit the knowledge of the atrocities that took place in the 20th century to future generations. Let it be engraved in their eternal memory that a strange creature descended to earth that murdered six million Jews – women, elderly, and children – in a modern fashion over the duration of a few years.

If humanity cannot understand this, then let them at least know about it!

[Page 257]

Glubokie Necrology

Translated by Eilat Gordin Levitan

Glubokie Jews who perished during the German Occupation in Glubokie, in the years 1941 to 1943 in the Glubokie Ghetto, which was among the very last in Belarus to be liquidated, the date of the final Action was August 20, 1943.

The families are listed according to their addresses:

Wilner Gasse

Surname	Head of household	No. of family members who died
FREYDKIN	Wolf	5
FREYDKIN	Zelig	2
FREYDKIN	Yitzhak	3
TEITCH	Max (Meir Begin's son-in-law)	2
BERNSTEIN	David (Zlata survived)	4
KREMER	(A glassmaker)	6
SIMKIN		2
BARKAN	Elie	3
PLISKIN	Mendel Leib	2
DRUTZ	Wulf (Mendel Leibe Pliskin's son-in-law)	4
KANTEROVICH	Yosef (Mendel Leibe Pliskin's son-in-law)	6
SLABODKIN	(Survived; Hirsh with the Partizan)	1
GITELZON	Lazar	5
AIGAS	Alter	4
TZIRLIN	Shmuel Motta	4
TZIRLIN	Shmuel Netta	4
MILSHTEIN	Nachman	4
SHPIER	Chaim Simha	5
KATZ	Katriel	2
AYGAS	Pesach	2
PAN	Reuven	3
FEYGELSON	Yosef (Survived; Zalman and Dan, with the partisans)	3
KOPYETZ	Moma	4
BODNAV	Yakov	2
KAZDAN		1
ZASPITSKY	Hertz	6
GELLER	Yehoshua (Doctor, and wife Zina)	3
BLANDT	Yuda	4
GITELZON	Natan	2
FERDER	Moshe	4

LEKACH	Shimon	4
ZALMANOVICH	Rabbi Hillel (son-in-law of Rabbi Katz, perished in Vilna)	3
SHAPIRA	Bela and Gutman	5
FEYGELMAN	Chaim	6
MAHLER (OR MILLER)	Mendel	3
GINDIN	Mendel	3
SHULHAIFER	David	5
KRAUT	Motta	4
ZINGER	Yermiyau	3
SVERDELIN	Zlata	5
YUNGELASON		5
GELMAN	Shmuel Nisan (Survived; Abba, he was with the partisans)	3
ZEITLIN	Berl	4
SCHLEISSER	Der Alte (old)	3
SWARDLIN	Bar	3
YUNGELSON	Dvora (Survived; Yuda and his family, son)	3
RUDERMAN	Mendel	3
SPEYER	Leib	4
VATKIN	Shmuel	7
	Aaron (the old wheel maker)	3
ITIN	Yosef (Survived; Rafael in the Red Army)	3
YUNGELSON	Wulf	5
SHAPIRA	Zalman	3
SHAPIRA	Mikhail	3
KAPILOVICH	Tanhum	6
KAPILOVICH	Yakov Bar	5
BADNYOV		3
YUNGELSON	Mottel	5
YUNGELSON	Katriel	5
FEYGELSON	Yakov son of Yeruchmiel	5
EPSTEIN	wife of Shmuel	5
ROSENBLUM	Falya- tailor	4
SIRMAN	Hirsch	4
KORMAN	Baruch ?	4
KAZDAN	David Zalman	3
KAZDAN	Yoseleh (wife and a child, Survived)	2
KAMINSKY	Yehoshua	5

SHEINKMAN	Yitzhak	3
GINSBERG	Yeruchmiel	4
MELAMED	Hirsch	2
MELAMED	Tuvya	4
MELAMED	wife of David Shimon	1
FEYGL	Husband of Pyatza, tailor. Survived; Mashka and Manya. He was killed in combat	8
ITIN	Peretz	7
KONIGSBERG	Yakov Melamed's son-in-law	4
GOTKINS	Shabtai	4
SHAPIRA	Leib	4
ITIN	(Carriage driver)	
KRAYNES	Moshe the Smith	4
AYGES	Zalman	12
AYGES	Chaim Reuven	6
AYGES	Zalman Moshe	2
BIRZAS	Chanach (Gershons Shayas	4
SHAPIRA	Roda (Shmuel Nisan Gelman's sister)	4
SHAPIRA	Chevel	5
FIDELHOLTZ	Kaskel and wife Dara	5
KANIS	Kopel and wife	5
WEINSTEIN	Mendel (a daughter survived)	2
MINDLIN	Alter	4
RAZAVO	Motta	5
YAFFE	Yashka	3
MAGILNIK	Yekutiel	2
YUNGELSON	Pinya	4
YUNGELSON	Zalman	2
MYATTAS	Ytzhak	5
KRAUT	Chaia Sara	2
KRAUT	Golda- husband Lazar was in the Red Army and survived.	2
KRAVITZ	Zalman the teacher	4
KRAMER	Sisters	2
GITELZON	Chaia Ethel (Survived; her husband Meir)	4
ZIYATCHIK	Moshe Yakov	3
ZIYATCHIK	Chaim son of Moshe Yakov	3
GLAVAN	Mendel	3
MANDELBOIM	Rabbi	5

Surname	Head of household	No. of family members who died
AYGES	Chianna (daughter of Berl Binyamin)	1
ALPEROVITCH	Avraham (Moshe Chana's son-in-law)	6
DIMMENSTEIN		
DREIZENSTOCK	Levi Itzhak	
GORDON	Zalman and his in laws	8
SHULAVITCH	Israel and wife Sara with their children	4
RABBINOVITCH	Meir Michik	4
RABBINOVITCH	Kalman' wife and 2 children (Kalman survived)	3
TREISTER	Yitzhak (Chana Eshka survived)	4

[Page 258]

Platz Kastyushki

Surname	Head of household	No. of family members who died
RUDERMAN	David (survived;Yankel, partisan and in the Red Army)	4
SALAVYECHIK	Moshe	2
GINDIN	Feyga	4
GINDIN	family of Moshe Meir	5
GILAVITCH	Chaim Hirsch	8
TITELBOYM		4
GILBERSTEIN	Mendel with wife Chana (née Titelboym)	3
TITELBOYM	Dvora	3
GITELZON	children of Binyamin (Survived; Binyamin and wife and child of a daughter)	2

[Page 259]

Dobrave Gasse

Surname	Head of household	No. of family members who died
IRMA	Yakov	3
VIRSHOV	(his in laws with wife and child and mother and sister)	5
SHAPIRA	Lazar survived; 2 sons, killed during combat?	6
GORDON	Chaia Bluma with the family of her son Isaac	8
MIRMAN	Binyamin	5
FEYGA	Riva and daughter	2

Surname	Head of household	
SHAPIRA	Kopel, wife Dvora	5
WEINSTEIN	Alte	7
WEITZKIN	Mattas and Ahinkender	4
MIRMAN	Hirsch	3
SHEINDELIN	Aharon and brother Yankel	5
ALPERIN	Chana wife of Kalabasnik Efraim Alperin	1
ZLOTKIN	Feyga	4
WACHSLER	Marim (the blind)	4
WEITZKIN	Zalman (survived son; David and in law; Avraham Shuv)	6
MINDELIN	2 sisters of Yekutiel Mindelin	2
MINDELIN	Yekutiel	3
GILBERSTEIN	Moshe (survived son Meir Invalid?)	4

Hoifisha Gasse

Surname	Head of household	No. of family members who died
LIPSHIN	Moshe	6
GLAZ	Zalman	3
DRUTZ	David	4
RUBASKIN	Zalman (survived son; Chaim)	4
TSIPILOVICH	Motte	3
WYMAN	David - tailor (survived daughter Rasha in partizan)	5
FRIEDMAN	Yosef	3
KAPILOVICH	Kopel	2
REICHEL	Chaia Sara (Avraham Yasha the Melamed's wife and daughter)	2
MILKIN	Sana -tailor (son Yeruchmiel was killed in combat while serving with the partisans)	4
MINDEL	Itzhak (Milikin's son-in-law)	3
FEYGELSON	Eli Meir	3
FEYGELSON	Itzhak	5
SHULMAN	Israel der Marazashnik	7
RIVKIN	Shmuel and his mother	2
AIDANSON	Avraham Itzhak	7
?	Yosef (Moshe Motta the Shamash son-in-law)	5
BINYAMINSON	Mikhail	5

Surname	Head of household	
WACHMACHER	Wulf	3
GLAZ	Chaim Eli and 2 sisters	3
WYMAN	Dvora	3
SARKIN	Rasha	2
GRABER	Nachum (survived daughter Michlia)	3
MARKMAN	Avraham Yitzhak (survived son Motta, was partizan)	7
MARKMAN	Batya	1
GINDIN	Zalman	3
GINDIN	Yakov	4
KATSCHARGINSKI	David	2
GRAMLIN	Zalik	3
ICHILITSIK	David (survived; son Shlomo, was a partisan)	4
HIDEKEL	Lazar (Ichilitsik's son-in-law)	3
SHMUSHKOVITCH	(Ichilitsik's son-in-law)	3
	Ichilitsik's daughter Bluma with child	2
GITLITZ	Mendel (survived; Rafael)	4?
KLIAT	Mendel	5
PUPKA		5
KNALL	Feyga Rachel	1
WEINSTEIN	Isaak	4
KLIAT	Yakov Isaac	5
HAVAS	Israel-Fruman	3
PIDELHOLZ	Gavriel	5
SHITZKIN	Beynash	4
TIVISHEVICH	Ber	2

Pashahadnya Gasse

Surname	Head of household	No. of family members who died
ZALDIN	the family of Shmuel (survived; Shmuel Zaldin, was with the partisans)	2
BIK	Lazar	6
GLAZ	Leib	3

[Page 260]

Palna Gasse

| Surname | Head of household | No. of |

Surname	Head of household	family members who died
SLUTZKIN	Chaia Sara	4
SLUTZKIN	Moshe Aharon	3
ZEMACH	Israel (survived; a son)	3
ZEMACH	Zavel	4
ZEMACH	Chaim	4
ZEMACH	Eli	3
HOYCHMAN	Zemach's sister	3
HOYCHMAN	Kalman Moshe	6
?	Avraham Itzha (savara)	5
KNALL	Mayte -porter	6

Kishalika (Lagyanava)

Surname	Head of household	No. of family members who died
CHANOVITCH	Ben Zion- shochet	5
GOTKIN	David	1
MELTZER	Alte (shoemaker)	5
PASSENSON		2
BAND	the family of the teacher Moshe Shmuel Band	6
LANKIN	Pesia the sister of Moshe Shmuel Band	5
SHPARBER	Zalman (survived the children Aidalia and Israel with the partizans)	2
PIASACHAVO	Zalman	2
SHPARBER	Shneyor	4
KAPLAN	Rafael	4
SHPARBER	Esar	1
GOTKIN	Yishaiyau	4
YAFFE	Bar (survived a son in the Red Army)	5
SKOLNINK		6
HIDEKEL	Lazar	4
?	Moshe named "the liver"	
NIYAMI	Batya	3
TYAMKIN		2
SZVATZ	Shalom	2
DRISAVIETZKI	Levik	5
DANILEVICH	Yisrael	4

FRUMKIN	Avraham Leib	6
KAKS	Avraham	3
GORDON	Reuven	5
SHULHAYPER	Motta and Moshe	6
MANKEVICH-SHULHAYPER	son-in-law	4
KAN	Zalman-Yasia survived; daughter Sonia)	
TSIPILEVICH	Esther	5
KAMINKOVICH	Bloyna	7
FAIMAN	Esther	6
YUNGELSON	Meir	6
DVASKIN	Yakov	5
FISHMAN	Malka	5
FISHMAN	Rasha (blind)	5
FEYGELSON	Yeruchmiel	8
GLAVMAN	Zelig	9
FEYGELSON	Moshe	4
TARNA	Bar- (Shlisar)	5
TSIPILOVICH	Sasha	1
LAPKA	a son survived, was in the Red Army	2
MINDEL	Yakov	2
FEYGELSON	Zelda?	7
SHIENDELIN	Liba	4
GATKIN	Shlomo	6
SHULMAN	Hevel	6
ZACH	Chaim-Chana	7
ATMAN	Leib	7
GORDON	Chaim David	3
YUNGELSON	Avraham	6
GITELSON	Alte	4
GANSHTEIN	Yitzhak	5
HADASH	Netta	3
BOYER	Chaim	6
TILAS?		5
FEYGELSON	Zalman	3
FEYGELSON	Eli Isaac	6
RAPAPORT	Lazar	4
ATMAN	Mendel	3
HOYCHMAN	Zalman	3
SCHEINKMAN	Zelig	8

GUTKIN	Yishaiyau	5
	Avraham the smith	4
	Yuda Leib the blinder	4
SASNOVICK	Hirsch	6
KNALL	Yosef	4
	Yuda Leib the shoemaker	5
FRIEDELAND	Hirsch the wagon driver	5
GINDIN	Shlomo Noach	4
SLAVIN	Leib	4
	Rachel Briana	2
BASS	Itzha David the tailor	1
	Etta	2
ZAK	Shlomo	2
GROSBEIN	Chana	4
POPKIN	Baruch	7
ZENDEL	Mendel	9
BLAICHMAN	Binyamin (survived; Meir was partisan)	5
GLANZET	Zalman	7
FINKELSTEIN	Mendel	2
BOYER	Efraim	7
GUREVICH	Motta	10
KATZOVITZ	Archik- wagon driver	5
ETTMAN	Rivka	6
RODSTEIN	Yisrael	2
MALIYESKEVICH		5
GUREVICH	Mendel	4
PEAK	Liba	1
BERNSTEIN	(Shamash) from Smorgon	3
GITELZON	Mendel	2
BODOVO	Archik- wigs maker	2
FISHER	Lipa who is the shamash of theTarnasher synagogue	8
GLAZMAN	Yankel - tailor	4
SHAPIRA	Malka and Yishaiyau	6
BLEICHMAN	Zalman	7

[Page 261]

Glucha Gasel

Surname	Head of household	No. of family members who died
ZEIDEL	Ruvel	4
LIPSHIN	Ben Zion	2
AIDIS	Moshe	2
	Liba (the mute)	1
VORABITZIK	Gordon Ruven survived; Yitzhak Voarabitzik in the Red Army- he was wounded)	12
POPKIN	Moshe Shmuel	9
REYNSTEIN		8
BODAVO	Avraham- wagon driver	12
MIRMAN	Leib	8
MIRMAN	Gershon (son was killed in battle while serving in the Red Army)	6
REICHEL	Lazar Aron	6
PLISKIN	Alter	
GOLDMAN	Hirsch (survived; son Heshel in the Red Army)	3
TSIPILOVICH	Draisa and son Zelig	2
SHULMAN	Yankel	11
SHULMAN	Moshe Shmuel	9
	Sonia the sister of Moshe Shmuel Shulman	5
SHEINKMAN	The glassmaker	10
KATZ	Efraim David and Sonia Chava- the mother. survived; son Zalman Berl? In the Red Army	5
FRIEDMAN	Meir Motte	6
REICHEL	Avraham?	5

Nya Gasse

Surname	Head of household	No. of family members who died
KOHEN	Alter	4
REICHEL	Nachum and Korkodianski	14
LEIBOVITZ	Avraham	6
PLISKIN	Gdaliyau and Bar-son (survived; son Aron Zelig)	6

Surname	Head of household	No. of family members who died
KRIVITZKI	Leib (Gdaliyau Pliskin's son-in-law)	4
ZLOTKIN		6

Moskva Gasel

Surname	Head of household	No. of family members who died
YAFFE	Kiva - wagon driver and daughter' family	14
KATZ	Zalman	6
GORDON		11

Warsawer Gasse (Dokshitzer)

Surname	Head of household	No. of family members who died
VORACH	Yitzhak	3
HOFFMAN	Asher	5
	Hirshl the "schmuck"	4
GLAZ	Avraham	3
DREIZENSTOCK	Berl	5
FEYGELSON	Avraham	7
BRASSEN	Avraham	5
YUDIN	Gdaliyahu	4
SCHMIDT	Aharon	5
SCHMIDT	Lazar	2
LIPSHIN	Yitzhak the tailor	6
SLAVIN	Zalman	5
BARYUDIN	Gita	2
HAVKIN	Tulia	1
HAVKIN	David	3
RAPAPORT	Lazar Bar	9
ZADLIN	Nachum	3
DINNESTEIN	family of Piyavesh (survived Fiyavish Dinnerstein with the partisans)	2
FEYGELSON	Meir	3
SROGOVICH	Chaim (survived; son Mulya?)	3
REICHEL	Leib son of Berl	3
GLAZ	Yakov	1
ZIZONOVICH		3

HIDEKEL	Leah	3
KOPILOVICH	Chana daughter of Kopel Zaliser	2
KROPIVNIK	Leah	3
ZLADIN	Bar?	4
SROGOVICH	Abba	3
CHODESH	Liba (survived; son Moshe)	4
FROGOVICH	Abba	3
KATZ	Rabbi Yosef Halevi	4
RAJAK	(survived; Mikhail and Tzvi, the editors of the book)	3
WEINSTEIN	Shalom	5
SHAKNOVITCH	Chaim Zelig (Weinstein's in law)	3
HAVAS	Yisrael	3
FINKELSTEIN	Zalman Eliyahu the shohet	5
SLAVIN	Mendel	4
FRIEDMAN	Chaim	4
FRIEDMAN	Motte	8
RABINOVICH	Chaia Rachel?	4
FEYGELSON	Chaim Hirsch	4
DIMMENSTEIN	Chana with son and in laws (survived daughter in law with her little girl in the partisans)	6
KRAUT	Nathan and brother	6
FEYGELSON	Mira - dentist	3
BADAVO	Shimon with the mother and brother and the family of the brother	8
TSIPILOVICH	Berl survived; daughter Pesia in the partisans	3
TZIPKIN	Efraim	4
TZIPKIN	Moshe	2
?	Shalom	3
VORBIATZIK	Chaim Pesach	2
DLUTT	Yaha	4
KONIGSBERG	Chaim	4
MIDYUK	Abba	3
MIDYUK	Dobba	2
MIDYUK	Moshe	5
FIDELHOLTZ	Zalman Yakov	7
FRIEDKIN	"Kalika"	4
ZLADIN	Yosef	3
ZLATKIN	Hillel	5
PALAVNIK	Fruma Chana	3
DAMSHKIN	Motte	3

WEITZKIN	Shmuel	5
PAN	Chana Liba	5
PAN	Peya Liba	2
PAN	Hirsch	2
ABBALEVICH	Yuda	5
PLAVNIK	Esther	2
SHER	Yakov	6
BROKOVSKI	Reuven- bookbinder	3
DAITCH	Moyta	2
HOYCHMAN	Yekutiel	2
HOYCHMAN	Tsipa	2
	the widow of Bar	3
GLAZ	Mendel Schneir	5
KATZ	Lazar Itzha	4
KATZ	Meir	3
GLAZ	Eliyahu	5
GLAZ	Pesach	2
GLAZ	Yente	1
FISHER	Avraham	4
GUREVICH	Chaia	3
ZIRLIN	Yakov Bar	1
HAVKIN	Hirschl	4
KATZ	Tuvya	2
KATZ	Moshe the son of Tuvya Survived daughter Ethel in the partisans	4
MIRMAN	Yosef	4
MEIROVICH	Yosef	4
TSIPILEVICH	Itzhak	4
TSIPILEVICH	Motte	3
GINDIN	Mendel	6
PLAVNIK	Yosef	7
SHAPIRA		4
SHAPIRA	Koppel	4
GEFFEN	Mulya	3
WEISKIN	Sonia	2
LANKIN	Shmuel	5
WEISKIN	the family of Eliyahu	4
SOLKIN	Israel	6
SOLKIN	Yosef	5
SPEYER	Aron and daughter Sonia	6

Surname	Head of household	No. of family members who died
HOYCHMAN	Batya	5
SROGOVITZ	the family of Yitzhak	8
SROGOVITZ	Reuven the son of Yitzhak	6
KRAMER	Moshe	6
BAKER	Moshe	6
PLAVNIK	Rasha	2
SAFRA	Matta	3
SAFRA	the family of Alte survived; Sapra Alte and one daughter	3
BLATT	Hirsch	5
HOYCHMAN	Nisam	7
HAVAS	Hirshel's wife Marusia (survived? He served in the Red Army)	2

[Page 263]

Lamzasher Gasse (Druyer)

Surname	Head of household	No. of family members who died
YUNGELSON	the family of Shalom (Yungelson Shalom survived in the partisans?)	4
KATZ	Yankel the son of Tuvya Katz	2
SHAPIRA	Shlomo Meir	7
FEYGELSON	Zalman	5
ROTTENBERG	Shmuel David (Krishnau)	4
KNALL	Poyba	3
RAPAPORT	Moshe Koppel the tailor	6
SOLOVYECHIK	Mulya	4
	Mendel of Halobitz	5
GINSBURG	Nicknamed "Kutiak"	11
	Eliyau the mulia	6
SESNOVIK	Pesach	8
KARASHNAVSKY		6
PALIACH	Shimon Hirsch and his in laws Levitanos	8
PLAVNIK		8
SHUKMAN	Yitzhak	7
BLATT	Itzhak, a hero of the Soviet Union died while fighting the Germans (the rest of the family survived and also his in laws)	1
	cemetery man (the printer) with all the families of his sons and daughters	28
KORILAVO		16

Surname	Head of household	No. of family members who died
FLEISCHER	Braha	5
LEVINSON	Salal son of Mendel	5
KATZ	Shmuel Lazar	16
LEVIT	Zalman	4
BINYAMINSON	Torah	4
	Zelig Itzha the teacher	8
SUPERNIK	Peretz	3
LEDERMAN	survived; son Mattke?	4
FIDELHALTZ	Chaim Chanoch	4
FIDELHALTZ	Avraham Yoshua	3
KOPILOVICH	From Vileyka	6
YUNGELSON	Motte	5
SHULKIN	Yidel Levi (Itzha Yungelson's son-in-law)	5
TILES	The tailor	3
KATZ	Chaia	5
	Lazar the family of Zerach?	8
MIRMAN	Itzha Bar	4
SCHNEIR		6

[Page 264]

Bialystoker Gasse

Surname	Head of household	No. of family members who died
MYAKININ		2
MUSIN	Zundel and wife Zelda. Shorshevsky Levin Raisel sister of Z. Musin (survived wife of the teacher David Levin)	3
SPER	the family of Hirsch (Sper, Hirsch survived)	4
GELBERSTEIN	Avraham	2
FISHER	Gasia	5
FRAN	Chaim; the photographer	1
	The son-in-law of Gasia Fisher	2
FREYDKIN	Zalman	5
FREYDKIN	Natan	3
KATZ	Shaptai	5
PRADER	the hair dresser	5
PRABER	Gita	2
FRIEDMAN	Chaim	4
ZAK	Solomon ; the tailor, survived; his wife Sima and his son and daughter	3

Surname	Head of household	No. of family members who died
KATZ	Batsheba	2
SHUCHMAN	Rivka	5
TILES	Wulf	3
REINAS	Zundel the musician	10
FISHER	Siffra	6
FEYGELSON	Lazar	3
ROZAVO	Chana	6
BRAUN	Nacha	5
BRAUN	David	5
REICHEL	Chaim Natan	5
MALISHKEVICH	Riva	2
KATZ	Leib	3
KATZ	Zisya	1
MARKMAN	Chaim Leib	2
MAHLER	Yitzhak	3
KRAUT	Motte	3
ZALKIN		
WYMAN	Reuven	4
KOHEN		4
KOHEN	Chaia	2
KOHEN	Shalom	4
ARNAS	Bar the tailor	3
CHADASH	Levick	3
CHADASH	Mulia	3
LIEBERMAN	Esther	3
LEKACH	Moshe	9
PATKIN	Gottlib	2
SWIEDLER	Leib daughter Henia survives	2
YIDEL	Slavins , a son survived and while serving in the Red Army was wounded	3

Palace of the 3rd of May Platz

Surname	Head of household	No. of family members who died
SHAPIRA	baker nicknamed "The Beard"	7
LAIMAN	Davids' family- David and a son survived. They were partisans.	2
KATZOVITZ	Mulia - son Izia survived. He was a partisan.	3
KOBOTSHNIK	Isar	

Surname	Head of household	
MINDEL	Yosef	4 ?
LEVIN		2 ?
	Chasia	
SHAMES?	A tailor	
SOLOVIETZIK	Mulia	

Krakover Gasse

Surname	Head of household	No. of family members who died
LEVITAN	Hirsh	11
SOLOVIETZICK	Chana	3
SOLOVIETZICK	Avraham	4
RUDERMAN	Zalman Wolf	4
PINTZOV	Yankel	3
PINTZOV	Shabtai	
YUNGELSON	Mote (The farmer/ builder)	
PLISKIN	Tisye	
TZENZIPER	Shalom (the butcher) survived; his daughter Freydel.	5
SOLOVIETZICK	Eisar	2
FRIEDMAN	Hirshel	3
ZISKIND	Nisan	
YUNGELSON	Hinda	
YUNGLSON	Ytzhak	
ELIANNAV	Shmuel (tailor)	
GENSHTEIN	Aharon (Shamash of the "Bloyer synagogue")	
KATZ	Yudel	3
FRIEDMAN	Rachel	
SHULKIN	Zadok (tailor)	5?
YUNGELSON	Shabtai	2

[Page 265]

Disner Gasse

Surname	Head of household	No. of family members who died
GORDON	Henia	
FRUMIN	Leib	4
FEIGELMAN	Heshel	4

MELAMED	Bracha?
FRIEDMAN	Chaim
VIGDERHOUS	David
SHAPIRA	Yosef- survived sons, Lipa and Michael with the partisans
SHERMAN	Mendel
RABINOVITCH	Eliyahu (Sherman Mendel's son-in-law)
WAXMAKHER	Leib
SLAVIN	Israel- Greynem
HAKNER	

Yatkave Gasse

Surname	Head of household	No. of family members who died
BEGIN	Meir with the families of son, Mote and daughter, Masha also Leja and husband Max.	8
VILNIN	Moshe	4
ZINGER	ben Zion-Leyzer	2
ALAY	Byenosh (Sherer)	
BOYDIN	Yosef - survived daughter; Ester	
FISHER	Moshe, son-in-law of Maudin	4
DVORKIN	Shlomo Meir and the family of his sister	6
ZAGAVEL	Chaim	5
SROGOVITCH	Yankel	5
LEVINSON	Mendel	
	Neighbor of Yankel Sragovitch	
MINDALIN	Bear	2
FEYGELMAN	Kopel- one daughter survived	4
SOLOVIETZICK	Yankel	2
SHULHAYFER	Chaim Leib	1
RUDERMAN	Chaim - Meir	
OSTROVSKI	Max	
FRIEDMAN	Yosh (the doctor)	4
FRIEDMAN	(brother of Dr. Yosh)	3
MINDALIN	Yekutiel	3
FALANT	Avraham	2
KATZ	Mendel (son-in-law of Falant) - his son Reuven survived; he was a partisan	
LISITZKI	Wolf	

Surname	Head of household	
MELER	Israel	3
BARKAN	Efraim- David	9
LEVIT	Michaels' family- Levit Michael survived, he was a partisan	4
MAZAVETZKI	Rachmiel Alperovitsh wife; Sonia and his in laws	4
ALPEROVITZ	Israels' wife and children	
AZESHINSKI	Michael - surivived;Son Pinye and one daughter	
NATANSON	Eliyahu (bookkeeper)	5
DVOSKIN	Chaia	3?
SHNEYOR	survived son David who was wounded while he was in the Red Army	5
SHMID	Ytzhak	6
SOLOVIETZICK	Zalman	
FRIEDMAN	Moshe	
LEVITAN	Aharons' Family- Aharon and son Avraham survived, they were partisans	3
KRAUT	Nechama	
KRAUT	Ytzhak	5?
Pintzov	Shimshel and in laws Kapilovitch Shimon	
KAZIEL	Aynik- wagon driver	
COOPERSTOCK		
GORDON	Rachel (wife of Yoel Gordon)	3
PECK	Mendel	
SHERZON	Meir and wife Chaia and daughters	

[Page 266]

Zomkove Gasse

Surname	Head of household	No. of family members who died
Pintzov	Chanan	4
GODIN	Wolf - son Aharon survived	5
BERKAN	Moshe- son Shalom survived	7
GITELSON	Zalman	6
PREN	Shlomo- David	5
CHEVLIN	Chaim	8
HOBERMAN	Mendel	8
ASMAN	Hinda - her husband, Yaakov Leib, survived	
ALPEROVITZ	Frieda - her son survived - he was in the Red Army	1
ALPEROVITZ	Zalman	3
PESENSON	Leja	3

ABRAMOVITZ	Moshe	6?
BRODNY	David	4
PODNOS	Yekutiel	3
	Family of Elia née Podnos (Yekutiels' daugher) - Elia and her husband survived with the partisans	
MELTZER	Alter (shoemaker)	5
MOSES	Reuven	4
BERKAN	Leyzer, Dvra	1?
SHENKER	Chaim	3
CHEIFETZ	Yehoshua- daughters; Malka and Bracha survived with the partisans;	4
CHEIFETZ	Yaakov Shmuel	3
VEINSTEIN	Sonia	6
KURENITZ	Shmuel- Leib	5
SHEPSENWHOL	sister of Moshe Abramovitch	5
SOLOVIETZICK	Moshe- watchmaker	5
	Toyber Shmid	
MUSHKAT	Zadok	5
GORDON	Shmuel- nicknamed "The black rooster"	1
TEITELBOIM	Ytzhak	3
RAPOPORT	Malka- daughter Rachel survived with the partisans	1
HOBERMAN	Reuven	6
RABINOVITCH	Leib	4
	Shabtai- the shoemaker and his wife.	6
GELMAN	Sonia and Alta- hairdressers	2
Pintzov	Ytzhak	1
CHEVLIN	Shimon- son Kopel survived	4
FRUMIN	Musia	2
UMBROS	Berl	5
ZAK	Leib	2
PIPIK	shoemaker	2
MONKITO	shoemaker	
ZALKIND	Meir- Leib- watchmaker	5
ALAI	Eliyahu- glassmaker	6
	two sisters - seamstresses	2
BIRNZVEIG	agronomy	4
KOSHER	Yaakov- owner of soap factory	4
RAYCHEL	Bear	3
SHPYER	Rivka, children of Pinia Shpyer; Ester, Yosef, Zishka shpyer	5

KRAUT	Mosay (Moshe) wife Rosa and daughter	3
GEFEN	Ytzhak- son Gershon survived	4
PREVEZKIN	Mota	3
HABERKORN	teacher in the Handels shul	1
SLONIMSKI	Leon - attorney	3
	the dentist from Disna	
ZAK	Yosef- son of Solomon, the accountant	2
	The old tailor near ?	
ZAK	Binyamin	1
KHAIT	Golda from Sharzan, husband Shalom and son David perished in the Vilna ghetto.	3
KAMINSKI	Chava and Leja- Chava joined the partisan and was killed in a mission.	2
SOGOVITZ	wife and three daughters; Riva, Slava and Tamara	4

Additional names given by Glubokie natives in America

Kishalika Gasse

FAYMAN	Ester
GENSTEIN	Ytza Fishel – tailor

[Page 267]

Warsawer Gasse

RAYDER	Shmuel - hotel

Mastava Gasse

SHACHNA	the water carrier
VEIRCH	A Porter

Wilner Gasse

SHPER	Hirshel died in the Soviet Union. His wife and 2 children perished in the ghetto. *
PILSKIN	Alter
SHNIEDMAN	Katriel
ZALKA	Avraham- The Printer

Mota- nicknamed "the Rooster"

Hipsha Gasse
DAITCHE

CHELVINA

3rd of May Platz
GOLDBERG and SHEINBAUM printers

Addition to the list from Glubokie natives in Israel
Krakower Gasse

Surname	Head of household	No. of family members who died
KATZ	Leib	4
KAZLINER	Mendel	4
BIMBAD	Zalman	3
Pintzov	Zelka	6
BUDAVO	Sara	1

Wilner Gasse

Surname	Head of household	No. of family members who died
FREYDKIN	Zalman	5
FLISKIN	Alter	6
NATANSON	book keeper	4
DANCHIN	Chana	2
MILSHTEIN	Chana	3
MILSHTEIN	Gdalia	1
SHAPIRA	Mendel	1
SHAPIRA	Pesia	1
SHUCHMAN	Rachel	2

Krakower Gasse

Surname	Head of household	No. of family members who died
ZIETLIN	Zavul	4
SWERDLIN	Shaul	4
BERZAN	Yaakov	3
YUNGELSON	Shmuel- Leib	4
FIDELHOLTZ	Shmuel	5
GELER	Pinchas	5
PILSKIN	Chaim Meir	3
HAP	Reuven	4
DZAIZINKAR	Berl	2
DZAIZINKAR	Motel	3
BARZAN	Efraim	2
ZAK	Yosef	1
?	Shayke – the "Shtefer"	4
LEVITAN	The daughter of Feiga and Chezkel	1
SWEDLER	Leib	2
FRIEDMAN	Natan	5
GELBERSTEIN	Avraham- Shaul	2

Dubrava Gasse

Surname	Head of household	No. of family members who died
RAM	Sara	3

Hipsha Gasse

Surname	Head of household	No. of family members who died

Surname	Head of household	No. of family members who died
MILER (MELER?)	Nachum	5
FIERMAN	Shaul	8

Kishlayka Gasse

Surname	Head of household	No. of family members who died
	Shimon Eliyahu- the butcher	6
GORDON	Yoske	3
FEYGELSON	Yosef	
SHEINKMAN	Ziomka	2

Warsawer Gasse

Surname	Head of household	No. of family members who died
CHAVES	Hirsh	3
CHAVES	Chalvina ?	

Lamzasher Gasse (Druyer)

Surname	Head of household	No. of family members who died
ALPEROVITZ	Israel	
FLIESHER	Meir	
MILER		
MUNEVEZ	David	2
MYATES	Leyzer	
MYATES	Michael	
BLOCH	Eliyahu	
DVESKIN	Yaakov	

[Page 268]

Glubokie Jewish partisans list

AZSHINSKI	Pina, son of Michael

ALPEROVITZ	Chana, daughter of Leib BLUT
ALPEROVITZ	Mota, Chana nee BLUT husband
AYGAS	David
BIRZESH	Aharon Gershon, Yeshaya's uncle
BARKAN	Shalom, son of Moshe
BARKAN	Nachum, son of Moshe
BADANIVO	Sonia
BARKAN	Yosef
BLUT	Ytzhak, son of Leib was killed as a hero
BLICHMAN	Meir, son of Binyamin
CHADASH	Hirsh
CHADASH	Tona
CHADASH	Leja
CHEIFETZ	Malka, daughter of Yaakov Shmuel
CHEIFETZ	Batia, daughter of Yaakov Shmuel
CHEIFETZ	Moshe Ytzhak, son of Yehoshua
DREIZENSHTOK	Reuven
DIMENSTEIN	Dina (daughter of Chaim and Chana FIDELHOLTZ)
ETMAN	Leib (was killed)
FEYGLSON	Zalman
FEYGLSON	Dan
FEYGELMAN	Sara, daughter of Kopel
FEGELMAN	Avner
FEYGEL	Michael (was killed)
FEYGEL	Sonia
FEYGEL	Moshe
FRIEDMAN	Yaakov
FREYDKIN	Hertz
GATLIB	Raia (was killed)
GENSHTEIN	Mota
GORDON	Eliyahu
GITELSON	Binyamin, son of Ytzhak Moshe
GITELSON	Sonia - wife of Binyamin
GITLITZ	Rafael
GELMAN	Abba, son of Shmuel-Nisan

ISRAELOVITZ	Hirsh
KATZ	Zalman-Ber
KATZ	Liba
KATZ	Reuven, son of Mendel
KATZ	Ester, daughter of Moshe
KOSOVSKI	Mina
KREMER	Zola (was killed)
KATZOVITZ	Ber- uncle of Moshe KATZOVITZ
KATZOVITZ	Eizia
LEKACH	Dr. Nachum
LEKACH	Dr. Nachum's wife was killed
LEDERMAN	Mota, son of Gershon
LEVIN	Raphael, son of David (was killed)
LEVIT	Michael
LEVIT	Rafael
LEVITAN	Aharon
LEVITAN	Avraham-Aharon's son
LAIMAN	David
MILCHMAN	Zalman
MILCHMAN	Raya-Zalman's mother
MINDEL	Yitzhak (was killed)
MELER	Myeta
MARKMAN	Mota
MIRMAN	Moshe
MELAMED	Ester
MELAMED	Rivka
MILKIN	Rechamia (was killed)
PINTZOW	Lucy (was killed)
PLISKIN	David
RAJAK	Michael
RAJAK	Zvi
RUDERMAN	Yaakov
RABINOVITZ	Kalman , son of Meir
RAPOPORT	Leib , son of David
RAPOPORT	Zalman

RAPOPORT	Rachel, daughter of David
SOLOVYETCHIK	Shimon, son of Mulia
SOLOVYETCHIK	Zipa, daughter of Moshe
SWIDLER	Mulia (was killed)
SASNOVIK	Pesach
SASNOVIK	Lipsha
SOSMAN	Shifra, daughter of Leibl RAPOPORT
SOSMAN	Yeshaya, Shifra's husband (was killed)
SLABADKIN	Hirsh
SRAGOVITCH	Abba, son of Chaim (was killed)
SRAGOVITCH	Chaim Hertz-Yitchak SRAGOVICH's uncle
SHOV	Avraham-Shmuel Nisan GELMAN's relative
SHPERBER	Aydele, daughter of Zalman
SHPERBER	Israel, son of Zalman
SHAPIRA	Leib
SHAPIRA	Lipa, son of Yosef
SHAPIRA	Michael, son of Yosef
SHAPIRA	Berka, son of Yosef (fallen)
SHRIRA	Elia, daughter of Padnas Yekutiel
SHRIRA	(husband of Elia)
TREISTER	Chana–Eska, daughter of Yitzhak
TZEPELIVITZ	Avraham (was killed)
TZEPELIVITZ	Pesi
TZALKIND	Mendel
TZALKIND	Mendel's daughter
VANT	Leib
WEIMAN	Rasha
WIENSTEIN	Moshe (was killed)
YECHILZIK	Shlomo, son of David
YUNGELSON	Shalom
YUNGELSON	Reuven
ZEMACH	Shimon
ZEMACH	Fishel
ZLADIN	Tulia
ZLADIN	Shmuel
ZAK	Pesach
ZINGER	Nachum

ZINGER	Mira-Nachum's wife
ZINGER	two daughters of Nachum and Mira

*Hirshel was sent to the Soviet Union. He survived and then immigrated to Israel in 1948. His wife and 3 daughters perished in the Ghetto. [Information received from his son, Isaac Shepher]

_ [Page 270]

Pictures

Translated by Jerrold Landau

Pictures extracted by Larry Gaum

A fur workshop of Glubokie

The ORT teaching workshop for women's tailoring

[Page 271]

A group of Hechalutz, 15 II 1931

A Hechalutz chapter

[Page 272]

A street in Glubokie

A street in Glubokie

[Page 273]

A street in Glubokie

A street in Glubokie

[Page 274]

A street in Glubokie

Firefighters of Glubokie

[Page 275]

At the mass grave of Glubokie Jews

Glubokie Jews accompany the Lubavitcher Rebbe to the train

[Page 276]

Children's performance

Jewish-worldly Folks School

[Page 277]

A group of Glubokie Jews

Glubokie Maccabee

[Page 278]

Mandolin orchestra

Wedding of the Glubokie native Yisrael Hanowicz in America

[Page 279]

Hashomer Hatzair chapter in Glubokie June 17, 1933

Hashomer Hatzair

[Page 280]

The *shochet* Ben-Zion Hanowicz, his wife and children

Michael and Tzvi Rajak in the partisans

[Page 281]

A group of children of the kindergarten affiliated with the school

A group of female students of the Hebrew School

[Page 282]

Eliahu (Elya) the Shamash

The communal grave of the Jews of Glubokie

**A communal worker in Glubokie
Chairman of the firefighters command**

[Page 283]

The *shochet* Ben-Zion Hanowicz

[Page 285]

Szarkowszczyzna

The Destruction of Szarkowszczyzna

by Szarkowszczyzna natives in Argentina
Translation supplied by Eilat Gordin Levitan

The shtetl Szarkowszczyzna is located in Belarus. The area is also called Kressen. However, for us natives, it is actually part of Jewish Lithuania. Even Though the Jews of Szarkowszczyzna did not speak a word of Lithuanian, they were still in character and culture true Litvaks. It was considered a part of the province of Vilna before 1939 , Dissner/ Disna County (Oyezd). Later on it was added to Glubokie County. It is situated a distance of 30 kilometers from Glubokieie, 50 kilometers from Dissne, 60 kilometers from Breslau, and lies on the banks of the small river Disenke, which empties into the River Dvine.

People used to float logs down the river to Dvinsk and Riga during springtime. The exact spot at which the shtetl is located is at a flat surface, no hills can be seen anywhere around. The earth is made of a lime soil. During times of heavy rains, or when the snow melts from the roads, the flooding is so bad that one cannot travel by cart. The town during such times would find itself cut off from the outside world.

Products were mostly delivered from Dvinsk, Disne and Polotsk. Later a railway station was devised at Varpaive, a distance of 25 kilometers from the shtetl, from there one could travel to Vilna.

The Czarist Russian government which controlled the area for more then 100 years (1790s – 1915), began to build a railway line in 1910, which was supposed to cut through Varpaive. In the end, they only built 7 kilometers., which extended only to the estate of the landowner, Rudzshinski. It was the worst stretch of land prior to the construction and after it the road was freed of swamps and mud. During the construction the Jews had good income for a few years. Many used to carry sand from the riverbank to fill the site.

During the year 1910, they also bricked over the only long street in town. The street cut through the shtetl and the marketplace. At that time the Street ended at the river's edge. From there one crossed to the other side on a ferry. The ferry was made of wood and a rope towed it. When the river overflowed, you couldn't ride the ferry. During such times one side was cut off from the other for a few days. They had started to build a bridge from both sides of the river where the ferry crossed. They poured large mounds of lime earth. But the building of the bridge was not completed. At the onset point of the highway, where one entered the shtetl, they erected a bridge during the outbreak of WWI (1914). Surrounding the shtetl there were exquisite forests. One forest, which was called the Zverinietz, was where Jewish youth would go to spend the holidays.

The Jewish population of Szarkowszczyzna included 1000 souls. About 500 Christian inhabitants also resided in town.

[Page 286]

Streets in the Shtet'l

The marketplace stood in the center of the shtetl. It resembled a long cardboard box. All of the stores were to be found there. Most of the buildings were made of wood, except for a few brick homes. The marketplace was not paved, after every rainy day one was unable to pass through it. Later on they made Special walks out of wooden planks in front of the homes and stores.

Five streets extended from the core of the marketplace. Disner Street was the longest of those Streets. It began with the house of Esther Itzes' Chidekel which served also as an inn. The pharmacy was also located there. It was the first street to be paved. It was a throughout street on which you could enter the shtetl from the main highway. About 20 Jewish families and 50 Christian families lived on this street. The youth would promenade Via Dissner Street during the summer and "frolic" on Sabbaths and holidays. They would go for strolls outside the shtetl through the verdant fields to the Christian cemetery. There is now a common brotherly grave near the place where the Jewish youth loved to walk during those bygone days. A large number of the Szarkowszczyzna Jews, our beloved who were so cruelly butchered by the bloody enemy, are buried at that grave.

Two synagogues were found in the shtetl; they were called the old synagogue and the new synagogue. The large empty space around them was known as the synagogue courtyard. All of the shtetl weddings were held there. A large crowd accompanied on foot the bride and the groom to the wedding canopy. Not only the couple's relatives, but also the entire shtetl would attend each and every wedding ceremony. Candles would be lit in each and every window of town houses. When a wedding took place during dry weather it was especially awe-inspiring site. But if ceremonies took place during the fall or after the snow melted it was misfortunate. In the dark you would find yourself struggling through mud. The men would wear boots, the women would lose their shoes, the musicians would play their marches and the shouts would echo through the shtetl. The bathhouse was located not far from the synagogue courtyard.

[Page 287]

There were no other long streets in Szarkowszczyzna., only short ones. One such typical street was called "The Tailors Street". It consisted of seven houses, which were the inheritance of the tailor, Leib Shulkin.

He left it to his children when he passed away. All of his children were tailors. When the river overflowed, it would always flood their homes.

The cemetery was located near the bank of the river, quite a distance away from the shtetl. The surrounding area was muddy much of the year, and one would approach the area with great difficulty. You would have to cross a small bridge, which was always broken. Quite often the floodwaters would carry it away and alternate Crossings would have to be found. You could assume that Szarkowszczyzna was an old shtetl considering the condition of the cemetery. An old mausoleum stood there. Unfortunately, no one ever thought of copying the inscriptions off the gravestones. A Jew, Jeremiah-Leib was his name, lived near the cemetery. He was the gravedigger, as well as the bath-keeper. He was a pious Jew.

The Shtetl up to the Onset of the First World War (1914)

The Sources of Livelihoods

The storekeepers subsisted on the market day, which occurred once a week. Every Thursday, peasants from the surrounding villages, would bring their products to sell in the marketplace. At the same time, with the money they earned, they would buy supply for themselves: Clothing, food products and work tools. They would bring to town all sorts of grains to sell: corn, barley, oats, and also flax, potatoes, fowl, eggs, butter, cows, calves and sheep. In the winter they would also bring wood and hay.

The trade in flax occupied a prominent place in the shtetl's economy. In order to procure the flax, Jews would travel to the estates of nobles, and through the villages. Since they needed large quantities of the raw substance, they did not wait for the market-day. Certain Jews, understandably the wealthy ones, had large silos where they would store the purchased flax. They would clean it-, sort it, pack it in large bales and send it off via the railroad. Only a few Jews owned such businesses, but many Jewish people worked for them as common laborers, as sorters and packers of the flax. Jews were also the wagoneers, who drove the bales of flax to the railroad station. This sort of production went on almost the entire year. The flax business was the main enterprise in the shtetl. People also dealt in grains, livestock and hides. There were also some fruit merchants. At the start of the summer, Jews would lease orchard land from the nobles. During the entire summer they cared for the orchards. As soon as the fruit ripened, it would be picked, racked in crates and sent to the big cities, all around the Russian Empire. They mostly grew apples and pears orchards. Very few fruits were sold for local consumption.

[Page 288]

Locally, people would buy fruits only at the very height of the season.

There were many tailors and seamstresses in the shtetl. There were entire families in which the craft would pass on from generation to generation. As we wrote before, the tailors inhabited a very delightful street. Children as well as adults worked at the- craft. They mostly sewed clothing to be used by the peasants of the villages. There were also those who traveled through the villages all week and sewed new clothes or patched the turn clothing for the peasants. They would return home only for the Sabbath. There were also tailors who sewed mainly for Jews, especially holiday and wedding outfits. This was the main industry of Szarkowszczyzna.

There were a few Cheders (elementary schools for Jewish religious studies). There were no Yeshivas in town. 1f someone wanted to provide further schooling for his children, he would send them to Mir, Vilna or other such cities. Most of those who went away to learn, would never return to the shtetl. Some Jews also sent their children to the Russian "gymnasia" (high school), in one of the surrounding towns. From there some would go on to attend the university. Several Szarkowszczyzna Jewish families had children who obtained a doctoral degree. However, not a single one of them, ever returned to live in the shtetl.

For many years the rabbinical position in the shtetl was occupied by the rabbi, R' Raphael. He was a very righteous Jew, possessing many refined traits. The immaculateness of his beard and the neatness of his appearance automatically commanded everyone's respect. He would teach a pane of the Talmud to the community on a daily basis, between the afternoon and evening prayers. His brother-in-law, R' Israel **(Israel Rabinowich)**, the Druyer Rabbi, who proceeded him, was entirely different in his outlook. He was extremely observant and exceptionally pious and unassuming. He was very careful and didn't even trust himself with important decisions. He always considered his responses very carefully in order to avoid being disingenuous to someone in the community. He was more fearful of giving the wrong idea during disagreements, than he was of the greatest sin. He perished together with rest of the Szarkowszczyzna Jewish community. Wrapped in his tallit, he led his flock to the slaughter. His only son, Hirshl, a doctor, embraced him the entire time until they perished.

{***Added in by Translator:*** Israel Rabinowich was born in Poland. He was a rabbi and married to Rivka nee Gintzburg. They had a son Zvi Hirsh. Prior to WWII he lived in Sharkavshchyna, Poland. Israel died in the Shoah. This information is based on a Page of Testimony submitted on 23/12/1956 by his wife's nephew; Zvi Gintzburg of Tel Aviv.}

[Page 289]

The most violent disagreements in the shtetl would come about as result of appointing new ritual slaughterers. There was a slaughterer's son by the name of Kalman, who wanted to take his father's place when his father passed away. The rabbis did not find him suitable for the job and did not give the O.K. He would not keep quiet about it. During every Shabath, he would interrupt the Torah reading and remind everyone that he had no livelihood. He was partially successful in obtaining a job eventually.

Young group of people of the Yiddish school

The most common source of livelihood in the shtetl was Storekeeping. Practically everything was for sale by everyone., from the best and rarest products to a cylinder of thread. Salt, sugar, kerosene and herring were the leading products. There were other occupations from which Jews made a living wagoneers, butchers, shoemakers, etc. There was one hairdresser in the shtetl, Itze-Leib Chazan was his name, who was also the doubling as town' clown {his son and daughter live in Argentina.)

The First World War (1914- 1918)

by natives of Szarkowszczyzna in Argentina

Translation supplied by Eilat Gordin Levitan

Life in the shtetl went on humbly until the year 1914. The effect of the First World War was immediately felt upon the shtetl. The Czar's army instantaneously called up the Jewish reservists for service. There was not a single family that did not have someone away at war. The sound of the wailing and crying echoed in the shtetl long after these reservists were sent away. Just as the families had begun to adjust to their new situation, the war began approaching the shtetl. The Russian-German front extended so deep into the Russian Empire that the images of Russian soldiers passing through the shtetl became increasingly frequent. Cavalry and infantry, as well as caravans of provisions, passed through. The caravans were so long they often proceeded for entire days and nights. No actions against Jews were carried out during that time. Eventually soldiers occupied the shtetl and they were quartered in every home.

[Page 290]

Most of the time the soldiers slept on the floor; the most important thing for them was having a roof over their heads.

We gradually became accustomed to the soldiers, though we did not grow to accept the other difficulties of being at war. It was arduous; not all were able to bear the burden, which the new situation created. Slowly, people began to deal with the soldiers. They were very good customers. Some Jews provided them with food. The baking of bread for the military became a prosperous industry. Not only the bakers were involved, but also many housewives. The military paid well. Also, other industries prospered. The tailors no longer had to travel for a livelihood. The soldiers and officers provided them with enough work.

Besides the material benefits, there was also a kind of cultural revival. Due to the war, people became acquainted with the new technical progress. For the first time in the shtetl history all kinds of automobiles and other new types of machines were seen. People became interested in what was going on in the world. The intellectual types, who read the newspapers, spread the news from around the world. Besides this local spread of information, the officers and soldiers also told of their own experiences at the front. Eventually this progress caused a break with tradition. Religious obligations loosened. Many no longer prayed with their former enthusiasm. The youth slowly began to throw off the yoke of religion. Very few continued to wear long curly side locks (payes). They would continue to go to synagogue, but mainly out of force of habit or regard for parents, but not of their own preference. In great anticipation the youth waited for earth-shattering events which were supposed to occur during wartime. Everything they did seemed exorbitant. The youth felt liberated from the traditional values - this was a personal revolution.

[Page 291]

In 1917 came the Russian Revolution. The rule of the Russian Revolutionary authority lasted but a short while in Szarkowszczyzna, since the Germans soon took over the area. Immediately during the first week, they conducted a census of everyone's possessions. Everything had to be listed according to exact detail, which included the number of horses, cows, calves, goats and fowl, as well as the number of eggs, amount of milk and other products that each one produced during a period of a week. This "innocent" census immediately became the guide used to determine from whom these products could be confiscated. "Fortunately," this bothered the local Jews very little because hardly anyone owned more than one cow, one horse, or one calf.

For the peasants in the villages this was entirely different. The Germans exactly what they wanted from them. Convoys of products such as eggs, milk, cheese, fowl, calves, sheep, and the like were sent daily to the railroad station.

The German Monarchy didn't last long. However, peace did not come to the area after the Germans left (1918).

In 1919 war broke out between the Russians and the Poles for control of the area. Authority in the shtetl passed often from hand to hand until finally the Poles gained the upper hand. At first no one felt secure with his life under the Polish control. It was enough if someone informed that someone else was a "Bolshevik". He would be taken away and never be heard from again. Besides this the Poles displayed a sadistic pleasure in beating

Jews. Everything was considered contraband. If something like salt, sugar, and alike was found in the possession of Jews, it was immediately confiscated, and the owners were badly beaten.

The firefighters of Szarkowszczyzna

[Page 292]

The fire of 1920

The Shmuel-Leibks' kitchen caught fire one day during the summer of 1920. The fire quickly spread to adjacent wooden homes. There was no fire extinguishing equipment in the shtetl. The Polish soldiers used this opportunity to throw firebombs at those Jewish homes that hadn't caught fire yet. In a short time, they managed to torch both synagogues and the bathhouse. From there the fire spread to all of the surrounding buildings until almost all of Szarkowszczyzna was burned to the ground. When the fire on Disner Street reached the non-Jewish homes, the priest appeared and asked the Polish soldiers to put out the fire. They did protect the non-Jewish homes. We can well imagine what took place in the shtetl at that time. All of the Jewish possessions had gone up in smoke. Only piles of ashes remained. There was no place to rest the head, and no food to put into their mouths. The cries of the children split the heavens.

Slowly people began to rebuild. The task turned extremely difficult. Mostly people obtained wooden frames bought from the peasants. They were brought to the shtetl and placed on the scorched plots. As long as there was a roof over the childrens' heads and a place to lie down, people were content. Completion of the building was done much later, after they had already lived in their temporary shelters for a long time.

An illness of epidemic nature broke out which claimed many victims. The Polish government began to make order and came up with oppressive new demands and edicts. As long as a livelihood was somehow earned the Jews became accustomed to the new conditions also.

Cultural activities

A fresh cultural organization was set up. A library was established, which was novel for the shtetl. Most of the volumes consisted of the new Yiddish literature.

A drama circle was formed, which presented plays from the well-known Yiddish theatre repertoire. They were mostly inspired by what some members of the circle had seen in Vilna. Some of the members were: Itzik Berels' Mindel, Dodke Berels' Mindel, Feige Mindel, Feige Milner, Moishke Chazan, Zelda Yudkin, Leibke Mindlin, Zalman Yankel's daughter, Rivke Estrin, Burshtein, Hirshke Berchon, Shlomo Reuvens' Yudin. The director was Itzik Mindlin. Later, some broke away, and set up a second drama circle. The director was the teacher, Rozshanski.

[Page 293]

There were two schools for children: A folkshule (Yiddish school) and a Tarbut (Hebrew spoken in all subjects) school. There was also a religious school, which lasted for a short time. Their administrators were Yisroel Tzimmer and Leibke Mindel. In the folkshule there was an organization named "Bin". The youth would gather there every night. They would arrange free discussions there. They also had presentations. There was a choir, which performed locally. All of the income would go to the folkshule. Besides that, the students paid tuition. There were about 100 students. The same was true of the Tarbut school. They also had enthusiastic youth who gave their best for the children's education. Their income was also from the same source. The folkshule administrators were Itzke Berl Mindel, his brother, Asher Mindel, Leib-Itze Estrin, and others. The brothers Chidekel administered the Tarbut School.

Sudden prosperity was brought about in all areas by the new railway line, which was set down in 1935. The station was in Zverinietz, one kilometer away, on the other side of the river. Everything became easier. One no longer had to travel tens of kilometers by cart through mud, to the train station. Also, a new steel bridge was built at that time. The tie to Vilna became easier and shorter in time.

The volunteer fire department was established in 1922, a few years after the great fire. [Most of the Jewish youth joined up. There were also non-Jew members. The Jewish leaders were: Hirshke Berchon, Lipe Shub, Zadok Rozov, and others.

[Page 294]

R' Yehoshua Estrin

R' Yehoshua Estrin

R' Joshua Estrin was among the oldest and most respected Jews in Szarkowszczyzna Torah and good deeds were combined in him. He was a "dyed in the wool Litvak". He passionately disliked everything that even smelled of affectation or ostentation. He made his life a holy crusade, lust as if he had a mission upon this sinful earth. Every excess word or unnecessary talk was distasteful to him. Even though he vas a Hassid of Rabbi Shneor-

Zalman's type, excessive enthusiasm and religious ecstasy were foreign to him. It would suit him just as if he were making a fool of himself. He was "dry" (did not drink) when he prayed or learned. The same consideration and understanding were present in every favor that he did for anyone. To sit at his table, one didn't need an invitation. It was an insult to him if someone left his home during mealtime without partaking in the meal. For a strange guest, the invitation was: "Nu, please go wash!" For an acquaintance, the "Nu" alone was enough. If someone didn't understand, he wouldn't repeat, even though he himself never attended anybody's affair unless he was asked three times. He died before the outbreak of World War II. His nephews are the brothers, Shlomo and Joshua Suskovitsh.

[Page 295]

When the Red Army Entered Szarkowszczyzna

Told by the partisans of Szarkowszczyzna:
Chana Chazan-Steinman, Tevka Milner, Shacha Steinman, and Beilka Chadash

Translated by Jerrold Landau

Donated by Anita Frishman Gabbay

In the autumn of 1939, Soviet Russia took Vilna and the entire region. The Soviet system was immediately implemented in Szarkowszczyzna. During the first few weeks, the shopkeepers were ordered to sell their merchandise at the price that was in place until the entry of the Red Army. At the beginning, both the Polish zloty and the Russian ruble were accepted. Later, the Russians exchanged the Polish zlotys for a pittance, and only the ruble remained. The end result was that the shopkeepers remained with paper currency of minimal value and the farmers "sold off" their merchandise to the Red Army. For the most part, the shopkeepers did not know what price to ask for. Often, the customers themselves set the price. Thus, all the Jewish possessions were liquidated within a matter of weeks.

The tradesmen (tailors, shoemakers, butchers, wagon drivers) were organized into Artels[1] (syndicates) controlled by the local authorities. The shopkeepers and businessmen sought work with the regime. Some found difficult work such as carrying lumber, sand, and the like. Others worked in the offices, educational institutions, or the police.

The two *Beis Midrashes* were left alone. Jews went to the synagogue as previously. The Jewish folk-school and cultural school were abandoned, because there was no financial means of upholding them. The prior income that the school activists used to give for its support fell through. The main factor was that it was not possible to conduct a program with Jewish-only quotas. Every undertaking had to be conducted with the participation of the entire population. Jews did not have the possibility of separate undertakings. There was a Jewish teacher, Gelman, in the Russian school who used to teach Jewish studies to the Jewish children one hour a day. The director of the school was Noach Kac (the son of Baruch-Shalom the baker).

[Page 296]

The Jewish library functioned as previously, directed by the Komsomol youth[2]. Programs were conducted solely in Russian. Yiddish theater was rarely performed.

The Arrival of the Germans

Life in the town changed on June 22, 1941, when Germany attacked Russia. As one can imagine, the news caused a panic in town. The Red Army quickly retreated. There was no ruling authority for several days. The peasants prepared to rob. They took whatever they could from the Jews. One peasant tried to convince the Jews to gather in one place at the time the Germans were entering. As was later verified, the intention was that the Germans would have an opportunity to liquidate the Jews immediately at the time of their entry. The end result was that the Germans shot that farmer first, when they found him on the street late in the evening.

The peasants from the surrounding villages pillaged the town for two days. At the beginning, the Jews organized a resistance. When they saw, however, that the robber was supported by several Germans who were already in the town, the Jews left everything open and hid wherever they could. This was merely the beginning.

The German army entered the town without a battle. They did not set themselves up there, but rather left. Some soldiers even asked the Jews for food and cigarettes. A group of about 20 young people left along with the Russians. The local authority was set up about a week later by the local Christian population. It was headed by a German. All the Jews – men, women, and children – were called together in the market. There, a Christian spoke in the name of the Germans. He said that the Jews must give over all their belongings to the authorities, including, for example, cattle, fowl, cushions, mattresses, furniture, etc. The Jews brought all the things to the local commander. Only cats were allowed to remain with the Jews. It was strictly forbidden for a Jew to have a dog.

[Page 297]

An edict was issued that males and females from the age of ten must wear two yellow patches. Jews were also forbidden from walking on the sidewalk.

Everyone still lived in their houses, as previously. Everyone was forced to work for the Germans. The work consisted of cleaning the streets, washing vehicles and floors, cleaning stables and horses, etc. At times, a German could have a desire and order that grain or straw be cleared out, and then order that it be gathered together again – beating them in the process. The Germans could bully as much as they wanted. Once, they ordered them to carry a dead dog around the synagogue and sing, and then to bury it in the synagogue yard. The Jews were not permitted to conduct any business with Christians, or even to talk to them. When the Germans entered, many Jews gave away their belongings to the Christians to hide. The Christians then waited for the death of the Jew.

A group of Szarkowszczyzna youths

The Jews chose representatives to represent them to the authorities. Early on, the Germans captured men on the street and sent them to work. If they needed anything, they would enter a house and steal it. When the council was set up, the sporadic robberies stopped for a bit of time. If the Germans needed anything, they turned to the Judenrat. Thus, the Judenrat had to provide people for work every day. During the winter, most of the work involved clearing the snow from the roads. The woman and children were not permitted to cover their heads with kerchiefs. They also sent Jews to the forests to chop wood, float rafts on the stream that led to the Dvina, saw lumber and thereby freeze their fingers, carry sacks to the mills, etc.

[Page 298]

That same year, the ghetto was set up. The ghetto consisted of two disparate sections. The market divided one ghetto from the other. At the beginning, Jews of Szarkowszczyzna were taken to a forest near Braslaw, and barracks were set up for them. Fate had it, however, that there was a Christian among the leadership, Mitzelitza, who was still friendly to the Jews. He made efforts for the Jews to be allowed to remain in their place, and that Jews from surrounding areas could be brought to Szarkowszczyzna. On the other hand, he sucked the blood of the Jews, extorting whatever he could.

Soon, Jews started to arrive from the surrounding towns and villages: Pohost, Germanovichi, Macolesce (Mishnevichi), Rymki, Holeve (Halubichy), Kosni (Konstantinovo), Bildzszewes (Buevshchina)[3], and others. The wagons stopped in the synagogue courtyard and let off the Jews with their meager baggage. The loneliness and agony were indescribable. The women and children began to weep so much that the town trembled. People saw death before their eyes. Slowly, they were set up in Jewish homes, whether with people they knew or people they did not know. Thus, four or five families often lived in one house.

There were two ghettos. One ghetto began from Itche Leib Chazan's (the hairdresser's) house and ended at Szprince's house by the bridge. There was a gate there through which the Germans would come to take Jews to work. The ghetto continued along the river until Hirshke Weksler's house. Both *Beis Midrashes* were located there. Services were only conducted there rarely, because the men had to go out to work at daybreak, including on the Sabbath and festivals. The gates and windows looking out toward the market were covered over with boards and surrounded with barbed wire. Entrance to the ghetto was through one gate that was located near the bridge. There were fewer Jews in that ghetto than in the other (approximately 700).

[Page 299]

The other ghetto began from Mote Ber Berchon's house (where the Judenrat was located), and continued until the field, from one side of Hershel Berchon's house, over the full length of Cerkowna Street, until Ephraim Eiten's house on the other side. The street was boarded up and surrounded with barbed wire. About 1,200 souls lived there.

Chana Chazan, the partisan woman with a group of friends

The cemetery was located outside the ghetto. One had to have a special permit to go there. Such a permit was given in the event of a death, however the funeral had to proceed through the ghetto and not through the free streets.

For the most part, people obtained their food through secretly bartering various items of merchandise, clothing, dishes, jewelry, and the like from the peasants. They always looked for a Christian neighbor, an intermediary, who would go in the darkness of night and throw the items over the fence or break through a board to transfer flour, potatoes, butter, milk, and other foodstuffs. Simultaneously, he would take the items that the Jews had prepared for him. Officially, the Germans rationed 100 grams of bread daily for each individual, big or small. They did not provide any other food, and this had to suffice for the entire day. Yet, they did not suffer from hunger, due to the aforementioned smuggling of food from the outside.

[Page 300]

The local Jews did not allow the poor families, especially the refugees who were brought in from surrounding towns, to suffer from any hunger. They used to share the bit of food they had with them. This was usually done by the neighbors themselves, but there were also cases where the Judenrat became involved with helping the poor people.

It was also a frequent occurrence that people would sneak out of the ghetto, venture far from the town to a peasant acquaintance, and bring back sacks of potatoes, flour, and other products. People did this before dawn by going through the ghetto gate, where the Jewish police would permit it. If one felt that there was a danger that the Germans might come, they would throw the products over the fence. Jews of various ages were among those who used to sneak out of the ghetto. It was easier to risk one's life than to see the family suffer from hunger.

The Judenrat provided a doctor, and, to the extent possible, medicine for the sick. The doctor was Hershel Rabinowicz, the son of the rabbi. It was permitted to fetch water from the river for only one hour a day. The two wells that were in the ghetto did not provide enough water. This was an issue for the ghetto in Jarzszefka. The other ghetto, on the bank of the river, did not have this problem.

There was no depression in the ghetto, the shadow of death did not show from the faces, and there no quarrels took place.

After about six months, the Germans began to say that those who are not working will no longer receive the 100 grams of bread. They therefore divided both ghettos into two sections; one for the productive people and the other for the non-productive people. The non-productive section was along the riverbank. The relationship with the peasants became more strained. They were simply waiting for the inheritance of the Jews.

[Page 301]

The First Victims

Within a short time, after approximately one month, the Germans came to search for Eliahu (Elia) Mindel, Tzadok Rozof, and Aharon the shoemaker, seemingly as a result of a report. They ordered them to take spades and dig pits next to the non-Jewish cemetery. The Germans shot them there, and these pits became their graves. They were not allowed to be brought to Jewish burial. A few days later, Yankel Baszewkin, Zalman-Mendel Muskat, and others were also taken out. They commanded them as well to dig pits, but they shot into the air. That time, they let them live. The next day, however, they came to look for them again, and they took them. They were never heard from them again. Nobody even knew where their remains were.

Szarkowszczyzna youth

David Pen and Yehoshua, Mashe-Zelda's husband, who worked at transporting grain to the Rudzik mill and bringing back the flour, also escaped a few times to fetch a sack of flour. Once, they were caught. First, they were confined to the ghetto itself. Then, they were led to Miory and shot there. Those murders cast a pall upon the Jews. Later, such murders became a daily occurrence.

[Page 302]

Thus, did one live with a constant deathly fear regarding what the next day would bring. Almost nobody believed that they could evade death. There were families who escaped from the ghetto, went to peasant acquaintances, spent about a week there, and returned to the ghetto. In every house, one or two people stood guard, watching to see where they [the murderers] would suddenly break into the ghettos and shoot everybody.

The Liquidation of the Szarkowszczyzna Ghetto

On Wednesday, July 17, 1942, the eve of the slaughter, a German S.S. man arrived in town from Glubokie on a motorcycle, to which a Pulemyot[4] was affixed. He summoned the oldest person of the Judenrat, Hirshka Berchon, and ordered him to prepare leather and jewelry for him, saying that the Jews need not fear, for they are going to conduct maneuvers. Then he called him again and ordered him to immediately give over that which he had gathered. This was extremely suspicious. A shudder fell upon both ghettos.

The entire town stood on guard. People noticed that it was not calm with the police. Unusual movement was taking place there. They had always guarded the ghetto on their own. The Judenrat was suspicious that the Germans were preparing an attack on the ghettos, to destroy them. They strengthened their guard and told everyone to be ready.

Zalman Cymer's daughter worked as a maid for the German police commandant. She hid in the attic of the commandant's house and listened from there as to what was taking place throughout the night. In that manner, she found out that the police were preparing to murder all the Jews. She snuck out of there and brought the dark news to the ghetto. Everyone was already prepared. When they noticed at 3:00 a.m. that the police were setting out for the ghetto gate, the leaders ordered that whoever could, should save themselves in whatever fashion they could. Thus, about 90% of the Jews of Szarkowszczyzna were saved. They escaped in the darkness of the night in whatever direction their eyes took them. Only the elderly, the sick, and children who had no energy to escape remained in the ghettos. A number of younger Jews also remained. They were near the river, which prevented them from escaping. The German police murdered all of them on the spot where they were found. Their communal grave is located at the edge of Disner Street, not far from the non-Jewish cemetery.

[Page 303]

The slaughter took place on a rainy early morning, on Tuesday, July 18, 1942 (Tammuz 3, 5702, 1942).

**In the Randhofer Camp in Austria,
a memorial ceremony for all who were murdered**

**Mendel Szoklin, Chana's husband,
and his brother Velvel**

The Jews themselves set the town on fire in order to cause a panic. In that way, the Jews made sure that the peasants, who were already on the lookout for Jews and ready to turn them in, would have their own difficulties. This was perhaps the first mass resistance against the Germans. The Szarkowszczyzners did not allow themselves to be shot.

The men, women, and children who escaped from the Szarkowszczyzna Ghetto that night spread out through the forests and the fields – barefoot, naked, and hungry. The Germans ambushed them and would shoot the escaping Jews every day along the paths in the fields. It was completely impossible for them to hide. They also had to seek that which was needed to sustain themselves. Thus did the escapees meet their deaths. The entire surrounding region is full of graves of the Jews of Szarkowszczyzna.

The survivors could not hold out for more than two months. Cold, and wandering about under the open sky, they were tired out. Many were sick and some were swollen. They had to seek a roof over their heads. Slowly, they gathered in the Glubokie Ghetto. Only a few young lads who decided that they would rather struggle with death than enter the ghetto remained in the fields. At that time, there were no organized partisans in the fields. The first Russian partisans were organized at the end of 1942.

[Page 304]

The Rajak brothers tell about the Jews of Szarkowszczyzna who went to the Glubokie Ghetto. It is not superfluous to tell it over:

In Szarkowszczyzna, in the manner of that time, thanks to the Judenrat that stood on guard the entire time and carefully tracked the deeds and intention of the Germans and police, over 50 percent of the Jews were saved. The Judenrat of that time, to be mentioned in a positive fashion, was almost the only one in the region that accurately evaluated the situation, was not fooled, and considered its primary goal as saving as much of the population as possible. In contrast to other Judenrats, the Szarkowszczyzna Judenrat did not calm the Jews with "it will be well for you," and did not simply give them empty promises. They did not assure them that they were "dear ones" to the Germans, exceptions, and that they would remain alive. On the contrary, they warned them that the situation was serious and dangerous, that the Germans will kill them, that a slaughter of the Jews of Szarkowszczyzna was inevitable, etc. Therefore, everyone must be on guard. The Germans will try to calm them with trickery, and one must not trust them. One must be prepared to run at any moment, which could come completely unexpectedly.

During those days, when the S.S. men were wandering through Glubokie and the region, the Szarkowszczyzna Judenrat was still performing its tracking activities regarding the German police and gendarmerie. Here, we must mention in a laudatory fashion the Judenrat member Hirsch Berchon, who, with an especially sharp glance, with special alertness, detected the preparations of the murderers. On the eve of the bloody day, from an "intimate friendly" conversation with the Uberwachtmeister Heit, he figured out the reason why he had come to Szarkowszczyzna from Glubokie. Heit told Berchon that he had come there to conduct "maneuvers," which will take place in the morning of the second day. He told him to assure the Jews that they need not fear. Nothing will happen to them.

[Page 305]

This was a sufficient sign for the Judenrat to quickly alert everyone that they must be prepared… Nobody slept that night. From the attics and other vantage points, they observed carefully what was taking place on the street, where they were going, and what they were doing.

When they noticed in the morning that the gendarmes and police were up earlier than usual, that their numbers were larger than usual, and that they were running armed back and forth from the gendarmerie, telling secrets to each other, etc., the Judenrat evaluated the situation as dangerous, and immediately ordered all the Jews to run…

The murderers were late. When they surrounded the ghetto, almost two thirds of the people were behind the town. When the S.D. drove in a half an hour later on vehicles, nobody was found in the ghetto other than the old, sick, and children. This time, the Jews tricked them…

Only a small bit of Jewish blood was left for the wild, German beast. They were upset with the Jewish "brazenness." The hatred flickered even more within them. Their skin cracked. They were mocked in such a way! Can it be? The Jews were so cunning, they went away! Their Aktion in Szarkowszczyzna fell through. Only a small amount of Jewish blood was left for them to suck.

However, they were not completely outwitted. The had vehicles, they had weapons, they were strong enough and could still teach a lesson to the constantly dismal Jews.

After murdering the elderly men and women and the children on the spot, which did not take the healthy Germans very long, they went back to their vehicles and pursued the Children of Israel[5] – they could make the fleeing Jews run.

To our misfortune, they captured many Jews and punished the "transgressors" harshly. Death was too little for them. They tortured them and caused them so much pain, in ways that only the Germans were capable of – and the extent to which the German capabilities in killing and murdering is well known. They stuck hot rods in the eyes, simply cut off live flesh, broke the fingers, tore out the teeth (especially when there were gold fillings), cut the tongues, etc.

[Page 306]

They murdered about 700 Szarkowszczyzner Jews that day, from among those remaining in the town together with those captured along the routes.

We must state that the Germans had a great deal of help from the local peasants, who captured Jews on the ways and gave them over to the murderous hands. The local police were especially diligent. However, this did not end with the 700 victims. The police did not tire, day after day and week after week, to search for the hidden and escaped Jews. They lay in the bushes, in the groves, in the rye stalks along the routes, and listened from there for the Jewish refugees.

One of the large impetuses for the police and the peasants to capture Jews was the belongings and money that the Jews had taken along. A peasant could find a watch, a ring, earrings, or just plain money on a murdered Jew. The murderers had a special appetite for a Jew with golden teeth.

The Jews knew that they were searching for them. They listened for them and would lie in the rye stalks and under the bushes, without moving from the place. They were even afraid to breathe loudly. They did not eat or drink. They lay under the rain and in the cold (to the bad luck of the Jews, June 1942 was wet and cold).

The extent to which the local police did not let up can be seen from the following fact: five weeks after the slaughter, a Jew from Szarkowszczyzna, Leibe Chazan, unable to bear the suffering of his children who were languishing terribly from hunger, crawled out from the rye stalks in front of everyone to get a bucket of water. When he bent over a swamp to fill a broken bucket with water, a policeman jumped out from under a bush and demanded money, saying that if he refused, he would lose his life... When Chazan gave him some of his money, the policeman shot him, wounding him severely. With his last energy, Chazan took out the rest of the money and tore it up quickly, so that the murderer would not benefit from it. The policeman immediately shot Chazan with another bullet and finished him off.

Chazan's wife and children witnessed this. They could not even express their pain with a shout or a groan. Unfortunately, they had to stifle their tears, for a cry, a sob, or a cautious rustle would have uncovered them. Even though they saved themselves at that moment, the cruel hands later found them.

[Page 307]

As has been said, many of the local Christians were the best searchers for the hidden people. Every peasant was very familiar with the pathways, trails, groves, and bushes in their region. They would murder the captured Jews with various implements, such as hatchets, spades, and pickaxes, or by giving them over to the hands of the police or the Germans. In return, the peasants received recognition from the authorities, and were also given material benefits, such as several kilos of salt, matches, soap, etc.

Thus, for example, Mekar from the village of Pialikes captured Zerach Kropivnik and murdered him. He also killed Motke Modow. He chased the family of Leizer Rodoskowicz into the river and drowned them. One of the residents of *Heifl* Bedi found three Jewish refugees. He tricked them, promised them protection, and then turned them over to the Germans. Wasztai Dawid tricked the family of D. Pildas with a promise to hide them, and later turned them over the Germans. He also tricked a young child, Estrin, and murdered him with a hatchet.

In the midst of such cruel acts, let us mention here in a positive way the brothers Marian and Adolf Stankewicz from Borsuchina, who helped the Jews during their time of tribulation. They helped hide them from the German murderers, provided them with food, and showed them places where they could hide and to where they could escape.

We must also mention with great praise a Stankewicz from that region, who simply sacrificed himself to save Jews. Jews set out to Stankewicz from all sides, knowing that they could find a refuge with him. He hid them where he could – in the stores, in the barns, in the attics, as well as with his acquaintances whom he trusted. Not only did he give food to those who turned to him, but he also carried food to Jews in the forest and in the stalks, if he knew where they were laying in hiding. More than one Jew was saved thanks to him.

The great benefactor, the rescuer of Jews, Stankewicz, was very popular in the area as a defender of Jews, and this was not appropriate. As I mentioned, the greatest portion of the peasants in the area helped the Germans greatly with finding the Jews. On account of that, the local peasant acquaintances decided to clear Stankewicz out of the way… Those "good neighbors" found out at one point that seven Jews were being hidden in the bathhouse, and two in the attic of his dwelling. They went to Szarkowszczyzna and told the local police about this secret. They immediately went covertly to the place of the "transgressor" and set the bathhouse on fire from all sides. The seven Jews in hiding immediately became a pile of ashes – one could barely recognize their bones. They also went to Stankewicz' house to search for Jews. Stankewicz, whose name must truly be inscribed with gold letters in the bloody pages of our annals, displayed exceptional self-sacrifice. Instead of himself fleeing from the murderers, he busied himself at that time with saving the remaining Jews. He quickly let them out of the windows, and he himself unfortunately fell into the hands of the bandits. The bandits took him to Glubokie, where they shot him.

[Page 308]

These were the few exceptions in the great, bleak desert.

A group of Szarkowszczyzna youth

Let us also mention here the Christian Lublinski. He did a great deal for the Jews. He would bring food and money to the ghetto, and act as an emissary. He would go from one ghetto to the other to keep families in contact with each other. More than once, he would hide Jews at his place and provide them with everything that he could. He was turned in, and the German murderers shot him.

[Page 309]

The house of the Szarkowszczyzna hairdresser Itche-Leib Chazan. His son Arke is standing here.

[Page 310]

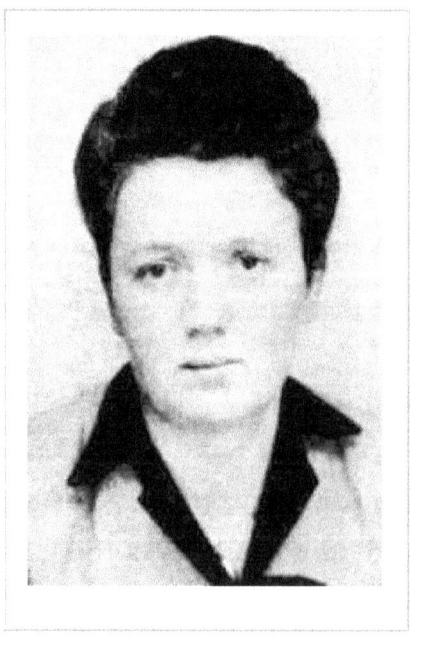

Chana Chazan-Steinman – a partisan woman

**Moshe Chazan,
the father of the partisan woman
Chana Chazan-Steinman**

Translator's Footnotes:

1. See https://en.wikipedia.org/wiki/Artel.

2. The Communist youth league. See https://en.wikipedia.org/wiki/Komsomol

3. Some of these shtetls or hamlets are hard to place, either because their names are pronounced in Yiddish differently from the actual Lithuanian name

4. A Russian machine gun: https://en.wikipedia.org/wiki/PK_machine_gun

5. Paraphrased from Exodus 14:8.

[Page 311]

Szarkowszczyzna Survivors Relate…

Told by Chana Chazan-Steinman, Moshe Chazan's daughter

Translation supplied by Jerrold Landau

Donated by Anita Frishman Gabbay

On the tragic Thursday of July 18 (Tammuz 3) 1942, at dawn, we began to run together with all the Szarkowszczyzners. As if to vex, my husband and my three children were sleeping. I had to awaken them. I could not even get the children dressed. Half-naked, I hurried them out of bed, and we started running. A few steps from the house, I lost sight of my husband Mendel and two children, five-year-old Shmuel and four-year-old Liba. I ran with my eight-month-old daughter in my hands. The shouting and crying pierced the heavens. From all sides, it sounded like everyone was calling out to their own. I found my way to Glubokie. We were a group of 50 people, but at the end of that same day, only 15 remained.

As we were running, my child was crying strongly in my hands. She was crying from terror, cold, and hunger. The Jews who were running with us yelled at me to silence the child, for I was liable to bring a misfortune onto them. I knew nothing of my husband and the two children. I left the group of Jews and set out to a nearby hamlet. I found a peasant woman in the hamlet. She gave me a bit of milk for the child and a rag to swaddle her. Of course, the peasant woman did not permit me to remain for an additional moment. She told me that she was afraid for her own life. I set out on my way again. I sat down at a highway. I was certain that the Germans or police would pass by and free me. Sitting there, I saw a man rise out of the stalks with a stick in his hand. It seemed that this was a peasant who was going to kill me. I did not raise my head and nestled my child to me. I waited for the end, but then I heard that he was speaking to me in Yiddish. I lifted my head and saw that this was Nathan Szulkin (the brother of Alter Szulkin, today in Argentina). He told me that I must move away from the road, for it is dangerous. I must go to hide in the stalks. He advised me to leave the child with a peasant woman to hide her for a bit of time, until I find a place to remain.

We went along the side of the rye fields. I knocked at a peasant's house and asked that they take the child for a few days. They chased me away and threatened to turn us in to the police. We continued further and met another peasant woman. She told us that the police are there in the village. Not far from there, we saw a village hut. We approached it. It was raining. We intended to rest there a bit and continue on. We entered. We barely succeeded in entering when we heard knocking. We heard someone speaking Yiddish. It was a woman with two children and an elderly mother. They were from Pohost. We took them inside. After a few minutes, we decided that Nathan and I should go to see what was going on outside. After walking about twenty steps, a wagon with a policeman drove by. He immediately began to pursue us. We ran to the nearby grove. We heard gunshots. The ground near us tore open. Nathan ran a bit father than I did. I saw how he grabbed his stomach and fell. He then lifted himself up and ran into the grove. I went deeper into the forest. I did not see Nathan again. Of course, I could not give him any help. I also never saw my child and the Pohost family again. I barely heard the voices that were coming from the hut.

[Page 312]

Thus, did I wander through the forest for a month. I only saw wild ducks at night. I did not find any other animals there. My greatest fear, however, was to encounter a human beast. I sustained myself with bitter berries and sour grass. The dress that I was wearing disintegrated into pieces. I was often thoroughly wet. I continued walking on and on, until I arrived one evening at the edge of the forest. I noticed a shepherd. I waited so he would not see me. He went away, and a crazy peasant woman came opposite me, singing and dancing. I was not afraid of her.

I went to the little house not far away. Near the house, I saw the peasant woman carrying milk in a pail. I came closer to her and asked for a bit of food. She directed me to a barn and told me to enter. I entered. She quickly brought me a pitcher of milk, and bread with butter. She also brought me a dress and a blouse. She told me that I could stay there for three days, until I regain my strength.

I dug a pit in the straw and lay down in the barn. The peasant woman brought me bread and milk once a day. I had to leave on the fourth day. She told me that her friends, who are very good people, are over there, one kilometer away. I set out to them. It was not far. I arrived at a house and knocked. The peasant crossed himself when he saw me. Apparently, he was frightened by my gait. He told me to enter the stable. There was hay in there. I made a place for myself. The peasant brought me milk and bread. He told me that not from him, the police killed the Szarkowszczyzner Chona Szulkin, his wife and child. A peasant to whom he gave over his possessions to hide, turned him in. If I do not want to meet the same end, I should go. The peasant woman wept over my bitter fate. She gave me a pitcher of milk, cheese, and bread, and I left.

[Page 313]

I walked among the rye stalks. I went, not knowing where I was going. I had food. Two days passed in that manner. I arrived at Pialikes, five kilometers from Szarkowszczyzna. I was afraid of entering the village. I first spent the night in a Christian cemetery. Then I dug a pit in a pile of hay. One early morning, a shepherd was leading cows, and one cow defecated on me. The shepherd saw me. I understood that I must leave. I continued on through the rye stalks and the fields. I was afraid to go on the road. At that point, it started to rain hard. It seemed that it would not stop raining. I came out from the stalks and sat under a tree. Then I went off to a nearby grove. This was a Christian cemetery. I spread myself over a gravestone and fell asleep.

I then set out again through the rye fields until I once again came to the village of Pialikes. From afar, I saw a peasant woman passing by. I ran after her and asked her to give me a bit of bread. The peasant woman crossed herself and wept over my bitter fate. She told me to go where a cow was standing tied up. She told me to take the rope and approach the cow. In this manner, I entered a stable. There was straw on one side. The peasant woman brought me water and a comb. I washed up and combed myself. I did not believe that this was possible. She brought me food. I did not eat anything non-kosher. The gentile woman lectured me that it was not for nothing that our G-d was punishing us. I spent a week there and then had to continue on. The name of the gentile woman was Fiene Tarases from Pialkes. She hid other Szarkowszczyzners, included Hershel Tabarowicz. After the liberation, I went to her and expressed my gratitude. She was indeed one of the few Christians who helped Jews.

[Page 314]

The peasant woman told me to go to her acquaintance in a hamlet. The peasant woman told me to hide in the rye stalks. I was afraid to remain in the house, the stable, or the barn. She brought me food.

A rainstorm broke out. All the rye stalks flattened. The peasant woman noticed that I could be seen from outside. She told me to run to the bathhouse. I spent the night there. The next day, I went back to the rye stalks. I spent another four days there in that manner.

I had to continue on. I arrived at a nearby hamlet called Pialikes, where there were a few householders. They knew that I was from Szarkowszczyzna. They had sewn [had clothes sewn] with my sister-in-law. The main thing was that one family drew me close. The head of the household was Lawanda Milanda and his wife Anfisia. I spent a few weeks with them. Since I was a seamstress, I sewed for them. I spent a month and a half in that manner.

That peasant told me about my husband Mendel and my two children: My son Molinka and my daughter Libechke were killed while fleeing the ghetto. As I have already explained, I lost track of them. My husband and the children entered a hut at the end of Jorzelka street in Szarkowszczyzna. This was on the same day. There, the Germans and the police captured them and took them through the market to the pit in which all the killed Jews of Szarkowszczyzna were lying. There, by the pit, they shot everyone. Their blood mixed with that of all the other martyrs.

From there, I set out to the peasant's sister. Her name was Luba. I remained with her for a month. I also sewed for her, all covertly. From there, I went to a relative off theirs, where I spent a month. After that, I returned to the Milanda family. I asked the peasant to transport me to the Glubokie Ghetto. He travelled specially to the Glubokie Ghetto to find out if any of our people remained alive. He told me that he found alive near the fence of the ghetto the Szarkowszczyzner Chaim Zalkes (the butcher's), who told him that my sister Frumka, her husband, and two children were in the Glubokie Ghetto. Her other two children were killed while fleeing the Glubokie ghetto: a twelve and a fourteen-year-old girl. Chaim Zalkes also told about my brother Nachman Chazan, his wife and two children. The older two children were burnt, and their mother went crazy as a result. Their names were Shepsl and Motka. Chaim also told the peasant that Sonia, the sister of the Suskowicz brothers, was in the ghetto. She was there with her husband Moshe Pajkin and their child. The older girl was Rivka. There were from among the finest in town.

[Page 315]

I remained with him for only a very brief period after that greeting. He was afraid that someone might turn him in. While I was hiding with him I found out that a Jewish family from Haleve was hiding with the widow Alsepsczicha, not far from Haleve. I met with them in my peasant's stable. We decided to go into the forests, where we heard that there were partisans.

I set out on my way the next night. We arrived at a bog. There we met the Szarkowszczyzners Meir Estrin, Nathan Estrin, Binyamin Estrin (all now in North America), and Yisraelke Estrin (now in Israel). We decided to go to the Kazan forests. We were told that partisans were there. We set out on our way. We indeed met Jewish partisans there. They were Gutman Foigl, whose sister is today in Argentina; Baruch Lipszin, Motka Lipszin, Yorka Lipszin, and Yechiel Hertz Lipszin – some of whom are now in North America, and some in Israel. I should also mention here Zalman Lewi from Druya and Shachna Steinman (my current husband). They maintained widows and orphans in the forests. They risked their lives to bring food for them.

There is a great deal to tell about my partisan life. One can write thick books about this alone. I understand that we cannot fill the Yizkor Book with me alone, so I will also mention here the Szarkowszczyzners who I met in the forests and about whom I heard. These are: Avraham Pajkin, Lova Mendel (Chaim Itshe's son), Shlomo Cymer, Tzipka Cymer, Frumka Chidelel, Chana-Sara Knel, Foiga Szulkin-Lipszin, Leizer Cipelowicz, Beilka Chadasz, Sonia Cymer, Etka Cymer, and Polia Cymer. All survived. A few Szarkowszczyzners survived in Russia.

Thus, did we survive until the liberation. We fought, risking our lives at every moment, starved, and hoped. After the liberation, I went to Szarkowszczyzna. I did not recognize the town. Everything was destroyed. I found two or three Jews there. All wept over the misfortune. The only thing that bound us together was the communal grave of our dearest beloved, in which my entire family was buried: my husband Mendel Szulkin, and my two children, five-year-old Mulinka and four-year-old Libetchke. My youngest girl, Malkele, was eight months old. As I explained, she was burnt in the hut. Their spilled blood will always demand revenge.

[Page 316]

Beilka Chadasz, Nachum Czale's daughter, Tells

I was seven years old when the Germans entered Szarkowszczyzna. I do not recall any details of that time, which I can tell over. However, I do recall what took place later. I will begin with the liquidation of the Szarkowszczyzna Ghetto. It was 3:00 a.m. We heard heavy shooting. I was picked up, and we began running. The entire town was burning. I lost my parents. I ran together with others. We arrived in the forest. In the evening, when we emerged from the forest to see where we were we encountered the police. They started shooting heavily. The bullets hit many of us. The rest fled. One of us had a Nagan[2] (revolver) and killed a policeman. The police consisted of the local peasants.

We ran further, and arrived at a far-off forest, which was larger and deeper than the previous one. We rested there a bit and looked for something with which to nourish ourselves. Once, I set out to ask for bread in a nearby village. I went from house to house. We were in luck. I collected a large sack of bread. When I returned to the forest, however, I had to cross a small stream on a wooden foot-bridge. Suddenly, a policeman approached me. He called to me. I began to run. I barely felt that he was shooting after me. Thus, did I enter the forest.

There were six of us in the forest. We did not know where to go further. Once, a peasant came to us and told us that there was a call from the Germans that all the escaped Jews who were hiding in the forests should come to towns that had ghettos. If we would pay him, he would lead us to the Postavy Ghetto. Since we were poor and naked, we collected a few gold chains and rings, and gave them to him. He took them, and indeed led us to the Postavy Ghetto.

[Page 317]

Memorial ceremony in the liberated Rondhoffen camp (Austria)

The Postavy Judenrat apportioned all of us up to families. The sent me to the Barkin family. I later heard that he survived. There, I found out that my parents were alive. A

Szarkowszczyzner told me that my father was coming the next day. My father indeed came to me. He was in the Glubokie Ghetto with my mother and two sisters. He received a permit from there to come to find me and bring me to Glubokie. However, I could not go with him, as my feet were swollen. We could not go by vehicle. It was 60 kilometers. I remained, intending to go later along with other Szarkowszczyzners who also had to go to unite with their families in the Glubokie Ghetto.

[Page 318]

The slaughter in the Postavy Ghetto took place before we could gather in Glubokie. Of course, the slaughter was not only of Postavyers, but also of all the Jews who were found there. I started to run, and luck was in my favor again. I found myself with other Jews in a thick forest. The town was surrounded by forests. We lay there for an entire day and set out at night to go closer to Glubokie. It was the winter, and the frost was great. My feet were bound with rags. We arrived in Glubokie at dawn. We broke open a board of the fence that surrounded the ghetto and entered. I immediately searched for my parents. They lived in a stable. The Rajak brothers wrote about life in the Glubokie Ghetto. I immediately set out for work. I cleaned fish that were packed like sardines and sent to Germany. I was nine years old at that time. We lived in that fashion for a year, until the second and final slaughter in the Glubokie Ghetto took place. This was in August 1943.

As you know, it was impossible to escape from the Glubokie Ghetto. The ghetto was surrounded by such armaments that it was impossible to penetrate. My parents and I ran into a bunker. About 500 Jews were hiding there. The entry to the bunker was through a well. We had worked on it for over a year. This was under Kontorowicz's brick house. We lay there in perpetual darkness. We hid there for three days after the slaughter, until we were uncovered. A German noticed how someone jumped into the well, which was the entrance to the bunker. A slaughter took place. Many of the Jews had weapons. We defended ourselves to the extent that we could. Some of the murderers also fell. The majority of us were killed.

My father, one sister, and I remained in the bunker for one more day after the slaughter. We were so closed off that they did not notice us. At night, we went out. We walked over dead bodies that were strewn over all the streets. We left the town. When we went a few steps further, near the Baraker Forest, we heard a shout, ordering us to halt. We started to run. My father was hit by a bullet. My sister was also shot. I was shot in the hand. A

German placed a gun on my shoulders to ensure that I was dead. The bullet went out through my mouth. I heard the German saying, "Four Jews kaput."

[Page 319]

I lay in the rye stalks among the tall sprouts for five days. I was covered with blood. I set out on the sixth day. I arrived at a hamlet. I knocked on a door. An elderly Christian woman came out. She took me inside. She washed my wounds and gave me something to eat. I could not chew or swallow. I spent a few days with her and set out on my way again. After going a few kilometers, I encountered an elderly Christian who immediately recognized that I was a Jew. He started to take me back to Glubokie to give me over to the Germans, for one would be paid for capturing a Jew. He took me for three kilometers until we arrived in a hamlet. He entered a house, dragging me along as well. However, I remained on the other side of the door. While he was inside, I banged the door and placed underneath it a shovel that was standing nearby and began to run. I threw off the sack with food that the gentile women had given me. I ran until I arrived in a field. When I sat down to rest, I noticed about twenty people near the edge. I asked a peasant where I was. He told me that these were partisans.

I immediately set out to them. The group of partisans was mixed, with Jews and Christians. Yitzchak Blatt of Glubokie was among them. They showed me where the surviving Jews were located, and I set out to them. When I told them about the peasant who was leading me to the Germans, they figured out that this was a known spy for whom they had been searching for a long time. They immediately set out to the hamlet, called to him, and took his documents to be certain that he was indeed the spy whom they were searching for. Then they locked him in the house and burnt the house down with him inside.

I met an aunt of mine in the forest among the surviving Jews. She was my mother's sister, Liba Lewitanus. She was rescued from the Druya Ghetto. We lived from the food brought to us by the Jewish partisans.

Needless to say, it was only the Jewish partisan youth who helped us with love and life. However, they scared us. Once, a terrible German blockade took place. They surrounded us. The only place remaining for us was a large, deep swamp, through which nobody could come. We lay there for two weeks. After that, when it was quieter, each of us looked for food. The orphans that remained were forgotten. Only one of them, Leib Baum from Kazian, took all of us orphans under his protection. He looked after us like his own children.

[Page 320]

Yitzchak Leib Chazan (the partisan) with his family

After the liberation, I went to Szarkowszczyzna. A large portion of the houses of the town remained. However, I could not remain. I escaped from there as quickly as I could, so as to see it no more.

[Page 321]

Sonia Szmuskowicz-Pajkin

Sonia Szmuskowicz-Pajkin

Beilka Chadasz tells:

Sonia Szmuskowicz, her husband Pajkin, and their five children were among the Szarkowszczyzners with whom I was together in the Glubokie Ghetto. (Sonia is the sister of Shlomo and Yehoshua Szmuskowicz). The children were Rivka, Arke, Yachne, Lyuba, and a young girl whose name I have forgotten. I worked at knitting gloves for the Germans together with Yachne, who was about ten years old. We worked from the morning until night. We received a bit of soup in return. The winter was difficult. Our hands and feet froze. Everyone had to work, including children from six or seven years of age.

During the liquidation of the Szarkowszczyzna Ghetto on July 18, 1942, Sonia and her family were saved. They all fled to their peasant acquaintance in a village and hid there for about a half a year. Then it became impossible for them to hide there anymore. When the deceptive call came from the Germans that the escaped Jews should come to the Glubokie Ghetto, they believed it and went to that ghetto. They lived in a house with other Jews. The crowding, hunger, and terror were indescribable. They lived in that manner until the second and final liquidation of the Glubokie Ghetto on August 20, 1943, 19 Av 5703. The entire family was murdered on that day.

[Page 322]

A Seder in the camp in Austria

A Szarkowszczyzner partisan

Translator's Footnotes:

1. Spelled as Szmuskowicz on page 321.

2. Probably Nagant (a type of Russian revolver).

[Page 323]

Dunilowicze
The Annihilation of Dunilovichi

Testimony by Nachke Svirsky

Translation supplied by Eilat Gordin Levitan and Daniel Wainer, grandson of Mayer Svirsky Z"L, the brother of the author

The Geographical Scene

Prior to World War II, the shtetl Dunilovichi formed part of the Vilna Region. Between the two World Wars, the region of Vilna was part of Poland. Today the region is split from Vilna and the eastern part of the former Vilna region, where Dunilovichi is located, is now in Belarus. Dunilovichi was situated about ten kilometers from the train station Varpaieve, where trains traveling through Vilna stopped. A highway passing through the shtetl connected the station with the town. Dunilovichi is situated about a hundred twenty kilometers from Vilna (Vilna is the Capital of Lithuania now) and thirty kilometers from Glubokie.

Two large lakes surrounded Dunilovichi. The young people of the shtetl would often go boating on the lakes during the summer and ice-skate on the frozen lakes during the winter. A river spanned by two bridges cut through the shtetl. One bridge crossed the river and the other linked the two lakes. Abundant with color, verdant and dense forests encircled the scenic town.

Dunilovichi up to the onset of the First World War (1914)

The Jews lived in the center of the shtetl. The Christians only lived on one street, the largest one in town. In the old days, the marketplace, encircled by Jewish owned shops, was located in the center of the shtetl, next to the White Church. Later,

the market was moved to the vicinity of the Town Hall. Every Tuesday, the peasants from the surrounding villages would gather in the marketplace, bringing their agricultural products for sale. They traded the money they earned to buy provisions from the Jewish stores. Examples of the provisions include salt, sugar, kerosene, haberdashery, metal products, pines, etc. The shopkeepers and grain dealers would sustain their families for an entire week from this one market day.

Although the owners of metal and fabric businesses tended to be better off then others in the community, few wealthy Jews resided in Dunilovichi.

[Page 324]

With no credited physicians in town, the barber-surgeon served as a doctor and the pharmacist was a Jew. Considering the size of the shtetl, too many poor Jews worked as wagon-drivers. If one of their horses fell dead, they would not allow Torah readings to continue on the Sabbath until one of the Gabbaim (beadles) promised to supply them with a new horse.

A significant number of tailors and shoemakers worked in the shtetl. Earning their daily bread with difficulty, they labored from the early hours of the dawn until the dark hours of the night. In comparison, the glaziers were better off since they were not stationary, traveling through the neighboring villages. Jews who sold soap, cartwheel grease and kerosene also earned their fill of bread.

There were three synagogues in Dunilovichi. There was a "mitnagid" synagogue (A traditional orthodox synagogue, as opposed to Hasidic). As the oldest and largest synagogue in town, the synagogue supported its own rabbi. Most of the poor Jews prayed in the small shul, the most strictly observant synagogue in town. The wealthy and not-so-observant Jews prayed in the "aristocratic shul."

The only bathhouse belonged to the Jews. The well-off Jews would rent this place out. Much of the income used for such services supported the rabbi and the doctor. There was also a gmilut chesed society with a small fund dedicated to "free loans." They loaned individual Jews a few rubles, which they could repay in small sums, free of interest.

There were three Heders (small schools) in the shtetl. Zalman was the Melamed (teacher of religious studies) for the beginners. He always carried a whip in his hand. The second Melamed was also named Zalman. He was nicknamed the "he-goat." He would teach Humash and Gemara. He also supplemented his income by baking buns and bagels. The third Melamed was Pesach Leib Mushkat, a teacher that followed the modern fashion. Besides teaching Chumash and Gemara, he also taught classes to develop proficient writing skills in Hebrew and Yiddish.

The War Of 1914 (The First World War)

Soon after the war broke out between the Russian empire and Germany, many Russian soldiers of the Czar passed through Dunilovichi, part of the Russian empire. As was the custom then, soldiers were quartered in private houses. Soldiers who came to town on their way west to the front, were found in every home. Since there were no alternatives, they had to sleep on the floor. With the coming of the soldiers, commerce picked up and Jews earned a good livelihood. They had almost gotten used to the "benefits" of the war, as long as the front would remain far from them.

[Page 325]

However, on one nice day the front suddenly came closer and shells began to fall on the shtetl. Amidst great panic and indecision, people asked each other, "Where should we go?" Others asked, "Should we remain here and hope that it will pass, or should we run away to the east, away from the rapidly approaching front?"

We saw many of the Jewish people running into Shmuel-Yehudah's cellar. When we arrived there, we met numerous families, loaded with all of their bedding. There were a few amongst us who were sick with very high fevers. Covered only with white sheets, the afflicted lay like corpses on the bare earth.

Deathly silence reigned there. No one dared utter a word. In this way we spent several days and nights. We found ourselves stuck between two fires. When it momentarily got quieter, we ran back home to take a look, to see whether the peasants had robbed us of our humble possessions. Many of the non-Jews did not hide. After the Jews left to their hideouts, they used this opportunity to wander about the Jewish homes and steal whatever they wanted.

After a few days, the bombardment finally ceased. During the battle between the two armies, many homes were damaged. Curious as to whether the shtetl belonged to the Germans or the Russians, the Jews began to creep out of their hiding places. Suddenly, Yisroel-Laizer appeared in front of us. Everyone found their tongues and began asking him, "Who controls the shtetl?" He said that he knew nothing about this. He quipped, "I only know that Merke, my wife, is cooking "shtshav" (sour leaves) and eating it." The crowd laughed at this sign that the danger was over and that we could allow ourselves a bit of fresh air. The children climbed out of the crypt. With their belongings in hand, everyone spread out onto the streets of the shtetl.

[Page 326]

The War Between the Bolsheviks and the Poles

The community of Dunilovichi experienced much of the ways of war by the time that Germany was defeated, and the Soviets took control of the Russian empire. Battles between the Bolsheviks and the Poles soon started over control of our area. Once again, the Dunilovichi Jews began to hide in the one suitable cellar, belonging to Shmuel-Yehudah. Some hid in the White Church, which belonged to the Russian-Orthodox. The bombardments were not as heavy as they had been previously, but we were still afraid to walk through the shtetl. Shells feel around every step that we made.

When it all quieted down, we came out and found that we were under Polish rule. The first meeting with them ended tragically. On the first day, the Polish soldiers seized a Glubokie Jew, who had all his life traveled through the villages and sold needles and soap. When they looked through his sack and found other merchandise, as well as a pair of Tphillin to boot, they were sure that they had captured an honest-to-goodness spy. They beat him brutally and then took him to the cemetery, where they shot him. This made a strong impression on everyone. It didn't take long before the Poles retreated from the shtetl and the Bolsheviks took over. The first person to come out of the hiding place and greet them was Tzire Gendel. She immediately ran back to the cellar and announced that "the comrades have arrived and there is no reason to fear them." Upon hearing these words, everyone grabbed their bedding and returned to their homes.

[Page 327]

Dunilovichi soon revitalized. The air was filled with proclamations, flowers and fiery speeches, which promised that good products were plentiful in Russia. People actually danced for joy in the streets. "An end to slavery arrived; everything belongs to us now: The forests, the fields, the lakes! All belong to the people. We are the proprietors of everything." We indeed went out to the forests and brought back enough wood for heating our homes for the winter. Whoever didn't have a horse, borrowed one, and brought back dry twigs. A rumor spread later that anyone who wanted potatoes could go into the nobles' fields and dig out as many as he wished. For many days people lay in the fields and filled their sacks with potatoes. We, the insignificant ones, went into the fields of Graf Sod, shook the trees and pulled off apples and pears. We used the fruits to cook up a compote, the best treat to eat with bread.

A group of youth

Once while sitting in the trees at the right height for putting apples into a sack or holding it in our bosoms, a non-Jewish boy ran up to us and began yelling at us to stop. But no one listened to him. Within a few days, nothing but leaves remained in the orchard. The Jewish-owned domestic animals also had a party. Previously they had the worst pasture, and now they pastured with the Graf's domestic animals.

[Page 328]

Within a few weeks the Bolsheviks had to retreat, and the Poles returned (c. 1920). The difference was immediately felt, and the atmosphere changed. People lost their confidence, and this was obvious on the faces of all. We found out that Mendl Abes had been shot for no reason while sitting on his own porch. Even though the front was now far from the shtetl, we were afraid to be on the street. The remaining few hooligans became the lords.

Slowly, life returned to normal. People began to work, stores opened again, peasants brought their produce to market on Tuesdays to sell and buy their necessities in the stores. The front had moved to the area of Glubokie-Disne.

At this point, I must recall a horrendous event. One early morning, I heard terrible screams piercing the quiet of the street. I ran out to see what had happened. Panicking people were running everywhere and filling the streets. What had happened? A soldier had passed by Michael the blacksmith's house and noticed a few girls on the porch. He had removed his rifle from his shoulder and shot one of them, hitting her in the head with a dum-dum bullet (which explodes), so that the entire wall was splattered with her brains. The town of Dunilovichi had never witnessed such a tragic funeral. They had to gather up pieces of the girl's skin and place it in a sack. Her uncle Shmuel-Yehudah Skiransky rolled on the ground and screamed with shrieking sounds. I had never before seen a whole shtetl cry with such anguish. When the public went afterwards to demand justice from the Commanding Officer (there was martial law and the military was in charge), the soldier excused himself by saying that he meant only to fool around and had not thought that his gun was loaded. The entire incident ended in this way. There was no one else to complain to. The fate of the Jews of the shtetl lay in the hands of a few hooligans. Since the border was far from the shtetl, it was there that trade (illegal trade with the Soviet Union) developed. There was a shortage of many products. Sugar, for example, couldn't be found at all. People started drinking tea with saccharine or dried fruits. There wasn't much of a supply of bread either. Salt was completely lacking. People struggled to sustain themselves until peace was declared between the Bolsheviks and the Poles and Dunilovichi became part of Poland.

[Page 329]

The new Polish rulers without delay demonstrated their capacity to govern. In a short time, they set up a city council, a bailiff (judge) and a Jewish village magistrate. His name was Aron-Zelik Drutz, a shoemaker, who couldn't read or write. Nevertheless, he held the position for 4 years. When he had to deal with documents concerning taxes, he would touch them with his fingers and say, "Here, this must be for you!" Interestingly enough, he rarely made a mistake. It was often said in the shtetl that Aron-Zelik reads with his fingers better than the bailiff reads with his eyes.

The Yiddish school in 1932

Dunilovichi became poverty stricken during the war years. The stores were empty and after being robbed so many times, the former wealthy had become poor. Many people left as the front came near and moved east to Russia. Some died during the war as soldiers, and a few remained as prisoners of war in Germany. In short, Dunilovichi was emptied of most of its populace.

The will to survive slowly caused people to forget the hard times. They started to look forward to the future. It seemed that everyone, each in his own way, set about looking for some source of livelihood. The Dunilovichi Graf, whose name was Tiskevitski, owned all of the walled stores, some houses and the well. Many of the buildings and homes were bought from those who had previously lived in them.

[Page 330]

The new Polish rulers quickly set about converting this old White Russian area into a Polish community. The local inhabitants had spoken their White Russian language for hundreds of years. No one there spoke Polish or even understood it. In a short while, the

White Russian Orthodox Church became a Catholic Church. This greatly angered all of the Belarusian villagers in the area. The root of the anger was the fact that the Holy Portraits had not been turned over to them in order to be transferred to the nearby village (Azun), 5 kilometers from the shtetl. In this White Church, many Jews had hidden during the crossfire that had taken place during the war.

Quickly a notice arrived from the government, announcing that a beginners' school would be set up to serve the entire population. The teaching would be done in the Polish language. Tuition would not be required, and it would be free for all. Despite this, a very small number of children enrolled in the new Polish school. I don't know the reasons, but it is a fact that from the entire shtetl, only ten Jewish children enrolled. The remaining children continued their studies in the Heders with Peise-Leib and Zalman Rozov. Rozov was by this time a qualified teacher and not just a "melamed" (Heder teacher). One could learn Yiddish, Hebrew and singing from him. I recall that one day during the period between the afternoon and evening services, Alter, the rabbi's son, told the group to take a break until the evening service. We all went outside. When we returned, the rabbi asked where we had all gone. When no one answered, he made us stand in a line and gave each one of us three heavy piles of logs to hold. Everyone kept quiet, but one kid by the name of David Skriansky threw the pile away. The rabbi "honored" us with a couple of smacks and sent us home.

Fulkshule (Yiddish School) In Dunilovichi

People began talking about setting up a Yiddish secular school. Notices were put up in all three synagogues, stating that all householders should gather for a meeting in the large synagogue. Since at that time no special political parties existed, it was unanimously decided to found a Yiddish school. The founders were Aron Ligumsky, Baruch Kolis, Moishke Lurie, Hirsh Barkin, Shalom Naratzky and Shmuel-Kalman Barkin. Two teachers were brought from Vilna, one a Rosenfeld, a student of Vilna University, and the second a Solomon, a graduate of the Vilna Gymnasia. Also, Shmuel-Kalman Barkin and Baruch Kolis became part time teachers. It took only a few days, after a short exam, the children were divided into classes. The school began to function. The first and second grades met in the ladies' section of the synagogue, the third grade in the synagogue at the table where Jews used to learn Mishne, and the 4th grade in the meeting room.

[Page 331]

Dunilovichi youth

As soon as the school began functioning, Dunilovichi changed her image and looked entirely different. Happy children's faces appeared on the streets. The youth revived, and something started to happen. Ploshe Lurie traveled to Vilna and brought back enough books, mostly textbooks for the children. Never had anything like this been seen in the shtetl. They ran to the library to grab a book as if running after "matzah water" (the special pure water used for the baking of matzos). The teachers had a difficult job in the school, because the children weren't graded properly and were behind in their studies. Many according to their ages should have finished school long before, but instead, they were in the first few grades and so forth. To top it off, there was poverty during those first few years. In fact, there wasn't even enough to cover the expenses of each day. At that time, in the entire Vilna province, there was a huge relief operation from North America. The school administration sent a delegation with Aron Ligumsky at its head to Vilna and it arranged for Dunilovichi to benefit somewhat from this help. On a fine morning, information arrived that a transport with clothing, mainly for children, had arrived. Entire days were spent standing until one got something and then it was "good for nothing"! Those who had hurried managed to get a pair of shoes or a few pairs of socks that the children could use, but those who were a bit late, got worthless things. A kitchen for school children was also established in the home of Shalom Naratzky. All the children, rich and poor alike, could eat a tasty lunch at that kitchen. The teachers had arranged this because of the poor children. At the beginning they had been ashamed to sit down at the table to eat, but when they saw the wealthy children, as well as the teachers, were all sitting around the table, they also sat down. The kitchen closed before the end of the school year because they stopped sending products from Vilna.]

[Page 332]

In time, the teachers prepared a children's presentation, the first which Dunilovichi had ever seen. Children performed in Yiddish and Polish and it was a pleasure to listen to them. No one had believed that in one year, so much could be accomplished. The fathers and mothers were very proud of their children. They saw that the Yiddish school was a noteworthy achievement. If not for the school, the children education and social life would have been completely neglected. When the school year ended, the administration called a meeting of all the parents to deal with the question of whether to build their own building for the folkshule because the synagogue was not appropriate. Besides this, they weren't sure if the more observant would approve of boys and girls learning together in the synagogue from books that were not holy.

Young girls during sewing class

Jews considered the possibility of a separate building, and immediately appointed a building committee composed of Dan Feigl, Zise Klionsky, Shalom Naratzky, Baruch Kolis,

Hirshl Barkin, Aron Ligumsky, Moishke Lurie, Yankel Abel, Motte Bergman, Flax Dratve, Yisroel-Chaim Gurvitsh and others. A large empty plot near the bathhouse was chosen and there the building was to be set up. The actual work began immediately, with the bringing of building materials. The singing of the builders could be heard and there was joy on everyone's face. When the building was completed, there was a dedication ceremony. It wasn't entirely comfortable since it had only two rooms, but all community activities were transferred there.

[Page 333]

A Group of Dunilovichi youth

With the start of the 2nd school year, the shtetl undertook the expansion of the school, as if trying to make up for lost time. Evening courses were set up for adults and two teachers were added, Aronovitsh from Vilna and Abraham Weinstein from Zamoshtsh. They took over the running of the school, as well as community activities. Tuition was very low, so that anyone who had the slightest desire to learn something could attend. It was truly a great success. The courses were well-attended, and the people learned math, Yiddish literature and Polish. A reading room was set up, packed with people every evening. They would gather there to live it up intellectually and read the newspapers which arrived, such as the Vilna Tog, the Folks Zeitung, Haint, Moment, the Literarishe Bleter, Der Folks-

Gezunt and a few Polish newspapers. The teachers also began to give lectures. Weinstein, a former student of Bialik, used to lecture regularly about Peretz. So many people came to his lectures that if you came a bit late, you had to remain standing on the street because there was no room inside. The library grew steadily, and the number of readers jumped. If an interesting book appeared, it was jumped upon. More than once, somebody would run to a borrower's home, and sit and wait for him to finish reading the book so that he could borrow it. It also led to arguments. Public readings also took place. The leading reader was Aron Ligumsky, who was a former Yeshivah student and an expert in both Yiddish and Russian literature. He would read Peretz aloud and everyone sat glued to their seats. When he read Shalom Aleichem, they would roll with laughter.

[Page 334]

Eventually, it was noticed that the building was too small for the school, since there had been an increase in the number of students. The people began to think about building a second building, larger and more comfortable. They also had in mind a larger plot, so that they could include an auditorium for theatre productions and children's activities. Until then they had had to use the Polish club, which wasn't at all suited for these things and not always available. Work started immediately. The people decided to turn to the Jews of Dunilovichi who immigrated to North America for financial help. The Americans contributed some money, but not enough to cover all expenses and we remained in debt. We began to search for ways to pay off the debts. Many helped with their own labor on the building. For example, Hirshke Trotzky and Elyakum Urevitsh rode into the forests to bring moss and other building supply.

A drama circle was founded under Hirshl Barkin's direction. Participants included Aron Ligumsky, Baruch Kolis, Liebke Tzefelovitsh. Abe Endel (today in Brazil), Rise Skiransky, Soke Tzefelovitsh (from Ostov), Sorke Feigel, the Eterise sisters, Rochke and Sonia Chodosh. These two sisters were especially distinguished in their performances, singing and recitals. The first production was presented with great success. It was Yakov Gordin's play "Chasye the Orphan." All profits went towards funding the school. When Zalman Reisin (author of a lexicon of Yiddish writers) once came to give a lecture in the shtetl, Eterise Chodosh presented a Sholom Aleichem monologue. He was very impressed by her presentation and he said that our little town had nothing to be ashamed of even in comparison to Vilna, when it had such talented artists. As a result of the great success, they consequently had several such evenings. Among other things, they presented "Motke Ganov" (Thief) and "Des Groise Gevins" (The Great Win). Hirshl Barkin, a conductor of sorts and a fiddler, formed an orchestra composed of Meir Svirsky, Yoshke Abel, Sayaiske Katzavitsh, Avrashke Cepelovitsh, Shmuel Barkin and Hirshl Barkin himself. Besides dance evenings for the youth, the orchestra played at weddings and the income went to the school.

Even with all these successes, there was still a lack of money to support the school. There were many children attending, but not all could afford to pay tuition. More teachers had to be brought in and they thought about setting up children's library, which was needed for the children's development. In order to establish it, money was needed, and they decided to attempt something new, something the shtetl had never known before. A mock trial, regarding Shalom Asch's "Motke Ganov", was planned. Announcements declared that anyone who intended to participate should prepare themselves and inform the organizers. Held in the second building, all of the rooms were packed. There were prosecutors and defense attorneys, among whom were Aronovitsh, Einstein, Abes, Ligumsky, Barkin, Kolis and others. The discussions continued for weeks until the matter was closed. Such evenings brought excitement to the monotonous life of the shtetl.

[Page 336]

Dunilovichi youth 1936

Suddenly, as if out of nowhere, there came about a split in the school. The new Hebrew teacher Hittelmacher with the support of Iruch Kolis, Rivke Feigel and others, planned to set up a modern "Tarbut school" where all subjects would be taught in Hebrew. They took away two teachers and about twenty children, and all of Dunilovichi went topsy-turvy. Immediately, two camps were formed: one loyal to the Yiddish culture and the other to Hebrew and Zionism. Unity disappeared. In the same way, all the parents and young people, who previously had been united on all matters of local community life, were now split into two sides. The same friends who had always worked together now suddenly became blood-enemies and there were frequent quarrels. They would run to the parents in order to get their children, each for his school. The "Tarbutniks" demanded a building for their school, and it had to be granted.

Fortunately, this disagreement brought hidden blessings since each side wanted to show what they could accomplish, and in this way drew more children into the schools. They appealed to the most poverty-stricken groups, pulling their children into the schools and giving them a fine education. Also, more youth were involved in various community projects. Hashomer Hatzair (Zionist, socialist Youth Movement) was founded, engaging in a broad spectrum of Zionist activity like founding hachsharot (farming communities to prepare young pioneers for life in Palestine). The Tarbutnikim had an influence on some of the orthodox Jews (they were called "beards"). They would support them as much as they could. For example, a Jew named Izik Dodkes, who used to get money from his family in North America, would pay $5.00 a month. (This was a very large amount at that time.) The only doctor in town, Dr. Brodny and the pharmacist were Zionists and supported the organization. The Zionists were a very happy and united group, self-confident and always ready to sing and dance.

[Page 337]

The hope of going to Eretz Yisrael gave them courage and aspiration. When they got together, they were always lively and animated.

Dunilovichi youth on the bridge

Meanwhile, the situation in the Folkshule worsened. They decided to look for children without charging a tuition fee. They had more children enrolled, but there wasn't enough money to support the school. They constantly had to search for new undertakings to raise money. It was hard because only a few hours before a performance, the police often would forbid its presentation. They could never be sure that they could complete an evening. The deficit grew. It also became obvious that many of the children attending the school were very weak. After a short investigation, they found out that this was due to improper nutrition. They then decided to provide a tasty breakfast each morning. A committee was formed which prepared a breakfast of coffee, bread and butter. In order to get these products, they had to go from household to household. The committee consisted of Shainke Yaffe, Itele, Rochke, Gesse Gurvitsh, Chana and Rochke Ginzburg. In short, it was very hard work; nothing came easy. Poverty was so great that they had to fire the woman who washed the floors and lit the oven. Her total monthly salary had been only ninety zlotys. The work was taken over by school alumni: Avrahamke Gurvitsh, Berge Zeitlin, Yona Kuritzky, Leibe Oks, Sheinke Kaminkovitsh, Rivke Oks and others.

[Page 338]

A few years passed in this way. Most of the elderly leaders passed away and the youngsters became the community leaders. To have an idea of the influence and accomplishments of the drama circle, it is enough to mention that Avrahamke Ginzburg, a graduate of the Folk school crossed the border to the Soviet Union, where he performed in the theatre under the direction of Michael Weicherts. Also, the choir of the shtetl became famous throughout the area. Under the direction of Abraham Gurvirtsh, it would travel through the surrounding villages including the town of Glubokie and give concerts.

Soon, however, the heavy hand of the reactionary Polish regime fell upon the shtetl. They began to persecute the Jewish Folkshule in every way. Still, Dunilovichi grew and with it, the accomplishments expanding cultural activities. In 1934, they already planned to build a large school with its own theatre auditorium. A large plot was bought not far from the slaughterhouse and a beautiful and comfortable building was put up. Not one of the surrounding shtetls had such a building.

It is worthwhile repeating what Nachman Maisel writes in his book "Once There Was a Life" about the Dunilovichi school. He writes that "it is interesting that the School Board of Dunilovichi told the emissary of the Vilna Central Education Committee, the writer Aaron Mark, 'We must have our own fireproofed building of stone and brick. Even if the government hadn't condemned our present location, we ourselves, for our children' sake, would have done something. The school in the last few years has grown in size and quality. We must push the narrow walls. We must have more room, more air and a broad horizon around the building.'" In this quote there is no date and no name is mentioned. All was done by an anonymous School Board.

From Yankale's Heder

They used to say that every cultural activity that took place in the shtetl started from Yankale's Heder. This meant that it was the spiritual inspiration of Yankel Abel that created the activity. He was the most intelligent and educated Jew in Dunilovichi. He was a Socialist and the first openly secular Jew in town. Thanks to him, the cultural organization was set up. Not a single cultural activity took place without his participation or his advice. He was the factual spiritual leader of Dunlovichi.

[Page 339]

Soon, however, the joy of building and cultural flowering at the apogee of its ascent was suddenly hacked into pieces ....

Translator's note:

Nachke Svirsky Z"L was born in Dunilovichi to Yoel Pinie (Pinchas) Svirsky and Ester nee Chanovitz of Vilna. In 1940 he immigrated to Argentina following his brother and his sister in law, Meyer Svirsky Z"L and his wifen Itke Z"L, daughter of Shmuel Ligumsky . Meyer and Itke arrived in Argentina in the 1920s. Nachke lived and worked with his brother. He was very attached to the family of his brothers' only daughter. There were two girls from the Svirsky family who survived the holocaust, they lived in the Soviet Union. The family, who mostly lives in Israel today, lost touch with them and wishes to reunite.

[Page 339]

June 1941, The Germans' Entrance to Dunilovichi

By Yitzhak Mushkat (A survivor, now in Argentina)

Translated by Eilat Gordin Levitan

Yitzhak Mushkat

At the onset of the second war world, in September of 1939, the Soviets annexed eastern Poland. After the difficult winter of 1940/ 1941, the Red Army had settled into the shtetl. In 1941, during the month of June, I worked as a gardener. In that year, almost all of the fruit trees froze. In the spring, we had to ride out to cut and count up the remaining trees. It was a very nice day. Suddenly, there was a commotion. Our hector ran over and told us the "good" news; we were at war again. Germany attacked the Soviet Union. No one rode anywhere, people believed in the strength of the Red Army. Two hours later we saw the "metal birds" and a mad rush. All of the Soviet/ Russian institutions began to pack in order to retreat from the rapidly approaching Nazis. At 3:00 A.M., they brought me a notice. I was to show up at the place of mobilization. At 6:00 A. M., they (the Soviet authorities) gave me two horses and a large wagon and told me to ride in the direction of Glubokie. On the road, there were already long columns. Oxen and goats were tied behind the wagons. Also the military was retreating to the Russian border (The former border pre 1939, east of Dunilovichi.) The full force of the panic could already be felt. All prisoners were released. Arriving at Glubokie, we stopped at a side road because by this time taller places had been bombed. I found about twenty of our young people in Glubokie. They were also fleeing closer to the border. Suddenly, they told us that it was already too late, and that everyone could go where they want to go; the border were sealed and the Germans took over the area of Minsk. I gave my horses to our townsfolk, and together with other Dunilovichi Jews turned back towards the shtetl. We had left our families there.

[Page 340]

When we got there, there was still light and Dunilovichi was filled with peasants from the villages who had come to the shtetl to steal. Jews were locked in their homes in fear and awaited their fate. They packed and some tried to ride away, but with children, it was impossible. They had to turn back. It was this way until the Germans arrived. Meanwhile, Jews made some order out of their bit of goods. Every Jew was somewhat acquainted with the peasants of the villages and of the shtetl. Everything was given to them to hide away. This added to our misfortune because later, every peasant helped the murderers in order to keep the Jewish possessions.

The Polish youth, organized as German spies, were as numerous as flies. Six days later, at 9:00 A. M., the first German tank arrived. In some places, individual Russian soldiers were hiding out. There was a small exchange of gunfire and we Jews paid for it. About two hours later, after the tanks' arrival, German soldiers poured in like sand. Our house was in the soldiers' path and the door just did not close. They immediately began to bother us, beating us.

Everyone was taken for forced labor. The first job was to repair the roads, since the heavy vehicles had ruined them. Jews had to immediately repair them. From the forests, they had to carry heavy logs on their shoulders. The murderers walked alongside to drive them on. Also, the Jews did other labor which suited them, such as washing the wagons and the horses and shining shoes. This was during the first few days. Some of the military stayed in the shtetl to set things in order. Polish police were organized under German authority. Decrees were immediately issued. At 9:00 A.M. everyone was ordered to be at the lake. Anyone found at home after that was to be killed. Understandably, everyone gathered even earlier.

[Page 341]

The first command from the murderers was "Assemble in a circle, women and men separately!" Hearts beating with fright, we heard the first decree: "All Jews must by tomorrow wear a yellow patch on both sides with the letter J for Jew. No Jew may walk on the sidewalk or go more than three kilometers out of the shtetl. Every Jew must report on time for daily labor." After scores of such decrees the Polish police ran rampant. I remember how they drove us into the lake to wash the German wagons.

Avraham Chaim Mushkat,
a partisan

Shaptel Ruderman

Once while coming home from hard labor, a peasant gave Yaakov Manfilk a head of cabbage. A German noticed this and he was given ten lashes, which immobilized him for two weeks. Every evening after work, the Polish police would herd all of the young people together in the bitter cold and order them to immerse themselves in the lake. Then they would drive them out and force them to roll in the mud. One day, when I was working on the gardens with ten other men and coming back late, a policeman came and ordered us to report to the police station in ten minutes. We knew what this meant, but we had no choice. When I got there, I was given a letter to take to the village of Zuferke, eight kilometers away. Ordered to leave the shtetl and return in three hours with an acknowledgement. I ran as fast as I could and brought it back.

[Page 342]

As I entered the police station, I noticed the worst murderer, a Polish non-Jew, whose only job was to torture Jews, standing there. When I saw him, I knew that I wouldn't get out unharmed. I simply asked if I was free to go. He quickly remarked that I wasn't yet free of him. He took me into a separate room and for no reason began to beat me until I fell. Then he took his gun and again beat me until he knocked out some of my teeth. When I began to scream, a second one came in and told me to go. He told me not to reveal who had beaten me. If I did, my entire family would be beaten. My only consolation was that I had escaped death. Even with my intense pain, I still had to go to work the next morning.

My father and brother were also badly beaten because they had given a wagon to a Christian acquaintance and another had informed on them. They were so badly beaten that they were swollen. The parents of children who had fled to Russia were called. Yoel-Pinye Svirsky, Shalom Naratzky, Barkan and many others came, and many didn't because there were too many to call. Whomsoever they wished to beat, they did so immediately.

They ordered that a Judenrat be chosen, given the responsibility for everything, including labor. They were Jewish Police, who would carry out everything that they were told to do.

One morning, they announced that shtetl Jews must gather in a ghetto. Our town was close to a lake and a river, and the street near the lake was set up as the ghetto. The thousand Jews of Dunilovichi had to gather in this one small street. All of the Jews had to be inside within twenty-four hours with no more than twenty-five kilograms of possessions. Furniture and valuable things, as well as cows and horses, were immediately confiscated.

[Page 343]

Chayke Mushkat

Lea Bar Lorens- Kagan

As much as people had, they surreptitiously carried into the Ghetto. The ghetto was sealed with a gate as an exit. The gate was near Kapekovitsh's home and that was also established as Judenrat headquarters. The thousand people were crowded in, a number of families assigned to each house. One could feel the closeness of death. I already mentioned how we were driven daily to the hardest of labors and so, regardless of living conditions, we were satisfied that at list they needed us. We ourselves sought out the creation of more work, because the shtetls with no work were immediately destroyed. Forty Polish policemen came daily and began to order things such as shoes and boots. Whatever they wanted had to be ready on time. The ghetto had to provide it all. If we didn't have it, we had to go to Glubokie, where everything could be had for money. On top of it all, we were often visited by the SS. This already involved with providing them with bribes of large sums of money, jewelry and other items. If not provided, the penalty was death. Understandably, one who no longer had anything to give was on the death list. As a result of fear and the daily depressing news, there was no strength for anything.

[Page 344]

Suddenly, we heard that several fleeing Sharkovshchyzna Jews, survivors of the slaughter in their town, had arrived. Many had fled to Glubokie and others to the forests.

In our ghetto, the Jewish police were ordered to go search for the escapees in the forests. It was also announced that any of the escapees who came forward on their own would not be harmed. Some actually went to other ghettoes, but tragedy also struck them and with each passing day, we heard of more slaughters. It was very bad for the escapees. If one came secretly into the ghetto and was discovered, the ghetto was no longer safe. Murderers used to wait impatiently for this moment. In this way, we lived for half a year. Some of our shtetl people worked in Lutzky, ten kilometers from the shtetl. Of the twelve men who worked there, eight perished.

On the thirteenth of Kislev (Nov. 22, 1942) at 3:00 A.M., all Jews in the Ghetto became very frightened. We realized that the Germans surrounded the ghetto. People began to flee like sheep, but there was nowhere to run. Whoever approached the fence was immediately killed. Everyone had prepared ahead some hiding place in the ghetto. There was no other alternative, so families ran to their hideouts and some, to their attics. There was such a panic that some died of fright. We had also made a hiding place in a stable, but there was room for only 8 people. In fleeing, we accumulated about twenty people and there was no air to breathe. Near our hiding place there was another one with about sixty people. As soon as a child cried out, the murderers heard it and they threw grenades, killing everyone. They began to search for our entrance, but with the coming of evening, they didn't succeed in finding it.

At 2:00 A.M., we exited our hideout. It was horrible; corpses and patrols were everywhere. It was impossible to remain safe. No matter what, we had to flee. It was bitter cold and the lake was frozen. At two in the morning, we exited. It was dark and we ran over corpses, ran through the street and began to race across the lake. To get to the forest, we had to run three kilometers. As we were running across the lake, they suddenly opened fire from all sides. We continued running. Due to our fright we were separated and some ran into their deaths.

[Page 345]

We came closer to the forest and there we saw that of the original twenty, only seven remained. Three members of the Ruderman family, Nehamke Shvimmer's grandson, Berl Zeitlin, my brother Abraham and I. We began to go back to see what had happened to the others, but we saw that we were being chased, so we went deeper into the forest. There, they again opened heavy fire on us, but in the forest, we were safe.

Aharon Ligumski, Rochester

We couldn't discover what had happened to the others. We stood for a while, not knowing what to do. Hungry and frightened, all we heard was shooting. We wanted to join the partisans but didn't know where the partisans were. We had simply heard rumors that in the forests there were partisans who came to fight the Germans, but we had never seen them. There was a small village of five houses named Cazinirovke, deep in the forest, seven kilometers from the shtetl. Christian acquaintances were there. We decided to go there, get some bread, and find out something, anything. We thought we knew the way, but no matter what direction we turned, we ended up in the same place. We didn't know why, perhaps the fear and hunger, but that's the way it was. Finally, we reached it. We carefully approached one house and knocked, but no one answered. Then we saw a small fire in one house. They had all already wanted to leave. I knocked and an old Christian came out. I asked him if we could enter to warm ourselves a bit, providing that no one was there. He answered yes, no one was there. We went into the house. It didn't even take five minutes before our sister, who is now with us in Argentina, ran out to us. Here, we became aware of the tragedy. She told us that when they had fled, Shalom Gurvitsh, his son, wife and child, and my two older sisters were with them. Fleeing to the village of Petrovitsh, a Polish murderer had caught up with them and killed them. She had hidden herself behind a stable and in that way, survived. Then she fled again, not knowing where to go. As she was fleeing, she heard about our parents and another sister who had also been chased. She hadn't known anything about us, so she decided to return to the shtetl. Going alone, upset with fear, an old man had suddenly come out of the forest and told her to go back, showing her where to go. She then came to that farm, where we met her in hiding. In this way, it was destined that we suffer together.

[Page 346]

We went out of the house and dawn was breaking. By day, we had to be careful not to be seen. We went deeper into the forest. The frost was fierce and we had nothing to wear. We didn't dare make a fire. We again went around in circles. Suddenly we saw a small boy sitting on a tree stump, eating a piece of bread. He was wounded in his leg. This was Reuven Furman's eight-year-old son. While running across the lake, he had been shot in the leg. He told us, "I made out as if I was dead. When the policeman went away,

[Page 347]

I ran into the forest. I was in the forest with my father and two brothers. Where they are, I don't know because I had fallen asleep. When I awoke they were gone." We couldn't understand why the father had abandoned his son. We asked him, "Where could they have gone?" He answered that he had simply heard them saying that they must go to the Shnitz Forests, where there were partisans.

Dunilovoitzers and Druiers

When we heard this, we had a shred of hope. We decided to go there since we might meet up with the partisans, but what to do with the boy? He wants to go, but he can't, since he is limping badly, and it is about forty-five kilometers to Shmitz. We bandaged his foot with a torn shirt. A rich peasant lived nearby. We brought him there and asked that he keep him until we find his father. We told the peasant that if he turns him over to the Germans, the partisans will come and burn down his entire farm. He took him and made a shepherd of him. We went in the direction of Shmitz and had to cover the distance in one night. Since we were very tired, we went to a peasant, a very good Christian, who lived in the forest about halfway there. There we found eight other Dunilovichi people. This peasant treated all of us like royalty.

[Page 348]

We ate something, rested and then continued on our way at about two in the morning.

We penetrated deeper into the forest. Suddenly, we heard a child's voice screaming, "Mama!" The echo was from a distance and upset us all. We went on until it got light. We stopped again, deeper in the forest, until dark. The trees were covered with light snow. Before our eyes, there seemed to appear different forms of palaces and mills. We couldn't understand it. Maybe it was a mirage, a result of fright, but that's the way it was.

When it got dark, we went on. We came to a village. From the village it was still about eight kilometers to Shmitz. We asked the peasants where the partisans were and they told us that we still had about six kilometers to go. And that's how it was. As we left the village we saw two people armed with guns and grenades. One was in civilian clothes and the other in a German uniform. As soon as they saw us, they stopped us and asked who we were. We didn't know who they were, but since they spoke Russian to us, we understood that they were partisans. They told us to go with them and about one kilometer away, a man on a horse galloped up, as drunk as Lot, and began shouting at us with such taunts that we thought we were caught. He chased us so quickly that we were exhausted. In this way we were chased for three kilometers, until we came close to a house. There they took us in. We met all sorts of people there, dressed in all sorts of uniforms, civilian as well as military. They lined us up, questioning us and taunting us until they ordered that we be taken into the forest. We had imagined it would be different and we wanted to flee. We were driven deep into the forest until we noticed patrols at their posts. One was an acquaintance from the shtetl. Then we understood that these were the partisans. We met people from

Dunilovichi such as Leib Gentzel and his daughter and Reuven Furman and his two sons. This was the father who had left his small son in the forest.

They told us to eat and rest and then to work on building huts. We breathed freely because we now found ourselves in the forest with the partisans. We were saved! There was a small brigade here of only about eighty, under the command of Markov.

[Page 349]

Dunilovichi Educational Society on Lake Narach

They brought us to the huts and we told the father that we had seen his son. One of his sons took a sleigh and horse and with another partisan went after the boy, whom they found three kilometers away. As the boy tells it, he hadn't wanted to stay and had followed us.

We traveled for six days and there was enough to eat. Unfortunately, the joy passed quickly. The commander came and told us that six thousand Germans were preparing to surround the forest in order to catch the partisans. Since we had no arms and the partisans were going elsewhere, we couldn't go with them. Our pleas and cries were of no avail. The commander simply gave us a document stating that we should be helped wherever we go. Since we had to cross the front lines, he wrote out where we should and shouldn't go. We had to travel about four hundred kilometers, crossing all of the German railway lines in order to reach the Russian side

[Page 350]

We gathered, cried for a while and decided to go. "Whatever will be will be!" Since a group of thirty can easily be spotted and find it difficult to procure food, we divided into three groups. We had to travel only by night and hide in the woods by day. We also had with us a pregnant woman, the wife of Shalom Gurvitsh. The problem of what to do with her was a serious one. Since she had a friend, Yitzhok Goldman, she remained with him and his group. He had many Christian acquaintances and she was hidden by one of them. The first group started out. The worst part the commander warned us about was crossing two railway lines and a bridge which the Germans had strongly fortified. If we could pass through those, the rest would be easy.

We covered very little ground the first night since we didn't know what to do. To travel in such a risky way where we had never been and where no one knew the area was hard. By the second night we traveled at full speed. We covered twenty to twenty-five kilometers each night. Tired, with frozen feet and half-starved, we had twenty-five kilometers more before the first railway line near Pohost. We entered a village and asked that they cook us a pot of potatoes. Since we weren't refused, we waited. Meanwhile, they alerted the police. Fortunately, we noticed that something was wrong and we escaped. In a few weeks we heard that the second group had also gone through the same village and two were caught, a father and a son. It was Mote the tailor and his son. They were tortured. We stayed in the forest all day. We couldn't sit or stand because our feet were broken in pain from traveling.

We dragged ourselves to the first railway line. It was two in the morning. We suddenly noticed fires near the line and Germans patrolling with dogs to protect the line. We lay down and searched for a way through. The entire line and station were blocked off with a wooden fence so that the snow wouldn't drift onto the line. Suddenly, while we lay there and listened, a train arrived. We then quickly and carefully broke through a few boards and ran speedily across the line into the woods. We came to a house, knocked and asked for directions. We were going the right way, just as the commander had told us. With the arrival of dawn, we went into the deep woods and waited for dark. Then we entered a house, cooked some potatoes, rested for a few hours and went further. The next day we found out that many Germans had been looking for us in the forest, but they had gone off in another direction. We knew how to camouflage ourselves in the winter woods, and this saved us from falling into a trap.

[Page 351]

The Choir of the Educational Society (1934)

We still had eighteen kilometers to go before the bridge. They told us to be very careful by the river. If we couldn't find a boat we would have to swim across.

The bridge traversed a nobleman's courtyard. The Germans were stationed in the palace, guarding the bridge. Since we didn't know exactly where the courtyard was, we ran through and met no one. Going through, we saw that in the palace the Germans were dancing in a drunkenly state. We later found out that it was a holiday and that they became so drunk that they neglected the bridge in order to go dancing. That was kismet.

[Page 352]

The second railway line wasn't difficult since we only had to cross a few kilometers further on. When we had already gone through, we noticed that we had come to a road that was full of German military. There were no woods nearby. We crawled into thick bushes and lay there a whole day until dark. We were lucky since we were only a few meters away from them. When it got dark we crossed the road and continued safely. We had only eighteen kilometers left to reach the Russian partisans.

Four hours later we reached a village. It was already nine at night. A Russian patrol stopped us at the edge of the village and requested our documents. Going with us in the dark, he asked who we were. When we told him that we were Jews, he immediately returned my documents and took us into a house where he told the village elder to feed us, prepare a place for us to sleep, and see to it that he heat a bath for us in the morning. During all our wanderings we hadn't once gotten undressed. We ate and rested. In this zone we were able to travel freely by day because the village was filled with Russian partisans. All of the men had been mobilized and the women did everything on their own. Every home had to provide several partisans with food.

At ten, we were told to gather in a house and to go to the unit commander because they couldn't confirm anything for us on their own. This meant another forty-five kilometers. We were pleased that at least we could travel unafraid, free and not in hiding. We traveled twenty-five kilometers before night fell. We entered the home of the village elder who gave us a place to sleep. We ate, and the next day we again traveled until we came to the commander. We gave him our documents, told him about our adventures and asked that we be accepted as partisans. He asked if we were armed. We didn't have any arms and therefore had to go to staff headquarters in Melnikov, about seventy kilometers from there. We went there but they didn't allow us into staff headquarters. They simply told us that if we have no arms, then we couldn't be accepted because at the time there was a serious shortage of arms. Partisans were joining up by the thousands. Disappointed that we couldn't accomplish our goal, we meanwhile wandered through the village. We were able-bodied and were hired for all sorts of work and well fed. We worked in the fields, rode into the forests for wood, repaired boots, sewed caps and did everything that had to be done.

[Page 353]

Hebrew Cultural School'

In this way we wandered for three months from village to village. It would have been good, but the partisans didn't leave us alone. They said that while they were fighting, we were hiding out. We couldn't convince them that we hadn't been accepted because we didn't have arms. They simply told us to go and kill several Germans with our bare hands and take away their arms. The fact that we had no place to stay or go disturbed us very much. A commander even took us aside and told us that if he meets us again in the villages, he'll shoot us. At the time, they didn't need an excuse, especially if it was a Jew. Before this we had already approached all of the partisan brigades and had gotten the same answer. After somewhat appeasing this commander, he wrote us a letter for the brigadier, Melnikov. His brigade numbered about fifteen thousand people, including many Jews. He told us to personally deliver the letter. At first, they didn't let us approach him, but with this letter we hoped we could actually go to him. We again had to travel forty-five kilometers, but this was our final journey and we set out.

[Page 354]

The staff headquarters was deep in the forest and partisans guarded many of the homes. Three kilometers away, we were stopped and questioned every fifty paces until we got there. Melnikov was there but they told us that he wasn't. A soldier took the letter to hand over to him. A young lady came right out to us and we saw that she was Jewish. In Russian, she told us to enter. She was the brigadier's secretary. The staff commissar was also there. With tears in our eyes, we told them of our bitter fate. We wanted to fight, but only as partisans. Our words moved them, and we were accepted as partisans. They sent us to a village where there was a Jewish unit of twenty who had survived the slaughter in Kurenitz and Krivichi. There we were given arms.

We patrolled a mountain top. The Germans were three kilometers from the mountain since the area was the right flank of the German advance. We had to be on constant guard because from that mountain we could see exactly where the Germans were headed.

A Russian commanded our Jewish unit. Every order was carried out. There were also six girls in our unit. They stood guard with their rifles and helped out in the kitchen. In this way, we Jews were by ourselves for five months.

We weren't far from Polotzk. When the Germans entered, the Russians torched the warehouse and armory nearby. After the partisans spread into the area, they would sneak in at night, bring the burned guns out and repair them until they were like new. There were many guns and in a short time all of the partisans were armed. Every night about thirty planes with arms would land and then carry off wounded partisans.

[Page 355]

Hechalutz – Danilovichi

A month later, the Jewish unit was divided up among the Russian partisans. We were ordered to report to the Boide Swamps near Disne. My sister and I went together while our brother was in a different unit. He was quickly promoted to be an officer. Once, while on guard, they noticed that Germans had come up to a point almost a meter away from them. He barely managed to escape. There was a battle, and he was lightly wounded in one leg. A week later we went off in the direction they told us to go, toward the Disne area. Riding our horses, we crossed the Disanke River.

In that zone there was still plenty to eat and that's why many partisans were sent there. Here, there began for us a chapter of constant battle with the Germans. The place was also terrible because of the peasants who had sided with the Germans. We had to be careful of every move.

[Page 356]

The unit of eight, including my brother, moved up closer to observe the Germans. We had meanwhile stopped at some houses near the woods. Suddenly we heard that the entire unit had fallen into a trap. Only the commander escaped; three were immediately killed and three were seriously wounded. When I asked where my brother was, he told me that he was lying wounded in the field and couldn't be reached. Our partisans immediately entered the battle. My brother managed to crawl on his stomach about half a kilometer until he came closer to the woods. Of the rest of the unit only two remained alive, although seriously wounded. There was no hospital nearby, but we had several nurses. We took up a position at another point. The wounded were sent to another place where there already was a makeshift hospital and a doctor. It didn't take long before there was another disturbance. It was winter and the wounded were taken on sleds into the Boide Woods. We again drove the Germans off and returned to our previous position. For a while it was quiet. The injured recuperated somewhat and went back to their previous tasks.

We got an order for all partisans to be on the ready. The Russians had beaten the Germans and since they were retreating through partisan territory, they had sent out a hundred thousand German troops with heavy armor and planes to wipe out the partisans. We retreated to the Boide Woods where there were huge swamps. We numbered about a thousand eight hundred eighty in three brigades. Shooting started and they began to surround the woods. At first the planes dropped leaflets calling for us to surrender. After five days, when we had nothing left to eat, the Germans surrounded the forest. A fierce battle took place. Blood ran like water and men died like flies. Those from Smolensk fought bravely and we were closer to death than to life. We finally found a way out. We ran through a swamp up to our necks in sludge for three kilometers. It was terribly cold. We everything away except for our guns and grenades, which we had to have with us.

[Page 357]

Dunilovichi Educational Society

The Germans meanwhile penetrated deeper into the forest. Dogs as big as horses led the way. Meanwhile we tramped through the muddy swamp and got away safely at the point where they couldn't imagine a human would be able to penetrate. After five kilometers we stopped. Here it was quieter. We had traversed it all in one night and we again had to cross the Disanke River, which was very wide at the time. We quickly made a raft of logs. In this way, exhausted, we stopped for a night near a forest.

In two days time we were given an order and also some good news. The Germans were fleeing, and we were to pursue them. We were ordered to blow up the entire line from Vitbesk to Lapel in one night, so that the murderers would have nowhere to flee. So, it was done. It felt as if the world were exploding. Then we went into the woods near the main roads so that we could take revenge on the Germans. It didn't take long.

[Page 358]

We began firing. They ran in a panic as if everything was too late for them. Then our unit saw the Red Army.

We turned the prisoners over to the regular Russian Army. In the last few days entire battalions had surrendered to us. The partisans were ordered to gather at a point near Pohost. We revenged ourselves as much as we were able, but it was still very little in exchange for the amount of our blood that had been shed. The partisans were quickly divided into different groups. The war continued. Some were sent right off to the front to fight again and some were allowed to make order in the towns. My sister (now in Argentina) and I remained to work in the shtetl Miory. Our brother Abraham was sent to the front. We worked there for about six months, until the war ended.

As soon as the war was over everyone ran back toto their homes, but we had nowhere to return. Only a pit remained, a pit containing a thousand Jews whose blood was still crying out. There were still many bandits circulating, murderers who had aided in the Holocaust. Unfortunately, we could no longer do anything. We just couldn't look again at the murderers, so we decided to leave the accursed land. Before leaving, we set up a monument and bade farewell to our dearest and most beloved who lay together in a common grave.

The 11th Yahrzeit of Hirshke Trotzky

The Jewish workers of Paris remember well the original and attractive figure of Hirshke Trotzky.

On a dark night on November 15, 1943, a battalion of SS, obviously told by an informer, encircled a Marquis (French underground) unit of Corez. There were eighteen combatants in the surprised group. Among them was Hirshke, his nephew Henri (son of his brother, Alexander) and a number of other experienced partisans.

[Page 359]

Ordered by the SS leaders to surrender, the courageous unit undertook an unequal battle rather than fall into the grasp of the murderers. They all died heroic deaths. Early the next morning, a young partisan photographed the eighteen fresh corpses, riddled with hundreds of bullets. A few days later, the photo calling for revenge was printed in a resistance newspaper and circulated among the population.

Hirshke was born on August 15, 1904 in a small shtetl not far from Vilna, named Dunilovichi. His father, a lawyer (Aharon Trocki, perished in Dunilovichi), strove to give his children a higher education and sent him to a gymnasia. Hirshke quickly joined the revolutionary movement. At first, he worked among the youth, bringing them his energetic and happy spirit. Later he went to work among the peasants ("KARAMADA").

Due to his association with these groups, he was forced to immigrate to France, where he settled in Paris, working first as a housing construction laborer and later as a furniture polisher. Gaining the sympathy of his fellow workers, he demonstrated his abilities, this time in "syndicalism." The Jewish and non-Jewish workers, especially the inhabitants of "Lila," very well remember his loving and temperate nature. When the civil war in Spain broke out, he volunteered for the International Brigade and distinguished himself on the battlefields of Spain in the fight against fascism.

During the tragic years of the Nazi occupation, Hirshke naturally was to be found in the front ranks of the partisans. With the same good-natured smile and always ready to help his comrades, Hirshke fought again with gun in hand. He was a superb marksman who was able to kill scores of the Hitler bandits.

The simple and proud life of Hirshke, the virtuous laborer, the sincere human being, the unbowed warrior; his heroic death on the fields of Corez set an example for us.

We honor his memory!

Translator's notes:

Others reported information to Yad Vashem:

(Tzvi) Hirsch Trotzki was born to Pesakh Aharon and Ester in 1904 in Dunilovichi. He was married to Reina Todres and had one child; a fifteen-year-old girl named Sara. He made his residence in Paris, France and worked as a clerk. During the war, he was in Turenne, France. He later died in the Correze District of France in 1943. This information was provided by a Page of Testimony from his brother Aleksander Trotzki in May 22, 1955.

Hirsch Trocki was born in Dunilowicze, Poland in 1904. He was a worker and married. Prior to WWII he lived in Wilno, Poland. During the war was in Paris, France. Hirsch died in 1943 in France at the age of 39. This information is based on a Page of Testimony submitted by his acquaintance.

Hirsch Trotzki was born in 1904 in Dunilovichi. He was married and lived in Wilno, Poland. He was a worker and lived in Paris during the war. He died in France on October 15, 1943 at the age of thirty-nine. This information was provided by a Page of Testimony written by an acquaintance, Sabina Elzon.

Hirsch Trocki was born in Dunilowicze, Poland in 1904. Hirsch died in 1943 in Correze District, France. This information is based on a list of deportation from France found in the Le Memorial de la deportation des juifs de France, Beate et Serge Klarsfeld, Paris 1978.

Hirsch Trocki was born on August 15, 1904 in Dunilovichi, Poland. He died in 1943 in the Correze District of France. This information was taken from a list of deportation from France. This 1978 list came from Le Memorial de la deporation des juifs de France, Beate et Serge Klarsfeld in Paris.

[Page 360]

Dunilowicze (Dunilovichi) Jewish residents in 1939

Translated by Eilat Gordin Levitan

Surname	Head of household	Number of family members
MEIROVITCH	Yeshaia – Rabbi	5
MUSHKAT	P. Leib	9
SHEREL	Avraham Yosel	4
SHEREL	Shmuel Zelig	3
KOPILOVITCH	Yitzhak Natan	5
CHADASH	Leib	2
CHADASH	Rachel	
ZAMIEVSKI		5
CHAIKIN	Chaim Zalman	4

BADANES	Leja	2
CHAIKIN	Rivka	1
SHAPIRA	Yosef	4
GUREVITCH	Gershon	4
	Leizer "the Dockshitzer"	3
FELSHER	Chaia Sara	3
ZAIANTZ	Nachum	2
ZAIANTZ	Leib	4
MUSHKAT	Raphael	3
BARKIN	Hirsh Tevel	6
MUSHKAT	Mordechai	3
AKS	Chaim Zelig	8
	Zerch the Shamash	3
KAPILOVITCH	Zusman	5
ZAK	Moshe	6
GUREVITCH	Siontsh	4
SWERDLIN	Michael	4
YAFFE	Chaim	3
BRODNE	Chaim	3
MUSHKAT	Pesach Raphael	3
BRODNE	Dr. Eliyahu	4
GOLDMAN	Eishi Gershon	2
GOLDMAN	Ytza Chone	4
GOLDMAN	Sara Leja	1
	Feygel nee Goldman	4
KLONSKI	Zisman	2
ZUKERMAN	Zalman	4
SARA?	Basha	3
MINDER	Ytzhak	2

MINDEL	Yoel	2
MINDEL	Yashke	3
LIVSHITZ	Mordechai	6
LIVSHITZ	Yshaya	2
GOLDMAN	Avraham Chaim	3
SWIRSKI	Yoel Pinia	3
GOLDMAN	Nachum Eliyahu	3
	Rubin	4
	Mordechai – the shochet	4
FRIEDMAN	Yeshaia - the shamash	8
LIGOMSKI	Shmuel Yaakov	2
LIGOMSKI	Aharon	5
	Shmuel Ytzhak	3
SWERDLIN	Israel Yankel	2
FORMAN	Reuven	9
GUREVITCH	Baruch	4
	Sara Beila	1
	Leybke, son of Sara Beila	3
	The "Shteper"	5
GORDON	Shmuel	1
TEPER	Frumka	7
	The "Prizerer"	4
ZIPILEVITZ	Pinchas	4
GAZ	Hirshel	2
GAZ	Peretz	2
GAZ	Beylka	3
GAZ	Chaim Dan	3
GENDEL	Leibka	6
CHADASH	Leybke	3

SWERDLIN	Leybke	4
GORDON	Binia	4
TROZKY	Aharon	2
TROZKY	Gdalia	3
ZIPELEVITZ	Pesia	3
ZIPELEVITZ	Sara	3
ZIPELEVITZ	Basha	2
SOLOVAY	Chaia Sara	4
GORDON	Zalman Leib	2
GORDON	Avraham – the Shamash	3
FISHER	Avraham	5
FISHER	Ester	3
KATZOVITZ	Feiga Simka	2
SKRANSKY	Avraham Meir	4
KATZIN	Ben Zion	4
ZIPELEVITZ	Moshe	4
ULMAN	Hinda	3
BENYA	Zalman	3
MANPIL	Shlomo	3
GAZ	Avraham Hirsh	1
	Disha Leja	4
CHADASH	Chaim Leib	2
KAGAN	Chaim Ytzhak	4
CHADASH	Mendel	3
SHNIEDER	Chaim Yashka	5
LINKOWSKI	Yosef	5
TAITCH	Aharon	2
SLAVIN	Eirma	4
DAZKES	Eizik	2
REYZEL	Chaim	2
	Reuven the	4

	"Shteper"	
GORDON	Yankel	2
KLINER	Zusman	3
GENDEL	Yankel	2
SHTEINGRAB	Ytzhak	4
RAYCHEL	Leib	7
SKRONSKY	Leib	6
GENDEL	Yudel	2
MINDEL	Wolke	6
MINDEL	Leib	
ZAIANTZ	Avraham	
SHIMON	Wolfovitz	5
BOROSOK	Baruch	3
ZIPELEVITZ	Leyzer	3
LURIA	Leyka	3
FEYGEL	Dan	7
ZIMCHAVITCH	Moshe	6
ZIMCHAVITCH	Binyamin	4
KLEINER	Shimon	4
MENCHES	Zadik	4
GRILICHER	Israel	3
	Chaim – the baker	2
ABILOVITCH	Noach	3
ABILOVITCH	Moshe	3
CHADASH	Avraham	2
CHADASH	Shimon	3
MINDEL	Noach	2
ZAITLIN	Meir Mordechai	2
ZAITLIN	Berl	3
BASS	Ester	3
PERLMAN	Meir Hirsh	3

GENDEL	Chana	2
FEIGEL	Ytzhak	2
GORDON	Israel Leyzer	1
ZIPELEVITZ	Natan	4
DLUT	Ruvke	5
GORDON	Baruch	9
KAMINKOVITCH	Berl	6
LEYKAS'S PARENTS	Zipa	2
ZIPELEVITCH	Shlomo	7
GAZ	Gershon	3
BLIAT	Israel	5
DRATWE	Max	6
KATZOVITZ	Abba Hirsh	2
DLUT	Gita Chyena	4
CHADASH	Chaim Yosef	6
CHADASH	Natan	6
	Chaia Rivka	3
	Meir - "the Blecher"	3
KAGAN	Zalman	5
GORDON	Geshe	4
SWERDLIN	Shepsel	2
KATZ	Yuda	4
	Pinile - the water carrier	1
RAZAVO	Zalman	5
ZINGER	Beinesh	2
SKRANSKY	Shmuel Yehuda	3
GUREVITCH	Shalom	3
CHADASH	Yehuda (Yudel)	6
RUDERMAN	Zalman	9

YASIN	Breine Ruderman and Yudel	2
DRUTZ	Aharon Zelig	3
MANPIL	Yosef	4
RAICHEL	Chaim Mordechai	3
	Nachum - the "Blacher"	4
	Chaim Gershon - the tailor	3
PEROVOSKIN	Shmuel Hirsh	2
KAGAN	Chaim	4
GORDON	Yankel	4
	Mota Zatzman – the "Beder"	4
PERMAN	Feivel	3
GINSBURG	Meir Bar	6
YAFFE	Chaze	5
BEIRACH	Yashka	3
GUREVITCH	Yisrael Chaim	3
GUREVITCH	Avraham	2
GUREVITCH	Shalom	3
GUREVITCH	Gershon	4
FISHER	Chaim	6
GORDON	Ytzka	2
GORDON	Gdalia	2
GORDON	Dinka	1
SHAPIRA	Yosef	4
ZIPELEVITZ	Myashka	4
IZIKSON	Feiga	3
BERMAN	Mota	4
ABEL	Yankel	3
RAICHEL	Leib	8

NARUTZKI	Shalom	7
TODER	David Meir	3
SHNEIDER	Leib	4
GORDOL	Ytzka	4
GUREVITCH	Michel	4
GUREVITCH	Ytka	3
KORITZKY	Shlomo Meir	5
GENDEL	Yudel the "ladiks"	2
	Chaim the "Zavorotker"	4
KLEINER	Aharon Leib	4
WOLLICH	Yosef	3
KLEINER	Zishka	2
KLEINER	Yzka	1
KLEINER	Pyase	1
ARKA	Aronovitch	4
GORDON	Yosef	4
SKRANSKY	Yisrael Eliyahu	3
MINDEL	Ytzka	7
ZIPELEVITZ	Hendel	4
DRUTZ	Eisar	8
GUREVITCH	Dvora	1
GORDON	Simka Eisars	3
	Leja Shmuel Ytzas	3
YANKOIF	Mota	5
SCHNEIDER	Miyashke	4
ZIPELEVITZ	Pinchas Ore	3
	David – the shoemaker	2
GUREVITCH	Eliakim	4
GARBER	Eliyahu Moshe	6

Surname	Given Name	Count
MINDER	Yechiel	4
GENDEL	Zire	2
YAFFE	Chaim	3
BENSON	Welwel	3
WEXLER	Yishaya	4

900 souls perished in Dunilowicze on November 22nd, 1942

[Page 362]

Jewish survivors who were in Dunilowicze during the war

Country where they resided when the list was made (c 1950)

The Soviet Union (Russia)

Surname	Head of household
KAMINKOVITCH	Avraham
GINSBURG	Hirshke
GINSBURG	Rachka
GINSBURG	Chana
GINSBURG	Pela
NARUTZKI	Chaim Reuven and another family member
KLEINER	Ytzka
RAZAVO	Michla
MINDEL	Libe (four family member survived)
MINDEL	Sonia
MINDEL	Leybke
MINDEL	Beynes
SWIRSKI	Frumka
FRIEDMAN	Shalom Bar
DRATOVE	Ziamke
DRATOVE	Chaia Dina
RUDERMAN	Shepsel

RUDERMAN	Breine
AKS	Rivka
AKS	Leyka
AKS	Ester

[Page 363]

Made aliyah after the war and reside in Israel

Surname	Head of household
AKS	Chana Gitka
ZAIATZ	Rivka
ZAK	Zalman
ZAK	Leybel
FORMAN	Yoel David
LINKOVSKY	Avraham Shlomo
WOLACH	Yashka
LINKOWSKY	Dan
KATZOVITZ	Cheika (two family members survived and now live in Israel)

Immigrated to Argentina after the war

Surname	Head of household
MUSHKAT	Yizka
MUSHKAT	Chayka
MUSHKAT	Avraham Chaim
DRUTZ	Frumka

Resided in Lida after the war

Surname	Head of household
KOPILOVITCH	Leibke
SHAPIRA	Leibe
ZAIANTZ	Leib

Immigrated to North America after the war

Surname	Head of household
YTZA	Chana (two family members)
GENDEL	Leibke
MINDEL	Abrashka
GUREVITCH	Avrahanke
ZEITLIN	Berke
TROTSKY	Tsherna
GARBER	Yechiel (two family members)
MINDEL	Mirka
FINKELSTEIN	Chaim Meir
FINKELSTEIN	Yehudit
RUDERMAN	Yitshka
CHADASH	Leibke (two family members)
ZIPELEVITZ	Myashka
MANPIL	Yankel
FISHER	Siama
SLAWIR (SLAWIN?)	Eirma
GORDON	Yankel with family (4)
GORDON	Wolka with family (4)
GORDON	Avrahamke
KORIZKY	Mirl

[Page 365]

Postavy

Postavy, Disna uyezd, Vitebsk gubernia

Latitude: 55°07' Longitude: 26°50'

As told by the Postavy partisans who survived and came to Argentina

The Topographical Situation

The shtetl Postov, (Postawy/ Postavy today in Belarus) was part of Vilna Province. It was located at a distance of 120 km. Northeast of Vilna (Vilnius- today in Lithuania). A railway station, also called Postov, was situated 2 kilometers away from town. The railway line ran from Vilna east to Vileika and from Vilejka north to Glubok (Glubokie). A river gashes through the shtetl. The river commences at Narutsh (the illustrious Narutsh Forest) and empties into the Dvine river north. During the summer the trees were cut down in the surrounding forests and the locals floated logs on the river northwest to Riga.

The shtetl is situated on high ground enveloped by lush forests. Because of this luxuriant nature, the shtetl and the surrounding area were considered a resort region. Vilna Jews would congregate there for rest and recuperation during the summer. Students, who studied in the big cities of the region, would also come there to relax in nature. There was a grand dazzling park where the Graf (nobleman) lived near by the shtetl. The graf owned most of the buildings in the area, as well as the surrounding fields. In the midst of the shtetl there was a small lake, which was called the "Blind River". The lake never dried up. There were all kinds of legends about it. Some of the legends connected the lake with the Turkish War.

The shtetl had four main streets and many smaller streets brunched out from them. There was a large busy market in the center of town. Every Monday was the weekly market day and farmers from the area would come to exchange goods and produce.

Postov was part of White Russia (Belarus) which was part of the Russian empire before the First World War. After World War I (c 1920), it became part of Poland. There were approximately 4,000 inhabitants, 2,500 of whom were Jews and 1,500 White Russians. Jews and Christians lived in peace.

Postavy History until 1914

Jewish life in the shtetl followed the stringently traditional pattern for hundreds of years until the onset of World War I. There were 3 synagogues in which the Jews prayed: The Beth Midrash (House of Study), the "mixed" synagogue and the Great Synagogue. Every day, when it had barely gotten light, shortly before dawn, young and old Jews, would ran to synagogue for morning prayer. In the afternoon you could also see Jews leaving their businesses they were joined by Jewish laborers and all would be rushing to synagogue for the afternoon service. Between the afternoon and evening services one would plunge into a holy book, looking into a Gmara (Talmud), Ein Yaakov (Talmudic Legends), or Mishna, and some would recite the Psalms.

[Page 366]

There were 2 Rabbis In the shtetl one was Hassidic and one a "misnaged" (opposed to Hassidism). There were 3 shochets (ritual slaughterers).. There was a "Chevra Kadisha" (Jewish Burial Society), an "Hachnasat Orchim" and "Linas Ha'Tzedek" (Hospitality committee and a bed for the night establishment, all free of charge). People would volunteer to sit with the sick through the night, especially the ill that were alone and had no family in town. There was also a local doctor. The Jewish occupations in town were diverse. There were storekeepers and laborers. Some were loggers who sent products to the faraway cities. Many made a living from the market day. The peasants from the surrounding villages would bring grain cattle and other products to sell. Wagoneers made their living by carrying passengers and products to and from the station, which was 2 kilometers away.

There were some traditional Heders for biblical studies. There was also a Russian elementary school with 7 grades and an Officer's school.

A Blood Libel

At the time of the Beylis trial (In the year 1913, the infamous lawsuit of Mendel Baylis took place in Kiev, Beylis was falsely accused of murdering a young Christian boy in order to use his blood for ritual purposes) This story took place at the same time in Postavy. There lived in the shtetl a Christian man who used to bake sugar ca tier daughter would sell them in the train station. When a train would arrive she would enter the coaches to sell her wares. One time shortly before Passover, she got involved with a purchaser in a coach. The train left the station and she couldn't get off. She got to the next station at Heidut There she met the Postov bagel-baker, Avraham-Itze. He took her in his cart in order to bring her home. They arrived in Postavy very late at night.

Meanwhile, her mother had run to the Rabbi screaming that Jews should return her daughter. Since it was just before Passover the Jews must have kidnapped her daughter. She knows Jews do this kind of evil, since such a trial of the Jew, Mendel Baylis, is now taking place in Kiev.

[Page 367]

A large crowd of Christians had gathered immediately and became enraged. The Jews were extremely frightened. Late that night the Christian girl rode in the shtetl with the bagel-baker and all quieted down.

Preventing a Pogrom

The following story took place in about the same time c 1912. There was in shtetl a young Jewish lady named Chana-Laike. She fell in love with a non- Jew and wanted to marry him. When her father found out about it, he beat her. Chana-Laike ran away to her non-Jew lover and told him everything. He discussed the matter with the peasants. They decided to avenge her fathers' beating, on the entire Jewish community. On a Monday, they decided to rob and kill the Jews. The Postavy Jews discovered this plan in time. A number of young Jews organized. They drove the turbulent peasants with sticks out of the market area. This was how a pogrom was prevented during that time.

Postavy river

The First World War - 1914-1918

The onset of the War hit the Jews of the shtetl worse than all other shtetls in the area. At the outbreak of the war the Christian neighbors began eyeing the Jews and looking at them unfavorably. Every misfortune and tragedy that befell on the residents was charged as associated with the Jews. When there was a shortage of silver money it was said that the Jews were hoarding it. The same type of blaming was true of other events.

[Page 368]

The most serious blame was the charge that Jews were in contact with the Germans. The youth was mobilized to revenge. Life became very hard for the Jews.

On the eve of Yom Kippur, the Germans entered Postov. Many of the Jews fled east to Russia. The Germans advanced towards Glubokie. Few German troops were left in Postovy. Eight days later the Russians launched an offensive. A mounted unit of Cossacks burst into the shtetl and with piercing shouts galloped towards the barracks on Vilna Street. No German troops were to be found there. The Christians joyfully congregated the streets in order to greet the Cossacks. The Jews hid in their homes in great fright. The Christ started to make up all sorts of stories about the Jews: That they are hiding Germans in their homes and that they had closed their stores in order to hide their merchandise for the Germans.

Suddenly there was an order announced by the Cossack commander; "All Jews must gather in the marketplace No Jew was to remain in his home."

The Rabbi advised all to go to the marketplace and he himself went. Even the ill Jews were carried over to the marketplace. From the marketplace the Jews, with the Rabbi leading, were led to the open field behind the barracks, where all were supposed to be shot. They took only the men, but the women and children chased behind them.

Rabbi, Shneur-Zalman approached the commander and attempted to convince him that the Jews were innocent. With that, the righteous Christian, Zacharov, in whose house the Rabbi lived, approached the commander. He was a retired Russian Army officer, who had been decorated with a gold medal, which was now pinned to his breast, and with the documents of extra ordinary service of the czar in his hands, he announced:

"All of my life I served the Czar Nicholas. For my honesty and devotion, I was given this medal."

"What do you want to tell me? Speak!" the commander said.

"I want to tell you that the Rabbi and the Jews are innocent. Everything that is being said about them is false. I plead with you to spare their lives. If you are going to shoot them, then shoot me together with them." (With these words he embraced the Rabbi and wouldn't let him go.)

"Zacharov, let it be as you desire, but with the condition that the Jews show us where the Germans are and that they immediately open their stores." Said the commander.

[Page 369]

The stores didn't need to be opened by their owners. The Cossacks had broken in and told the Christians to take what they wanted. Quickly all the merchandise was stolen.

The Germans returned again two days later, and the front remained stationary for a long period of time. The region of Postavy remained volatile for 3 years. Because of the crossfire and the constant fear, it became impossible to continue living in the shtetl. The Jews fled Postov during the 10 Days of Penitence (between Rosh Hashanah and Yom Kippur) in 1915. Many went to Vilna and many settled in Panevezys (Lithuania, The native Jews of Panevezys were sent to Russia earlier). There was no lack of hunger and need for the refugees. They lived with the hope that they could return to Postavy as quickly as possible.

A street in Postavy

Return to Postavy

When World War I ended most of the Postavy Jews returned to their demolished homes in Postavy. Nothing remained of their possessions. The buildings were so badly damaged that it was impossible to repair them. In spite of all Jews began to build new homes.

It didn't take long before a new war broke out between the Poles and the Bolesheviks. For a year the shtetl was besieged with fighting troops. The area kept passing from hand to hand, from the Russians to the Poles and vice-versa. Each of them would search for their enemies in Jewish homes and businesses. The Christian population supported the looting and helped both sides and once again the shtetl was looted and impoverished. The population suffered famine and temporarily fed themselves only on vegetation.

[Page 370]

The war came to an end and the region became part of Poland c 1920. Shortly, the Jews began again to revive the economy, community and cultural life. A bank for storekeepers and businessmen was founded. A free loan fund was established for Laborers and craftsmen. A burial society, a synagogue for prayer and an elementary school, for the majority of Jewish children were founded. Even though there were free Polish schools, the parents made the effort and sent their children to the "Tarbut School," in order to get a Jewish education in Hebrew. When the school could no longer support itself by tuition alone the Jewish youth organized a drama circle and preformed plays and charged the audiences in order to help the school financially. They presented Yiddish Theatre. A large library was established, in Postavy. The library contained Yiddish, Hebrew and Russian books.

Zionist organizations started flourishing in town. There was a children's' club and Chalutz organization in the Tarbut school, which gave the children a Zionist education. When the school officials couldn't agree on the language of instruction, Yiddish or Hebrew, the Yiddishists broke away and set up a school under the auspices of the Jewish Socialist Bond. The Tarbut School remained under Zionist supervision. This split led to greater accomplishments. Each side sought to bring in the best teachers for the children and the best lecturers for the adults. The youth benefited from the cultural creativity. The Yiddishists maintained that Jewish life must be improved for Jews wherever they lived. The Zionists prepared the youth in Hachsharo (training camps for communal and agricultural living); for the aim of Aliyah (migration) to Palestine/ Eretz Israel. Many youngsters did indeed go on aliyah. They are scattered throughout the land of Israel. Several young people went to Argentina, where they set up their homes.

Expanded up to the year of 1933, a peaceful period involved for the Jews. When Hitler came to power in Germany, the ill Nazi "spirit" also invaded Poland and even reached the small shtetl of Postavy. The Polish anti-Semites set up picket lines at Jewish stores and businesses. Jewish artisans were denied work. Jewish children weren't admitted into Polish schools. Often, Polish and White Russian hooligans administered beatings to Jews.

[Page 371]

A self-defense Jewish circle was formed. All parties were united. The struggle was difficult, but eventually the Jews felt more secure. So it went until September of 1939, when Germany invaded Poland....

As soon as the news arrived that Germany had invaded Polish territory, the Christian hooligans beat and robbed the Jews.

Postavy Jewish cemetery

[Pages 371]

The Soviets Entry in September of 1939

The Germans and soviet divided the territory of Poland. Our area was annexed by the Soviets.

With the arrival of the Soviet Russians (Sept. 17, 1939), the Jewish situation changed. All Zionist parties and groups were officially disbanded. Jews had to adapt to a new way of life. The Socialist system was established. Merchants and owners of businesses had to search for other ways to earn a livelihood. Shortly they found new professions. For the Postavy Jews the Russian occupation came as a great relief. They greatly feared the Germans. After the soviets entered Anti-Semitism was "officially" disallowed. When the Soviets came with all their might they were hoping now that they would avoid the war and also avoid German-Nazi domination.

[Pages 372]

The Arrival of the Germans

The sudden German attack on the Soviet Union took place on June 22, 1941. German planes flew low over the shtetl and bombed the area before we even had a chance to realize what was happening to us. The panic that spread in the shtetl was indescribable. Many Jews fled east to Russia. The roads were dark with thousands of Jewish men, women and children. We awaited a miracle, but it never came to us; most did not make it to safety.

The fate of the Jews who remained in Postavy was even worse. The local hooligans came out of their hiding places as soon as it was known that the Germans were coming and began beating and robbing Jews. The hatred of the local Christians towards Jews became even more virulent than it, had been previously, before the Soviet occupation.

The First Victims

The first thing the German troops did after entering Postavy was to take 50 Jews hostage. They lined them up with their faces to a wall, their hands behind their backs. they aimed with machine guns at them They informed the entire Jewish population that if a Jew were to harm one German soldier, they would shoot all 50 Jews. Fortunately, the Jews at this point got off with only a fright. The 50 Jews were freed after a short time.

The Germans did commit some murders on the 1st day. Gershon the carpenter's son, was standing near his house watching the German army pass through. For no apparent reason a German officer ordered that he be taken and shot. His father, who saw through the window that his son was being marched off, ran to the officer and begged him to release his son. The German ordered that the father be taken also. The other 3 children, who were watching, were also taken. They were all taken to the Christian cemetery and shot. This took place at about 4:00 P. M At the fence of the Christian cemetery.

That same night two Christians informed on a group of Jews, saying that they were communists. They were Velvel Friedman and his 2 sons: Moshe and Yaakov. They were all shot and a son-in-law, Zelik Chodosh, Ole Shuvitz, the midwife, Chava Shapiro of Vilna Street, Zelig- Itze's daughter and a Russian lawyer. The police and the Gestapo agents took them all out of their beds in the middle of the night. The women and children weren't harmed. They were all taken to Zalman Cepelevitz's house and there imprisoned in a dark cellar. They were kept there until the following evening. Afterwards, to the accompaniment of music, they were taken to the outskirts of Vilna Street, where they were all shot.

[Pages 373]

The Germans did not tell anyone that they were shot. They said that they were sent to Germany for forced labor. The Christians who dug the pit in which they were all buried, told the Jews that they were shot. Permission was obtained to give them a proper Jewish burial only 4 months later, after paying heavy bribes.

A short time later the German forces took a few more Jews. They were Chaim-Elye Tzepelovitsh and Weiner's two sons-in-law, Leibe Reichel, the brick-maker, and Misha Zaslavsky.

Each day brought new victims and new rules set against the Jews. Jews couldn't walk on the sidewalks. They had to walk in the middle of the street like livestock. If a Jew happened to walk on the sidewalk, he was immediately shot.

[Pages 374]

Jews wore two yellow patches on which there was a Star of David. One patch was over the right breast and the 2nd on the shoulder.

Translator's notes:

Yaakovs' son, Meir Bar Shalom nee Friedman survived and lived with his wife Shulamit in Kvuzat Yavne. Also see story of Dvora at the end. Two other sons, Avraham Ytzhak and Chanoch died as heroes. They were partisans. His wife, Ettel nee Shulman perished.

Yaakov Leibe Reikhel was married to Yokheved nee Khodosh. His granddaughter survived and lived in Kibbutz Naan but it could be another Reichel- there were many Reichels in Postavy.

Moshe Zaslavski was born in Kiev, Ukraine in 1892. He was a metalworker and married to Sonia nee Shnitzer. During the war was in Postawy, Poland, his daughter survived.

Incarcerating the Postavy Jews in the Ghetto

All Jews were crammed into a sealed Ghetto during August 1941. During that month about 2,000 Jews were driven into the Ghetto. It was located on Barzilan and Dvortzov Streets, and one side of Braslavsk Street. It was sealed off with a fence of 3 meter high. At the top of the boards there were 3 layers of barbed wire. A wide gate of about 3 meters was erected at the entrance to the ghetto. Polish police guarded the gate. The home of Shmuel-Shlomo Rabinovitsh, the blacksmith was near the gate.

The order to enter the Ghetto was given by the police at 6:00 A.M

The Jews were given 6 hours to move. In other words, by 12 noon, no Jew was to be found walking outside of the Ghetto. Entering the Ghetto, everything had to be left behind. Only a small hand package was allowed. This "package" contained objects that would serve as "furniture, clothing, bedding and food".

They ordered us to set up a Judenrat committee that would serve as a "go between" the Jews and the Germans. The members of the Judenrat were the dentist, Rubenstein, Michael Toibesh, Shimon Lubotzky and Pesach and Shia Shubitz. They also organized the Jewish police to guard the Jews from inside the ghetto.

Four or five families lived in each room In the Ghetto. They slept wherever they could find a spot. In some of the rooms there wasn't even enough standing room. Filth was excessive in all the dwellings. All sorts of diseases spread in the ghetto rapidly. Food consisted of 100 grams of bread a day per person. Each one was also given a plate of watery soup.

All men, women and children were marched off by the Germans to do their duties in the forced labor troop. Jews would start working each morning at 7:00. They worked until 4:00 P.M.

[Pages 375]

They would load and unload wagons, plow fields, sweep and clean and do all the hardest and filthiest jobs. When Jews left the ghetto in the morning, no one believed that he would return to his family, that he would see his dearest again. Before leaving for work they would all bid each other farewell. They would kiss and embrace.

Besides the filthy labor, the Germans set up workshops for knitting, baking, upholstery, tailoring and others All the residents of the ghetto worked as slaves to the Germans; even 13-year-old children.

Each day brought new victims. Each day someone failed to return from work. It took little for the germans to kill Jews. Some were killed for trying to bring some kind of food into the Ghetto. If during inspection at the Gate, someone was found with a piece of bread or a potato under his shirt, he would be brutally beaten and then stabbed to death on the spot.

A street in Postavy

[Page 375]

The Liquidation of the Postov Ghetto

The bloody day of the inhalation of the ghetto occurred on Dec. 25, 1942, 3rd of Teveth, 5703. About 1,500 Jews were still alive in the Ghetto at the time. At 3:00 A.M. of that night, the Jews heard muffled voices. Immediately there was an order from the police for everybody to vacate the Ghetto. Children were awakened. Everyone became extremely frightened. They knew what it meant. They were ordered to line up in rows of 4. This time old and young, men, women and children were lined up. The Germans ordered everyone to march to the railway line. While crossing the railroad trucks, it was clear to everyone that they were being led to the slaughter. A few Jews used the darkness, they began to run to different directions. Other Jews followed them. The Germans began firing at everyone from all sides. The weak ones amongst the Jews, who couldn't keep up the speed, were instantly shot.

A street in Postavy

[Pages 376]

Very few Jews arrived alive to the huge pit, which had been prepared earlier by the Germans and their local assistants. This mass grave was filled later with the corpses, which were spread all about. This common grave of all the murdered Postov Jews is to be found on the other side of the railway line at the end of Bazielan Street.

A Street in Postavy

[Pages 377]

The Survivors of the Postov Ghetto

Motel Katzavitsh – in Postavv

Moshe Katzavitsh – in Postavv

Abraham Roichman and wife in Israel

Moshe Roichman and wife in Israel

Raya Roichman (now Eisenman) in Israel

Abraham Friedman in Israel

The child, Tzipora Golomb (parents perished) in Israel

Fanye Tzepliovitsh and 3 children - In Postov.

Devora Friedman - in North America.

Rivke Friedman in Postov.

Tzipe Friedman in Postov

Pese Friedman in Postov

Yitzhok Barkman in Postov

Yaakov Foigl in Postov

Yoel Veksler and his wife Nechama - in North America.

Chaim-Ber Veksler & wife in North America'

Rivke Veksler in North America

A street in Postavy

[Pages 378]

Partisans of the Postiv Ghetto

Zalman Roichman tells:

Abraham-Mitze Friedman, a Postov partisan, was in Dolhinov, a shtetl not far from Vilejka, when most of the Dolhinov Ghetto was annihilated. He and another, Shimon Shapiro, managed to escape from the Dolhinov Ghetto and attached themselves to a Soviet partisan group in the forest led by Tymzok. (For more information go to the Dolhinov Yizkor book to Avraham Friedman Story). Shortly afterwards they began to search for ways to save Jews from the Postov Ghetto. After 3 days of steady wandering he arrived in Postov Ghetto. The news that he and other partisans were in the Ghetto spread promptly. They simply could not believe such an accomplishment, until it was ascertained that this hero was in contact with the Judenrat, and had asked them to let all able-bodied, fighting Jews out, so that they could go to the partisans and carry on the fight against the German murderers. The Judenrat refused. They argued that it must be either the entire Ghetto or no one. Since he couldn't take all, he left the Ghetto, taking only his sister, Leah Shapiro, and her 3-year-old child, Shlomele, and his brothers, Moshe and Henech Friedman.

But Abraham-Mitze did not stop there. He undertook a difficult journey of hundreds of kilometers till he reached a Christian acquaintance, who had connections with partisans. He asked him to take a letter to his friends in the Postov Ghetto. This Christian, named Naumtship, who lived in a village between Postov and Kabilnik, carried out his request.

When we got the letter, we organized a group and sent them into the forest. In this group were: Michall-Itze, Zalman and Abraham Friedman., Milke Zaslavsky, Chaya Ruchman, Devora Friedman (Gordon) and Abraham Ruchman. They met at the designated spot and from there went into the forest to the partisans. Abraham Ruchman went back into the Ghetto to await news from the group.

Leib and Moshe Katzovitz with their mother Rachel

Chaim Zalman Izikson with his family in Postavy
- they all perished

In this way several weeks passed. Once this same Christian came running and asked that I hide him so that no one would meet him. I worked for Rache Estrin, outside the Ghetto, where there had once been a bakery. I hid him away there and he gave me a letter from Abraham-Mitze Friedman. The letter read as follows: "I await you a week from Wednesday at the same spot as previously. This was 6 km. from Postov and you had to pass through the Jewish cemetery. The partisans received word that they are ready to liquidate the Postov Ghetto, so come immediately since you may be too late to save your lives if you wait."

[Pages 380]

I only told the men about this letter. On the 2nd Wednesday, I also told the women about the contents of the letter and told them to prepare to leave. In a half-hour we were all finished with our preparations, and armed, we left the Ghetto. First, we tore off the yellow Shields of David, which the German murderers had ordered us to wear, sewn to our clothes on both sides. Afterwards we cut the barbed wire fences, removed three boards from the barrier, and carefully, with great difficulty, we managed to save ourselves, only a few days before the Postov Ghetto was completely annihilated.

The following were in the group: Zalman the tinsmith and his wife, Reizel from Heidutzishok (now in America). Zalman, Nachman, Abraham, Fanye and Rachel Roichman; Tzvia and Feigele (One-year-old) Golomb; Dobe Shapiro; Sonia, Leah and Gese Zaslavsky; Chaval, 'Czipe and Fechke Friedman; Chaim-Eliyahu Katzovitsh; Nehama, Zlatke, Esther and Mindel Gordon. With this, the work in Postavy of the heroic partisan, Abraham-Mitze Friedman, ended. There simply were no more Jews left in Postovy. There was no one left to save. Abraham-Mitze Friedman died a heroic death during the unequal battle against the German murderers. This occurred in September, (I don't remember the day) 1943. May his name be remembered forever. Nachman.

When the young partisan-Nachman, (His father was the gravedigger in the Postovy cemetery.) came to me to request that we take him along to the forest. I asked Zalman, the tinsmith, about it. Zalman agreed to take him only on condition that he brings arms with him. Nachman answered that he had arms, and with this statement he told the following story: "At the start of the War, as soon as the Germans entered the shtetl, I noticed a German lying near our house. The German was still breathing. I immediately took an axe and killed him. I buried him in the Jewish cemetery together with the arms which he carried." He told no one about this, not even his parents. I went with him to the cemetery and saw with my own eyes what this young Nachman had actually done. After prolonged effort, we arrived to partisans' camp in the forest. Nachman allowed me no rest, asking that we return close to Postov to search for escapees from the Ghetto. We went in groups of threes: Nachman, one Kopel from Baranovitsh (who died in the forest) and I. When we came to a village, 10 km. from Postov, we went into the house of a Christian to warm ourselves a bit. Warming ourselves and having something to eat, we asked the peasant if he knew something about the Postovy Ghetto. He didn't answer. To the question as to whether he knows anything about where to obtain arms, he also didn't answer. When we assured him that no harm would come to him, he told us about a non-Jew who had hidden arms in a well. When we came to that peasant's house, we first asked if all that were present were with us. Afterwards we began to talk about the arms. At first, he denied everything. But when we took him outside, tied him and lowered him into the well near his home, he begged that we spare his life and he would give us the arms. As this was happening, he told us that a stranger was among those in his house, whom he didn't know, and that he couldn't be sure that that one wouldn't inform the Germans in Postov that he had had partisans in his home.

[Pages 381]

Right off we went back into the house and asked the stranger to get out of bed and show us his documents. When he dressed himself and put a large cross around his neck, Nachman recognized him. He was a Postov priest as well as a German spy who used to look for partisans as well as Jews in the villages, he looked for Jews who had fled from the Ghettoes. He had a revolver as well as documents proving he was a spy. We took him with us. Riding out a few kilometers., we promised to let him live and return everything to him, provided he told us something about his "good deeds". This person began telling us about how he had had no small part in the murder of the Postov martyrs, as well as in other Ghettoes. Of course, we quickly felt the urge to take at least a small bit of revenge on him. But we disagreed among ourselves as to who should have the privilege to kill such a disgusting priest-spy-murderer.

[Pages 382]

We drew lots and it was young Nachman who was actually able to taste some sweet revenge.

Nachman was not satisfied with this alone. He still wanted us to go to Postov. Perhaps we would still find someone there. But when we came to our liaison officer, Naumtshik, he warned us not to take the risk because the danger was great, and the entire area filled with many German murderers. There was suddenly a banging on the window of the peasant's house in which we were sitting. The peasant led us out the back door to the bath-house, thinking it was Germans. It was a groundless fright. It turned out to be an escaping Jew, Clendl Tzepelovitsh (son of Zalman), who had saved himself from the Postov slaughter and banged on the window searching for a haven. He told us in detail about the destruction of the Postov Ghetto. He said that his mother and sister, PJylime, had also saved themselves. They were about 20 kilometers away. Nachman went with him immediately to the place and brought them back to us. All of us then went further. On the way we met three other survivors: Leibke Einhorn (later killed as a partisan); Yaakov Foigl (a tar dealer now in Postov); Yitzhok Barkan (also in Postov for a while and later in Israel). All were naked, barefoot and hungry. In a nearby village, we were able to get clothing and food for them. In this way we brought them into the forest to the partisans. There, the heroic young Nachman fell courageously, after a prolonged battle with the Nazi murderers. This occurred October 25, 1943.

[Page 383]

Druya

Druya (also known as Druja)

Latitude: 55°47' Longitude: 27°27'

Translation supplied by Eilat Gordin Levitan

The shtetl Druya lies on the border of Latvia and Belarus. It was part of the Disna County in the Vilna Province before the war. The river Dvina splits the shtetl into two parts. It flows from Druya, passed the Latvian border, through Dvinsk (Denenberg), Riga, and then empties into the Baltic Sea. Droike, another small river, flows out of the Breslav Lake and ends in Druya, where it empties into the Dvina River. The shtetl was divided into three parts: Druya, Zadroye, and Zadvine. Before WWI, Druya rested on the borders of four provinces of the Russian Empire: Vilna, Vitebsk, Kovno, and Kurland. During the year between the war the Vilna province was in Poland, Kovno in Lithuania, Kurland in latvia and part of Vitebsk in the Soviet Union.

A favorite saying in Druya was, "When a rooster crows in Druya, all four provinces hear it."

Druya had two railway lines, a small local line running from Dukst and the second one, which was a major line, was completed in the year 1935. It went through Varpaieve, Vilna, and Warsaw. About 4,000 souls resided in Druya in the year 1939. About 2,500 inhabitants were Jews and 1,500 inhabitants were Christians. There were eight synagogues. The Great Synagogue with its about 250 years of history, was famous throw the region since it had the largest and most beautiful ark in the entire Vilna district. The ark was topped with a Russian-Romanov style eagle which stood on top of the heads of two lions. The Synagogue had been built by Duke Sapehi as a gift to the Jewish population. At that time, he had also built a Catholic church. The second synagogue, which was called the Great Beth Midrash, stood opposite the Great Synagogue. There was a house of study on its premises, where there once had stood a yeshiva. In later years, the scholars and Mithnagdim used to pray there. The third synagogue was called the Hassidic Minyan. Those worshippers had their own Rabbi and they conducted themselves as Hassidim of Shneur-Zalman's sect, the (Lubavitsh) Chabad. The remaining synagogues were the Kapustzer Minyan (Hassidic), Kalman's Minyan (Mithnagdim), Ishe-Meir's Minyan (Mithnagdim), Zalman's Minyan, and on the other side of the small Zadruike river, a very small synagogue. Besides Heders, there was also a Talmud Torah for the poor children.

[Page 384]

Among the well-known Jews in the shtetl was David the Cantor. He and his son were both accomplished musicians. Shmuel Moldin was famous as a prayer leader, while Getzl, the sexton, was well-known as a sermon giver. He would lead study groups in the Beth HaMidrash. He also had the first Jewish library in the shtetl and for a small fee he would lend his books out. The prayer leader in the Great Synagogue was Itze-Leib, the ritual Slaughterer.

The Holy Ark from the Druya Great Synagogue

[Page 385]

The following organizations existed in Druya:

1. A Burial Society,

2. A Charitable Society,

3. A Society to aid the Sick (members would stay overnight at the homes of the ill),

4. The Jewish Bank. It had been built in small sums from shares. Credit was extended at low interest only to shareholders and under very liberal conditions. The Bank was administered by a Directorate, chosen by the shareholders. Moshe Tubman was always the Chairman.

Aside from the cheders, there was a Talmud Torah for the children of the poor.

The Great Synagogue of Druya, which existed for 500 years

[Page 386]

The Druya Folkshule (school)

Druya Drama Circle

The Druya Folkshule was conduct by Tzisho (central Jewish school organization) and seventy-five children attended this school. The school was supported by a small tuition, which was paid by some of the parents, and by the occasional performances of the Drama Circle. The Drama Circle had twenty members of both genders. They would present the plays created by Yaakov Gordin, Kobrin's "Village Boy," Schiller's "Robbers" and others. Ephraim Kogan directed it (now he lives in Argentina). One of the participants was Benjamin Feinweitz (also in Argentina). The Drama Circle worked very hard to support the Jewish Folkshule (school). The Folkshule also had a wind instruments orchestra that played during weddings and arranged-dance evenings. All the income went towards supporting the Folkshule.

[Page 387]

Some members of the orchestra (Kasriel, Benjamin Feinweitz, and Baruch-Zalman Entin) reside today in Argentina.

The Volunteers of the Fire Department

We know that the fire department existed in Druya for a long time, but today no one remembers when it had begun. Most of the members were Jewish and it was run by the Tubman family. Some of the former members live in Argentina now.

A group of Jewish partisans, all from the shtetls of Szarkowszczyzna, Dunilowicze, Druya, and Kaziany

The Youth Organization (Hechalutz)

HeChalutz youth organization was founded in 1925 and concerned itself with Hachshara, preparing pioneers for immigration to Palestine. They would engage in agriculture, logging, and the training at various other trades. The income supported the organization itself. There were about thirty members.

The Society to aid the Sick

This organization helped the destitute sick. The contributions of shtetl Jews and Jewish merchants who came to the shtetl supported it. This organization had a doctor who would treat the sick people free of charge. In its final years, the organization was run by Ephraim Kogan (now in Argentina).

[Page 388]

Beitar (Revisionist youth movement)

A branch of this organization was founded in 1934 and named for Trumpeldor. Shlome Levin (who perished) was the leader and it contained about 250 young members. A considerable number went through Hachshara before the war and went to Israel, where they are found today. (One member, Leib Entin, is in Argentina.) They had a Drama Circle, a library, and a choir. They would dress in their brown uniforms for most activities.

Teachers and directors of the Druya Folkschule

Vocations in Druya

There were many shopkeepers and laborers, but there weren't many large enterprises in Druya. There was a beer brewery, which belonged to the Tubman family. The beer brewery supported the livelihoods of many Jews. There were Jews who dealt in wood, flax, seeds, grain, hides, geese, etc.

[Page 389]

About twenty families subsisted on agriculture. The farms were mostly privately owned and they planted corn, oats, barley, potatoes, and alike. Besides this, there were also Jews who managed vegetable gardens, leased orchards, and owned tanneries. A public library was located near the bank.

From September 1939

Leib Entin relates:

The Russians entered Druya in September 1939. The Jewish as well as Christian populations welcomed the Russians with joy. They commanded that the shops remain open, and that the merchandise be sold for Polish zlotys. Then they declared that only 100 zlotys per person can be exchanged for 100 Russian rubles. The remaining zlotys that people had were lost. Private business was destroyed in that manner.

A flooded street in Druya

After that, the regime ordered that cooperatives and Artels be set up. Everything belonged to the regime. Some merchants were hired as employees. Others worked at manual labor.

[Page 390]

The tradespeople, such as tailors, shoemakers, and furriers were organized into cooperative workshops.

The ruling authority was formed from the local population. The police chief was a Jew. Later, he was sent to Siberia with his family. Thus was his family saved. Today, they are in Israel.

The Great Synagogue was turned into a grain warehouse. The Jewish Folkschule was turned into a Russian school.

Druya Noted Personalities

Alter Drunanov
1870-1938

Druyanov Abba- Avraham- Asher (Alter) was the son of Eliyakum- Pesach - Getzel. His father, Pesach-Getzl, and grandfather, Yaakov-Mendl, were the rabbis of Druya. On his mother's side, he was also descended from rabbis.

Theatrical performance for the benefit of the Folkschule

Author, folklorist and Zionist public official. Alter was born in Druya in 1870 and studied in the Volozhin Yeshiva. Later he moved to Odessa and was the secretary of HaChultz. Member of the center of the Russian Zionists. Editor of "HaOlam" (1909-1912), "Reshumot" and "Miyamim Rishonim". Published "'Ktavim Letoldot Chibat Zion Veyeshuv Eretz Yisrael", "The Book of Tel Aviv" (1935), "Pinsker and his times", He also worked for different Hebrew periodicals. His Yiddish works appeared in Peretz's "Yom-Tov Bletter" (Holiday Pages), in "Yid" and in "Friend." His two volumes on Jewish folklore were published in Hebrew and printed in Odessa and in Jerusalem in 1922. He also published a large collection of Jewish jokes (more then 1,400) in 1922. Three-volume anthology of Jewish humor, Sefer HaBdikha ve-HaKhidud [Book of Jokes and Wit]

[Page 391]

He also edited the chapters of Modern Hebrew literature, folklore and geography of Eretz Israel in the Hebrew and German Encyclopedia "Eshkol". He died in Tel Aviv and his grave can be found near Bialik's grave, since they were intimate friends. A collection of his assays "Ktavim Nivcharim" was published in two volumes in Tel Aviv.

Toviev Yisrael Chaim
1858-1920

Yisrael Chaim was a writer and a linguist. He was born in Druya to a well to do family. When he was still a child the family moved to Riga. He received a Jewish education from private tutors. Graduate of the Technion in Riga; department of economic and commerce. Wrote assays in "Hamelitz" and was renowned by the readers for his rich and expressive language, and his unique style. Wrote educational books; "Eden Hayeladim", "Moreh Leyeladim", "Torat Hanigud", Hamachin", Egron Lebnay Haneurim" (all published in Warsaw). "Ozar Hasira ve Hamelitza" was published in Tel Aviv. All his books were very well received.

A flooded street in Druya

In 1905 was a member of the editorial committee of "Hazman". Was the publisher of "Hachaver" a newspaper for the youth. He was very dedicated to the Hebrew language. During the First World War he settled in Moscow and translated some classical French and English literature to Hebrew. (Oscar Wilde, Charles Dickens, Mark Twain, Viktor Hugo)

In Moscow he experienced some great tragedies, the Bolsheviks murdered his son and his son in law died at a young age. He returned to Riga were he died in 1920 of a heart attack. Books written by him;

'The writing of Y. B. Toviev- research topics of literature and language" (Berlin, 1923) "Ozar hameshalim vehapitgamim" (Odessa) "The Hebrew origin in the jargon." "Jewish Names" two plays; "Bimkom Drasha" (Warsaw) and "Hashorer Bebeito" (Piotrkow).

[Page 392]

Chaim Tzernovitsh (Rav Tzair)

He was a well-known Hebrew teacher and writer. The author of a basic work on the Talmud, he was a son-in-law of a Druya inhabitant, Kisin. His wedding took place in Druya and he also lived there for a short time.

A street in Druya

Moshe Paikin

Paikin was the first owner of the only bookstore in Druya. He was an intimate friend of S. Anski (Yiddish author and playwright of "The Dybuk") and Dr. Chaim Zhitlovsky (Yiddish writer). His son was the Israeli Consul in Iran.

Hillel Vichnin

Born in Druya in 1879, Vichnin translated Leo Tolstoy's booklet, "Whose Faith is Better?" into Yiddish. He was editor of "Der Folksfriend" (Vilna, 1901). He emigrated to North America in 1901, where he worked for a while for the "Jewish Daily Forward" and the former Philadelphia Yiddish daily, "The Jewish World." His son, Yisroel Vichnin, is known as a piano virtuoso.

Footnote:

1. The translator embellished the original narrative in this section.

[Page 393]

Snapshots of Druya School Life during the 20th Anniversary of the Druya Folkshule

From speeches during the 20th Anniversary

At the beginning of the first school year, the school managed with much difficulty to find a location to be held. There was also a general shortage of teachers. Not many wanted to move to "our Siberia". (The northern part of the Vilna region was called "Polish Siberia" because it was the coldest and furthest part from the center of the Polish Republic.) A month passed and finally some teachers came. Intensively, they worked on the curriculum, and did everything with great enthusiasm. The school was their scene, their center of life. "What we ate gave us energy!" Day and night they worked at the school. The children bound themselves to the teachers and acknowledged them with great love. The fathers and mothers were blessed to have them. The school administration and the teachers formed one big happy family for a while. Then, all of a sudden, the teachers lost favor in the eyes of the administration. They were all fired!

The burial of sheimos (worn out holy books), 1931, near the Great Synagogue

[Page 394]

The school was closed, and a deep sadness engulfed the children, parents, leaders, and friends of the school.

The beloved Chaim Buzak wrote the school administration letter after letter, demanding that teachers would be rehired. Each word held a pained cry of "Have pity and save the school!" as if a mother, who is saving her only son, uttered the words. There were still no teachers. Weeks flew by and dispatches were sent out. Heartrending letters continued to be issued. Chaim Buzak threw aside his own matters. He traveled to Vilna's Central School Board, and demanded, "I can't and won't go home without teachers!" The school reopened. All was fine, but the rent still needed to be paid. The financial situation of the school was desperate. What could be done to improve it?

Four children of the Luria family (Druya)

[Page 395]

The members of the school administration and close friends of the school came together and raised a limited sum of money. During those years a livelihood in Druya became grievous and with many obstacles, so they managed this feat only with great toil and headaches. However, with the school in danger, would there have been any excuse not to give? They gave! But why did they give? It was not just to fulfill an obligation or to get notoriety. The newspapers didn't publish names and they didn't dream of recognition by the powers that be. They gave because of their love to the children!

A flooded street in Druya

B.

As months passed the teachers were not able to pay their rent. They've come to the limit of their credit lines at the grocers. A proposal from the administration came: "we must raise the tuition!" The devoted and loyal female teacher Kazvan was opposed. "This cannot happen," she argues. "The parent's livelihoods become smaller day by day. Poverty grows and we are increasing tuition? What for, to increase the salaries of the teachers? It is bitter for the parents. We do not have to be a privileged group. No gestures or poses! No declamations! We give from the depths of the heart!"

[Page 396]

And so, they continued to serve the Jewish secular school.

This was the way that a small group of stubborn teachers and supporters worked, day in and day out. It is easy to mention twenty years of the past, but for these twenty years, there were all sorts of obstructions and complications. There was a constant effort made to survive the events, to struggle with problems as they come and not to break . . . not everyone could do this! Our school was honored by these sacrifices. Let us all therefore stretch out a hand, put our shoulders to the wheel, and help support the school in its difficult struggle to exist. Let us become partners to this sacred work of the Druya school officials!

A flooded street in Druya

The Liquidation of the Druya Ghetto[1]

The Soviets came to our area first. They annexed eastern Poland.

Leib Entin relates the story of the Russian arrival, September of 1939:

The Russians came to Druya during the month of September of the year 1939. The Jews, as well as the Christians, greeted the Russians with joy, since they were fearful that the Germans would take control of the area. However, soon they were displeased with the system. The Soviets first ordered that stores would stay open and that merchandise could only be sold for the Polish zlotys. Afterwards, it was announced that only a hundred zlotys per person would be exchanged for one hundred Russian rubles. The remaining zlotys which people had plenty of, completely lost their value. Private enterprises died immediately. Later, the government ordered that co-ops and workmen's associations be set up. Everything belonged to the state. Some merchants were hired as managers and others as common laborers. Skilled craftsmen such as tailors, shoemakers, and carpenters were organized into cooperative workshops. The regime was made up of members of the local population. The former police chief was a Jew and his entire family was sent to Siberia as a punishment. Because of this sentence, the family survived and they now live in Israel. The Great Synagogue was turned into a flour warehouse and the Jewish Folkshule became a Russian school.

In June of 1941 Germany attacked Russia. As the Germans arrived they established two ghettos in Druya. One was actually in the shtetl and it began at Leib Pukin's house at the bank of the Droike River. The second ghetto was beyond the cemetery. Unfortunately, we weren't able to gather more details here in Argentina, since very few escaped and survived the slaughter. All the rest were shot and all the Druya Jews were buried in one common grave. The slaughter took place on the second day of Tammuz 5702 (July 17, 1942). For more details read the Druya Yizkor book which was published in Israel.

Footnote:

1. The translator embellished the original narrative in this section.

[Page 397]

Kaziany

The Destruction of Kazan
(Kozyany, Belarus)
55°18' 26°52'
Translation supplied by Eilat Gordin Levitan

Geographical Position

The shtetl Kazan (Kaziany) was situated on high ground surrounded by forests. It was twenty kilometrs from Postovy and fifty from Szarkoviszizna, on the little Disenka River, which flowed into the huge Dvine river. The river was the source of livelihood for the Jews of the shtetl. During the summer, the logs of the surrounded forests were floated on this river to Riga. The Jewish population consisted of three hundred souls. Since there were about five thousand Christians, the Jewish population was barely noticed. The main Jewish occupations consisted of business in flax, wood, grain, and hides. They were also storekeepers. Some stores, where you could buy almost everything, were quite affluent and profitable. The only laborers in the shtetl were the tailor, shoemaker, and blacksmith.

After World War I, the shtetl experienced a cultural revival. A Folkshule (school), based on Yiddish traditions, and a more modern Hebrew Tarbut School were established. A Drama Circle was also organized and it performed the well-known plays of the Yiddish theatre repertoire, such as Gordin's *Slaughter*, Kobrin's *Village Boy*, *Sale of Joseph*, and others. The main performer was Shlomo Blacharovitsh, who also was the director. He had acted in the Moscow State Theatre. A second performer, who was also well-known, was Moshe Beigel. He had played in troupes together with Marevsky, Bulov, Kaminski, and others.

[Page 398]

The Drama Circle had a library which also served as a gathering place for the youth to engage in discussions.

Chona Feigel of blessed memory. From Kazan. Killed in the Glubokie Ghetto at the age of 58

Velvel Reichel of blessed memory. From Kazan. Killed in the Glubokie Ghetto.

In this way, the shtetl lived under the September of 1939, when the Russians arrived. The new regime instituted the order mentioned in the stories of previous shtetls. The only difference was that the rich Jews of Kazan were sent deep into the Soviet Union. Meir-Aaron Reichel was in this way saved from the destruction and now lives in Israel. The misfortune struck Kazan just like all other shtetls, with the coming of the Germans in the June of 1941. The first victims were the Feigel family. In the middle of the day, they took Chono Feigel, his son Hishke, and his daughter Rivke to Shlomo Hochman's garden, where they were all shot. In Kazan itself, no ghetto was set up. Most Kazan

[Page 399]

Jews fled into the forests, where many hid and fought with partisan movements until the end of the war. Some Jews fled to the Sz. ghetto and shared the fate of the Sz. Jews. The Jews that hid in the forests saved themselves from destruction. They were helped by the fact that Kazan was surrounded by large and thick forests. The high-command of the partisans was actually in that area and also the famous Tshapaiev-Otriad.

Leizer Shulkin and his wife Chaya-Feiga.

Gele Foigel with a few of her family members. All were killed in Kazan.

The Kazan Jews avenged themselves on the murderers – the Germans as well as the local Lithuanians and White Russians, taking them from their homes, "repaying" them, and then setting fire to their houses. The Germans got their repayment in another way. Bridges, warehouses, and railway lines were blown up and German-occupied villages were encircled, bombarded, or put to the torch.

[Page 400]

In these operations, the youth of Kazan were especially distinguished. Gutman Feigel and Leib Reichel were decorated more than once for their courage by the Russian partisan high-command. The German regime even put a high price on their heads. Guman Feigel survived, and he now lives in Vilna. After the liberation of Kazan, Leib Reichel voluntarily enlisted in the Russian Army. Unfortunately, he didn't live to see the murderers' final collapse since he fell in battle near Berlin.

The communal grave in Poligon

Baile Reichel

Also, of great help to the partisans in the Kazan forests was the mother of Leib Reichel. When the Germans entered Kazan, she was sixty-two years of age. She refused to wear the yellow Star of David and she dressed herself as a peasant in order to travel to surrounding villages in search of food for her family. As mentioned, many Kazan Jews had fled into the surrounding forests. At the time, there weren't any partisan groups yet. By themselves, they had to obtain provisions to live, as well as arms to defend themselves against the bloody enemy who lurked on every side. Baile Reichel displayed unusual heroism. She devoted herself completely to helping the Jews hiding in the forests. With her disguise as a peasant, she brought food, arms, and important news to the most dangerous places. In this way, she maintained communication between the Jews of the forests and those in the ghettos. In those trying times, a simple message that someone was still alive was very happy news. However, this was not her only task. She would also take Jews out of the Sz. and Glubokie ghettoes and show them where to find the partisans. Many Jews were saved in this way.

[Page 401]

Hirshke Foigel. Killed in Kazan.

**Leizer Shalkin's two children.
They were killed.**

Once, after she had led a young lad into the forest, she returned to find missing her husband Velvel and son Berke. The Jewish police had taken them to Glubokie for liquidation. There, the local regime demanded Jewish victims on a daily basis. She immediately went to Glubokie and came to the head of the Judenraat, Liderman. She begged that her husband and child be allowed to leave the ghetto. She promised him gold, but he wouldn't hear of it. They died in the Glubokie ghetto. She returned to the forest and this was understandably risky. She continued dressing as a peasant and acting as the contact between the partisans and the ghetto. When she arrived at Poligon Station near Sventzian, she was once more to experience tragedy in her life. The Germans had set up a ghetto in Poligon, into which they had driven the Jews from the surrounding small shtetls and villages. In this ghetto were her daughter Malka with her husband Meyer Gedud and their four children. Baile had arrived at the ghetto just before the eve of the slaughter. The Germans hired her to wash pots because they thought that she was a Christian. She wanted to take the son-in-law and a couple of the children out of the ghetto, but her daughter was tired and sick and didn't want to remain alone. A few days later, the slaughter took place and nine thousand Jews were butchered in one day. A huge pit was dug. They would put the victims on a board over the pit, shoot them with machine guns, and dump them into the pit. Many were buried alive in this fashion.

[Page 402]

Beile Reichel. Lives in Israel.

Beile Reichel with her daughter Rivka, Rivka's husband Mitelman, and their son Velvel.

[Page 403]

Baile Reichel, together with other peasants, witnessed this slaughter. She saw how her daughter Malka and her family were put on the board. . .

Returning the forests, she continued her work with the partisans. She eventually found one of her grandchildren who now lives in Kovno. To this day, many surviving partisans of the area speak with amazement about this wonderful and heroic woman. Fate brought her to Israel, and she lives there with her son Abraham who arrived during the Third Aliyah. Her daughter Rivke also lives there and she spent the war in Russia.

Baile is now seventy-five-years-old and she still helps her daughter with household chores. Jews come to her as to a saint. Unfortunately, until now, no one has undertaken the writing of her biography.

Hechalutz of Kazan and Vidz, 1932

[Page 404]

Former Kazan Partisans in Israel

As we mentioned, a good number of Kazan Jews, mostly the young, survived. They now live in Israel. Together with the Chalutzim who had arrived before the war, they are quite a group! They are: Tzvi Sversky, Sonia Chatzkels, Yentke Groisdorf, Abraham Reichel, Miriam Boim, Yosef Lipshitz, Baruch Lipshin, Shlomo Notels, Yisroelke Notkowitsh, and Fradke Sversky. In Argentina, one can find Hertz Reichel (Baile's son), Genye Feigel-Modlin and Yisroel Reichel.

[Page 404]

Pictures
Translated by Jerrold Landau
Pictures extracted by Larry Gaum

Paczurkes, a village near Kazan. The Reichel family stands near their mill.

[Page 405]

Public school, from Postavy, 1922

Dramatic club of the Zionist organization in Postavy

[Page 406]

Chapter of "Haoved" of Postavy parting from a Postavy family on the occasion of their aliya to the Land of Israel

A Postavy family

[Page 407]

The Postav teacher Kocikowicz with a group of students and friends, 1935

Postavy cemetery

[Page 408]

Chapter of "Haoved" of Postavy parting from a Postavy family on the occasion of their *aliya* to the Land of Israel

Luskier Folks School near Szarkowszczyzna

[Page 409]

Avraham Yitzchak, Gershon Bunimowicz's grandfather, from Postavy

A Jew of Postavy with his granddaughter

[Page 410]

The tailor Norodcki from Dunilowicz. He was killed in Dunilowicz

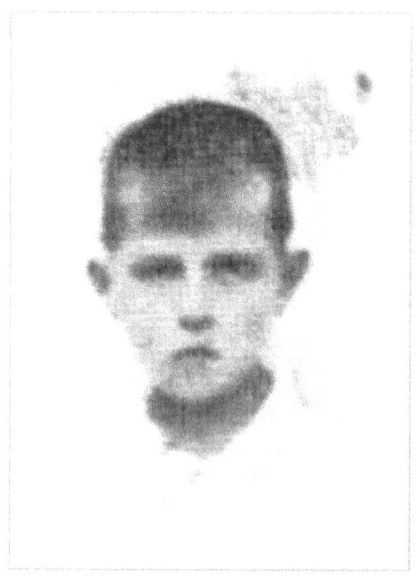

The child Herzl Icler of blessed memory. Child of Kopel Icler of Kazan. Died on July 26 in Buenos Aires at the age of 8.

Avraham Feigel from Kazan

[Page 411]

Yisrael Shpunt of blessed memory, died in New York at the age of 78 on January 2, 1949. **Rachel Leah Shpunt** of blessed memory, born in Dvinsk, lived all the years in Glubokie, then she traveled to her husband Yisrael Shpunt in America. She lived there for four years. In 1936, she went to her children Reuven and Yentl Shpunt in Argentina. She died in Buenos Aires at the age of 94 on November 12, 1955. Both are from Glubokie. A large crowd came to her funeral.

Translator's note: The dates here do not seem to present an accurate timeline

Yekutiel Rivkind – teacher from Postavy

[Page 412]

Sonia Chazan from Szarkowszczyzna. She was killed.

David Icler and Chieb Icler from Postavy. They were killed.

Moshe Paikin. Husband of Sonia Szmuszkowicz from Szarkowszczyzna. Killed in the Glubokie Ghetto.

Translator's note: I suspect the name is Chaim, and there is a typo

[Page 413].

Sara Devora Entin, born in 1913 in Lozowka. Lived in Druja. She was a Yiddish-Hebrew teacher in the towns of Horodziej and Lozszki. It is surmised that the peasants with whom she lived killed her.

[Page 414]

Zalke Gordon of blessed memory. Born on July 31, 1908 in Szarkowszczyzna. Died in Buenos Aires on the eve of Rosh Hashanah, September 27, 1954.

Professor of botany, a cousin of Sonia Kacowicz, born in Vilna. Lives in Poland.

[Page 415]

Motel Kacowicz. Nephew of Noach.
A partisan. Lives in Postavy.

Kopel Icler's brother from Postavy. Perished.

David Dorf, Shimon and Itshe Tiles, Cashe Tiles, Malka Tiles, and the children of Yisrael and Leizer of Glubokie. All perished.

[Page 416]

Moshe Paikin's mother and brother from Szarkowszczyzna. Perished.

Rachel-Lea Szulkin of blessed memory from Szarkowszczyzna. Died at age 65.

Kopel Icler's mother from Postavy

Shlomo Szulkin. 14 years old. Perished.

[Page 417]

Avraham Entin. Born in Druja, 1914. Served in the Polish Army. Underwent *hachsharah* in Beitar. Died fighting against the Germans.

A gravestone from the Druja cemetery. Our dear father, a pure, upright man. Kalman Uri Teitz the son of Reb Aharon Chaim of blessed memory. Died 13 Cheshvan 5637 (1936). May his soul be bound in the bonds of eternal life.

**Yehoshua Teitz. A partisan.
Lives in Druja.**

[Page 418]

Yoel Pinia Swirsky with his wife, children and grandchildren from Dunilowicz. All perished, aside from Noachke, who lives in Buenos Aires.

[Page 419]

Beilka Chadasz from Szarkowszczyzna with her friends after the liberation. The story of their experiences is included in the chapter "The Destruction of Szarkowszczyzna".

Leib Baum. A partisan from Kazan.

[Page 420]

At a celebration of the L'L organization. Shmerke Koczerginski of blessed memory is in the center.

Youth of Glubokie at a celebration in 1934

[Page 421]

Yentel Reichel de Povodofsky z"l

Yentel Reichel was the daughter of Yitzhak Reichel. Her mother was Laia-Reizel. Yentel was born in 1897 in Postov. She was orphaned very young and was raised by relatives. At a young age she left for Vilna where she worked in a bakery. Later, after the second World War, she returned to Michalishok. She was married in Postov to Yedida Povodofsky who came from Ozorkov, near Lodz. Yedida served in the Polish army, after the war ended he remained in Postov. In 1929 Yentel arrived in Argentina. She made her home in the Jewish quarter, "Wisha Krespa". Here Yentel became the "mother" of all the Landsleit that came from all the shtetls around Postov. Her home was the meeting place for all the expatriots. We felt the warmth radiating from our "old home". Her death, November 24, 1955, left a hole in our hearts. Her friendship will always be remembered. Her funeral drew a large crowd. Her eulogy was read by Ruben Lewin.

[Page 423]

Landsleit Organization of Skarkowszcyzna, Dunilovitch, Postov, Glubok and Environs
Translated by Anita Gabbay

Founding and Activity

December 14, 1946, at the home of Ruben Weinunsky, 15 Landsleit met with the vision to form an organization. It was at the time when the bitter news started pouring in about the survivors of the Holocaust, the survivors of our old home. We leaned on each other and we decided to do whatever was necessary.

The organization met and it was decided to locate and help those that survived from S./D./P./ and its surroundings, and even from other places if need be. The name decided was "Landsleit Organization for S./D/P. and others". At another meeting Glubokie was added to the name.

March 29, 1947, our first undertaking took place. All the Landsleit and their families met, which took place in Buenos-Aires. The meeting was very festive, never again were the numbers so large. Sholem Asch's book "The Thorn that Burns" was auctioned. We raised a lot of money. The moral enthusiasm was even greater. All the Landsleit felt that they belonged to one family.

The organization sent packages to the refugees who were still in Germany, Austria, France and Italy.

[Page 424]

We also sent papers to six Landsleit, who where in Italy. These papers were from the Paraguayan regime, although none of them wanted to remain in Paraguay.

Every year the organization leads a memorial service for our nearest and dearest. In the first years we conducted the service in a synagogue. We organized it in an evening, every detail. Most of the Landsleit came. In 1950 our organization presented 2 bronze covers for the monument to our Holy Martyrs, which can be found in the "Tablada" cemetery. Every year there is a memorial is at the cemetery, in the month of November-Sunday morning. A Chazzan says the prayers and we say the Kaddish. The monument: one part to remember the shtetls Skarkowszcyzna, Dunilovitch, Postov, Glubokie. The second part is for the memory of Druya, Kazan, Svir, Kobylnik, Pahost, Opsa, and Dokshitz.

[Page 425]

Such evenings were performed for the Landsman Ruben Weinunsky, on his return from North America, where he went on a search mission. As it turned out he read a list of our survivors. Many such acts were performed through the organization. Half the Yiskor book was subsidized by Nahum Katevitch and his wife.

Fellow townsfolk at a farewell evening for Noach Kacewicz and his wife upon their journey to the State of Israel

Our fellow townsfolk at a memorial ceremony at the monument for the martyrs at the cemetery in Toledo

Rivka Rifkind (da) Greenberg also contributed to various causes, she came from Israel. Also, from Minia Kohen, North America. Mrs. Schpunt, the sister of Ruben Schpunt, from Glubokie, came for a short visit from North America. To Zelig Modlin who went for a visit to North America, for Hertzke Reichel who went for a visit to Israel. A wonderful farewell evening was prepared for the Skarkowczcyzner Leib Schulkin, on his departure for North America. He was one of the most active volunteers of the organization. An evening for the chairman Shloime Suskevitch when he issued his philosophical journal "Dvaka". Another important event took place to honor the pioneer

[Page 426]

Mendel Reichel, who made Aliya to Eretz Israel. We welcomed the Landsleit from America Benia and Ethel Brezg. They were Kopel Itzler's sister and brother-in-law.

The organization welcomed the refugees from the old home. April 9, 1949, the first known faces arrived, Shachna and Chana Schteinman, and the Dunilovitcher Chaia Muskat, Yitzhak Muskat and Avraham Muskat. They endured the entire Nazi occupation and liquidations of their shtetls. They told their stories for hours about their struggles, life and liquidations. This was the first news of our old home.

November 7, 1951, Beilka Hadash was the second to arrive. Her survival is outlined in the Yiskor Book. That evening we heard a few words about her struggle for survival.

A separate joy was the evening the organization gave praise to Avraham Reichel, who came for a short visit from Israel. He was in Israel over 25 years. He was one of the most active Halutzim that came from our region. He also gave us a greeting of good wishes from our Israeli Landsleit.

Current Management of the Landsleit Organization

Chairman:	Shlomo Suskevitch
Vice-Chairman:	Nahum Katavitch and Hertz Reichel
Secretary:	Berek Weinunsky
Treasurers:	Nachke Swirski and Ruvke Schpunt
Board members:	Alter Schulkin, Zelig Modlin, Meir Swirski, Shloimke Feigelson, Ruben Lewin, Tanchum Pintzov, Chaim Tiles, and Moishe Chazan
Translators/Accountants:	Kopel Itzler, Yehoushe Schuskevitch
Women's committee:	Malka Steinberg, Yente Tiles, Sonia Katavitch, Rosa Reichel, Itke Swirski, Gesia Modlin, Chana Steinman, Itke Gurevitch, Rocke Schpier, Sheindel Schpunt, and Chana Schulkin

[Page 427]

The current committee of the Landsleit organization of Szarkowszczyzna, Dunilowicz, Postavy, Glubokie, and region in Argentina

[Page 428]

A group of town natives in the first years after their arrival in Argentina, 1930

[Introductory Spanish pages]
Typed up by Genia Hollander

M. y Z. RAJAK
IN MEMORIAN DE LAS COMUNIDADES
JUDIAS DE GLEBOKIE, SZARKOW-
SZCZYZNA, DUNILOWICZE,
POSTAWY, DRUJA, Y KAZIANY,
EXTERMINADAS POR LA BARBARIE
NAZI – GERMANA.
DESTRUCTICCION DE COMMUNIDADES JUDIAS DE
RUSIA BLANCA – LITHUANIA (PROV. DE WILNA).
Redactor: SALOMON SUSKOVICH
* * *
Editado por la Sociedad de Residentes de Szarkowszczyzna,
Dunilowicze, Postawy y Glebokie en la Argentina.
BUENOS AIRES
1956

Translation:
M. and Z. RAJAK
IN MEMORIAL OF THE JEWISH COMMUNITIES
OF GLEBOKIE, SZARKOW-
SZCZYZNA, DUNILOWICZE,
POSTAWY, DRUJA, AND KAZIANY,
EXTERMINATED BY THE
NAZI-GERMAN BARBARIAN.
DESTRUCTION OF JEWISH COMMUNITIES
OF WHITE RUSSIA - LITHUANIA (PROV. OF WILNA).
Editor: SALOMON SUSKOVICH
* * *
Edited by the Society of Residents of Szarkowszczyzna,
Dunilowicze, Postawy and Glebokie in Argentina.
BUENOS AIRES
1956

Printed in Argentina

THIS BOOK FINISHED PRINTING ON MAY 24, 1956,
AT THE GRAPHICS WORKSHOPS "ZLOTOPIORO
BUENOS AIRES, REPUBLIC OF ARGENTINA.

Este libro ésta dedicado a la memoria de nuestros seres
queridos, mujeres, jóvenes y ninos que sin excepción fueron
exterminados por la barbarie nazi-germana.
DESTRUCCION DE GLEBOKIE. 6,000 almas:
20 de Agosto de 1943.
DESTRUCCION DE SZARKOWSZCZYZNA. 1,800 almas:
18 de Julio de 1942.

DESTRUCCION DE DUNILOWICZE. 900 almas:
22 de Noviembre de 1942.
DESTRUCCION DE POSTAWY. 2,500 almas:
25 de Diciembre de 1942.
DESTRUCCION DE DRUJA. 2,500 almas:
17 de Julio de 1942.
DESTRUCCION DE KAZIANY. 300 almas:
20 de Agosto de 1943.
Rogamos a nuestros connacionales que no organicien fiestas privadas a reuniones sociales en la fecha de estos aniversarios. Rogamos a nuestros connacionales que en la fecha de estos aniversarios lean capitulos de este libro.

Translation:
This book is dedicated to the memory of our loved ones, women, youth and children who without exception were exterminated by Nazi-German barbarism.

DESTRUCTION OF GLEBOKIE. 6,000 souls:
August 20, 1943.
DESTRUCTION OF SZARKOWSZCZYZNA. 1,800 souls:
July 18, 1942.
DESTRUCTION OF DUNILOWICZE. 900 souls:
November 22, 1942.
DESTRUCTION OF POSTAWY. 2,500 souls:
December 25, 1942.
DESTRUCTION OF DRUJA. 2,500 souls:
July 17, 1942.
DESTRUCTION OF KAZIANY. 300 souls:
August 20, 1943.

We ask our nationals not to organize private parties or social gatherings on the date of these anniversaries. We ask our compatriots to read the chapters of this book on the date of these anniversaries.

NAME INDEX

A

Aarons, 42, 43
Abbalevich, 245
Abel, 321, 323, 326
Abel, 354
Abes, 316, 323
Abilovitch, 352
Abramovitsh, 155, 156, 169
Abramovitz, 251
Abramowitz, 140
Abrarnovitsh, 174
Aditska, 125
Aditzka, 151
Agranat, 190
Aidanson, 237
Aidis, 242
Aigas, 233
Aks, 349, 357
Alai, 141
Alai, 252
Alay, 250
Aleichem, 21, 322
Alexander, 183, 346
Almer, 61, 64, 117, 143
Alperin, 237
Alperovitch, 28
Alperovitch, 236
Alperovitsh, 130, 140, 142, 161, 176, 251
Alperovitz, 251, 256
Alter, 143, 176, 177, 196, 233, 235, 242, 252, 253, 254, 300, 318, 386, 423
Alyasha, 152
Anski, 389
Arie, 194

Arka, 355
Arnas, 248
Aronovitch, 355
Aronovitsh, 321, 323
Aronson, 191
Askerka, 190
Asman, 251
Asmans, 44
Atman, 240
Aygas, 233, 256
Ayges, 235, 236
Azeshinski, 251
Azshinski, 256
Azshinsky, 143, 176
Aztinsky, 57

B

Badanes, 349
Badanivo, 257
Badavo, 244
Badnyov, 234
Bagin, 125, 128, 138, 143
Baker, 246
Band, 239
Baoudin, 18
Baravak, 59
Barkan, 331, 377
Barkan, 233, 250, 257
Barkin, 305, 318, 321, 322, 323
Barkin, 349
Barkman, 372
Baryudin, 243
Barzan, 255
Bass, 241, 352
Baszewkin, 290

Bat Shimon, 30
Baum, 307, 417
Baylis, 360
Baziki, 191
Becker, 124, 142, 148, 189
Begin, 250
Beigel, 395
Beirach, 354
Bemma, 83, 84
Bemmo, 189
Benson, 356
Benya, 351
Berchan, 148
Berchon, 282, 283, 288, 291, 293
Berchov, 140
Bergman, 321
Berkan, 151, 180, 193
Berkan, 251, 252
Berkowitz, 71
Berman, 101
Berman, 354
Berniakovitch, 59
Bernstein, 233, 241
Berzan, 255
Bialik, 115, 322, 387
Bielinske, 22
Bik, 238
Bimbad, 254
Binyaminson, 237, 247
Bipkin, 228
Birnzveig, 252
Birsh, 217
Birsz, 220
Birzas, 235
Birzesh, 257
Birzsh, 98
Birzsn, 186
Blach, 84
Blacharovitsh, 395

Blaichman, 241
Blandt, 233
Blant, 69, 149, 162
Blatt, 69, 152, 187, 194, 195, 215, 218, 222, 226, 229, 307
Blatt, 246
Bleichman, 241
Bliachman, 228
Bliat, 353
Blichman, 257
Bloch, 256
Blut, 256, 257
Bodavo, 242
Bodnav, 233
Bodovo, 241
Bogin, 16
Boim, 401
Bok, 59
Borosok, 352
Botvinick, 81, 143
Boydin, 250
Boyer, 240, 241
Brassen, 243
Braun, 248
Brezg, 422
Britanishske, 133
Britanishsky, 15, 33, 35, 49
Britanistisky, 27
Brodne, 349
Brodny, 324
Brodny, 251
Brokovski, 245
Brown, 161
Buchhalter, 57
Budav, 139, 160
Budavo, 254
Budin, 141
Budniov, 69
Budov, 63, 103

Bulov, 395
Bunimowicz, 407
Burshtein, 282
Butchko, 59
Buzak, 391

C

Cantor, 119, 379
Catkin, 148
Cepelevitz, 367
Cepelovitsh, 323
Chachalka, 63
Chadash, 163, 284
Chadash, 248, 257, 348, 350, 351, 352, 353, 358
Chadasz, 304, 309, 417
Chadshan, 163
Chaikin, 348, 349
Chaim, 387
Chamtzenko, 196
Chanovitch, 239
Chanovitsh, 25
Chasash, 187
Chatzkels, 401
Chaves, 18, 24, 78, 92, 149
Chaves, 256
Chaveson, 49
Chavkin, 159
Chazan, 102, 103, 135, 210, 279, 282, 284, 287, 288, 295, 298, 299, 300, 303, 308, 410, 423
Cheifetz, 252, 257
Chelvina, 254
Chevlin, 18, 133
Chevlin, 251, 252
Chidekel, 130, 275, 282
Chidelel, 304
Chodesh, 244
Chodosh, 96, 116, 322, 367

Cipelowicz, 304
Cohen, 108, 143, 174, 176
Cooperstock, 251
Cymer, 291, 304

D

Daitch, 245
Daitche, 254
Dambrovski, 59
Damshkin, 244
Danchin, 254
Danilevich, 239
Dazkes, 351
Dimenstein, 257
Dimmenstein, 236, 244
Dinnestein, 243
Disvitsky, 180
Dlut, 353
Dlutt, 244
Dombrovski, 74
Dratove, 356
Dratve, 321
Dratwe, 353
Dreizenshtok, 257
Dreizenstock, 236, 243
Dreizin, 230
Drisavietzki, 239
Drisviatskes, 93
Drisviatzky, 159
Drizenshtok, 63
Drotz, 56
Drunanov, 386
Drutz, 139, 316
Drutz, 233, 237, 354, 355, 357
Drutzs', 125
Dubrovski, 59, 191
Dvaskin, 240
Dveskin, 256
Dvorkin, 250

Dvoskin, 251
Dworszecki, 4
Dzaizinkar, 255

E

Ehrenberg, 37, 136
Einhorn, 377
Einstein, 323
Eisenman, 372
Eiten, 288
Eliakum, 26
Eliannav, 249
Elzon, 348
Endel, 322
Entin, 382, 383, 384, 394, 411, 415
Epstein, 234
Estrin, 103, 282, 283, 296, 303, 374
Eterise, 322
Etkin, 194
Etman, 257
Ettingaff, 140
Ettingoff, 107
Ettman, 241

F

Faigelson, 28, 108
Faiman, 240
Falant, 250
Fayman, 253
Fegelman, 257
Feigel, 153, 195, 216, 217, 220, 322, 324, 396, 397, 401, 408
Feigel, 353
Feigelman, 26, 141, 152, 195
Feigelman, 249
Feigelson, 126, 140, 153, 162, 224, 423
Feigl, 320
Feinweitz, 381, 382
Felsher, 349
Ferder, 233
Feyga, 236
Feygel, 257, 352
Feygelman, 234, 250, 257
Feygelson, 233, 234, 237, 240, 243, 244, 246, 248, 256
Feygl, 235
Feyglson, 257
Fidelhaltz, 247
Fidelholtz, 175, 179, 217, 220
Fidelholtz, 235, 244, 255, 257
Fierman, 255
Filipak, 191
Finkelstein, 241, 244, 358
Fisher, 93, 247
Fisher, 241, 245, 247, 248, 250, 351, 354, 358
Fishers, 125
Fishman, 240
Fleischer, 246
Fleisher, 159, 163
Fliesher, 256
Fliskin, 44
Fliskin, 254
Foigel, 397, 399
Foigl, 304, 372, 377
Forman, 350, 357
Fran, 247
Freeman, 109
Freidkin, 141
Freidkins, 96
Freydkin, 137
Freydkin, 233, 247, 254, 257
Friedeland, 241
Friedkin, 244
Friedman, 28, 44, 69, 140, 150, 169, 195, 367, 372, 373, 374, 375
Friedman, 237, 242, 244, 247, 249, 250, 251, 255, 257, 350, 356

Frishman, 1, 197, 230, 284, 300
Frogovich, 244
Fronovitsh, 98
Frumin, 249, 252
Frumkin, 240
Furman, 335, 337

G

Gabbay, 1, 197, 230, 284, 300, 420
Gadenson, 184
Galberstein, 139
Galitzianer, 155
Ganshtein, 240
Garber, 355, 358
Gatkin, 240
Gatlib, 257
Gaum, 260, 402
Gaz, 350, 351, 353
Gebell, 67
Gedud, 399
Gefen, 252
Geffen, 245
Geidenzon, 181
Geiler, 191
Gelberstein, 247, 255
Geler, 255
Geller, 28, 63, 137
Geller, 233
Gelman, 165, 173, 182, 235, 285
Gelman, 234, 252, 257, 259
Gelvan, 143
Gendel, 314
Gendel, 350, 352, 353, 355, 356, 358
Genichavitsh, 195
Genichovitsh, 151
Genshtein, 249, 257
Genshteyn, 228
Genstein, 253
Gentzel, 337

German, 28
Gidenson, 185, 186, 187
Gilavitch, 236
Gilberstein, 236, 237
Gildin, 149, 175
Gilevitch, 69
Gilevitsh, 180
Gilewicz, 223
Gindin, 234, 236, 238, 241, 245
Ginsberg, 28
Ginsberg, 235
Ginsburg, 246, 354, 356
Gintzburg, 278
Ginzburg, 325, 326
Gitelson, 140, 142, 159
Gitelson, 240, 251, 257
Gitelzon, 81, 84, 92, 119, 128, 184, 186, 191
Gitelzon, 233, 235, 236, 241
Gitelzons, 93
Gitlitz, 238, 257
Gittelzon, 44
Gittleman, 35
Glanzet, 241
Glass, 63
Glassman, 160
Glavan, 235
Glavman, 240
Glavnitzki, 198
Glaz, 18
Glaz, 237, 238, 243, 245
Glazman, 140
Glazman, 241
Glezer, 153
Godin, 18, 161, 162
Godin, 251
Goldberg, 141, 142, 160, 189
Goldberg, 254
Goldman, 338, 349
Goldman, 242, 349, 350

Golomb, 372, 375

Gordin, 1, 2, 5, 8, 10, 30, 47, 48, 50, 54, 57, 58, 59, 60, 62, 64, 67, 70, 71, 72, 73, 74, 83, 85, 86, 88, 90, 91, 94, 97, 100, 106, 108, 115, 123, 128, 132, 137, 139, 144, 150, 155, 156, 158, 166, 168, 170, 172, 174, 179, 185, 232, 274, 279, 311, 322, 327, 348, 377, 381, 395

Gordol, 355

Gordon, 44, 52, 69, 84, 93, 110, 116, 119, 126, 140, 141, 148, 153, 154, 163, 164, 165, 177, 188, 195, 228, 242, 251, 373, 375, 412

Gordon, 236, 240, 243, 249, 251, 252, 256, 257, 350, 351, 352, 353, 354, 355, 358

Gotkin, 239

Gotkins, 235

Graber, 238

Gramlin, 238

Greenberg, 422

Grilicher, 352

Grinevitsh, 190

Grishkevitsh, 81

Grod, 154

Groisdorf, 401

Grosbein, 241

Grudman, 190

Gurevich, 241, 245

Gurevitch, 423

Gurevitch, 349, 350, 353, 354, 355, 358

Gurevitsh, 18, 139

Gurvirtsh, 326

Gurvitsh, 137, 143, 161, 321, 325, 334, 338

Guta, 30

Gutkin, 241

Guzava, 163, 190

H

Haberkorn, 141, 159

Haberkorn, 253

Haberman, 96, 141

Hadash, 33, 423

Hadash, 240

Hait, 142, 189

Hakner, 250

Hanowicz, 269, 270, 273

Hap, 255

Haradishz, 78

Havas, 238, 244, 246

Havkin, 243, 245

Hazan, 81, 210

Hebel, 142, 147, 154, 162, 188

Heberling, 142, 143, 189

Heinliat, 142, 160, 189

Heit, 165, 293

Hershman, 193

Hertz, 167, 233, 257, 259, 304, 401, 423

Hidekel, 196

Hidekel, 238, 239, 243

Hidekels, 93

Hirshman, 194

Hite, 101

Hittelmacher, 324

Hlarkov, 195

Hoberman, 196

Hoberman, 251, 252

Hochman, 142, 154, 188, 396

Hochmann, 62

Hoffman, 56

Hoffman, 243

Hoichman, 182, 184, 190

Hoychman, 239, 240, 245, 246

I

Ichilitsik, 238

Ichiltsik, 69, 124

Icler, 408, 411, 413, 414

Igeses, 98

Irma, 236
Israelev, 153, 154
Israelovitch, 257
Itin, 234, 235
Itkin, 177
Itzes, 275
Itzler, 422, 423
Ivanov, 53, 54
Izikson, 374
Izikson, 354
Izraelov, 139

K

Kac, 285
Kacewicz, 421
Kacowicz, 412, 413
Kagan, 332
Kagan, 351, 353, 354
Kahn, 49
Kaks, 240
Kalmanovitch, 27
Kaminkovich, 240
Kaminkovitch, 353, 356
Kaminkovitsh, 325
Kaminska, 194
Kaminski, 395
Kaminski, 253
Kaminsky, 234
Kan, 240
Kandratin, 191
Kanis, 235
Kanovitch, 28
Kanterovich, 233
Kantorovitsh, 175, 176, 177
Kantrovitz, 56
Kapekovitsh, 332
Kapeliavitsh, 195
Kapenberg, 151
Kapenvald, 142

Kapfenval, 112
Kapfenvald, 189
Kapilovich, 234, 237
Kapilovitch, 349
Kaplan, 230
Kaplan, 239
Karashnavsky, 246
Kardiel, 155
Kasar, 141
Kasdan, 228
Kasher, 93
Kasovska, 175, 176
Kaspzshitzki, 192
Kasriel, 27, 111, 139, 140, 197, 382
Katavitch, 423
Katevitch, 421
Katscharginski, 238
Katsherginsky, 141
Katz, 24, 25, 26, 33, 44, 47, 61, 68, 89, 117, 119, 141, 142, 160, 197, 234, 246
Katz, 233, 242, 243, 244, 245, 246, 247, 248, 249, 250, 254, 257, 258, 353
Katzavitsh, 141, 153, 323, 372
Katzin, 351
Katzovitch, 6, 28
Katzovitsh, 130, 375
Katzovitz, 2, 374
Katzovitz, 241, 248, 258, 351, 353, 357
Kazdan, 229
Kazdan, 233, 234
Kaziel, 251
Kazliner, 158
Kazliner, 254
Kazshdan, 184, 185, 186, 187
Kazvan, 392
Kern, 139, 142, 154, 159, 163, 165, 166, 167, 189
Kevlin, 44
Khait, 253

Khodosh, 367
Kiselevski, 105
Kiupt, 180
Klave, 193
Kleiner, 352, 355, 356
Klianer, 151
Kliat, 238
Kliner, 352
Klionsky, 320
Kliot, 71
Kliyupt, 180
Klonski, 349
Knall, 238, 239, 241, 246
Knel, 140, 304
Kochanovski, 231
Kocikowicz, 405
Koczerginski, 418
Koenigsberg, 98
Koenigsbergs, 93
Kogan, 381, 383
Kohen, 422
Kohen, 242, 248
Kolis, 318, 320, 322, 323, 324
Kolye, 92, 183
Konigsberg, 235, 244
Kontorowicz, 306
Koopershtok, 27
Kopilovich, 243, 247
Kopilovitch, 348, 357
Kopyetz, 233
Korilavo, 246
Koritzky, 355
Korizky, 358
Korman, 234
Korolenka, 63
Kosher, 252
Kosovski, 258
Kotz, 5, 8, 10, 30, 69, 140, 186
Kozliner, 54, 63, 193

Kozlovski, 59
Kozshdans, 181
Kozyol, 190
Kramer, 235, 245
Krapivnik, 103, 160
Krashnevsky, 161
Kraut, 114, 119, 160, 164
Kraut, 234, 235, 244, 248, 251, 252
Kravietz, 118, 140, 197
Kravitz, 57
Kravitz, 235
Kraynes, 235
Kreines, 140, 160
Kremer, 140, 197, 223
Kremer, 233, 258
Krieger, 189
Krivitchanin, 59
Krivitshanin, 74
Krivitzki, 242
Krivitzky, 98, 142
Kropivnik, 296
Kropivnik, 243
Kulbis, 137
Kurak, 141, 186, 216, 217, 220
Kurenitz, 131, 342
Kurenitz, 252
Kuritzky, 325
Kurkudiansky, 92
Kutchak, 223

L

Labanak, 82
Lablanka, 159
Laiman, 248, 258
Landau, 1, 3, 4, 7, 106, 111, 139, 159, 197, 230, 260, 284, 300, 402
Lankin, 239, 245
Lapka, 240
Lavanak, 59

Lederman, 61, 67, 68, 110, 117, 137, 144, 146, 152, 153, 154, 156, 157, 158, 161, 169, 176, 195, 196

Lederman, 247, 258

Leibl, 69, 148, 162, 187, 194, 259

Leibovitz, 242

Leiman, 196

Leizer, 81, 196, 296, 304, 349, 397, 399, 413

Lekach, 27, 29, 80, 96, 139, 140, 193

Lekach, 234, 248, 258

Lenkevitch, 59

Lev, 14

Levandovski, 49, 59

Levendovski, 74

Levin, 149, 174, 247, 383

Levin, 248, 258

Levine, 196

Levinson, 246, 250

Levis, 141

Levit, 246, 250, 258

Levitan, 1, 2, 5, 8, 10, 30, 35, 47, 48, 50, 54, 57, 58, 59, 60, 62, 64, 67, 70, 71, 72, 73, 74, 83, 85, 86, 88, 90, 91, 94, 97, 100, 106, 108, 115, 123, 126, 128, 132, 137, 139, 144, 150, 155, 156, 158, 166, 168, 170, 172, 174, 179, 185, 232, 274, 279, 311, 327, 348, 377, 395

Levitan, 249, 251, 255, 258

Levitanos, 26, 246

Lewi, 304

Lewin, 218, 419, 423

Lewitanus, 307

Liderman, 399

Lieberman, 248

Lifshin, 194

Ligomski, 350

Ligumski, 334

Ligumsky, 318, 319, 321, 322, 323, 327

Linkovsky, 357

Linkowski, 351

Linkowsky, 357

Linushkin, 139

Lipshin, 191, 401

Lipshin, 237, 242, 243

Lipshitz, 401

Lipszin, 304

Lisitzki, 250

Livshitz, 350

Lublinski, 297

Lubotzky, 368

Luria, 391

Luria, 352

Lurie, 318, 319, 321

M

Magilnik, 235

Mahler, 234, 248

Maisel, 326

Makar, 103, 164

Malishkevich, 248

Maliyeskevich, 241

Mandelbaum, 27

Mandelboim, 235

Manfilk, 330

Mankevich, 240

Manpil, 351, 354, 358

Marevsky, 395

Mark, 4, 30, 127, 326, 388

Markman, 228

Markman, 238, 248, 258

Markov, 337

Martzinkevitsh, 84

Marx, 136

Masnavick, 174

Mazavetzki, 251

Mazavetzky, 141, 176

Mazovetzky, 130

Meierovitch, 64

Meirovich, 245
Meirovitch, 348
Mekar, 296
Melamed, 98, 235, 237, 313
Melamed, 235, 249, 258
Meler, 250, 255, 258
Melnikov, 340, 341, 342
Meltzer, 139
Meltzer, 239, 252
Menches, 352
Mendel, 27, 44, 139, 174, 233, 234, 235, 236, 238, 240, 241, 244, 245, 246, 250, 251, 254, 257, 259, 290, 292, 300, 303, 304, 351, 360, 422
Mentkowitch, 44
Metler, 180
Meyerovitch, 61
Miakinin, 49, 140
Michelman, 138
Michl, 195
Midyuk, 244
Milanda, 303
Milchman, 141, 153, 196
Milchman, 258
Miler, 255, 256
Milkin, 153
Milkin, 237, 258
Miller, 234
Milner, 282, 284
Milshtein, 233, 254
Mind, 186
Mindalin, 250
Mindel, 125, 217, 282, 290, 375
Mindel, 237, 240, 248, 258, 350, 352, 355, 356, 358
Mindelin, 237
Minder, 349, 356
Mindlin, 24, 282
Mindlin, 235

Minushkin, 160
Mirlin, 119
Mirman, 125, 130, 133, 142, 228
Mirman, 236, 237, 242, 245, 247, 258
Mitzelitza, 287
Modlin, 401, 422, 423
Modow, 296
Moldin, 379
Molotov, 34, 37
Monkito, 252
Moosin, 174
Morre, 189
Moses, 252
Munbaz, 61
Munbez, 176
Munboz, 180
Muncaz, 114
Munevez, 256
Munkaz, 177
Munvoz, 16
Mushkat, 313, 327, 329, 331
Mushkat, 252, 348, 349, 357
Musin, 141, 247
Musin, 247
Musins, 218
Musiz, 61
Muskat, 290, 422
Myakinin, 247
Myates, 256
Myattas, 235

N

Nalanzokn, 57
Naratzky, 318, 319, 320, 331
Narutzki, 355, 356
Natanson, 143
Natanson, 251, 254
Natarius, 140
Naumov, 54, 75, 142, 191

Naumtshik, 376
Naumtship, 373
Niedzieletz, 178, 191
Niyami, 239
Norodcki, 408
Notels, 401
Notkowitsh, 401
Novick, 35

O

Oks, 325
Olmer, 56, 148
Ortoyav, 211
Ostashevski, 54
Ostrovski, 190
Ostrovski, 250
Ostrovsky, 61, 82, 158
Ozshinsky, 173

P

Padnas, 167, 259
Padnos, 228
Paikin, 389, 411, 414
Pajkin, 303, 304, 309
Pak, 140
Palant, 141
Palavnik, 244
Paliach, 246
Pan, 233, 244
Passenson, 239
Patkin, 248
Paulski, 190
Peak, 241
Peck, 251
Peikin, 196
Pen, 291
Peretz, 113, 116, 129, 130, 193, 194, 235, 247, 322, 350, 386
Perlman, 352

Perman, 354
Perovoskin, 354
Pesenson, 251
Peterson, 189
Philipak, 82
Piasachavo, 239
Pidelholz, 238
Pildas, 103, 139, 164, 296
Pilskin, 253, 255
Pinczow, 221
Pines, 109
Pintzov, 57, 61, 69, 163, 195, 196, 251, 252, 254, 258, 423
Pintzov, 249
Pipik, 186, 223
Pipik, 252
Plavin, 124
Plavnik, 245, 246
Pliskin, 18, 56, 165, 233, 242
Pliskin, 233, 242, 249, 258
Pobalski, 59
Podnos, 141, 174, 186, 252
Podnos, 251
Polyak, 125
Pomieto, 192
Popkin, 241, 242
Povodofsky, 419
Prader, 247
Pren, 140
Pren, 251
Prevezkin, 252
Pupka, 238
Pupko, 93

R

Rabbinovitch, 236
Rabinovitch, 250, 252
Rabinovitsh, 186, 368
Rabinovitz, 258

Rabinowich, 277, 278

Rabinowicz, 289

Rabinowitz, 138, 140, 142

Rabinzon, 26

Radaskovitsh, 103

Radianov, 166

Raiack, 112, 116

Raiak, 109, 135, 142, 161

Raichel, 354

Rain, 162

Rajack, 78

Rajak, 1, 2, 7, 8, 9, 10, 11, 13, 15, 21, 24, 27, 30, 31, 36, 37, 39, 40, 42, 47, 66, 96, 210, 231, 271, 293, 306

Rajak, 244, 258, 425

Ram, 162

Ram, 255

Rapaport, 240, 243, 246

Rapoport, 252, 258, 259

Rappaport, 79, 136, 186

Raskin, 53

Rayak, 130, 184

Raychel, 252, 352

Rayder, 253

Razavo, 235, 353, 356

Reichel, 367, 396, 397, 398, 400, 401, 402, 419, 422, 423

Reichel, 237, 242, 243, 248

Reichl, 92

Reichles, 93

Reikhel, 367

Reinas, 247

Reynstein, 242

Reyzel, 351

Rifkind, 422

Rivkin, 237

Rivkind, 409

Rodoskowicz, 296

Rodstein, 25

Rodstein, 241

Roichman, 372, 373, 375

Rosenblum, 234

Rosenfeld, 318

Rosentreter, 165

Rothenberg, 141

Rottenberg, 246

Rozavo, 248

Rozet, 193

Rozof, 290

Rozov, 283, 318

Rozshanski, 282

Rubashkin, 61, 157, 169

Rubaskin, 237

Rubenstein, 368

Ruchman, 373

Ruderman, 149, 153, 160, 161, 195, 330, 333, 354

Ruderman, 234, 236, 249, 250, 258, 353, 356, 357, 358

Rudstein, 227

Rudzik, 291

Russkevitsh, 179

Rutshakavsky, 151

Ryder, 44

S

Safra, 49

Safra, 246

Salavaitshik, 126

Salavyechik, 236

Samasianek, 153

Sapehi, 378

Sara, 349

Sarkin, 238

Sasnovick, 241

Sasnovik, 259

Satnowik, 219

Sazikin, 194

Scheinkman, 240

Schleisser, 234

Schmidt, 243

Schneider, 355

Schneiderman, 111

Schneir, 247

Schpier, 423

Schpunt, 422, 423

Schteinman, 422

Schulheifer, 44, 211

Schulkin, 422, 423

Schultz, 142

Schuskevitch, 423

Schwartz, 79

Sesnovik, 246

Shachna, 253

Shachnovitsh, 26

Shaindlin, 109

Shaknovitch, 244

Shalkin, 399

Shamash, 81, 139, 237, 241, 249, 272, 349, 351

Shames, 248

Shapira, 24, 69

Shapira, 234, 235, 236, 237, 241, 245, 246, 248, 249, 254, 259, 349, 354, 357

Shapiro, 18, 43, 69, 92, 140, 153, 154, 156, 193, 222, 223, 367, 373, 375

Sharaveika, 161

Shaynkman, 24

Shebeka, 81

Sheinbaum, 141

Sheinbaum, 254

Sheindelin, 237

Sheindlin, 69

Sheinkman, 69

Sheinkman, 235, 242, 256

Shell, 159

Shenker, 252

Shepsenwhol, 252

Sher, 245

Sherel, 348

Sheres, 195

Sherman, 250

Sherzon, 35

Sherzon, 251

Shiendelin, 240

Shitzkin, 139

Shitzkin, 238

Shmid, 251

Shnayerson, 43

Shneider, 355

Shneidman, 139

Shneir, 125

Shnell, 149

Shneyor, 251

Shnieder, 351

Shniedman, 253

Shnitzer, 368

Shov, 259

Shparber, 24, 69, 92, 153

Shparber, 239

Shpeer, 142

Shper, 189

Shper, 253

Shperber, 223

Shperber, 259

Shpier, 140

Shpier, 233

Shpunt, 409

Shpyer, 252

Shrira, 141, 167

Shrira, 259

Shteingrab, 352

Shtshebes, 191

Shub, 186, 191, 196, 283

Shubitz, 368

Shuchman, 139

Shuchman, 247, 254
Shukman, 246
Shulavitch, 236
Shulevitsh, 108, 126, 149
Shulhaifer, 234
Shulhayfer, 250
Shulhayper, 240
Shulheifer, 24, 108, 113, 114, 133, 143, 149, 175, 179, 187
Shulheiser, 61
Shulkin, 276, 397
Shulkin, 247, 249
Shulman, 107, 125, 242, 367
Shulman, 237, 240, 242
Shulovitch, 28
Shultz, 93, 160
Shulvitsh, 140
Shutav, 130
Shuvitz, 367
Shvimmer, 333
Simkin, 233
Sirman, 234
Sivka, 63
Skiransky, 316, 322
Skolnik, 196
Skolnink, 239
Skransky, 351, 353, 355
Skronsky, 352
Slabadkin, 259
Slabodkin, 18
Slabodkin, 233
Slavin, 241, 243, 244, 250, 351
Slidzevskes, 95
Slobodkin, 223
Slonimski, 253
Slonimsky, 57
Slutzkin, 239
Smids, 189
Smolski, 191

Sodenkovitch, 59
Sogovitz, 253
Solkin, 245
Solomon, 318
Solovay, 351
Soloveitshik, 153, 154, 180, 195
Solovietzick, 249, 250, 251, 252
Solovietzik, 249
Solovyechik, 246
Solovyetchik, 258
Sosman, 259
Spakovski, 191
Sparber, 61
Sper, 247
Speyer, 234, 245
Sragavitch, 69
Sragavitsh, 115, 142, 167
Sragovitch, 259
Srogovich, 243, 244
Srogovitz, 245
Stankevitch, 216, 218
Stankevitsh, 103
Stankewicz, 296
Statzevitsh, 104
Steinberg, 423
Steinman, 284, 298, 299, 300, 304, 423
Subbatin, 190
Sudinkovitsh, 74
Supernik, 247
Suskevitch, 422, 423
Suskovich, 425
Suskovitsh, 284
Sverdelin, 234
Sverdlin, 130, 161, 230
Sversky, 401
Svidler, 18
Svirsky, 311, 323, 327, 331
Swardlin, 234
Swedler, 255

Swerdlin, 255, 349, 350, 351, 353
Swidler, 258
Swiedler, 248
Swirski, 423
Swirski, 350, 356
Swirsky, 416
Szmuskowicz, 309, 311
Szmuszkowicz, 411
Szoklin, 292
Szulkin, 300, 301, 304, 414
Szvatz, 239

T

Tabarowicz, 302
Taitch, 351
Tarases, 302
Targanski, 59
Targonski, 74
Tarna, 240
Teitch, 233
Teitelboim, 252
Teitz, 415, 416
Teller, 177
Teper, 350
Tilas, 240
Tiles, 413, 423
Tiles, 247
Tiskevitski, 317
Titelboym, 236
Tivishevich, 238
Toder, 355
Todres, 347
Toibes, 109
Toibesh, 368
Toimkovitch, 59
Treister, 82
Treister, 236, 259
Trilop, 178, 191
Trocki, 347, 348
Trotsky, 358
Trotzki, 347, 348
Trotzky, 322, 346
Trozky, 351
Trumpeldor, 383
Tsanger, 189
Tshapaiev, 187, 194, 396
Tsipilevich, 240, 245
Tsipilovich, 237, 240, 242, 244
Tskhapaiev, 194
Tubman, 379, 382, 384
Tyamkin, 239
Tymzok, 373
Tzalkind, 259
Tzefelovitsh, 322
Tzeitel, 18
Tzentziper, 18, 132, 160, 161
Tzenziper, 249
Tzepelivitz, 259
Tzepelovitsh, 367, 377
Tzepliovitsh, 372
Tzernovitsh, 388
Tzimer, 142, 194
Tzimmer, 195, 196, 282
Tzipkin, 244
Tzirkavetz, 130
Tzirkovetz, 132, 133, 134, 135, 136, 165, 184
Tzirlin, 137
Tzirlin, 233

U

Ulman, 351
Umbros, 252
Urevitsh, 322

V

Vachstman, 125
Vaitzechovski, 59
Valakevitsh, 140

Valstein, 18
Valyukovitch, 190
Vant, 63
Vant, 259
Vashtai, 103
Vatkin, 234
Veinstein, 252
Veirch, 253
Veitzkin, 18, 24, 113
Veksler, 372
Verachavsky, 118
Verch, 121, 170
Vichnin, 389
Vienstein, 43
Vigderhous, 249
Vigodsky, 24
Vildt, 142, 189
Vilkamerska, 27
Vilkomirski, 40
Vilnin, 250
Virshov, 236
Vitvitski, 36, 189
Vitvitzken, 130
Vitvitzki, 9, 130, 132, 133, 134, 135, 136, 142, 165, 184
Volov, 59
Voogdman, 189
Vorabitzik, 242
Vorach, 243
Vorbiatzik, 244
Voroshilov, 187, 194, 195

W

Wachmacher, 238
Wachsler, 237
Wainer, 311
Waxmakher, 250
Weicherts, 326
Weiman, 139, 186
Weiman, 259
Weiner, 367
Weinstein, 25, 33, 49, 69, 150, 163, 164, 177, 204, 244, 321
Weinstein, 235, 237, 238, 244
Weinunsky, 420, 421, 423
Weiskin, 245
Weitzkin, 237, 244
Weksler, 287
Wexler, 356
Wienstein, 259
Wilkomirska, 7
Wolach, 357
Wolfovitz, 352
Wyman, 237, 238, 248

Y

Yachelman, 153
Yachelson, 150
Yaffe, 325
Yaffe, 235, 239, 243, 349, 354, 356
Yankoif, 355
Yaramek, 59
Yaremek, 49, 74, 161, 191
Yash, 28, 118, 130, 159
Yasin, 354
Yechiltzik, 61
Yechilzik, 259
Yeshurun, 26
Yevgeni, 209, 210, 211, 212
Yidel, 248
Yididovitsh, 39
Yotzkevitch, 59
Ytza, 358
Yudin, 282
Yudin, 243
Yudkin, 282
Yungelason, 234
Yungelman, 69, 126

Yungelson, 109, 162, 187, 246, 247
Yungelson, 234, 235, 240, 246, 247, 249, 255, 259
Yunglson, 249

Z

Zablotzki, 59
Zach, 240
Zacharov, 362
Zack, 64, 121
Zadlin, 243
Zagavel, 250
Zaiantz, 349, 352, 357
Zaiatz, 357
Zaitlin, 352
Zak, 241, 247, 252, 253, 255, 259, 349, 357
Zakravski, 74
Zakrevski, 59
Zaldin, 238
Zalka, 253
Zalkes, 303
Zalkin, 248
Zalkind, 130
Zalkind, 252
Zalmanovich, 234
Zalmanovitsh, 27, 89
Zamievski, 348
Zashtoft, 136
Zaslavski, 368
Zaslavsky, 367, 373, 375
Zaspitsky, 233

Zatsepitzke, 69
Zatzman, 354
Zawisker, 203
Zeidel, 242
Zeif, 189
Zeitlin, 325, 333
Zeitlin, 234, 358
Zeldin, 71, 119, 141
Zemach, 239, 259
Zemf, 142
Zendel, 241
Zhitlovsky, 389
Zietlin, 255
Zimchavitch, 352
Zimer, 194
Zimmer, 69
Zinger, 79, 89, 116, 124, 187, 228
Zinger, 234, 250, 259, 353
Zipelevitch, 353
Zipelevitz, 193
Zipelevitz, 351, 352, 353, 354, 355, 358
Zipilevitz, 350
Zirlin, 245
Ziskind, 249
Ziyatchik, 235
Zizonovich, 243
Zladin, 243, 244, 259
Zlatkin, 244
Zlotkin, 237, 242
Zud, 170
Zukerman, 349

www.ingramcontent.com/pod-product-compliance
Lightning Source LLC
Chambersburg PA
CBHW081420160426
42814CB00039B/242